Grounded Nationali:

MW00824198

Globalisation is not the enemy of nationalism; instead, as this book shows, the two forces have developed together through modern history. Malešević challenges dominant views which see nationalism as a declining social force. He explains why the recent escalations of populist nationalism throughout the world do not represent a social anomaly but are, in fact, a historical norm. By focusing on ever-increasing organisational capacity, greater ideological penetration and networks of micro-solidarity, Malešević shows how and why nationalism has become deeply grounded in the everyday life of modern human beings. The author explores the social dynamics of these grounded nationalisms via an analysis of varied contexts, from Ireland to the Balkans. His findings show that increased ideological diffusion and the rising coercive capacities of states and other organisations have enabled nationalism to expand and establish itself as the dominant operative ideology of modernity.

Siniša Malešević is Professor of Sociology at the University College, Dublin. He is also an elected member of the Royal Irish Academy and Academia Europaea. His recent books include, as author, *The Rise of Organised Brutality: A Historical Sociology of Violence* (Cambridge University Press, 2017, recipient of the ASA outstanding book award 2018) Nation-States and Nationalisms (2013) and, as editor, *Nationalism and War* (Cambridge University Press, 2013). His publications have been translated into eleven languages.

Grounded Nationalisms

A Sociological Analysis

Siniša Malešević

Professor of Sociology, School of Sociology, University College Dublin

CAMBRIDGE
UNIVERSITY PRESS

CAMBRIDGE
UNIVERSITY PRESS

University Printing House, Cambridge CB2 8BS, United Kingdom

One Liberty Plaza, 20th Floor, New York, NY 10006, USA

477 Williamstown Road, Port Melbourne, VIC 3207, Australia

314–321, 3rd Floor, Plot 3, Splendor Forum, Jasola District Centre, New Delhi – 110025, India

79 Anson Road, #06–04/06, Singapore 079906

Cambridge University Press is part of the University of Cambridge.

It furthers the University's mission by disseminating knowledge in the pursuit of education, learning, and research at the highest international levels of excellence.

www.cambridge.org
Information on this title: www.cambridge.org/9781108425162
DOI: 10.1017/9781108589451

First published 2019

Printed and bound in Great Britain by Clays Ltd, Elcograf S.p.A.

A catalogue record for this publication is available from the British Library.

ISBN 978-1-108-42516-2 Hardback
ISBN 978-1-108-44124-7 Paperback

In memory of my teacher Ernest Gellner and recently deceased friends and colleagues Ben Anderson, Michael Banton and Anthony D. Smith.

Contents

Acknowledgements

This book would not see the light of day without the support and help of many people. I have benefited greatly from the insightful comments of friends and colleagues who have read individual chapters or the entire manuscript. I am also grateful to the colleagues who had opportunity to hear me presenting some of this work and who provided useful critiques at various events including the London School of Economics; McGill University, Montreal; Princeton University; Yale University; University of Copenhagen; European University Institute, Florence; University of Edinburgh; Inter-University Centre, Dubrovnik; Free University of Berlin; University of Vienna; Loughborough University; Comenius University of Bratislava; European University of Tirana; Oxford University; University of Hamburg; Queen's University Belfast; the Georg-von-Vollmar-Akademie e.V. in Kochel am See, Munich; and University College, Dublin. In particular I would like to thank: (late) Ben Anderson, Saša Božić, Gerry Boucher, John Breuilly, Rogers Brubaker, Miguel Centeno, Randall Collins, Tom Crosby, Lea David, Francesco Duina, Jon Fox, John A. Hall, Chris Hann, Jonathan Hearn, John Hutchinson, Atsuko Ichijo, Tom Inglis, Richard Jenkins, Dietrich Jung, Deborah Kaple, Krishan Kumar, Simona Kuti, Steve Loyal, Michael Mann, Aogan Mulcahy, Niall O'Dochartaigh, Umut Ozkirimli, Kevin Ryan, Joe Ruane, Stacey Scriver, (late) Anthony D. Smith, Stefan Steter, Ori Swed, Jenifer Todd, Tamara Pavasović Trošt, Gordana Uzelac, Iarfhlaith Watson and Andreas Wimmer.

Although this book draws on the previously published papers and presentations, all chapters have been substantially revised, expanded and updated so that in most instances they look very different from the original version. I would like to thank the following publishers for their permission to draw on the previous publications: Chapter 1 is an extensively revised version of 'Do National Identities Exist?' (2017) *Social Space* 1(13): 49–64. Several sections of Chapter 2 draw on 'Nationalism and Longue Durée' (2018), *Nations and Nationalism* 24(2): 292–9. Chapter 3 is a revised and expanded version of 'The Foundation of

Statehood: Empires and Nation-States in the Longue Durée' (2017), *Thesis Eleven* 139(1): 145–61. Chapter 4 draws in parts on 'Nationalism and Imperialism as Enemies and Friends: Nation-State Formation and Imperial Projects in the Balkans' (2018), in F. Duina (ed.), *Nation and States, Power and Civility*, Toronto: University of Toronto Press. Several sections of Chapter 5 draw on 'Small Is Beautiful' (2016), *Dublin Review of Books*, July, p. 79. Chapter 6 draws in parts on 'Irishness and Nationalisms' (2014), in T. Inglis (ed.), *Are the Irish Different?* Manchester: Manchester University Press. Chapter 7 is a substantially revised version of 'Wars that Make States and Wars that Make Nations: Organised Violence, Nationalism and State Formation in the Balkans' (2012), *European Journal of Sociology* 53(1): 31–63. Chapter 8 is expanded and revised version of 'The Mirage of Balkan Piedmont: State Formation and Serbian Nationalisms in the 19th and early 20th century' (2017), *Nations and Nationalism* 23(1): 129–50. Chapter 9 is an extensively revised and expanded version of 'From Sacrifice to Prestige: Visualising the Nation in the 19th and 21st century Serbia and Croatia' (2017), *Visual Studies* 32(3): 212–23. Chapter 10 is expanded and revised version of 'Globalisation and Nationalist Subjectivities' (2018), in D. Jung and S. Stetter (eds.), *Modern Subjectivities in World Society*, London: Palgrave. Chapter 11 is an expanded and updated version of 'From Mercenaries to Private Patriots: Nationalism and the Private Military Contractors' (2018), in T. Crosby and U. Swed (eds.), *The Sociology of the Privatization of Security*, New York: Palgrave.

Finally, I would like to thank my family for being patient and sticking by me all these years even though I keep coming up with yet another book project. Thank you for your love, patience, and support Alex, Luka and Vesna.

Introduction: The Tenacity of Nationalisms

Intellectuals have always had a strange relationship with nationalism. For one thing, nationalism was rarely taken seriously as a coherent ideological doctrine. Most classical liberals from John Locke and James Mill to Friedrich Hayek and Karl Popper ignored or completely dismissed nationalism as no more than irrational 'tribalism' (Chen 2007: 22). The socialists and radical thinkers from Karl Marx and Rosa Luxemburg to contemporary neo-Marxists understood nationalism as a largely unpleasant side effect of class conflict. Hence, Marx and Engels (1998 [1848]: 39) scorned 'national one-sidedness and narrow-mindedness' while, Luxemburg (1976 [1908]: 135) argued that '"the nation" as homogeneous socio-political entity does not exist ... only classes [exist] with antagonistic interests and "rights"'. Although some classical thinkers, such as Lord Acton, John Stuart Mill, Otto Bauer and Lenin, among others, developed more articulate interpretations of nationhood, their approaches were still highly instrumentalist in seeing nationalism as an underdeveloped set of sentiments lacking ideological complexity and pronounced autonomous qualities. Even contemporary theorists are adamant that nationalism has no coherent and articulated doctrine. Michael Freeden (1998: 750–1) characterises nationalism as a 'thin ideology' that, unlike liberalism, socialism or conservatism, lacks a comprehensive system of principles and ideas that address a wide range of political issues including 'its own solution to questions of social justice, distribution of resources, and conflict-management' that other, what he considers to be, well-established political ideologies provide. In his view, nationalist ideas are rarely independent but are better understood as 'embellishments of, and sustainers of, the features of their host ideologies'. In a similar vein, Andrew Heywood (2003: 136) argues that 'nationalism is not an ideology at all' as it lacks a 'developed set of interrelated ideas and values'. Even the classical theorists of nationalism such as Gellner and Anderson believed that nationalism is conceptually inchoate. For Gellner (1983: 124–5) the nationalist doctrines 'are hardly worth analysing . . . [as they] suffer from a pervasive false consciousness . . . we shall not learn too much about nationalism from the study of its own prophets'. Similarly, Anderson (1991: 5) insists that nationalism is a set of beliefs characterised by 'philosophical poverty and even incoherence'.

For another thing, nationalism has regularly been understood as a doctrine whose pinnacle was long in the past and whose decline was inevitable. This attitude was succinctly expressed in Albert Einstein's famous quip that 'nationalism is an infantile disease. It is the measles of mankind' (Dukas & Hoffman 1979). Hence, over the last two hundred years many academics have pronounced its imminent death. Initially, nationalism was viewed as an unexpected offshoot of the French and American Revolutions and was perceived as a temporary aberration bound to disappear once the Enlightenment project penetrated all spheres of social life. By the mid-nineteenth century, the rise of nationalist movements in Europe was interpreted as a transitory phenomenon linked to the inevitable collapse of imperial rule. By early to mid-twentieth century, the violent nationalist excesses were yet again perceived as a historical anomaly rooted in the peculiarities of the German and Italian 'incomplete' and 'belated' unification. The post-WWII decolonialisation triggered another wave of nationalist movements throughout the world and the mainstream intellectuals tended to interpret this situation as a transient phenomenon linked to the disintegration and de-legitimisation of European colonialism. The rise of new social movements from the 1960s onwards, including the nationalist parties and associations in Northern Ireland, Scotland, Catalonia, Basque country, Flanders and further afield, largely came as a surprise to many analysts. These 'new nationalisms' were yet again described as fleeting occurrences reflecting asymmetric centre–periphery state relations or class inequalities and as such were seen as unlikely to last. The collapse of state socialism in 1989–91 brought another wave of nationalist uprisings, which too came as a surprise to most intellectuals. These nationalist movements were yet again dubbed as temporary, assuming that once the former communist states undergo full transition to liberal democracy these nationalist sentiments will inevitably wane. The similar type of social diagnoses was pronounced in the wake of largely unsuccessful Arab Spring of 2010. More recently, the Brexit referendum, the Trump election and the rise of the far right in Europe have all been described as another temporary nationalist glitch spurned by unregulated economic globalisation, intensified mobility of people and the rise of sharp economic inequalities.

It seems that these dominant views of intellectuals fly in the face of historical reality. If nationalism is no more than a simple, immature and emotional attachment to a particular collectivity or territory then one could not explain why such popular attachments were largely non-existent before the late eighteenth and early nineteenth centuries and why they have continually gained in strength over the last two centuries. Furthermore, the conventional mainstream accounts of nationalism as a temporary aberration cannot explain why this 'transiency' has constantly been 're-occurring' over and over again. If this phenomenon keeps 're-appearing' at regular intervals and has been doing this for the last two hundred years than it makes no sense to describe nationalism as a historical anomaly.

It is important to recognise that nationalism is not a juvenile disease that one can outgrow or cure. Nationalist movements are not some kind of marginal nuisance that periodically interrupts a natural flow of human development. It is crucial to acknowledge that rather than being a historical abnormality and a temporary irritation, nationalism is in fact the dominant form of modern subjectivity. Just as with other modern ideological projects, nationalism too is a child of the Enlightenment. Instead of viewing nationalism as an unsophisticated and inchoate bundle of sentiments, it is paramount to conceptualise and analyse nationalism as a fully fledged ideology and a dominant form of subjectivity in the modern era. Nationalism is not a thin ideology as Freeden sees it; it is in fact a very rich and diverse set of ideas, principles and practices that are integral to the organisation of everyday life in modernity. This ideology is associated with a long list of theorists, ideologues and practitioners – from the classics such as Herder, Mazzini, Fichte, Hegel, Rousseau, Garibaldi, Michelet, von Treitschke to its more recent proponents from the political left to the far right, including Tagore, Gandhi, Fanon, Farrakhan, Bannon, Dugin and so on. Just as with other political ideologies, the nationalist ideologues have published numerous books, pamphlets and political manifestos that clearly outline the key ideas and principles of this ideology and many have also offered the specific solutions to the key social and political issues – from the distribution of resources to social justice and conflict management issues (Ozkirimli 2017; Smith 2008; 1999). For example, all separatist movements – from the Scottish National Party, the Euzko Alderdi Jeltzalea, Vlaams Blok to Sinn Fein or Junts per Catalunya – have published extensive political programmes that address nearly all relevant social issues. Furthermore the principal ideologues of these movements have all articulated their visions of the social order they envisage independence would bring. The same applies to the non-separatist nationalist movements and parties from the French Front National to the Austrian Freedom Party, Danish People's Party, Independent Greeks, BJP or Polish Law and Justice. In this sense, nationalism could not be regarded as a conceptually inferior ideology as it provides comprehensive answers to key social and political questions just as any other political ideology does.

Nevertheless nationalism is much more than an ordinary political doctrine. It is also a social practice embedded in the everyday life of modern societies. While an average citizen of any modern nation state might not be familiar with the idiosyncrasies of liberal, socialist or conservative ideologies, she is very likely to know what nationhood means to her. In other words, precisely because nation-centric understandings of social reality are so pervasive in the modern world, it is almost impossible to escape this ideology in everyday life. Hence, in a sociological sense, nationalism is a super-thick ideology, a meta-ideological doctrine, which penetrates daily interactions of human beings and as such also shapes how modern individuals see and act in their social world.

Furthermore, the popular perception that nationalism is something that belongs to the past, a 'measles of mankind', is completely inaccurate. The conventional depictions of the nineteenth century as the heyday of nationalism, which are still taught in history classes all over the world, are simply wrong. In fact nationalism as a worldwide sociological phenomenon only gains significance in the twentieth and twenty-first centuries. Whereas in the early nineteenth century only a very small number of political, cultural and economic elites developed a strong sense of national attachments, in the twentieth and early twenty-first centuries nationalism has become a mass phenomenon that impacts on the thoughts and actions of billions of individuals globally. The popularity of nationhood is well attested in the social surveys conducted all over the world. These surveys show that ordinary citizens now identify much more with their respective nationhood than any of their predecessors ever could (Duina 2018; Gallup 2015; Medrano 2009; Antonsich 2009, Smith and Kim 2006). This is not to say that such periodic snapshots of public opinion are the best way to gauge the changing character of nationhood. There is no doubt that the intensity of national attachments is contextual and dynamic and as such is bound to wax and wane as social, economic and political conditions change. Nevertheless, while individual attitudes do change, the organisational and ideological context in which these ideas and practices are developed and operate are much more stable. Since we now live in a world where the nation state is the only legitimate form of territorial rule and where nationalism is the dominant and most popular mode of operative ideology, it is almost impossible to escape the nation-centric understandings of social reality. In a world of nation states the rulers can successfully justify their right to rule only by invoking nationalist principles – the view that the nation is the fundamental unit of human solidarity and political legitimacy. While rulers and those who aspire to rule can deploy different intensity and type of rhetoric used, they still have to rely on nation-centric tropes. In other words, there is no escape from nationalism in modernity. The rulers and the wider public can be more or less nationalist; their nationalist ideology can be more or less inclusive; they can utilise more civic or ethnic idioms of nationhood; such rhetoric can be more or less aggressive, but there is simply no way to avoid nationalism in a world whose legitimacy resides in the principle that the nation state is the only legitimate form of territorial organisation. It is here that the nation states differ from pre-modern forms of polity where there was no place for nationalism as their rulers invoked very different sources of rule justification – mythologies of kinship, the divine origins of kings, specific religious traditions, civilising missions and so on. Thus there is no modernity without nationalism. While this ideological doctrine might escalate only intermittently, it nonetheless dominates persistently.

Grounding Nationalisms

The recent dramatic rise of 'nativist', 'populist' and various 'identitarian' movements from India, Turkey, the Philippines, Russia, China, Japan, Israel, to the United Kingdom, the United States, Germany, Brazil, France, Hungary and Poland, among others, has prompted lively debate on their character and their causes. The largely unexpected victories of Donald Trump in the 2016 US elections and the United Kingdom's 2016 referendum leading towards the decision to leave the EU, together with the proliferation of far-right movements and populist parties in many European countries, have led commentators to conclude that these developments are best characterised as 'new nationalism'. The argument is that the main features of the new nationalist ideology include strong resistance towards immigration, anti-globalisation, preference for the introduction of economic protectionism, identity politics, support for populist leaders and nativist policies and general hostility towards cultural and religious differences. For example, Takis Fotopoulos (2016) argues that this new nationalism differs from its old, nineteenth century, counterparts as it primarily appeals to those who see themselves as the victims of globalisation and who aim to 'minimise the power of the elites'. Other analysts such as David Goodhart and Eric Kaufmann emphasise the cultural sources of new nationalism. Rather than being rooted in economic inequalities and the unevenness of globalisation, they argue, the new nationalism is engrained in firmly held values that reject multiculturalism and cultural diversity as such. Hence Goodhart (2017) identifies an ideological schism between the majority nationalist 'somewheres' and the elite globalist 'anywheres'. Kaufmann (2018) also sees new nationalism as primarily driven by cultural concerns linking it to the rejection of 'open border' policies and popular dissatisfaction with ever-greater cultural and religious diversity that now characterise many Western societies. Rather than seeing anti-immigrant sentiments as a proxy for economic inequalities, as Fotopoulos does, Kaufman argues that the surveys show that the new nationalism is a cross-class phenomenon, often driven by middle classes as much as by impoverished groups.

The principal problem with these and similar interpretations is their overemphasis on recent events and lack of engagement with the long-term historical trends that have shaped the dynamics of nationalist ideologies. Hence, rather than singling out specific, ad hoc, individual factors such as the economic costs of neo-liberal globalisation or conflicting cultural worldviews, it is crucial to analyse the rise and transformation of nationalisms through much longer periods of time. Firstly, the very concept of 'new nationalism' is vague and misleading. The idea of 'new nationalism' has been deployed and reused on so many occasions to account for the variety of political events that took place from the early twentieth century to today. For example, this concept was used by Theodore Roosevelt in the series of public speeches that were later published as a book *New Nationalism* (1910). In these speeches Roosevelt articulates his vision of a strong federal government that would unify US society through the protection of welfare rights and private property. The same term was deployed during WWI and in its aftermath when Wilson's and Lenin's ideas of national self-determination were linked directly to popular aspirations for national sovereignty and the rise of 'new nationalism' (Rosenthal and Rodic 2014). This concept was also used to describe the anti-colonial and post-colonial movements that strived to establish independent states from the 1950s to 1980s. The rise of separatist organisations in 1960s, 70s and 80s Western Europe has also been termed 'new nationalism', as was the collapse of the communist federations in the 1990s (Ignatieff 1994; Tiryakian & Rogowski 1986; Snyder 1968). More recently the notion of 'new nationalism' was utilised yet again to describe popular resistance to economic globalisation (Delanty 2000). This overuse of the concept is more than a sign of scholars' lack of imagination. Rather this is a symptom of the larger problem – the widely shared misperception that nationalism is a transient phenomenon bound to eventually evaporate. Hence, instead of tracking down and analysing these diverse forms of nationalism's transformation through time and space, many analysts tend to confine this phenomenon to a set of very narrow temporary causes. In this context, the designation 'new' does not stand for a novel phenomenon but for the analyst's surprise that nationalism has not gone away.

Secondly, using the term 'new' could wrongly imply that either there was no nationalism before these recent political developments or that what is happening now is profoundly different from what was there before. However, I would argue that rather than seeing these developments as being qualitatively different or utterly novel it is much more productive to treat them as the particular variation of social processes that have been in place for the past 200 years. In other words, nationalism did not and could not emerge suddenly and out of nowhere in 2016. Instead, the recent political events such as Brexit or the election of Trump have only made its prevalence and persistence much more palpable. To track down its historical dynamics it is paramount to recognise that nationalism has been, and remains, the dominant mode of political legitimacy and collective subjectivity in the modern era. Hence, in contrast to pre-modern polities such as empires, city states, patrimonial kingdoms or tribal confederacies, where the rulers legitimised their right to govern by invoking mythological origins, royal prerogatives, civilising missions, kinship rights or religious authority, nation states are unique in a sense that their very existence is justified in terms of popular (i.e. national) sovereignty. In other words, the strength of nationalism in the modern era stems in large part from the organisational dominance of the particular form of polity that underpins the modern world – the nation state. In this context, all modern states and social movements that aspire towards political or cultural sovereignty inevitably appropriate nation-centric discourses and practices. As Ernest Gellner (1983: 6) made clear, in the modern world nationhood is so normalised and naturalised that there is a near-universal expectation that 'a man must have a nationality as he must have a nose and two ears; a deficiency in any of these particulars is not inconceivable [. . .], but only as a result of some disaster, and it is itself a disaster of a kind'. This stands in sharp contrast with the pre-modern world where the overwhelming majority of people identified in local, mostly kinship-based, terms or perceived their world through the more universalist prism of religious beliefs and practices. With the rise and expansion of nation states worldwide, nationalism has gradually become the dominant cognitive framework for understanding wider social relations. Although one can trace the origins of this ideology in the influential intellectual movements such as the Enlightenment and Romanticism and the political revolutions of the late eighteenth and early nineteenth centuries, it is really in the twentieth and early twenty-first centuries that nationalism has become fully grounded in the institutions of modern state – from the educational system, mass media, the military and civil service to the public sphere. Furthermore, its organisational and ideological potency is also rooted in the workings of civil society, private corporations, NGOs and the wider networks of kinships, friendships, neighbourhoods and peer groups. It is only it the last century or so that nationalist ideologies have managed to finally penetrate much of the globe, whereby, as various surveys show, most contemporary individuals perceive their nations as being one of their primary sources of identity.

Why has nationalism proved to be such a potent, protean and durable force in the modern age? Why has the nation state established itself as the central organising mode of social and political life in the last two hundred years? Why is nationalism still the dominant form of collective subjectivity?

The principal aim of this book is to explain why nationalism remains the most potent operative ideological discourse in the modern era. More specifically, the ambition is to explore the social origins and the organisational, ideological and micro-interactional dynamics of nationalist ideologies. In this context I work with a broader, sociological, understanding of nationalism. This means that nationalism is not to be associated solely with separatist doctrines, anti-immigrant nativism or far-right politics, rather this concept aims to capture the variety of historical and contemporary nationalist experiences.

I see nationalism as an historically shaped and constantly changing phenomenon defined by its organisational capacity, its aptitude to articulate popularly enticing ideological narratives and its ability to link wider ideological projects with the emotional and moral universes of face-to-face interactional networks. In other words, nationalism is an organisationally and ideologically embedded process that has historically proven to be extremely successful in tapping into the micro-world of everyday life. The conventional perspectives which focus extensively on separatist movements or periodic surges of nativist and populist politics often overlook the centrality of nationhood in the modern era and as such are unable to provide coherent explanations of this phenomenon. Rather than being a bizarre anomaly, nationalism stands at the basis of modern social order. To emphasise the importance of the organisational and ideological structures as well as the interactional dynamics that foster the creation, reproduction and proliferation of this doctrine, I develop and utilise the notion of grounded nationalism. This concept is intended to capture several features of the nationalist phenomenon.

Firstly, nationalism is historically grounded in a sense that once it developed it became sturdy and has subsequently expanded and proliferated in different directions. Initially, it captured the hearts and minds of intellectuals, the property-owning strata and other political, economic and cultural elites. It then gradually incorporated other social groups – the middle classes, civil servants, soldiers, police officers, workers, farmers and the urban poor, among others. This gradual, vertical, mostly top-down, expansion was soon followed by the more horizontal and external augmentation as nationalist ideas and practices were slowly but surely diffused throughout the globe. Scholars still disagree whether nationalism originated in Europe or the Americas (Wimmer 2012; 2002; Breuilly 1993; Anderson 1991). However, there is a great deal of agreement that once the ideas of popular sovereignty, national independence and cross-class cultural homogeneity spread, they took firm root among different groups. Hence, once established, nationalist ideas and practices tended to grow and expand through the various social movements, civil society groups and state institutions. This is not to say that this was in any way inevitable or that nationalism has quickly displaced other ideological projects. On the contrary, the rise of nationalism has been profoundly contingent and was strongly resisted by the representatives of the ancien régime, the rural population, the religious establishment, monarchists and many others. Furthermore, for much of the nineteenth and early twentieth centuries, nationalism was incorporated into other ideological projects – from liberalism, socialism and feminism to imperialism, conservatism and racism, among others. It took a long time for nationalism to become a dominant operative ideology of the modern era. Although its historical entrenchment was gradual and rather slow, once established, nationalism tended to become grounded and expansive. Much of this expansion was fostered by its malleable character. Nationalist ideas and practices were constantly reformulated in order to attract diverse social groups. Hence, in the early and mid nineteenth century, nationalism was firmly aligned with the progressive causes advocated by liberals, socialists, feminists, anarchists, republicans, secularists and others. In this period, most nationalist movements were largely dominated by the middle classes. By the end of the nineteenth and early twentieth centuries, nationalism attracted a much wider following but by then its central discursive tropes had become amalgamated with right-wing ideas ranging from imperialism, colonialism, monarchism, fascism to eugenics and racism. After WWII, nationalist ideas become even more grounded. With the collapse of colonial structures, the nation state model was firmly established as the only legitimate form of polity organisation. In this context, the dominant nationalist discourses underwent yet another ideological shift, moving firmly to the left of the political spectrum and coalescing with socialism, revolutionary republicanism and anti-colonialism. Nationalism widened its support base further and was gradually embraced by populations all over the globe. Hence the historical grounding made nationalism into a strong and persistent social force that continued to develop and expand together with the growth of the organisational and ideological capacities of the state and non-state actors.

Secondly, nationalism is organisationally grounded. For nationalist ideas to have any impact on the thoughts and behaviour of many individuals they require forceful social organisations. Hence, nationalism developed and proliferated with the growth and expansion of organisational power. Initially, the spread of nationalist doctrines depended on relatively small organisations such as secret revolutionary societies including the Italian Carbonari, Portuguese Carbonária, Greek Philiki Hetairia or the Turkish Committee of Union and Progress among many others. Such organisations were successful because they operated highly disciplined, yet very flexible models of organisation involving small covert cells dispersed throughout their respective countries and abroad (Rath 1964). Later nationalist ideas were promulgated through the large social movements that were involved in a variety of social, cultural, political and military actions. For example, Irish nationalism grew in part through the establishment of the Gaelic League and Gaelic Athletic Association, both of which promoted 'traditional' Irish activities – sports, dancing, music, language and literature. Initially, the members of GAA were small farmers, shop assistants and barmen but gradually the organisation spread throughout Ireland and its membership base expanded dramatically. At the core of GAA success was its ever-expanding organisational capacity – with the hierarchical and parish-based structure of boards, committees and councils (Cronin et al. 2009). In addition, Irish nationalism developed through the successful organisation of over fifty 'monster rallies' that were organised by the supporters of Daniel O'Connell's campaign to repeal the Act of Union between 1843–45 (Coakley 2013). Such activist-led meetings, involving hundreds of thousands of participants, were highly instrumental in spreading nationalist messages and in fostering a nation-centric understanding of social and political life in Ireland. The other nationalist movements deployed different organising strategies, ranging from petitions, mass-scale strikes, civil disobedience campaigns, protests, boycotts, the establishment of parallel institutions, rebellions and violent insurgencies, among others. In all of these cases it was organisational power that proved crucial in spreading nationalist ideas.

However, the centrality of organisational grounding is most clearly visible in the rise of state capacity. Over the last two hundred years, the state authorities have invested heavily in the development of their infrastructure, including transport and communication networks as well as the capacity to control their borders, resources, taxation and their population. The rising organisational capacities provided for the increased size of administrative, juridical, military and police apparatuses, all of which have allowed for the greater control and monitoring of the population. While these developments have strengthened state power, they have also contributed substantially towards the expansion of nationalism. From the nineteenth century onwards, state authorities have utilised these organisational powers to forge more uniform and standardised institutions that would help mould their citizens into a relatively homogenous population. The nation state has been the decisive vehicle for what Mosse (1975) calls 'the nationalisation of the masses'. In this context, nationalism proliferated through the ever-increasing organisational power of state institutions. At the heart of this organisational power is coercion. Historically, nationalism emerged as an ideology centred on forging (national) unity out of local and kinship-based diversities. Much of its historical triumph is rooted in the state's coercive policies whereby national unison was often achieved through the destruction of local pluralism. It is no historical accident that the egalitarian and democratic promises of the French and the American revolutions were also built on top of mass murders of royalist Catholics in Vendée and Brittany and the native populations on the 'American frontier' respectively. For much of the nineteenth and early twentieth centuries, nationalism expanded through coercion and violence: the relative cultural homogeneity of European states came about as a result of ethnic cleansing and violent 'exchanges of population' (Mazower 2009). This explicit virulence has largely disappeared during the Cold War era in the global North but the nation-centric foundations of modern states have remained in place. Obviously this was always a highly contested process that generated a great deal of resistance. Nevertheless, increased coercive capacity, combined with greater ideological penetration was highly instrumental in advancing the nationalist organisational structure. In this context, modern nation states have deployed assimilationist policies whereby nationalist projects often resembled Procrustean beds: to become a full citizen one had to display a substantial degree of cultural uniformity. Even when a degree of cultural diversity was tolerated, no nation state could give up on the organisational push towards standardisation. Thus, the organisational grounding was pivotal in the emergence, growth, transformation and expansion of nationalisms.

Thirdly, nationalism is ideologically grounded. The coercive-organisational might of the state and non-state agencies makes the spread of nationalist ideas possible, but ideas matter just as much. Nationalist ideologies offer the grand vista of collective liberation and emancipation. They invoke the moral principles of justice, liberty, equality and fraternity and posit the nation state as the pinnacle of human progress – the territorial organisation that in moral terms supersedes its traditional pre-decessors such as empires or kingdoms. Nationalist messages are couched in the language of righteousness often emphasising the injustice of foreign oppression and the sacrifices of one's co-nationals: 'Ireland unfree shall never be at peace' (Patrick Pearse), 'We hold our heads high, despite the price we have paid, because freedom is priceless' (Lech Walesa), or 'One individual may die; but that [national] idea will, after his death, incarnate itself in a thousand lives' (Chandra Bose). In the eyes of nationalists, human beings cannot fully develop and express themselves outside inde-pendent and sovereign nation states. Nationalist doctrine is premised on the idea that every nation should have a state of its own and that every individual should be loyal to their respective nation. Nationalism also emphasises cultural similarity and political solidarity where the nation is understood to be the central form of collective existence. In the discourse of nationalism each nation possesses a unique character and unrivalled distinct features. Nationalist doctrine recognises the significance of other types of social identity. However, the underlining principle of all nation-alist perspectives is the idea that the attachment to one's own nation surpasses all other collective allegiances. As both Kedoruie (1993 [1960]) and Smith (2008) emphasised, in the age of nationalism the dominant expectation is that all individuals belong to a specific nation and that having no national identity is perceived as a moral flaw. In addition to these strong ethical imperatives, nationalism also invokes a sense of shared collective interests – being a full and committed member of a nation means that one is likely to benefit materially and symbolically from the national successes in the world arena, ranging from economic prosperity to geo-political dominance and cultural prestige, among many others.

Nevertheless, the power of ideology resides not only in the specific ideas and practices but also in its legitimising and mobilising capacity. Nationalism is ideologically grounded in a sense that it provides popular justification for a particular course of action. Much more than any other modern ideological doctrine, nationalism appeals to very wide sectors of the population. This appeal is in part rooted in the ever-increasing orga-nisational capacity of modern states which have institutionalised nation-alist discourses in their public sphere, educational systems, mass media and other influential outlets, and in part in the changed social profile of their citizenry. While in the traditional and the early modern world, the majority of the population consisted of illiterate peasantry that had little or no contact with state institutions, in modernity one is constantly exposed to nation-centric discourses. In this context the populations of modern states are engaged in an ongoing ideologisation processes that involve not only the central pillars of the state but also private corporations, religious organisations, civil society groupings, kinship networks, friendships, peer groups, neighbourhoods and many other non-state agents. This is not to say that citizens of modern nation states are simply and deliberately manipulated by their governments, powerful private corporations and other entities. Instead this continuous ideologisation is a structural phenomenon grounded in the organisational configuration of the modern world. Since we all now live in the world of nation states, their institutions inevitably reproduce the structural contexts that continuously produce nation-centric understandings of social reality. There is no doubt that these ideological tropes can and are periodically resisted by different groups. However the nationalist coding often operates in a very similar way to the programming algorithm – it is flexible at identifying new solutions and novel answers to the specific problems but these solutions still remain firmly embedded in the already established systems – the nation-centred universe.

Finally, nationalism also depends on micro-interactional grounding. It is difficult if not impossible to envisage successful nationalism without the effective coercive-organisational structures and articulated ideological narratives. Nevertheless, nationalism is not only a structural phenomenon but also involves thinking, reflective individuals who actively or habitually reproduce nation-centric realities. As Skey (2011, 2009), Fox and Miller-Idriss (2008) and Billig (1995) convincingly argue, nationalism is reproduced through everyday practices at the grassroots level. Hence Fox and Miller-Idriss (2008) demonstrate how nationhood is discursively constructed through routine talk in interaction, through the everyday choices individuals make, through their periodic involvement in the ritual enactments of the nation and through their everyday consumption of national symbols and products. In other words, to have a lasting impact, nationalism has to be grounded in the daily interactions of ordinary individuals. To make an impact and to resonate with the widely diverse audience, nationalist narratives have to speak in the language that ordinary individuals can recognise as understandable and meaningful. Some scholars, such as Cohen (1996) and Hechter (2000), have emphasised this individualist allure of nationalist rhetoric. In this context Anthony P. Cohen refers to 'personal nationalism' and argues that all nationalist performances, from the ritualist gatherings that commemorate fallen soldiers to the speeches of politicians, resonate only when they appeal to our diverse individualities: 'We watch these rites and, as individuals, in interpreting them we remake them in the sense that we are able to make of them ... we hear their voices [of politicians] but listen to ourselves' (Cohen 1996: 807). It is certainly true that nationalist rhetoric is more likely to make a durable appeal if it addresses some personal concerns and provides a sense of ontological security for individuals. Nevertheless, if the nationalist messages targeted only individual interests they would resemble personalised marketing campaigns and as such could not maintain a long-term influence. Instead, nationalism is potent precisely because it operates at the trans-individual level: its strength resides in its micro-interactional grounding. More to the point: since nationalism is rooted in specific emotional commitments and ethical imperatives, its massages and practices have to relate not only to individual selves but also to other people. Nationalist ideologies derive their force from the micro-world: from the sense of loyalty and the intense micro-level emotional attachments that human beings develop and maintain with significant others. In this sense, nationalism is deeply grounded in the micro-universe of daily interactions.

Nevertheless, these small group bonds do not generate nationalism on their own. While Fox and Miller-Idriss are absolutely right that nationalism thrives on the everyday routine interactions, such interactions cannot make nationalist realities by themselves. The ritualistic events, the nation-centric consumption and nationalist conversations all contribute towards the reproduction of nationalist habitus, but these agency-driven actions do not create nationalism. Instead nationalism originates and is maintained in the structural realm over long periods of time. Nationalist ideas and practices are grounded in large-scale organisational and ideological structures and it is only when such structures are firmly in place that one can see the society-wide proliferation of nationalist doctrines. In other words, nationalism is generated in the structural sphere but its continuous existence is heavily dependent on the everyday micro-interactional grounding. What is central in this process is how the structural and the interactional grounding come together. Hence, in this book I analyse how social organisations penetrate the micro-world of everyday interactions. To disseminate nationalist narratives, social organisations have to tap into the grassroots: the well-established networks of close kinships, friendships, neighbourhoods, peers, lovers and other face-to-face groupings. Since human beings are first and foremost emotional and moral creatures who attain solace, security and fulfilment in very small groups, the social organisations have to emulate the language and practices of the small group bonds. Hence, the successful nationalist projects are premised on the organisational translation of the ideological grand narratives into the micro, family and friendship-based, stories. An effective and firmly grounded nationalism entails a stable coordination of organisational, ideological and micro-interactional realms.

Thus, is this book I explore how grounded nationalisms develop, operate and expand. The focal points of my analysis are the organisational, ideological and micro-interactional underpinnings of nationalisms. I argue that the strength and worldwide proliferation of nationalist ideologies is firmly linked with the character of social organisations, the scale of ideological penetration and the depth of the micro-level solidarities that shape specific nationalist habitus.

Nationalism is a flexible and malleable ideology that has survived and expanded precisely because it was able to adapt. However, the organisational properties that sustain this ideological doctrine and also feed upon it (i.e. the bureaucratic structure of the nation state), inevitably pull this ideology towards privileging some form of cultural homogeneity. Hence, even when rulers and state administrators express genuine sensitivity towards cultural diversity, the organisational structure of the nation state often makes it impossible to overcome the centrifugal forces of cultural homogenisation. In this context, the cultural patterns of majority population regularly provide the dominant content for hegemonic nationalist ideologies. In this sense, contemporary nationalism is similar to its nineteenth-century predecessors – it speaks in the language of community cohesion but its very existence is premised on the obliteration of cultural diversities. The principal difference here is that whereas nineteenth-century nationalist ideologies were carving unity by denigrating the local and regional differences, contemporary nationalisms forge national cohesion by establishing and maintaining boundaries vis-à-vis immigrant populations. Nationalisms do change, evolve and transform but they remain firmly tied to their organisational shells – nation states. Hence, what we are witnessing now is not 'new nationalism' that suddenly and out of nowhere attacks cultural pluralities. Instead, this is the same historical phenomenon that has been in operation for the past three hundred years: an organisational and ideological attempt to mould and maintain (national) unity by negating inherent diversities.

In theoretical terms, this book follows in the footsteps of my previous work (Malešević 2017, 2013a, 2010, 2006, 2002), emphasising the historical interdependence of coercive bureaucratisation, centrifugal ideologisation and the envelopment of micro-solidarity networks. However, a substantive part of the book focuses on empirical case studies aiming to show how organisational power, ideological penetration and micro-solidarity operate in practice. The main case studies are the Balkans and Ireland, although I also discuss other parts of the world. Hence, the first part of the book provides a theoretical framework (Chapters 1–3), the second part applies these ideas to the variety of historical and geographical contexts (Chapters 4–9) whereas the third part brings these findings together by looking at the general patterns of nationalist ideas and practices in the global environment (Chapters 10–11).

The Book's Layout

Chapter 1 focuses on the concept of national identity. The leading approaches disagree over the questions such as: How old are national identities? Are such identities real or socially constructed? Do individuals have multiple or singular identities? Whereas the constructivists see national identities as novel, socially constructed and multiple, the perennialists emphasise their historical longevity, popular supremacy and genuineness. I challenge both of these interpretations and argue that belief in the existence of national identities is in itself a contingent historical product of the specific organisational, ideological and microinteractional processes that have moulded the world over the last three centuries. I explore the social context of this belief in the substance and universality of national identities. I also historicise the social origins and the expansion of this belief system.

Chapter 2 provides a theoretical framework for the modernist longue durée approach. More specifically, I contest the hegemonic attempts to identify the longue durée type of analysis with ethno-symbolism. The chapter aims to show that the modernist theories of nationalism are fully compatible with the longue durée perspective. In this context I explore the modernist alternatives to ethno-symbolism and then provide a critique of the existing approaches to the study of nationalism, both ethno-symbolist and modernist. In the final part of this chapter, I articulate a different modernist longue durée approach and zoom in on the organisational capacity, ideological penetration and the envelopment of micro-solidarity.

Chapter 3 explores the relationship between empires and nation states. Conventional historical and popular accounts tend to emphasise sharp polarities between empires and nation states. While an empire is traditionally associated with conquests, slavery, political inequalities, economic exploitation and the wars of yesteryear, a nation state is understood to be the only legitimate and viable form of large-scale territorial organisation today. This chapter challenges such interpretations by focusing on the organisational and ideological continuities between the imperial and the nation state models of social order. In particular, I analyse the role coercive-organisational capacity, ideological penetration as well as the transformation of micro-solidarities play in the formation of polities over long periods of time. I argue that although empires and nation states are different ideal types of polity, they are highly compatible and as such prone to metamorphosing into each other. I also explore how, when and why specific coercive-organisational, ideological and micro-interactional processes make this periodic historical metamorphosis possible.

Chapter 4 follows this empire vs. nation state debate but zooms in on the ideological projects that underpin them: imperialism and nationalism. I am to show that just as empire and nation states are not necessarily a mutually exclusive form of state organisation, the same applies to imperialism and nationalism. However, I differentiate between the capstone and modernising imperialisms and argue that the only the latter attained sufficient organisational and ideological power to penetrate their societies in a similar way to that of nation states. I also explore how in the nineteenth and early twentieth centuries, imperialism was often utilised to strengthened nationalist projects. In this context, the chapter compares the Serbian and Bulgarian historical experience and their reliance on the imperialist and nationalist discourses.

Chapter 5 problematises and dissects the idea of a small nation. This concept has often been deployed to illustrate the relatively distinct historical pathways of Ireland, Belgium, Denmark, Norway and the Balkan states, among others. The term is regularly used in a very descriptive and self-explanatory sense indicating an unproblematic statement of fact. However, in this chapter my ambition is to show that the notion of 'small nation' often has less to do with the size and much more with the specific strategic and ideological goals of a specific nationalist movement. Hence, I analyse how the Irish and Balkan nationalists have utilised this concept with a view of legitimising their respective nationalist claims and also de-legitimising their adversaries throughout the nineteenth and twentieth centuries.

Chapter 6 analyses the historical dynamics of nationalism and state formation in Ireland. Many historiographical and social science accounts emphasise the unique features of Irish nationalism – its unusual blending of civic and ethnic dimensions, its blurring of left and right-wing divisions, its religious particularities or its specific geographical position. Furthermore, much of the scholarship on Ireland shares the view that Irish nationalism reached its peak in the early twentieth century and that ever since this ideology has experienced a steady decline. In this chapter, I try to show that neither of these two claims are empirically sustainable. The chapter shows that in sociological terms, Irish nationalism resembles other European nationalisms. Moreover, by focusing on the rise of organisational capacities, ideological proliferation and their link with the micro-solidarities I argue that Irish nationalism has become much more grounded over the past fifty years and as such has experienced an upward trajectory.

Chapter 7 investigates the character of grounded nationalisms in the Balkans. More specifically, I explore the relationship between organised violence, state formation and nationalism. Since the beginning of the nineteenth century the Balkans has been a synonym for aggressive nationalism and unbridled violence; the two phenomena traditionally understood to be key obstacles for its social development. This chapter contests such views by arguing that it was the absence of protracted warfare and coherent nationalist doctrines that distinguishes the history of south eastern Europe from the rest of the continent. The chapter makes a case that it was not the abundance of nationalism and organised violence but rather their historical scarcity that proved decisive for the slow pace of social development in the Balkans. The focus is on the link between the weak organisational capacity and the feebleness of popular nationalisms in the nineteenth-century Balkans.

Chapter 8 continues this analysis by zooming in on the case of Serbia. The continuous rise of the Serbian state in the nineteenth and early twentieth centuries is often described as a typical example of Piedmont-style national unification. The conventional historiography emphasises the role popular nationalism has played in this process, making little if any distinction between forms of Serbian nationalisms within and outside the Serbian state. This chapter challenges such interpretations and argues that the formation and expansion of Serbia had less to do with society-wide national aspirations and much more with the internal elite politics within the Serbian state. Moreover, the chapter makes the case that rather than being a driving force of national unification, expansionist nationalism was a by-product of the state's organisational development.

Chapter 9 explores the changing representations of the nation in nineteenth and twenty-first-century Serbia and Croatia. I analyse how the changed structural conditions influence different visualisation strategies of a nation over long periods of time. More precisely, I attempt to show how the dominant nineteenth-century visual representations of nationhood were centred on violent images: representations of battlefields, personal sacrifices, national martyrdom, large-scale forced migrations of the nation and the past military glories of medieval kingdoms. In contrast to this mode of representation, the imagery of twenty-first-century nationalism tends to focus on the nation's international achievements in the fields of economy, science, technology, art and sports. Whereas the nineteenth century was saturated with violent images of the nation, in the twenty-first century such representations are less visible. On the surface, this significant visual shift would seem to indicate that nationalism was a far more influential force in nineteenth Serbian and Croatian societies than is the case today. However, I argue that the opposite is the case: the changing representations of the nation in fact reflect a greater organisational and ideological penetration of nationalism in the present-day. While in the nineteenth century's violent images of the past largely served as a didactic tool for the socialisation of mostly peasant, and thus nationally ambiguous populations, in the twenty-first century there is no need to perform such a role, as most citizens are already highly nationalised. Instead the visualisation of national success in sports or science and the relative absence of violent images reflects the organisational and ideological strength of grounded nationalisms.

Chapter 10 looks at the impact globalisation had on nationalism. Much of contemporary analysis is premised on the idea that globalisation and nationalism are mutually exclusive processes. While nationalism is generally associated with the preservation of national sovereignty and the protection of cultural authenticities, globalisation stands for open borders, economic interdependence, the mobility of peoples and worldwide integration. However, in this chapter, I challenge such views by demonstrating how globalisation and nationalism have historically constituted each other. I argue that the expansion of globalisation is a precondition for the worldwide proliferation of nationalist ideology. The first part of the chapter offers a brief critique of the approaches that overemphasise the historical novelty of globalisation while also perceiving nationalism as an ideology in decline. The second part aims to show how and why modern global subjectivities remain wedded to grounded nationalist practices.

Chapter 11 tackles the relationship between grounded nationalisms and capitalism. Neo-liberal capitalism is often perceived to be a force bent on undermining the sovereignty of nation states and weakening national identifications. In particular, the ever-present privatisation of state institutions has been associated with the decline of nationalism. In this chapter, I question these assumptions by exploring the social dynamics of privatised coercive organisations – the private military and security contractors (PMSC). The members of these organisations are often described as the profit-seeking mercenaries of the twenty-first century. However, in this chapter, I aim to challenge such simplified historical analogies by focusing on the different ideological and organisational dynamics of PMSCs and their pre-modern mercenary counterparts. I aim to show that unlike mercenaries who had no sense of loyalty to any nation, the employees of PMSCs were born and raised in nation-centric environments and as such are inevitably ideologically and organisationally wedded to the grounded nationalist realities of modern life. The chapter explores how private military contractors manage and negotiate the organisational aims of profit maximisation with the often-conflicting ideological goals set by national governments and the wider public.

Concluding chapter recapitulates the main points advanced and explored in the book. It also briefly situates and analyses the recent articulations of grounded nationalism. I emphasise that the periodic excesses of nationalists should not be conflated with the rise and decline of nationalist ideology. Instead, I argue that nationalism should not be judged by its visibility but primarily by the scale of its organisational, ideological and micro-interactional ground-ness.

Nationalism is a highly pliable ideological doctrine that has endured many historical changes and was able to adopt, transform and survive. Rather than being a stubborn nineteenth-century relic, nationalism has actually just started its proper sociological development in the twentieth century and has reached all social strata and much of the globe only in the twenty-first century. This is an ideological doctrine and social practice that is still developing, expanding and becoming more grounded in every-day life. Whether we like it or not, nationalism is here to stay.

1   Making Sense of Nationhood

Introduction

There is no doubt that an overwhelming majority of people in the world believe that national identities are real and discernible entities. The academics and social commentators might disagree profoundly over questions such as whether national identities are modern, primordial or perennial, or whether nationhood is essential or socially constructed, but they too generally do not doubt the existence of national identities. Some scholars might focus on the plural and the multiple character of all identities, including national ones, but they would seldom question the relevance of this concept and its empirical manifestations. In this chapter, the attempt is made to challenge such dominant understandings. More specifically, I argue that the contemporary belief in the existence of established, omnipresent and durable national identities is in itself a contingent historical product of the specific organisational, ideological and the micro-interactional processes that have shaped our world over the last three hundred years. In this context, the chapter emphasises that it is paramount to historicise the origins and the rise of the popular beliefs in the substance and universality of national identities. In this and the next two chapters, I elaborate a theoretical framework for the study of such popular beliefs. In particular, the focus is on the role that three long-term historical processes have played in the formation of 'national identities' as we understand them today: the cumulative bureaucratisation of coercion, centrifugal ideologisation and the envelopment of micro-solidarity.

Do National Identities Exist?

Sociology is an academic discipline that is generally not associated with producing scientific formulas and theorems. Nevertheless one of its few theorems, the Thomas theorem, has largely stood the test of time since its first formulation in 1928. This quite simple, yet rather potent, theorem states that 'if men[sic] define situations as real, they are real in their consequences' (Thomas and Thomas 1928: 571–2). What this means is that the popular perceptions of a specific situation are likely to influence their actions. In other words, all social actions are shaped by the individual and collective interpretations of a situation. For example, if a large number of individuals believe in a particular understanding of social reality, then their actions will ultimately contribute towards making this belief into an actual reality. In some respects, the Thomas theorem works as a self-fulfilling prophecy (Merton 1948). Typical examples include the 1973 toilet paper panic and the so-called New Thought philosophy's law of attraction. The toilet paper panic was triggered during the worldwide oil crisis following the widely circulated rumour of an imminent shortage of toilet paper caused by the decline in the oil imports (Malcolm 1974). As the rumour spread, people stockpiled large quantities of toilet paper thus directly causing the shortage. The law of attraction, derived from nineteenth-century ideas of mesmerist Phineas Quimby, stipulates that 'like attracts like' suggesting that focus on positive or negative thoughts will bring about positive or negative experiences. Although the law of attraction evades scientific criteria of falsifiability and testability, and as such has regularly been termed a pseudoscience (Shermer 2007), it has substantial appeal for those who subscribe to a view such as one's happiness can always be interpreted in relation to focusing on the positive thoughts.

The Thomas theorem applies just as well to the contemporary notion of national identity. Judging from the various surveys around the world, it seems quite obvious that an overwhelming majority of individuals believe in the existence of national identities (Duina 2018; Gallup 2015; Antonsich 2009; Medrano 2009; Smith and Kim 2006). Such surveys also indicate that the populations of many countries score very high in terms of personal sense of attachment towards one's nation. For example, Israeli, Chinese, Japanese and Filipino populations regularly top various polls in terms of highest levels of national identification (Tang and Barr 2012; Smith and Kim 2006; Brym and Araj 2006). One recent study found that China, Japan and the Philippines were among the top ten countries in the world according to the level of national attachment (Tang and Barr 2012). USA and many European nation states also top such 'national pride' tables. For example, 90–92 per cent of Americans from all social classes expressed views that they are proud or very proud of their national identity (Duina 2018: 19). Similarly, the Eurobarometer surveys indicate that most Europeans feel strongly attached to their nations. When asked 'Would you say that you are very proud, quite proud, not very proud, or not at all proud to be Greek, Finn or Irish', more than 95 per cent of respondents stated that they feel very or quite proud of their nationhood (Antonsich 2009: 286–9).

Moreover, national identities are perceived as tangible, natural and normal states of being that every individual has or ought to possess. Such beliefs also have real consequences in a sense that they help reproduce and maintain nationcentric and identity-centric views of social reality. While disagreeing on the question of whether national identity is primordial, perennial or modern, genuine or constructed, the scholars of nationhood generally do not question the existence of national identities as such (Malešević 2013a, 2011; Brubaker 2004). Hence, they too operate in line with the Thomas theorem and their actions and analyses generate real consequences whereby national identities are understood as objective and material social realities.

Nevertheless, while the Thomas theorem does tell us a great deal about the impact of collective perceptions of reality on social behaviour, it does not help us explain the social and historical origins of such perceptions. Furthermore, using this theorem one cannot find out how such social interpretations change through time. For example, to most of our pre-Socratic predecessors the Earth was unquestionably flat. From ancient Greece until the classical period, to the Bronze and Iron Age societies of the Near East, to India until the beginning of the first century, to China well into the late sixteenth century, the majority of intellectuals were convinced that human beings live on a flat disc floating in the large ocean (Garwood 2007).[1] Such a belief retained its popularity for many more centuries among ordinary individuals worldwide. Yet today only a small minority of people share such a view. Furthermore, the fact that our precursors defined their social reality in terms of living on the flat Earth did not make this planet any flatter than it actually is.

I would argue that something similar can be said about the national identities. While today, the majority of world populations perceive themselves through the prism of a specific national identity (i.e. Lithuanian, Vietnamese, Croat, Indonesian, etc.) our predecessors did not and could not see the world in such terms. Instead their social realities were much smaller (i.e. village, close kinship and clan networks, neighbourhoods, etc.) or much larger (the universe of eschatological religions, empires and the unyielding nature; Breuilly 1993; Gellner 1983; Anderson 1991 [1983]). Even at the onset of modernity it was only small number of people who did think of themselves in national categories. Moreover, one could go even further and argue that regardless of how many individuals

---

[1] Apparently, leaders of Boko Haram still hold the view that the Earth is flat (Boyle 2009).

perceive their immediate social world through the category of national identity, this in itself does not make national identities any more real than they were at the dawn of human history. They did not exist then and their contemporary material existence is just as doubtful today.

Perhaps the comparison of the Earth structure and the collective sense of national identity might be farfetched in a sense that an astronomical object is much more stable and durable than human perceptions. However, our focus is not on the intrinsic material features of these two very different phenomena but on the changing popular understandings of social reality. In this sense, widely shared belief in the existence of a permanent and stable flat Earth is to be evaluated in a similar way to a widely shared belief in the existence of permanent and stable national identities. Both such sets of beliefs have a profound impact on the behaviour of those who share such beliefs. The idea that the Earth is flat had direct implications on the popular perceptions that the human beings constitute the pinnacle of existence. In a similar way, the belief in the existence of national identities regularly leads to popular views that a membership in one's nation represents the most important form of collective existence.

To understand the popular impact of such perceptions it is paramount to briefly explore their social and historical origins. Leaving the Flat Earth debate aside and focusing on national identity alone, it is necessary firstly to decouple its two constituents: 'national' and 'identity'.

As argued previously, the notion of identity is an imprecise umbrella term with limited conceptual power (Kaplan 2018; Malešević 2013, 2006; Brubaker 2004; Brubaker and Cooper 2000). This is a historically novel idea with a very specific and quite narrow origin – Western modernity. Comparative sociologists and anthropologists have demonstrated convincingly that the identitarian concepts such as 'self', 'personality', 'character' and 'self-identity' develop late in human history and have very different meanings in different parts of the world. Outside Western modernity, one often encounters understandings of the individual and the social which are not bounded by either individual or collective agency. In some traditional orders, there is also no firm distinction between nature and human beings. For example, as Handler (1994: 32) documents, for many traditional groups in South Asia there is no concept of personhood reduced to one's corporal experience. Instead, individuals together with other beings are in constant motion where there is no 'separability of actors from actions'. In Hindu tradition, one does not encounter bounded individual units but people and animals are all seen as divisible 'composites of the substance-codes that they take in' and as such prone to continuous change. Geertz (1973: 369–70) too depicts Balinese concepts of personhood as having deeply depersonalised features. This is reflected in the arbitrarily coined personal names which are made up of 'nonsense syllables' and which are rarely used in everyday interaction. In each of these two cases, as Handler (1994: 33) emphasises, 'there is no sense of an essential human personality that is continuous from birth to death. Rather, persons orient themselves to a divine and unchanging cosmic realm in which the details of an individual's unique personality have no importance.' Very similar attitude is present among the contemporary Ju/'hoansi in Namibia. Their origin myths invoke stories about the age 'when identities of both animals and people were fluid and during which different species intermarried and preyed on one another' (Suzman 2017: 72).

Bendle (2002) and Baumeister (1986) have demonstrated convincingly that the notion of identity did not have much popular resonance in pre-modern and early modern Europe either. In a traditional, hierarchical orders, an individual's position was largely defined by her birth and the social strata she inhabited. In such rigidly stratified social environments, there was neither possibility nor wish to make individual choices on the basis of one's preferences. It is only with the onset of modernity that these social relationships have been transformed radically. With the gradual disintegration of the traditional order, individuals were forced to assume new social roles and consequently to develop new sense of who they are. Furthermore, as the traditional world order was undermined, it also provided new opportunities for social and geographical mobility thus placing individuals in new social constellations. The questions of identity only become relevant when 'factors that underpinned a sense of continuity (geography, community, employment, class, etc.) were destabilised', while at the same time the factors 'that provided a sense of differentiation (ancestry, social rank, gender, moral virtue, religion, etc.) were delegitimized' (Bendle 2002: 16).

The concept of identity has also been challenged on empirical grounds. Brubaker and Cooper (2000) and I (Malešević 2011, 2006) showed how the porous nature of this concept allows for proliferation of rather weak and ambiguous theoretical models and inadequate operationalisation strategies. Laitin (2007) and Kumar (2003) have emphasised that identities 'have no obvious empirical referents' and as such tend to evade analytical rigour. Brubaker (2004) has also singled out the reifying and essentialist properties of identitarian discourses. For example, many academic studies on identity tend to attribute human features to such an abstract and metaphoric entity. Hence, one can often read how identities are in conflict with each other or 'how people come to assume and inhabit . . . identities, and how identity then shapes what they do' (Reicher and Hopkins 2001: 3). This very common practice tends to anthropomorphise identities by assuming that such concepts possess a will of their own and can act in the same way individuals or organisations do (Malešević 2013a, 2006). Hence, despite its enormous popularity, identity is far from being a useful analytical concept.

The concept of a nation also exhibits some of the same problems: it lacks clearly recognisable empirical referents, it is prone to essentialisation and reification, it is conceptually ambiguous and it has highly diverse meanings which tend to change in time and space (Malešević 2013a; Brubaker 2004; Eriksen 2002). However, unlike identity which is so wide that it can incorporate almost any form of individual and social activity, the idea of nationhood has much more limited scope: it is something that refers to a particular collective experience associated with a specific historical period and a limited group of people. As Ben Anderson (1991[1983]: 5) emphasised, regardless of their size, which can range from few hundred thousand (Maldives, Singapore, Bahrain, Iceland or Montenegro) to over a billion (China, India), nations are always imagined as limited in terms of their population and territory: 'the nation is imagined as limited because even the largest of them encompassing perhaps a billion living human beings, has finite, if elastic boundaries, beyond which lie other nations. No nation imagines itself coterminous with mankind.' This point is deeply linked with the specific historical context of nationhood as the typical pre-national forms of social organisation tended to encompass either much larger or much smaller groups of people. Whereas our pre-historical predecessors lived in very small, flexible and unstable nomadic bands of foragers, the birth of civilisation resulted in the establishment of large scale, internally highly diverse, imperial polities. Hence, neither of these two organisational models were well suited for the establishment of national projects: while the world of hunter-gatherers lacked any firm attachment to a specific territory or codified and written cultural practices, the empires were structurally too hierarchical and culturally too diverse to attempt to forge the commonly shared national ideas and practices. So the notion of nationhood develops quite late in human history and the model of the sovereign nation state becomes dominant only in the last two centuries (Malešević 2013; Mann 1993, 1986; Hall 1986; Gellner 1983; Anderson 1991[1983]).

Finally, unlike 'identity', which is so wide that it can incorporate great variety of universalist projects, nationhood is first and foremost a form of particularism. In contrast to the religious doctrines and imperial creeds which speak in the language of universalism, nations are as a rule conceptualised as communities of specific groups defined by what Anderson (1991[1983]: 7) calls 'deep, horizontal comradeship'. In this sense, nation states differ sharply from empires: whereas the imperial rulers legitimised their existence in reference to the entire world, nationalist leaders confine their rhetoric to the members of their nations. For example, King Philip of Spain was regularly depicted as 'the heir of the universe' and 'lord of the world' (Kumar 2017: 153–4). When Pizarro encountered Incas, he described his master as 'a king of Spain and the universal world' (Diamond 2005: 74). In contrast, the contemporary Indian, Serbian or Peruvian politicians always address their audiences in strictly particularlist terms emphasising that their loyalty resides in their membership of a particular nation (the Indians, the Serbs or the Peruvians).

Therefore although the concept of nation is also deeply problematic, its relatively limited scope allows a bit more precision. While 'identity' is not very useful tool for analytical purposes it is difficult to completely dispense with the idea of nationhood. However, to fully understand the social origins of 'national identity', it is paramount to focus our attention on the three historical processes that have made the national identity paradigmatic in the contemporary world. These three processes are: the centrifugal ideologisation, the cumulative bureaucratisation of coercion and the envelopment of micro-solidarity.

Ideological Penetration

The almost universally shared perception that every human being has or ought to possess a national identity is, historically speaking, a very recent development. As historical sociologists show, before the modern era, the majority of individuals conceptualised their daily existence in terms of much broader, mostly religious, worldviews, or much narrower, kinship, clan and residence focused, attachments (Mann 1995, 1993, 1986; Gellner 1983; Anderson 1991[1983]). The idea that every individual is primarily a German, Pole, Zimbabwean or an Uzbek would make little, if any, sense to our pre-modern ancestors. Since the traditional world was defined by stark hierarchies, there was little, if any, congruence between the state and culture. This was the world inhabited by the ruling aristocracies focused on their inherited social status and the masses of illiterate peasants. In addition to the sharp political and economic divisions, these two principal strata were also culturally divided. As Gellner (1983) argues convincingly, this was a universe where 'the high culture' of nobility stood in opposition to the ocean of 'low', mostly oral, cultures of peasantry communicating through thousands of distinct, and often mutually incomprehensible, vernaculars. Moreover, the key legitimising principles of these traditional orders reinforced these cultural divides as the rulers were universally understood to have 'the divine right' to rule. In this type of social environment, there was neither need nor capacity to forge a degree of cultural homogeneity that characterises most contemporary nation states. Simply put, national identities could not exist in a world where the primary source of group solidarity for the majority of, essentially peasant, population was deeply local: clan, village or kinship. Moreover, even the elites were for the most part ignorant of nationhood as their loyalties resided in the transnational aristocratic network connected by intermarriages.

For example, for most of its contemporary citizens, Thailand is an ancient nation that has been in existence for over a thousand years. The influential Simhanavati legend describes a Thai chief Simhanavati as a founder of Chiang Saen City around in 800 CE after which Thais adopted Buddhism and Sanskrit royal names. The conventional historical accounts emphasise the continuity of Thai tradition in the existence of various small kingdoms such as Sukhothai Kingdom (thirteenth century) where allegedly every citizen could approach a king directly and ask for help. Nevertheless, the idea of a Thai nation is a very late development. Although some scholars point to the significance of King Wachirawuth and the Sixth Reign (1910–25) for development of nationalism, it seems that the key period followed the Siamese coup d'état of 1933. The new rulers were inspired by German nationalism and attempted to establish the dominance of the Central Thais throughout the entire country. Throughout the twentieth century, Thaisation was enforced through the promotion of the king as a symbol of the nation and the introduction of compulsory practices such as twice daily broadcasts of the national anthem (Phleng Chat), the ritual of saluting the Thai flag in the schools and the military and the nationalist imagery in the mass media and educational system (Chaloemtiarana 2007; Peleggi 2007). Although Thai nationalists pride themselves on having a unique cultural tradition that encompasses all Thais, here too, just as everywhere else in the world, nationalist ideology emerges very late, culminating in the twentieth and twenty-first centuries.

Similarly, the Russian national identity is popularly understood to have deep, well established and durable historical roots. The conventional historiographic accounts usually start from the ninth century migrations of East Slavic tribes to what is today Ukraine, Belarus and Western Russia. In this narrative, the establishment of Kievan Rus' state under the Verengian Rurik, and his progeny, Oleg, Igor, Olga and Sviatoslav, represents the beginning of Russian polity that by the eleventh century was already one of the most powerful states in Europe (Ziegler 2009: 9–10). According to The Tale of Past Years/The Primary Chronicle, a twelfth century document that combines mythical with the real events, the Kievan

Rus' state experienced its peak under the reign of Vladimir the Great and Yaroslav the Wise. The nationalist accounts regularly emphasise the significance of this period, seeing it as the cornerstone in the development of key pillars of the Russian identity – Orthodox Christianity and distinct cultural tradition associated with unique language and legal codes. During the reign of Vladimir and Yaroslav, Orthodox Christianity became the state religion and the Old Church Slavonic was established as the liturgical and official language. In addition, this period also witnessed the creation and implementation of the first East Slavic written legal code – *the Russkaya Pravda* (Ziegler 2009: 10–11). The conventional interpretations also emphasise other foundational events, seen as having played a critical role in the rise of Russian national identity – Alexander Nevskii's victory over Teutonic Knights in 1242, Ivan I's inauguration as the Grand Prince of Moscow in 1325, Ivan the Terrible's expansionist sixteenth-century reign that transformed Russia into a large empire and the establishment of the Romanov dynasty in 1613. The very long reign of the Romanovs (1613–1917) has in particular been marked as crucial in the rise of Russian national identity. Hence, the nationalist interpretations starting from Count Sergey Uvarov tended to associate Russian identity with the three central ideas – the preservation of the Russian Orthodox Church, the loyalty to the House of Romanovs and the glorification of the 'Russian national spirit'. These three idioms were later institutionalised by Emperor Nicholas I as the official ideology of the Russian state. With the collapse of the Soviet Union, many of these ideas, together with the pre-Soviet Russian Slavophile tradition, have been revived and re-established as being 'the very essence of Russian identity' (Laruelle 2008: 43).

Nevertheless, just as in the Thai case, here too nationalist narratives project present concepts and contemporary social realities deep into the past. Rather than exhibiting any form of shared national identity for much of its history, Russia was a deeply hierarchical polity where nobility had no sense of cultural or any other type of attachment with the peasantry under their control. Furthermore, as Carter (2010: 70) shows, despite their nominal commitment towards the Russian cultural project, Romanovs were largely ignorant of Russian identity: 'Almost nothing about Romanovs was "Russian" . . . their lives were those of Westernised aristocrats. Their court etiquette was German, their parks and palaces were neoclassical, their home comforts were English. Even by blood they were barely Russian at all, the product of endless marriages into German royal families.' Moreover, just as in the other aristocratic polities, the ordinary population also lacked any sense of society-wide attachment as their primary sources of identification were either local (family, village, parish, clan) or supranational (religion, mythology). The majority of the Russian population spoke different dialects and until Lomonosov's standardisation of Russian language in the eighteenth century there was no possibility of establishing a language based on shared national identity. It was only in the mid-twentieth century that the Soviet state successfully killed off the dialects through the compulsory imposition of the standardised Russian language in the educational system (Brickman and Zepper 1992). Hence, the notion of society-wide Russian national identity is a very recent development.

For nationalism to emerge as a dominant ideological narrative, it was paramount that the idea of divine origins of monarchs became replaced with the new principle of political legitimacy – the notion of popular sovereignty. This idea, fully articulated by the Enlightenment thinkers, and for the most part realised in the French and American revolutions, replaced social strata with a nation as the epicentre of social and political life (Malešević 2013a; Schulze 1996; Mann 1993; Gellner 1983). Consequently, nationalism became the new dominant ideological force, capable of mobilising large numbers of, now increasingly literate, populations. Well equipped with the egalitarian ethos, emancipatory politics and discourses of solidarity (*liberté, égalité* and *fraternité*) the nationalist leaders were able to legitimise new models of rule as well as to galvanise large numbers of people to support these new regimes. In such an environment both the state and the civil society became vehicles of mass-scale nationalist socialisation throughout the world. The ever-rising literacy rates and the establishment of mass-scale educational systems focused on inculcating a nationcentric understanding of the past and present thus helped forge new generations of young nationalists all over the world (Gellner 1983). The invention and proliferation of the printing press together with the global expansion of capitalism fostered emergence of the public sphere where ordinary individuals were able to buy and read cheap mass media and novels that reproduced nationalist visions of social reality (Anderson 1991[1983]; Calhoun 1994). The introduction of compulsory military service together with the proliferation of warfare were crucial in moulding new recruits into loyal members of their nation states (Tilly 1985; Mann 1986, 1993; Conversi 2008). Even the expansion of the welfare state and the gradual widening of the civil liberties and citizenship rights was tightly linked with one's membership in a specific nation state (Breuilly 1993; Mann 1993). All these large-scale structural processes contributed substantially towards making nationalism a dominant ideology of the modern age.

Although the contemporary rhetoric is saturated with ideas that nations make states and that national identities generate nationalism, the sociological reality shows otherwise: it is the states that make nations and nationalism that forges the popular idea of national identity. All modern social organisations, including the nation states, require specific ideological glue to hold their diverse memberships together. In modern contexts, this is achieved through the process I term centrifugal ideologisation: a mass-scale structural and historical phenomenon through which social organisations project and temporarily forge a degree of ideological unity out of complex diversities that inevitably characterise all such large entities (Malešević 2013, 2010). While all nation states are composed of heterogeneous individuals and collectivities that possess different interests and values, nationalist ideologies aim to paper over these facets and project a widely believable image of society-wide homogeneity. Ideologisation is a contingent, uneven and contested process which, when successful, manages to integrate and mobilise socially diverse populations around a set of commonly shared principles. This ideological practice is not confined to the marginal movements at the extreme right or left of the political spectrum. Instead it is something that incorporates most political parties, civil society groupings and large-scale social movements that, in the modern era, inevitably embrace the nationcentric rhetoric. The fact that nationalism is more ambiguous than most other ideological discourses makes it more protean as it allows that its central principles can be rearticulated by a variety of social and political forces throughout the political spectrum. None of this is to say that centrifugal ideologisation is some kind of giant brain washing device that imposes certain beliefs on the unsuspecting public. On the contrary, this process entails a great deal of popular consent which is achieved in direct collaboration with the civil society groupings, family networks, residential associations and many other non-state actors. Centrifugal ideologisation is a process that constantly reinforces already held beliefs and practices. Although historically this process was initiated by the cultural and political elites, once fully in operation ideologisation proliferates throughout entire societies. With the ever-increasing literacy rates, expanding educational systems and the multiplication of the mass media outlets there is a greater ideological penetration. Modern technological advancements facilitate even greater ideological diffusion while the open borders stimulate nationcentric understandings of reality.

In this sense, despite periodic ups and downs, the centrifugal ideologisation has continued to increase over the past three hundred years. It is this broader social context that gave birth to the idea, and also helps maintain the perception, that one's national identity is something stable, tangible, durable and deeply personal. When asked about the meaning of national identity today, most 8–13-year-old schoolchildren in the world will reply that they are proud of their nation and that having a particular national identity has a distinctly personal significance for them (Stephens 1997; Gullestad 1997;

Hengst 1997). If one is to take such statements at face value, it would be easy to conclude that national identities not only exist but are highly potent forms of individual and collective identification. However, the key point here is that what is ordinarily perceived as an expression of national identity is in fact a historical product of the specific ideological processes. Saying that one feels proud to be Kazakh, French or Korean is much more than a personal reflection on one's own state of being. It is something that demonstrates the inner workings of ideological processes that are historically specific and organisationally mediated. Such statements reflect the impact of ideological power and its society-wide penetration. They tell less about the inner feelings of individuals and much more about the strength of nationalist discourses worldwide. For example, in 2014 over 80 per cent of the Asian population described their national identity as being very important or important ranging from Qatar where 98 per cent of respondents expressed that they are very proud to be Qatari to Uzbekistan, the Philippines, Jordan, Yemen, Pakistan and Malaysia where over 90 per cent of population stated that they are either very or quite proud of their nations (www.worldvalues survey.org/WVSNewsShow.jsp?ID=154). These trends are not unique to Asia and are just as visible all over the world. For example, over 94 per cent of European Union citizens described their national identity as very important form of group attachment (Eurobarometer 2010). Similarly the US population is also very proud of their national identity. As the recent Gallup survey (2015) shows, 81 percent of Americans say that they are either extremely proud or very proud to be Americans with more than half of all respondents (54 per cent) declaring themselves 'extremely proud'. However, if we were to travel in time and conduct similar survey in 1610, it is most likely that over 90 per cent of individuals interviewed would have no comprehension what national identity is (Anderson 1991 [1983]; Mann 1993). Hence using such survey results just to say that national identities are very strong today does not really tell us much. What matters more is how are such collective understandings of social reality shaped and maintained. Focusing on the process of centrifugal ideologisation allows us to assess how much such collective perceptions are dependent on the continuous ideological work – from the banal, everyday practices that reinforce the nationcentric images of social reality to the coercively enforced social actions that exclude, delegitimise or even criminalise alternative ideological discourses.

Coercive Organisational Power

There is no doubt that nationalism is a potent ideological force. Over the past two hundred years, nationalist ideology, in a variety of forms, has become a dominant source of political legitimacy and has established itself as the principal operative ideology of modernity (Malešević 2013a, 2006). However, no ideology, regardless how forceful and popular it might be, can achieve much without the concrete institutional support. Even the powerful monotheistic religions such as Christianity and Islam attained worldwide impact only after they became official belief systems of the three mighty empires – the Byzantine, the Ottoman and the Safavid respectively. The secular ideologies are no different: the rise of Marxism-Leninism was entirely dependent on the organisational capacity of powerful communist states – from Soviet Union and China to much of Eastern Europe. Similarly Fascism, Francoism and Nazism rose on the back of the Italian, Spanish and German polities. The state is not the only social organisation capable of institutionalising ideological doctrines. From the big private corporations to the powerful Churches to the terrorist networks and political movements, many non-state organisations have proved capable of galvanising influential ideological creeds. Nevertheless, the modern nation states possess more, what Michael Mann (2012, 1993, 1986) calls, despotic and infrastructural powers than other entities to enact and diffuse ideological doctrines. Thus, with the rise and expansion of nation states as the dominant form of polity, nationalism became the principal ideological discourse of the modern era.

However, to fully comprehend the link between the nation state and nationalism it is necessary to take a brief look at the historical process that underpins this relationship – the cumulative bureaucratisation of coercion. This concept stands for an ongoing structural process that involves constant increase in the organisational capacity for coercion and the ability to pacify the social realm under the organisation's control. Despite the occasional reversible trends throughout history and the periodic disappearance of specific social organisations, the coercive organisational power has, for the most part, experienced a cumulative trend over the centuries. This is particularly noticeable in the increased territorial scope, infrastructural reach and societal penetration of various social organisations. The cumulative bureaucratisation of coercion has been in existence for the past 12,000 years and has accelerated over the last 250 years (Malešević 2013a, 2010). It is no accident that this acceleration coincides with the emergence and the worldwide proliferation of nation state as the dominant model of territorial organisation. The rulers of premodern empires, patrimonial kingdoms and city-states utilised some organisational powers to maintain a degree of proto-ideological consensus among the aristocratic elites. However, modern polities require much more organisational capacity to preserve social order and to maintain legitimate grip on power. To achieve this, the leaders of nation states have to rely not only on the ideological concord (nationalism) but also on the coercive tools that they have at their disposal. Hence, all effective nation states monopolise the use of violence on their territory through the control of military and police (Collins 1975). This control of force also allows for the further monopolisation of taxation, judiciary and education, which in the authoritarian states usually extends to the full control of mass media. Unlike their pre-modern counterparts, the nation states also require and rely on the large administrative apparatuses, extensive and efficient transport and communication networks and many other advanced forms of infrastructure.

In addition, nation states have compact territories, fixed borders and centralised governing structures emanating from the capital cities. They often have substantial impact on the economy, culture, politics and welfare of their citizens. All of these are ingredients of organisational and coercive power that makes nation states infrastructurally much more potent than most of their pre-modern counterparts. As Mann (1984: 114) emphasises, nation states are unique in a sense that they can 'assess and tax our income and wealth at source, without our consent'; they store and can recall immediately 'a massive amount of information about all of us'; they can enforce their 'will within a day almost anywhere' in their domains; their impact on the economy is huge and they also provide the subsistence of most of us (in state employment, in pensions, in family allowances, etc.). This enormous organisational and coercive capacity, coupled with the greater level of popular legitimacy attained through grounded nationalism, allows nation states to enact and maintain a specific interpretation of social reality codified as 'the national identity'. Since nearly all social organisations that compose nation states are created and maintained with a view of performing a specific task in relation to preservation or enhancement of the nation state, their organisational roles (and the ideological discourses deployed) are inevitably centred on reproducing the existing nation state. Thus in the modern era we are all born in nation states, raised in the educational institutions run by and in the name of nation states, are employed by nation states and in our old age and illness are provided and cared for by the nation states. Even the private corporations that operate in this world have to follow the rules and regulations of nation states. Simply put, in organisational terms, we live in a deeply nationcentric environment and our livelihoods are regularly dependent on a substantial degree of loyalty to the respective nation states. In such an environment, the idea of national identity is less of a personal choice or an emotional/cognitive state of one's self-being and much more a reflection on the organisational and ideological realities of the world we live in.

As scholars of everyday nationalism emphasise, this nationcentric universe is maintained through banal and unnoticeable daily practices, from the nationcentric weather reports and tabloid newspaper headlines, the hanging flags on the government buildings, the everyday use of the national coins and postal stamps to the competitive international sporting events such as Olympics or World Cups (Brubaker et al. 2006; Edensor 2002; Billig 1997). Nationhood is also enacted, performed, talked about, and entrenched through the nationcentric consumption habits and even video games (Fung 2014; Skey 2011; Fox and Miller-Idriss 2008). For example, in Chinese online games 'gamers imagine themselves as part of the national history ... the way they perform the role and communicate with other gamers co-constructs the cultural definition of being Chinese' (Fung 2014: 36). In a similar way, the Japanese pop culture has gradually become integrated into the everyday nationalist practices. Hence, the pop idol bands have been systematically linked to the past cultural nationalist movements such as *nihonjinron* in order to reinforce an image of the Japanese nation as unique and culturally superior (Mandujano 2014).

However, what is crucial here is that all these practices entail the presence of specific social organisations – games are produced by large-scale private corporations and approved by the state's censorship boards, weather reports are generated by the government-created and financed meteorological agencies, and the mass production of newspapers, coins, stamps and national flags requires both public and private organisations. Even the pop idols are now manufactured by the corporate mass media and, often, with the tacit support of the consumerist state. The state budgets allocate substantial financial resources for the ritualistic commemorative events, monuments, celebrations and other practices associated with the preservation of nationhood. In other words, nationhood is firmly grounded in the variety of institutions. Moreover, open dissent against such commemorative events is regularly policed though ritualistic shaming or direct coercive acts. For example, describing the Delhi Republic Day parade, taking place every year on 26th January at Rajpath, New Delhi, as a celebration of militarism will automatically invoke hostility from both the state officials and many civil society groups (Pathak 2016). Although the practice of wearing a red poppy flower on the Remembrance Day, 11 November, is firmly associated with the United Kingdom and Canada, this ritual is also present in Sri Lanka where the commemoration ceremonies of Poppy Day take place at the War Hero cenotaph in Vihara Maha Devi Park, Colombo. Nevertheless, some political groups oppose this practice, seeing it as an imperial leftover and instead promote alternative forms of commemoration – from sunflower campaigns of the leftist movements (Suriyamal) to the more vigorous celebrations of 22nd May as Sri Lanka's true and only Remembrance Day (de Silva Wijeyeratne 2013). This is very similar to the British case where the resistance to the traditional commemorations is associated with wearing a white poppy (Melville-Smith 2014). Hence, the very presence and proliferation of 'national identity' is heavily dependent on the organisational and ideological scaffolds that prop up its existence. There is no 'national identity' without potent social organisations. The power of nationalism stems from its ideological and organisational ground-ness.

Framing Micro-Solidarity as National Identity

Anthony D. Smith (2010, 1991 [1983]) and other neo-Durkhemian theorists of nationhood insist that national identities are real in a sense that they provide intense meanings and emotional attachments to individuals. For Smith (1991: 16–17) national identities 'fulfil more intimate, internal functions for individuals in communities'; they are 'called upon to provide a social bond between individuals and classes by providing repertoires of shared values, symbols and traditions ... members are reminded of their common heritage and cultural kinship and feel strengthened and exalted by their sense of common identity and belonging'. This rather conventional view of national identities is built on a wrong premise that nationhood by itself automatically generates affection and meaning. Nevertheless, if this were the case, there would be no need to invest enormous energy and resources into making and keeping ordinary individuals loyal to their nation states. If such emotional attachment was natural and straightforward, politicians, intellectuals and generals would not have to regularly make appeals for national unity, solidarity and the duty to sacrifice for the nation. Historians and historical sociologists have convincingly demonstrated that transforming disloyal peasants into enthusiastic Frenchmen, Germans, Czechs or Indonesians was an extremely difficult and protracted historical process that has never been finalised (King 2005; Anderson 1998; Sato 1994; Breuilly 1993; Mann 1993; Weber 1978). Despite two and a half centuries of intense nationalist socialisation, nationhood is still not universally accepted as the primary source of one's emotional bond. Even in times of wars and other national calamities, most individuals value their family members, friends and local communities more than their nation states (Malešević 2017, 2010). Moreover, as Collins (2012) rightly argues, the intensity of nationalist attachments remains dependent on specific institutionalised and non-institutionalised events. Although group-experienced nationalist attachments can be powerful and intense, such Durkhemian collective effervescence cannot last for a long time. Killing of a prominent co-national by a government from the hostile nation state might provoke ad hoc movements characterised by strong nationalist intensity but such feelings usually do not last. For example, 1999 US bombing of the Chinese embassy in Belgrade that killed three Chinese journalists and injured another 20 people sparked furious nationalist reactions and large-scale demonstrations in China but this ad hoc movement dissipated very quickly after this event (Weiss 2014; Zhao 2014).[2]

None of this is to say that emotions and meanings do not matter. On the contrary, human beings are first and foremost affective creatures in constant search of meaningful action. Although in the short term, human actions might be often instrumental, strategic and driven by rational choices, in the long term, motivation and internal fulfilment regularly stem from meaningful and emotionally satisfying activities. In contrast to the utilitarian action which is premised on mutually interdependent interests, emotional bonds do not necessarily entail reciprocity. Instead, affective bonds require prolonged and dedicated, small-scale, face-to-face interaction that one usually experiences within family networks, deep friendships, among committed lovers, close neighbourhoods, peers, clans, gangs and other tightly bound groupings. As micro-sociological and socio-psychological studies demonstrate, an overwhelming majority of human beings derive their emotional fulfilment, comfort and sense of ontological security from such small-scale groups (Malešević 2015; Collins 2008, 2004; Dunbar 1998).

Hence, one of the key issues for all modern social orders is how to reconcile the instrumental demands of the large-scale social organisations with the micro-level emotional attachments that mobilise social action. In most respects, these two represent the polar opposites: while social organisations such as nation states or business corporations are bureaucratic, formalised, anonymous, instrumental and emotionally detached, the family and friendship-related micro-groups are built on the sense of familiarity, intimacy, affective bonds, spontaneity and shared morality. Whereas nation states are generally huge conglomerates of millions of people who will never meet each other and who constitute an abstract and, for the most part cold, entity, the micro-world of face-to-face interaction is premised on emotionally shared warmth where everybody knows everybody else. Therefore, to successfully close this enormous gap, all social organisations have to devise adequate mechanisms which would

---

[2] As Zhao (2014) emphasises, initially the government was highly supportive of student demonstrations spreading throughout over 20 cities in China. However, once it realised that it could lose the control of the demonstrations, they were not permitted any longer.

project the image of micro-level solidarities onto the screen of large-scale social organisations. Since the nation states, unlike business corporations, can better utilise the rhetoric of kinship, they are often much more successful in emulating the affective bonds of the micro world.

Hence, regardless of whether the particular nation state adopts the predominantly ethnic or the civic discourses of popular legitimacy, there is a pronounced tendency to frame the central principles around the myth of common descent. In some cases, the ethnic mythologies invoke the sacrifices of 'our shared ancestors', such as in the Indian heroic myths of Shivaji Maharaj and Lakshmibai, the Rani of Jhansi or in the Israeli myths of Masada (Heimsath 2015; McLane 2005, Zerubavel 1994). In other, more civic, myths, the shared common descent is linked to the values espoused and fought for by the 'founding fathers', as in the case of José Rizal in the Philippine national project or Ahmad Shah Durrani in Afghan nationalist movements (Go 2011).[3] In each of these, cases common descent is not conceptualised in terms of the literal blood relations as nearly everybody is well aware that such links with the ancestors are not genetic. Instead, the focus is on the moral responsibility that the common descent invokes. As Mock (2014: 87) emphasises, the 'perception of distant familial ties alone does not translate into national community unless it is accompanied with a sense that those common ancestors suffered and sacrificed to maintain the group as a group'. In other words, the institutions of nation state deploy the imagery and rhetoric of micro-level solidarity to continuously legitimise and mobilise social action of individuals under their control. This is occasionally done through the deliberate acts of political entrepreneurs, nationalist intellectuals or military figures but in most other cases it is almost a habitual practice that all modern nation states are involved in. In this context, organisationally generated, deep ideological penetration is a precondition for organisational success. The cumulative bureaucratisation of coercion provides the long-term built organisational environment but it is the ideology of nationalism that 'translates' genuine micro-solidarities into an attachment to a specific nation state. What is externally and colloquially perceived as having a strong 'national identity', is in fact reflection of the long-term structural development: the capacity of nation states or

---

[3] In some instances, the same mythology could be used for either ethnic or civic understandings of the nation. For example, the Chinese concept of 'minzu' has been redefined significantly throughout recent history: from Liang Qichao's Volkish notion that stood for a racial definition of a Chinese, Han-dominated, nation towards more inclusive understandings of Maoist intellectuals such as Li Weihan and Fan Wenlan who developed a notion of a 'multi-minzu' country and the more recent designations of China as being comprised of 'super-minzu' (Leibold 2013, 2007).

social movements (in cases where the ambition is to secede) to ideologically and organisationally penetrate the micro-level universe and to connect the disparate pockets of micro-solidarity into a society-wide macro-level narrative of ideological unity. There is no 'national identity' without ideology, social organisation and micro-solidarity. It is the unique, historically produced, combination of these three processes that make what we perceive as 'national identities' possible. Obviously, this in not to say that one's feelings of attachment to nationhood are insincere or a result of indoctrination. On the contrary, precisely because the discourse of 'national identity' is organisationally and ideologically so grounded in our everyday life, such feelings of attachment are possible and, almost universally, seen as normal and natural.

Conclusion

To question the existence of national identities does not imply that the individual feelings and cognitions of billions of individuals throughout the world do not matter. Moreover, this argument does not support the traditional Marxist premise of nationhood as a form of false consciousness. On the contrary, in the contemporary world, most expressions of national identifications are sincere and genuine and an overwhelming majority of individuals perceive their national identities as real, tangible and meaningful pillars of one's selfhood. The point of this chapter was to historically and analytically probe the structural context of such pervasive beliefs and practices. Rather than taking such statements of belief at face value, it is crucial that they are historicised and contextualised. Once this is done properly, then it becomes clear that all claims to collective identities rest on the specific ideological and organisational scaffoldings that frame, integrate and ultimately control human feelings of attachment (to the small-scale groups). To understand the significance of national identity in the contemporary world, it is paramount to move beyond the conventional present-centric narratives of identification in order to realise that there is no identity without ideology, organisation and micro-solidarity.

2   Grounded Nationalisms and the Sociology of the Long Run

Introduction

The main representatives of the longue durée perspective in nationalism studies are the ethno-symbolists Anthony D. Smith and John Hutchinson. Ethno-symbolism has often been characterised as the most significant alternative to the modernist theories of nationalism. In the conventional understanding, the modernist accounts are deemed to be shackled by their 'blocking presentism' and as such confined to a rather blinkered view of long-term social change. In contrast, ethno-symbolism is perceived historically to offer a much more nuanced explanation of nation-formation processes. In this chapter, I challenge such conventional interpretations. More specifically, I argue that the longue durée perspective is fully compatible with modernist approaches to nationalism. The chapter briefly explores the four modernist sociological models of the long run, explains how each of these approaches relates to the study of nationalism and identifies their strengths and weaknesses. The third part of the chapter provides a critique of ethno-symbolism and long-run modernism by outlining an alternative, grounded, version of the longue durée perspective.

Ethno-Symbolism and the Longue Durée

In the multidisciplinary field of nationalism studies, the concept of longue durée is firmly associated with the ethno-symbolic approach as initially articulated by John Armstrong (1982) and then fully developed by Anthony D. Smith (2009, 1986) and John Hutchinson (2017, 2005). The principal idea behind this position is that the rising significance of nationhood and nationalism in the contemporary world cannot be explained solely by focusing on recent social changes. Instead, as Smith (2004: 197) argues, 'the study of nations and nationalism requires a long-term approach, one that seeks to trace patterns of development and change over la longue durée in collective cultural identities'. Similarly,

Hutchinson (2000: 651) insists that 'by examining the ethnic character of modern nations in la longue durée, we can identify more convincing recurring causes of national revivals, the role of persisting cultural differences within nations, and the fluctuating salience of national identities with respect to other social allegiances'. Both of these scholars view ethno-symbolism as an explanatory alternative to the modernist accounts of nation-formation. They point out that the modernist theories of nationalism overemphasise the role of relatively recent social changes, industrialisation, secularisation or urbanisation, while downplaying the significance of long-term factors in the nation-formation processes. Drawing on John Peel's (1989) idea, Smith (2004: 197) contends that the modernist approaches suffer from 'blocking presentism', that is, the inability to move away from the focus on present generations and their interpretations of the past, 'at the expense of that past'. In particular, Smith insists that most modernist theories provide top-down explanations that exaggerate the centrality of political or economic elites in the process of nation building. While both Smith and Hutchinson recognise the role political and other entrepreneurs play in manipulating ethnic and national solidarities for self-interested purposes, they are adamant that that there are objective limits to how far such instrumentalist policies can go. For example, Smith accepts that an overwhelming majority of nationalist narratives are based on selective and romanticised readings of actual past events but he argues that such interpretations can never be arbitrary or based on random choices. In his own words:

If you don't have cultural materials, what are you going to select? And if you do have them, what are you going to leave out, and what criteria do you employ for the selection? My point was that in order to appeal even to some of the population that the elites wished to mobilise, they had to select elements that possessed some meaning and significance ('resonance') for that particular population ... At its most basic, this means that elites had to remain within the cultural traditions of the populations they wished to rouse; it was – it is – no good trying to rouse the English with appeals to French history or Russian literature or German football! (Smith 2003b: 362)

In many respects, ethno-symbolism emerged as an attempt to rectify what Armstrong, Smith and Hutchinson saw to be the main pitfalls of modernism: a) the present-centric understanding of nation formation where nations and nationalism are conceptualised as being largely a product of modernisation; b) the overemphasised, instrumentalist character of nationalism where there is little room for explaining the emotional resonance of nationalist narratives; c) the top-down explanations which focus on elite actions and as such cannot fully capture the dynamics of mass behaviour and the intense popular appeals of nationhood.

Although Armstrong's *Nations before Nationalism* (1982) laid foundations for the longue durée cultural approach, it was Anthony Smith's *The Ethnic Origins of Nations* (1986) that emerged as a fully developed articulation of ethno-symbolism. In this book and many other publications since, Smith has developed a distinct longue durée approach that is built around three central ideas: a) modern-day nations are often developed around the cores of previous ethnies that have existed for very long time; b) the strong elements of continuity between pre-modern ethnies and modern nations are regularly rooted in their shared symbolic properties – myths and memories; c) the power of nationalism resides in its emotional and moral appeal where ethnies and nations are often perceived as sacred communities.

For Smith, the popular resonance of nationalist narratives is rooted in the commonly shared transgenerational values. Although the pre-modern ethnies and modern-day nations differ in many respects, Smith emphasises the symbolic continuities between the two. In particular, he identifies the myth of common descent as a building block of the shared moral universe that binds the members of a particular nation with their pre-modern ancestors. Although such links might be fictitious, they are still regarded by many members of the nation as highly significant. In Smith's view, since the myth of common descent contributes towards the perception of the nation as a durable and meaningful moral entity, it also helps foster shared collective action around the idea of the nation. In this context, as Smith argues, nationalism is akin to a civil religion which incorporates specific ritualistic practices such as the periodic worship of sacrificial symbols that help establish and reinforce the ethical parameters of one's membership in a particular nation. For example, the annual commemorations dedicated to the soldiers who lost their lives in wars for the national cause (i.e. wars of independence or liberation, etc.) contribute towards maintaining strong symbolic links between the present and the past. In other words, Smith contends that to fully understand the strength of national identifications, it is essential to explore how such ritualistic events, which often commemorate individuals who have been dead for centuries, still can generate potent emotional responses among the contemporaries. For Smith, this behaviour can only be explained through the longue durée analysis that centres on the reproduction of shared moral universes shaped around transgenerational values that impose certain ethical obligations towards one's ethno-national predecessors. In his view, the idea of 'the glorious dead', an epitaph written on many WWI and WWII cenotaphs in the United Kingdom and elsewhere, captures quite well this sacred and temporal dimension of nationhood. In his own words:

The cult of the glorious dead gives the most tangible expression to the idea of the nation as a sacred communion of the dead, the living and the yet unborn. But more important, the cult of the glorious dead, and rites and ceremonies of national commemoration that accompany it are themselves seen and felt as sacred components of the nation intrinsic to its 'sacred communion' of history and destiny'. (Smith 2003a)

In this understanding, such rituals only reinforce what is already there – shared traditions and symbols and the rich mosaic of common myths and memories. Hence, for ethno-symbolists, the strength of national identifications in the modern era stems in large part from their historical rootedness: although not all contemporary nations have traceable or recognisable ethnies, many do and the majority of nationalist movements draw inspiration from the past. Furthermore, for ethno-symbolists, and Smith in particular, the past that really matters in the nation-formation processes is the cultural past. While recognising that nations might inherit some economic or political heritage from ethnies, it is the cultural resources that are seen by the ethno-symbolists as central in perpetuating the longue durée link between the pre-modern and modern worlds. For Smith, nations are, in cultural terms, the modern incarnations of ancient ethnies. Although nationhood involves much more complex organisational forms, it still preserves the vital cultural ingredients that underpinned pre-modern ethnies, including common myths and elements of common culture. As Smith (1986: 157) emphasises, in modernity, ethnies are faced with a choice of becoming nations or disappearing: 'a transition from *Gemeinschaft* to *Gesellschaft* finds confirmation in the more limited but vital sphere of ethnicity: in the modern era, ethnie must become politicised ... and must begin to move towards nationhood ... [and] take on some of the attributes of *Gessellschaft*, with its features of rational political centralisation, mass literacy, and social mobilisation'.

There is no doubt that ethno-symbolism offers a potent and coherent alternative to the conventional modernist accounts of nation-formation. The ethno-symbolists rightly challenge those modernist perspectives that ignore the significance of past events or the long-term historical dynamics of social change. For example, John Hutchinson (1994) is absolutely right that one cannot fully nor adequately understand nationalism from the rather narrow 'revolutionary' model of modernisation as the long-term social transformations in Western Europe and elsewhere have also developed in more evolutionary ways. For example, Gellner's (1996: 366) rather radical statement that 'the world was created round about the end of the eighteenth century, and nothing before that makes the slightest difference to the issues we face' seems to be indicative of such a problematic hypermodernist view. Similarly, Smith's criticism that some modernist concepts of the nation are tautological and Eurocentric also makes sense. Smith (2008: 13–14) points out that some modernist definitions rule out 'any rival definition of the nation, outside modernity and the West. The Western conception of the modern nation has become the measure of our understanding of the concept of the nation per se, with the result that all other conceptions become illegitimate.'

Although these general criticisms are well founded, the ethno-symbolist emphasis on the centrality of culture is simply inadequate. While one can readily agree with the view that nationhood is not something that just springs suddenly out of nowhere without accepting the idea that nations emerge from long-lasting cultural cores, there are three key problems with the ethno-symbolist version of longue durée analysis of nationhood. Firstly, Smith's central idea that nations emerge out of, and in some crucial sense resemble, ethnies ignores the historical realities of their respective social worlds. As Breuilly rightly points out (1996: 151), much of the pre-modern world had no institutional frameworks for the development and maintenance of large-scale group identities. Consequently, most social attachments tended to remain local, fragmented and discontinuous. In the European context, such institutional structure could have been provided by the church or the well-established dynasties, but neither of these two were well equipped for the advancement or preservation of ethnic or national attachments. Instead, both of these institutions were ideologically and organisationally shaped around trans-local and universalist principles that emphasised religious transcendentalism and aristocratic privilege where there was no room for ethnies or nations. Hence, there is no automatic transition from ethnies to nations, as nations, unlike ethnies, entail presence of complex organisational and institutional shells.

Secondly the ethno-symbolists utilise very wide, and as such quite imprecise, catch-all concepts of culture that cannot adequately discriminate between different social processes involved. Speaking about shared transgenerational cultural values in the pre-modern and modern contexts as if they are very similar or nearly identical is empirically unfounded. Although Smith (2003a) argues that this cultural continuity involves gradual transformation from the largely traditional notions of chosen people and sacred covenants towards more modern ideas of shared ethnohistory or collective memories, his conception of culture remains very static. For one thing, the ethno-symbolist assumption that cultural values persist through time is not corroborated by any meaningful evidence as we have little or no information on the popular beliefs of most premodern populations. As Laitin (2001) shows, Smith tends to illustrate his arguments with anecdotal examples, many of which have not undergone any proper methodological scrutiny. For another thing, Smith and other ethno-symbolists tend simply to assume that the ancient records about the collective perceptions and feelings of various groups are reliable. Nevertheless, such documents can never be taken at face value as many ancient writers tended to exaggerate and misinterpret their social realities by labelling different groupings as if they were one and same group, by inventing ethnic groups where none existed, by not differentiating between temporary warrior coalitions and specific ethnic communities and by not recognising the highly dynamic and volatile internal group structures (Steuer 2006; Geary 2002, 1988). In reality, we have no reliable evidence on what the thoughts of most pre-modern individuals on these matters were. More importantly, one should not project contemporary concepts such as 'nation', 'identity' or 'ethnicity' that were created in, and devised for, modern mass societies into the pre-modern world of localised, dispersed and often rather isolated small communities (Malešević 2006). In this context, ethno-symbolists conflate culture with ideology: whereas in much of the pre-modern world, cultural practices rarely if ever transcended locality, close kinship networks or a small village, in the modern world, cultural resources are often interwoven into the powerful ideological narratives and practices. Hence, while many traditional myths and memories were confined to the microcosm of one's village, clan or family, the contemporary societywide nationalist commemorations entail presence of powerful organisational and ideological apparatuses.

Finally, the ethno-symbolist accounts tend to conflate the micro and macro realities of the social world. Although Smith clearly distinguishes between small-scale ethnies and the usually much larger nations, his approach is still shackled by a very static understanding of group solidarity. In his approach, the size of collectivities has no bearing on the quality and intensity of their attachments. Ethnies, just as nations, are perceived to be cohesive and, for the most part, homogeneous entities held together by strong moral and emotional ties.[1] For example, Smith (1986: 97) writes about ethnies as 'a cluster of populations with similar perceptions and sentiments generated by, and encoded in, specific beliefs, values and practices'. Similarly, nations are understood as 'sacred communions of

---

[1] Smith (1991) identifies two different ideal types of ethnies and nations – lateral ethnies that largely transformed into the modern civic nations and vertical ethnies that often became ethnic nations. However, this distinction does not focus on group size and how size influences the character of solidarity. As I have argued before, Smith's typology is congruent with Durkheim's dichotomy of mechanical and organic solidarity and they both tend to ignore the question of group size (2013: 172, Malešević 2006: 117).

citizens' who share common political religion of nationalism 'with its own scriptures, liturgies, saints and rituals' (Smith 2010: 157). This conflation of the micro and macro worlds leads Smith and other ethno-symbolists towards the view that all collectivities, regardless of size, experience the same type of social attachment. However, the plethora of micro-sociological studies has established clearly that individuals tend to act differently in groups of different size (Weininger et al. 2019; McClelland 1985; Collins 2008, 2004). From Simmel (1955[1917]) to Collins (2008), sociologists have demonstrated how the intensity of solidarity tends to decrease as group size increases. Hence, the social ties that ethno-symbolists attribute to ethnies and nations are not built of the same interactive material. Whereas small face-to-face interactions often involve genuine emotional ties, most large-scale anonymous collectivities emerge and are sustained through the protracted organisational and ideological work. Therefore, one cannot assume that national attachments involve an all-encompassing, societywide and synchronised expression of feelings towards all members of a particular nation. Instead, such rather temporary states of macro-level cohesion can only be generated through the active involvement of specific social organisations such as the state, educational system, military, mass media and so on.

Modernism and the Longue Durée

Although ethno-symbolists insist that modernist perspectives as such tend to completely ignore the pre-modern world, this has not been the case in all instances. In fact, even staunch modernists such as Gellner or Hobsbawm engage extensively with the past and explore how and why the pre-modern world, which dominated much of human historical experience, suddenly transformed into something profoundly different – the epoch of modernity. For example, in his *Plough, Sword and Book* (1988), Gellner provides a subtle historical sociological analysis of the long-term social transitions that have gradually changed the world over the course of human history: from foraging bands to agrarian civilisations to industrialised modernity. Although Gellner emphasised the centrality of industrialisation for the emergence of nationalism, the account presented here is much more nuanced than some of his blunt statements that completely dismiss the role of the past. Nevertheless Gellner, Hobsbawm and Laitin, among others, do subscribe to the strong modernist position that sharply differentiates between the traditional and the post-traditional world. This is exemplified by Gellner's (1997: 17–20) Big Ditch thesis, where the pre-modern Agraria is counterposed to modern Industria. In this view, the Agraria is built on the Malthusian system dominated by a stagnant economy where there is 'a ceiling on possible production, though not on population growth' and where people 'starve according to rank'. In contrast, Industria, which stands on the opposite side of the Big Ditch, is characterised by perpetual scientific development, economic growth, innovation, complex division of labour and intense social mobility. The Big Ditch thesis also invokes the sharp cultural differences that underpin these two social universes: whereas in Agraria culture serves to 'reinforce, underwrite, and render visible and authoritative, the hierarchical status system of that social order', in Industria, culture operates as a social glue that forges new citizens capable of functioning in a highly dynamic environment. For Gellner (1997), the semantic character of work relations in industrial societies entails the presence of a universal, context-free literacy that allows for 'frequent and precise communication between strangers involving a sharing of explicit meanings', which ultimately establishes conditions for greater social and geographical mobility. While Gellner's perspective is insightful, he and other representatives of strong modernism fail to account for the elements of continuity present in the nation-formation processes. In other words, one can readily accept the argument that modernity represents a qualitatively different model of social order without necessarily accepting the view that such order springs *deus ex machina*. The pre-modern and modern social realities differ but modernity develops on top of already existing organisational, institutional, ideological, micro-interactional and other scaffolds. There is no Big Bang that gave birth to the modern world. Even the Big Ditch metaphor is too one-dimensional to capture the complexity of long-term historical change. Thus, to understand the historical dynamics of nationalism and nation-state formation, it is paramount to take the long-term past seriously and to not only trace discontinuities and sharp differences but also to look for the continuities and similarities where they exist. Nevertheless, these are not necessarily the cultural continuities so dear to the ethno-symbolists. Instead, one could zoom in on the economic, political, biological and other sources of historical continuance.

In this context, one could identify several modernist sociological traditions of research that develop a longue durée approach to the study of social phenomena, including the world system approach, the Eliasian tradition and the neo-Weberians approaches, among others. Although some of these schools of thought do not focus extensively on nationalism, nationhood or nation-state building, they all provide coherent analyses of these phenomena. Even the original longue durée perspective articulated by Fernand Braudel and other representatives of the second generation of French Annales school, developed a distinct interpretation of nation-formation which combines the modernist and perennialist elements.

This approach developed in opposition to the dominance of event-centred historical analysis. In contrast to conventional historiography that focuses on significant historical events (i.e. the invention of the printing press, or the French revolution) or influential personalities (i.e. Napoleon or Stalin), the Annales school centred on identifying the long-term patterns of social change. Furthermore, this type of macro-historical analysis was capable of shifting the focus from the traditional historical narratives steeped in methodological nationalism towards analyses that transcend specific political boundaries and fixed time frames. Hence, rather than studying France, Italy or Spain as individual trans-historic entities, Braudel explored the historical dynamics of the entire region of the Mediterranean. Although Braudel and his followers were primarily focused on the macro-economic and social factors, they also articulated a distinct longue durée view of nationhood. For Braudel (1988: 303–5), nations are historically dynamic entities that change through time and space. Hence, modern-day France is not a singular and fixed society but, as he puts it, 'many societies'. However, unlike the conventional modernists who deny the existence of nationhood before modernity, Braudel argues that nation formation was a long-term creative process where 'the crucial events occurred in fact millennia ago'. For example, unlike Hobsbawm or Gellner, who see the French Revolution as the pivotal moment in the formation of the French nation, Braudel (1988: 72) argues that France was not born in 1789 but emerged gradually and over a long period of time in the village construction and kinship ties of the 'pre-Roman Gaul'.

World-system scholars such as Wallerstein, Arrigi and Chase-Dunn, among others, also offer a distinct modernist longue durée interpretation of social development where nation-formation is also discussed. Although much of their attention is on the transformation of capitalism over the course of human history, world-system scholars relate the nation-formation processes to the changing dynamics of world systems. Thus, Wallerstein (1987, 1980) understands the development of nation states through the prism of capitalist expansion throughout the world. He contends that, unlike classes, which are the primary generators of social action, nations are historical inventions that develop quite late in human history. However, this modernist interpretation is also built on an idea that nations do not emerge ex nihilo but are the result of long-term social development in the structuring of the world system. For Wallerstein (1987: 381), 'the nation hinges around one of the basic structural features of the world economy' that is 'the political superstructure of this historical system, the sovereign states that form and derive from the interstate system. In other words, nations emerge on the backbone of the states that are themselves products of the capitalist world system. In Wallerstein's theory (1987: 387), nations are modern entities but their development involves a longue durée processes: nation is 'in no sense a primordial stable social reality, but a complex clay-like historical product of the capitalist world-economy'.

The Eliasian approach also offers a modernist interpretation of nation formation which is grounded in the longue durée model of analysis. For Eliasians, the long-term development of states was a historical precondition for the emergence of nationhood. In *The Civilising Process* (2000), Elias writes about the historical competition of the small pre-modern 'survival units' that gradually become larger, more powerful and more centralised states capable of monopolising and controlling physical power. In this interpretation, state development does not automatically lead towards shared national identity. Instead, as Elias (2000) points out, it takes a long time for states to become nations. For example, the seventeenth century French absolutist state was not an entity that most of its population could identify with: this polity still did not inspire a sense of 'subjective integration' that characterises contemporary attitudes towards one's nation state. For Elias and his followers, nations entail shared feelings of belonging, a developed national conscience and the existence of the 'national habitus'. The Eliasian longue durée model identifies four historical mechanisms through which the nation states and nationalisms came into being from the Middle Ages until the contemporary period: 1) the gradual decline of small-scale identifications and the growing interdependence of individuals on the wider state level; 2) the increased significance of statewide institutions such as taxation, education and jurisprudence and the increased density of societywide networks of interaction; 3) the vertical diffusion of tastes, standards and practices whereby the middle and lower strata imitated the upper-class standards of self-restraint; and 4) the emergence of national 'we-feelings' that follow structural transformations (Kuipers 2013; Elias 2000, 1996).

However, the most significant modernist longue durée approach is represented by the neo-Weberian tradition of scholarship. Charles Tilly (1992, 1985), Michael Mann (2012, 1993, 1986) and Randall Collins (1999), among others, have developed an organisational materialist interpretation of nation-state formation. Although this perspective insists on the quintessential modernity of nation states they also emphasise that the creation and development of statehood is a long-term process involving gradual institutional transformations that took thousands of years. For Tilly (1992), war was a decisive catalyst of state building. Zooming in on early modern Europe, Tilly argues that protracted and costly inter-state wars forced European rulers to engage in capital accumulation and the extraction of more resources for wars. They also had to widen their recruitment base by introducing universal military conscription. To achieve this, rulers fostered the development of state infrastructure: transport and communication networks, proper systems of administration and revenue collection, census taking and so on. Consequently, from the seventeenth century onwards, state power become much more centralised and territorialised and rulers expanded their geo-political influence while also establishing monopolies on the use of violence within territories under their control. As Tilly (1975) demonstrates, this long-term process of state making was dependent on intensified coercive control at home and the expansion of warfare abroad resulting in the dramatic reduction in the number of European states: whereas there were around 1,000 states and statelets in fourteenth century Europe, by the early sixteenth century this number dropped to 500 and by the early twentieth century there were only thirty states left. For Tilly (1996: 303–6), this long-term development of state structure was a precondition for the emergence of nation states and nationalisms. He identified two dominant forms of nationalism that developed out of different state-making trajectories: the top-down trajectory where central rulers were directly involved in the process of state-enforcing nation formation and the bottom-up trajectory where peripheral elites embarked on state-seeking nationalism. In his view, the top-down model was centred on challenging and erasing 'all particularisms' while bottom-up nationalism was spearheaded by minority elites with 'strong investments in alternative definitions of language, history, and community' and who as such articulated nationalist rhetoric centred on victimhood and resistance to oppression.

Mann provides a similar interpretative account that focuses on the gradual increase in the organisational capacity of states. He, too, traces the long-term processes that underpin the expansion of infrastructural powers of states, as well as their geopolitical transformation, often shaped by the dynamics of warfare. Mann understands state formation through the prism of changing power network dynamics. He identifies political, military, economic and ideological powers as 'overlapping networks of social interaction' that 'offer alternative organizational means of social control' (Mann 1986: 2). In this account, nation states do not emerge ex nihilo but develop gradually through the historical interaction of military capacity, the struggle for the control of material resources, the changing dynamics of ideological legitimacy and the political power linked to the state's control of a particular territory. Utilising this power-centred analytical model, Mann (1995) identifies three distinct historical periods through which nation states and nationalisms developed in Europe: 1) the emergence of elite-based proto-nations in the eighteenth century rooted in the expansion of state power, commercial capitalism and the gradual spread of discursive literacy among intellectuals, bankers, merchants and high ranking officers; 2) the late eighteenth and early nineteenth century diffusion of nationalist ideas and practices among property-owning groups and other middle classes caused by war-induced fiscal pressure that forced rulers to grant some civil rights to middle-class groups; and 3) the advent of mass-scale nationalisms in the nineteenth and early twentieth centuries, underpinned by the continuous growth of commercial capitalism and state power, both of which increased the infrastructural capacities of states (i.e. the statewide transport, communication and educational networks, etc.). Mann (2016, 2012, 1993, 1986) also emphasises the role of the state in the development of nationhood. In particular, his vision of longue durée involves tracing the historical dynamics of state formation from the ancient civilisations in Mesopotamia to the contemporary dominance of US and Chinese states. Much of his focus here is on the long-term historical process that he calls social caging – a gradual but pervasive territorial and social containment of people within established institutional structures. In his view, both the formation of states and the regulation of private property relationships contributed towards the social caging of individuals throughout the course of history. In this context, both nation states and nationalism develop and are sustained through the caging institutions of the state and capitalism.

These four distinct longue durée perspectives – the Annales school, the world system approach, the Eliasian tradition and the neo-Weberian perspective – all offer well-developed modernist theories of nation-formation. Rather than ignoring the past or engaging in the 'blocking presentism', these four approaches provide comprehensive theories of long-term social change. Hence, not all modernist accounts ignore what Smith refers to as 'the pre-modern bases of nationhood'. While some modernist and constructivist scholars might be guilty of overemphasising 'the agendas and activities of recent political elites' and the views 'that nothing before the eighteenth century mattered, and therefore no account need to be taken, and no enquiry made, of conditions before that time' (Smith 2004: 196), that certainly is not the case with these four modernist longue durée perspectives. Therefore, the standard ethno-symbolist critiques require a serious qualification. Moreover, the ethno-symbolist contention that the only past that matters is the cultural past is as reductionist as it is empirically unfounded. What these four modernist accounts show is that it is quite possible and plausible to develop a longue durée theory of nation-formation which is neither culture-centred nor perennialist/ethno-symbolist in character. Nevertheless, this is not to say that these four alternative perspectives are without problems. On the contrary, I would argue that although these theories offer more persuasive interpretations than the ethno-symbolists, they also suffer from three pronounced epistemological weaknesses.

For one thing, these approaches overemphasise the role the state plays in nation-formation. There is no doubt that the state has historically been a pivotal structure for institutionalising nationalist ideas and practices, as well as for providing a unified locus of attention for the nationalist movements that resisted its power and fought for independence from the existing states. However, the state is only one type of organisational power and there is a need to explore the impact of many other social organisations that have historically been instrumental in this process, including private corporations, religious organisations, social movements, armed groups, civil society groupings, clandestine agents, transnational communities and so on. This is particularly relevant for understanding the historical context of the pre-modern world where no social organisation had uncontested monopoly on the legitimate use of violence, taxation, education and jurisprudence over a fixed territory. In this type of environment, state power was just one of many organisational forms that shaped social relations. Although Tilly clearly recognises the significance of social movements and other forms of 'contention politics', his approach remains firmly state centric where the success and failure of specific social movements is largely determined by their relationship with the state (Tilly 2003). Furthermore, even the concept of the state is in itself problematic as it papers over historically very different forms of polity ranging from city states, city leagues, khanates, sultanates, patrimonial kingdoms, empires, nation states and so on. In order to understand the origins and development of nation states and nationalisms one can, and should, not treat all these different forms of polity as if they belong to the same type – the state (see Chapter 3).

Secondly, the four modernist longue durée perspectives remain too instrumentalist in their explanation of nationalism. The neo-Weberians and the world-system theorists operate with a staunchly materialist and utilitarian understanding of nationalism. As Brubaker (2010: 375–81) rightly points out, in Tilly's theory of nationalism, cultural elements 'were subordinated to an underlying structural logic' which can deal with the changing incentives of rulers but can not explain 'why the claims-making of threatened elites takes the form of speaking in the name of a "nation," or why resource-hungry rulers themselves begin to use the language of nationhood to frame their claims on resources and loyalties'. The same criticism applies to the world-system theorists who advance even more economistic and instrumentalist theories where nationalism is completely determined by the forces of capitalism or, as Wallerstein puts it, nationalism is no more that a 'complex clay-like historical product of the capitalist world-economy'. Although Mann, Braudel and Elias leave more space for the role ideas, values and cultural practices play in the process of nation-formation, they, too, subscribe to the overly rationalist understanding of historical change. All these approaches see nationhood as a by-product of state formation where ideological action remains a subsidiary to economic or political forces. Even scholars such as Mann, who identify ideology as an autonomous source of social power, tend to downplay its significance for much of history. Hence, Mann (1986: 371) argues that, before modernity, ideological narratives 'had no general role of any significance, only world-historical moments' and that ideological power, including religion, has been in decline over the past two centuries. Such an instrumentalist perspective cannot fully or adequately account for the historical sources of the popular support for nationalism. In other words, what is missing in these modernist theories is the greater emphasis on ideology.

Finally, the four modernist approaches offer overly structuralist accounts of nationalism and nation states. Not only do they see nationhood as something that emerges through the top-down engineering of elites or specific institutions, but they also misunderstand or downplay the popular appeal of nationalism. The focus in these theories is on the working of specific state institutions, such as the military, the educational system or state-controlled media, in forging a shared nationhood. Hence, while they are good at explaining these long-term organisational dynamics, they are not so good at tackling the popular motivations. In other words, it is not so clear why at some point in history nationalist narratives start to appeal to the majority of a population. Why and how this ideological discourse, which remained a preserve of a small, mostly intellectual minority in the not so distant past, suddenly becomes a dominant source of political legitimacy and personal identification for billions of individuals in the present? It is certainly plausible to see this profound social change in terms of greater social caging of state power (Mann), the increased self-restraining practices of those who aspire towards faster social mobility (Elias), or through the prism of the greater diffusion of capitalist practices in the everyday life of individuals (Wallerstein). However, none of these explanations can fully capture the emotional and moral appeal that nationalist narratives and practices invoke. None of these four perspectives engage properly with the micro-interactional level of analysis. Since their focus remains macro-structural, they largely ignore the emotions and ethical imperatives that sustain and motivate much of human action. Even the Eliasian tradition, which acknowledges the importance of emotions, does not provide a sound micro-sociological explanation of social action. Instead of linking the structural and micro-interactional sources of social change, the Eliasians tend to deploy highly problematic, and explanatorily futile, Freudian categories devised for the clinical level of analysis to explain the emotional motivations of millions of individuals (Malešević and Ryan 2013).

Hence, although these four accounts demonstrate clearly that one can move beyond ethno-symbolism and articulate a modernist longue durée perspective on nation-formation, the existing approaches still can substantially be improved upon.

Grounded Nationalisms and the Sociology of the Long Run

The starting position of any modernist perspective is the idea that nationhood and nationalism are modern phenomena. Although scholars disagree on the precise timing and place of their origins, there is a general consensus among modernists that nationalism and nationhood appear quite late in human history: between the eighteenth and nineteenth centuries. There is also widespread convergence around the idea that nationalism develops together with the other pillars of modernity: capitalism, urbanisation, industrialisation, secularisation and the rise of specific forms of the modern state. Furthermore, the modernist school of thought emphasises that whereas, in traditional societies, cultural difference had little or no political meaning, in the modern world, nationalism becomes a sociological necessity. The new world of modernity fosters, and is dependent on, strong national attachments (Breuilly 1993; Anderson 1991[1983]; Gellner 1983).

These central premises of classical modernism make a lot of sense. It is difficult to see how the pre-modern empires, city states or patrimonial kingdoms could generate and maintain the cultural homogeneity of their populations. Even if such polities had organisational and ideological means to create this homogeneity, it is not clear why any ruler would be willing to politically mobilise or arm their subjects when they could then easily turn against that particular leader. It is also far from being obvious why any pre-modern sovereign would invest enormous resources to mould the subjects under their control when the borders, and hence also populations, of these territories were constantly shifting. Furthermore, since the traditional polities were as a rule deeply hierarchical – where there was no sense of moral equality between individuals belonging to the different social strata – it is difficult to envisage how and why such individuals would share the same cultural practices.

Nevertheless, claiming that nationalism and the sense of nationhood are quintessentially modern does not automatically mean that they emerge suddenly and out of nowhere. On the contrary, just as any other historical phenomenon, nationhood and nationalism have a distinct past. To say that nationalism is a modern ideology does not imply that the ideas and practices that underpin this ideological discourse have not been around before modernity. The same applies to the nation state and the sense of nationhood: while these phenomena attain their full sociological meaning in the modern era, their organisational ingredients have been around for much longer.

Hence, to understand the historical dynamics of nation formation, it is paramount to explore the organisational, ideological and micro-interactional processes that gave birth to, and then fostered, the emergence of nation states and nationalisms. More specifically, it is crucial to zoom in on the changing dynamics of organisational capacities, the scale of ideological penetration through time and the how these two structural processes are related to the micro-level solidarities.

The Coercive Organisational Capacity

The neo-Weberian perspective, as articulated by Tilly, Mann and Collins, provides the most advanced analysis of institutional and organisational processes involved in nation-formation. In particular, Mann's notion of 'social caging' and Tilly's concept of 'political racketeering' capture quite well the ever-increasing organisational developments that stand at the base of state power. The neo-Weberians demonstrate convincingly how and why once the state comes into existence, it soon becomes the most effective source for the accumulation of resources, people and capital. They also show how social development, including the rise of science, technology, transport, communication, education, administration and so on, often emerges as a by-product of a state's expansion. Once state rulers embark on creating larger military forces, more powerful weapons and the better control of their territories, they inadvertently foster the continuous advancement of the infrastructural capacities of their polities. However, what is missing in these statecentric accounts is the recognition that historically the organisational power has emerged and developed in the variety of guises. If one is focused solely on state power one is likely to miss the wider organisational sources that provide ingredients for the future development of nationhood and nationalism. To better understand the historical dynamics of nation-formation, it is crucial to explore all these different forms of organisational power – from independent armed groups, religious-military orders, private corporations, merchant guilds, religious associations to civil society agents and further afield. Although states are powerful social organisations that influence the trajectories of nation-formation, this has not always been the case as many pre-modern social orders operated in very weak polities. Furthermore, just as ethno-symbolists wrongly project nations into the past and see cultural homogeneities where there they did not really exist, so do some neo-Weberians wrongly perceive the state as a relatively uniform and historically continuous entity that has been in existence for thousands of years. Nevertheless, just as ethnies are not nations and small-scale ethnic attachments have nothing in common with modern-day nationalism, so the Sargon's Akkadian empire of twenty-fourth century BCE has very little in common with nineteenth century empires or twenty-first century nation states. Hence, to better understand the rise of organisational capacities over the course of human history, it is paramount not to conflate different forms of polity and to acknowledge that the sources of these capacities are highly divergent.

To capture these complex historical dynamics, it is necessary to zoom in on the patterns through which one can identify increased organisational capacities such as the expansion of military might, the development of administrative apparatuses, the increased economic capabilities, the growth of transport and communication networks, the centralisation of authority and so on. Since, in the modern era, nation states monopolise the legitimate use of violence, education, taxation and legislation, they tend to dominate all these indicators of organisational capacity. However, to fully understand this historically unique situation, one has to look deep into the past and explore the pre-modern realities where polities were generally much weaker in this respect and where organisational advancements materialised outside the central authority. For example, as Hintze (1960) shows, many regions in seventeenth and eighteenth-century central Europe had rather weak polities that operated as a Ständestaaten ('polity of estates'), where political, economic and military powers were split between rulers and the powerful estates. In this context, rulers could not impose their will on the powerful aristocrats but were obliged to consult them when introducing new legislation or planning military actions. Often, the nominal rulers were much weaker than the estates: the Duchy of Mecklenburg-Schwerin was militarily much stronger than the monarchs of German Confederation it formally belonged to. Similarly, the economic capacities of such nominal rulers were deeply inferior to those of independent city leagues such as the Hanseatic League (Hansa), which was a confederation of merchant guilds that dominated Baltic maritime trade for centuries (fourteenth to seventeenth century). The cities that belonged to Hansa had their own legal system and their own military force. Although some of the member cities were also part of various other polities, they maintained substantial autonomy in many areas.

Moreover some of the leading cities such as Hamburg were wealthier and more developed than the capital cities of other European polities. Hence, in this context and many others, the focus on the all-state orga-nisational capacity (i.e. German Confederation) would provide us with an inaccurate picture of historical reality as such polities were very weak and the real military or economic powers resided in different, non-state, social organisations. In both of these cases, Hansa and the polities of estates, one can find the organisational seeds of what eventually would become a sense of German nationhood. Whereas the Hanseatic League was complex organisation that included many cities with culturally diverse populations, its core membership base consisted of Low German speaking merchants. The League was subject to law of German polities and its free cities owed allegiance to the Holy Roman Emperor. More importantly, since Hanseatic cities were economically, and also militarily, much stronger than other parts of the Holy Roman Empire, they could significantly influence imperial policy. In this context, what was crucial in this relationship with the wider empire was not the cultural factors, as ethno-symbolists would claim, but the organisational strength of Hansa around which any future German nation state could and would have been built. The fact that Hanseatic cities had efficient and indepen-dent legal systems in place and were in possession of potent military organisations have all contributed towards providing the organisational building blocks of the future German nation state. The same applies to the polity of estates as it was these independent and militarily powerful estates that eventually fostered the rise and expansion of the militarily and bureaucratically most advanced German polity – Prussia. This long-term structural development was rooted in the ever-increasing organisational capacities of different historical agents: from the military-religious Catholic order of Teutonic Knights to the Duchy of Prussia to Brandenburg-Prussia and eventually to the Kingdom of Prussia which lead the successful 1871 unification of 'German lands' into the German empire under Prussian hegemony.

In addition to these powerful and independent merchant guilds and estates, one can also identify a variety of other robust social organisations which played an important part in creating structural conditions for the future development of nationhood. For example, Serbian and Greek nationalist narratives insist on cultural continuities in the development of their nations by tracing their 'unbroken' origins to the medieval Serbian empire under Dušan and the ancient Greek and Byzantine civilisations respectively. However, these pre-modern empires were deeply stratified and as such defined by intense vertical allegiances between aristocracies that had not, and could not, recognise 'their' peasants as being of equal moral worth to them. Hence, apart from the vaguely defined common religious denomination, there were no culturally shared practices between these two or any other social strata. Hence, the ethno-symbolist insistence on cultural continuity makes little sense here as the Serbian and Greek aristocracies and peasantries were not involved in joint trans-class commemorations nor have they shared the common myths of origins. Instead, the Byzantine and the medieval Serbian nobilities both had narrow, family-based, mythologies and genealogies of descent that were utilised to differentiate the nobility from the rest of the population. Thus, any claim towards cultural continuities of medieval and modern Serbs and Greeks is spurious (Pantelić 2011; Roudometof 2001).

Nevertheless, recognising the modernity of Serbian and Greek nation-hood does not automatically suggest that they emerge ex nihilo. Instead, in both cases, the emergence and rise of nationhood was rooted in long-term organisational development. While, as I demonstrate in Chapters 7 and 8, modern state formation played a central role in the growth of national awareness in the nineteenth and early twentieth centuries, it was the other social organisations that made this long-term structural transformation possible. One of the most important such social organisa-tions was the church. However, rather than focusing on the cultural sources of religion, as ethno-symbolists and also nationalists regularly do, the focus should be on the organisational capacities that the Christian Orthodox religious institutions provided. During the long per-iod of Ottoman rule, the Orthodox Church maintained institutional presence in much of the Balkans. Although the Ottomans converted some churches into mosques, such as Hagia Sofia and the Parthenon, they also allowed other churches and parish-based religious organisations to continue their existence. Moreover, they centralised the Orthodox Church by appointing a head of the entire Christian Orthodox popula-tion – the ethnarch. In addition, the Ottomans established a complex organisational vessel, the millet system, that helped not only preserve the presence of Orthodox Christianity in the Balkans but also fostered further institutionalisation of the church throughout the region. While before the Ottoman conquest the Christian aristocracy and peasantry had little or no interaction, during the Ottoman period the Church acquired the organi-sational and proto-ideological means to bring together different social strata into something that will later be recognised as a common Christian community. The fact that the patriarch /ethnarch was the religious and administrative ruler of the entire Orthodox millet meant that central church authorities gained greater control of the Christian populations in the Balkans. Initially, the millet system provided for the setup of a single Rūm millet (*millet-i Rūm*), but this was later reorganised to accommodate different cultural and religious traditions. During the Ottoman rule, the millets had substantial organisational powers, including the creation and implementation of their own laws, collection and distribution of their own taxes, control of their own administration and the monopoly on the educational and spiritual care of their flock (Mylonas 2012). These rather substantial organisational capacities were highly instrumental in providing institutional means and resources for the latter-day development of nationalisms in the Balkans. Both the Greek and Serbian nationalist movements drew on the religious heritage of Orthodoxy vis-a-vis the Muslim 'Other', but even more important in this process was the possibility of relying on the organisational means put in place by the Orthodox millet – the parish organisations, local churches and schools, the legal system, the financial resources collected by taxation, etc. In other words, the organisational structure of the millet system was highly beneficial for the latter-day establishment of nationalist movements that utilised already existing organisational infrastructure to challenge the Ottoman empire (Case 2010; Roudometof 2001; Mazower 2000).

Ideological Penetration

Modernist accounts emphasise that nationalist ideology differs substantially from pre-modern belief systems. Both Gellner and Anderson insist that nationalism involves a completely novel way of understanding relationships between human beings. In contrast to the traditional world where the focus was on eschatology, the afterlife and inherent hierarchies, modernity provides new social conditions that allow for the moral equality of all individuals. Hence, instead of 'the sacred script communities' where the high clergy would mediate between heaven and earth, in the modern world, people inhabit the moral universe of sovereign imagined political communities where they develop a sense of 'deep horizontal comradeship' with their co-nationals. Furthermore, the new economic conditions foster greater spatial and social mobilities where individuals have to develop new communicative and other skills to survive in ever-changing social environments. In this context, being educated in uniformed cultural practices and being proficient in standardised state languages becomes a necessity of everyday life. Hence, nationalism only makes sense under modern conditions.

These classical modernist accounts are correct in a sense that nationalism is, for the most part, incompatible with the traditional understanding of social relations. The pre-modern world was culturally too stratified and too centred on eschatological questions to leave much room for the concept of a unified, trans-class, nationhood. However, to fully comprehend how popular belief systems and practices change over long stretches of time, it is important to recognise this as a gradual process. In other words, although nationalist ideology is distinctly modern, it, too, develops slowly by expanding, transforming and reformulating already existing ideas, values and everyday practices. Hence, what is worth exploring is how different pre-modern beliefs and practices change and become redefined and incorporated into modern nationalist narratives. For example, many nationalist discourses invoke kinship-related metaphors such as 'our Peruvian brothers', 'a sacrifice for the Russian motherland', 'the sisterhood of Serbian daughters' and so on.[2] Nationalist rhetoric also utilises totemistic metaphors, conceptualising nations as totemic images deserving devotion and worship (Marvin and Ingle 1999). In this sense, one can notice a strong association with the imagery used by the hunter-gatherers and other pre-modern collectivities. This has already been recognised by Durkheim (1976: 387) when he compared the totemic rites of the Arunta in Australia to modern rituals such as 'a reunion of citizens commemorating the promulgation of a new moral and legal system or some great event in the national life'. Ethno-symbolists such as Smith (2000: 797) make much of this analogy: 'what Durkheim wrote about the Arunta and other Australian aboriginal tribes applies with equal, if not greater force, to nations and nationalism. This comes out clearly in his discussion of society's tendency to create gods, even secular ones, as during the first years of the French revolution, and of the totem as the flag or sign of the clan which evokes sacrifice on its behalf.' However both Smith and Durkheim are profoundly wrong in treating modern citizens and pre-modern hunter-gatherers as somehow being engaged in the same practice (Malešević 2006: 109–35). There is a huge difference between a small group such as the Arunta involved in their face-to-face interaction and the elaborate, and institutionally mediated, rituals devised for the celebration of an abstract entity involving millions of individuals that is a nation. Whereas the former entails performing a specific set of rites within a tiny, largely isolated, community that worships its only known deity, the latter encompasses a highly secularised social environment where the state and the specific social movements utilise their organisational powers to communicate and reinforce

---

[2] Lauenstein et al.'s (2015) study of national anthems, which included a meticulous content analysis of 203 lyrics from 204 countries, indicates that majority deploy kinship and friendship-related terms, thus attempting to tie micro-level solidarities with societywide nationalist narratives. Hence 53.2 per cent of all national anthems invoke family terms such as fatherland, motherland, sons, daughters, brothers, sisters, progeny, family, etc.

a particular ideological message that aims to project a sense of unity among millions of individuals that will never meet each other. Hence, there is no equivalence here at all. Nevertheless, the fact that similar imagery can be used in such diverse social orders indicates that nationalism can successfully draw upon already-existing rhetorical and other tropes. The key issue here is how, why and when such pre-modern imagery can find a substantial degree of resonance in the modern world? For example, why the idea of common ethnic descent still appeals to so many people. Although most individuals are well aware that such large entities as are nation states are composed of biologically heterogeneous populations, there is still widespread acceptance of the myth of common descent. One could recognise that more than a billion people could not possibly have the same biological predecessors, yet the citizens of India and China cling to the idea of common ethnic descent just as do citizens of much smaller nation states. To understand the strength of these beliefs and corresponding practices, it is necessary to zoom in on the role ideology plays in this process. As I emphasise in my previous work, human beings are ideological creatures that search for meaning, and internal as well as external justification of their actions (Malešević 2013a, 2010). In the pre-modern world, mythology, animistic beliefs, kinship-centred values, imperial doctrines and various religious creeds often operated as the principal proto-ideological discourses that helped legitimise a particular course of action. However, as most traditional orders were either very small, or if larger then highly stratified, there was neither organisational means nor the demand to forge societywide ideological unity. It is only in the modern era that ideological power takes centre stage in a sense that modern organisations and social movements aim to mould individuals into ideologically coherent wholes. Furthermore, since large-scale ideological penetration entails the presence of a robust organisational structure, it is only in modernity that one can rely on such advanced organisational capacity to generate, disseminate and reinforce specific ideological values and practices.

Nevertheless, although distinctly modern, this process of ideologisation builds upon previous proto-ideological processes. In other words, ideological penetration often relies on well-established idioms and actions, which are often reformulated and repackaged to appeal to a much wider (modern) audience. For example, the notion of common descent and the symbolism associated with flags and coats of arms, both of which are the cornerstones of contemporary nationalist imagery, emerged and developed from the already-existing pre-modern idioms. However, while in the pre-modern world, common descent, flags and coats of arms were a sole prerogative of a small cohort of aristocrats who used these cultural markers to differentiate themselves from non-aristocrats, in modernity, these cultural symbols became the central components of nationalist ideologies regularly utilised to demarcate one nation from the other. Hence, to understand the social significance and ideological potency of nationalist symbols, one has to trace this historical transformation from the proto-ideological symbolism of nobility to the societywide ideological narratives that dominate modern-day nationalist discourses. For example, most strands of Polish nationalism are deeply rooted in the belief that the Polish nation has been in existence for a very long time. These nationalist discourses invoke the historical longevity of Polish nobility (*szlachta*), whose descent is occasionally traced to biblical or ancient historical figures such as Noah's son Japheth or Alexander the Great and more commonly to the ancient Iranian tribe of Sarmatians (Davies 1982). Nevertheless, much of the focus here is on the Middle Age warrior clans who fought for the kings and dukes during the Polish Lithuanian Commonwealth (1569–1795). These members of mostly lower nobility had the right to display their own coat of arms and it was a common practice that families belonging to the same clan used the same coat of arms. This symbolised their shared descent and as such provided an organisational and proto-ideological structure for the higher social status of szlachta families. During the late Middle Ages there were only around 200 such noble families. However, by the early eighteenth century, this organisational and proto-ideological mechanism was utilised effectively by many to climb the social ladder (mostly through marriages and ennoblement) resulting in as many as 40,000 members of szlachta (Frost 2015). This number continued to increase dramatically and by the early twentieth century no fewer than one million individuals (13 per cent of the Polish population) were considered to be members of szlachta (Choloniewski 2016). They were all entitled to use common coats of arms and to claim shared descent with 'their' noble predecessors. Hence, with the rise of Polish nationalism in the nineteenth century, the szlachta tradition become a cornerstone of Polishness where the imagery and practices associated with szlachta become synonymous with the Polish nation. Hence, the original symbolism of common descent, expressed in family crests/coats of arms, become gradually extended to the much larger population and eventually transformed into a nationalist narrative that would encompass all Poles.

In this process, even the proto-ideology of early szlachta, sarmatism, was reformulated and incorporated into the dominant nationalist discourses. Traditionally, sarmatism was derived from the myth of szlachta's origin among the ancient Sarmatians. This belief system was associated with pacifism, the preservation of a traditional rural lifestyle, peaceful conduct and the possession of extensive personal freedoms. During the nineteenth and twentieth centuries, this Sarmatian proto-ideology, together with a distinct interpretation of the Catholic faith, was fully integrated into the Polish nationalist narratives that emphasised stoic victimhood and peaceful resistance to foreign domination. Furthermore, a key symbol of nobility, namely the distinct coat of arms indicating an aristocratic lineage, has gradually been reformulated to include a million individuals and eventually became a national symbol representing up to 40 million citizens of Polish nation state. Thus, the contemporary imagery associated with Poland, including the white crowned eagle with the golden beak and talons on a red background, is really a historical product of the long-term organisational and ideological transformation: an aristocratic symbol designed to differentiate nobility from 'their' commoners has gradually been appropriated as a symbol that distinguishes 'those commoners' (i.e. members of one nation state) from other 'commoners' (i.e. members of other nation states). This long-term historical shift indicates a degree of continuity in the process of nation formation. However this has little or nothing to do with cultural continuity, emphasised by ethno-symbolists, but is a process rooted in, and dependent on, ideological penetration which itself rests on the expansion of organisational capacities. In other words, it was not the cultural symbols themselves that were central in the transformation of an aristocratic myth into a nationalist narrative but it was the organisational and proto-ideological scaffolding of the szlachta system that made this transformation possible.

The Envelopment of Micro-Solidarity

One of the key criticisms of the modernist paradigm in nationalism studies is that they are too rationalist and too instrumentalist. Anthony Smith and other ethno-symbolists have claimed repeatedly that modernists largely ignore the emotional appeal of nationalism and when they see passions they tend to interpret this as a form of simple elite manipulation. In Smith's (1998: 128) own words:

[modernists argue that the] passivity of the masses must have its counterpart in the manipulations of the elites, that the emotions of an inert mass are waiting to be aroused and channelled by the elites as part of an exercise in social engineering ... this view fails to account for the passion and fervour of mass followings for nationalist movements and the frequent willingness on the part of the unlettered and poor to make great sacrifices and even court death to defend their countries.

Some of this criticism is well founded. Several strands of modernism, from Gellner and Hobsbawm to Laitin and Hechter, do operate with overly rationalist and elite-centred views of social reality (Malešević 2006, 2004). Furthermore, as Heaney (2013) shows convincingly, such accounts reproduce the highly problematic dichotomy where reason and emotions are assumed to be mutually exclusive phenomena and where passions are often conceptualised as the Other of rationality. In this context, emotions are often associated with violence and conflict while reason is linked to civic and liberal forms of nation-formation. However, the ethno-symbolists, too, are just as guilty of this analytical neglect of emotions. While they do regularly emphasise the centrality of passions, affects and 'fervour' in nationalism and generally do not associ-ate emotions with violence, they rarely, if ever, provide in-depth analyses of how emotions work in nationalism (Averill 2018, Collins 2012). Hence, instead of engaging with the sociology of emotions by identifying the historical trajectories of popular sentiments or by dissecting the subtleties of changing emotional states of individuals and specific collec-tivities, they tend to take the specific emotional states for granted and treat the emotional power as given, fixed and unproblematic. For example, Smith often singles out one's willingness to die as a prime example of strong emotional attachment to one's nation. Nevertheless, such state-ments, even when pronounced by soldiers who are facing death at the battlefields, can never be simply taken for granted. The decades of research on the motivations of soldiers, but also other individuals engaged in similar life and death situations, such as revolutionaries, terrorists, insurgents and others, indicate that in most cases individuals do not necessarily die for abstract entities such as nation, religion or political ideology. Instead, in most instances, one's emotional commitment remains on the micro level – towards one's family, friends and peers (Malešević and O'Dochartaigh 2018; Malešević 2017, 2010; Collins 2008, 2004; Bourke 1999; Gabriel 1987). Thus, to understand how nationalism and nation-formation processes operate, it is paramount to analyse the social or historical dynamics of emotional power (Malešević 2016, 2013a; Heaney 2013).

There is no doubt that emotions play an extremely important role in human motivation. As Turner (2007) and Barbalet (2002, 1996) show, humans are highly emotional creatures, more emotional than any other species on the planet. Moreover, despite enormous structural changes that have transformed the character of social orders under which humans live, there is a strong element of continuity in how emotions affect their behaviour: just as their foraging predecessors 80,000 years ago, contem-porary humans experience fear, anger, sadness, happiness, shame, guilt and many other emotions. A plethora of recent studies has also established that human beings are psychologically wired for life in very small groups. Not only do humans lack cognitive and emotional capacities to successfully maintain long-term interaction with a large number of individuals, but for much of their existence they had no organisational means to form and sustain large groups. Hence, for over 98 per cent of their existence on this planet, human beings have lived in very small, egalitarian, nomadic and malleable groups rarely consisting of more than fifty individuals (Fry 2007; Collins 2004; Damasio 2003; McCarty et al. 2000; Dunbar 1998). In this type of environment, emotional attachments had to remain on the very micro level: face-to-face daily interaction with close kin, peers, friends, neighbours and extended family.

However, recognising that human beings are first and foremost emotional creatures does not by itself tell us much about the strength of nationalism in the contemporary world. Since nationalism is for the most part a modern ideological discourse and practice, it is necessary to explain how, when and why this ideology acquired strong emotional appeal among the vast majority of modern individuals. To understand why and how this ideological discourse, which remained a preserve of a small minority in the not so distant past, suddenly became a dominant source of political legitimacy and personal identification for billions of individuals in the present, it is necessary to historically contextualise this social transformation. This long-term structural shift was facilitated through the highly contingent confluence of increased organisational capacity, ideological penetration and the envelopment of micro-solidarity. More specifically, nationalism could become a dominant (operative) ideological discourse only when the universal micro-interactional attachments were integrated into the wider organisational and ideological processes. In other words with the growth of coercive-organisational powers, and ideological mechanisms capable of justifying their aims and courses of action, large-scale organisations were able to successfully tap into the intimate microcosm of friendships, peer groups, neighbours and family networks. Since most efficient large-scale social organisations are entities driven by bureaucratic principles of goal maximisation, clearly defined and regulated division of labour, disciplined hierarchies of subordination and the accomplishment of specific tasks, they are, by definition cold, rational and impersonal. In contrast, our family and friendship networks are shaped by emotional warmth, personal intimacy and a close sense of belonging. It is these universal emotional and moral ties that make human life meaningful for millions of individuals. It is precisely because humans highly value these micro-social ties that they are often willing to endure great hardships and sacrifices for such micro-groups. This emotional power, which largely resides in the micro-world, has historically been an object of envy for many representatives of social organisations. Since Alexander the Great, who often forged omens and soldiers' family imagery to motivate his armies to fight (Taylor 2003: 29), the leaders of various organisations have attempted to harness and utilise the emotional and moral power of micro-solidarity.

Nevertheless, before the modern era, this was very difficult to achieve as most social orders lacked the organisational and ideological structure to mimic and embed micro-interactional ties within their entities. With the development of technology, infrastructure, communications, educational systems, transport networks and other forms of organisational and ideological capital, this has become not just a possibility but rather a common practice. Thus business corporations such as Microsoft, Apple or Google tend to depict their organisations as friendly entities that 'empower one's future'. For example, on their website, Microsoft is presented in the following words: 'We are a *family* of individuals at a truly global company, united by a single mission. We work together, building on each other's ideas and collaborating across boundaries to bring the best of Microsoft to our customers and the world' (https://careers.microsoft.com/mission-culture) [my italics]. Similarly, police and military forces throughout the world frame their activities and their raison d'etre in the discourse of micro-solidarity. From the US Navy to the Russian Army to the Chinese People's Armed Police, all these organisations invoke the centrality of internal cohesion and camaraderie among the organisational units while also emphasising their role as protectors of citizens and their families. In this context, the nation state is not different: it is yet another social organisation that derives much of its legitimacy from the claim that it represents something that most of its citizens cherish – the sense of emotional and moral attachment with people that matter. Thus, the strength of nationalism in modernity stems from its organisational and ideological ground-ness and its ability to mimic and replicate the language and practices associated with the face-to-face intimacy. Since the bureaucratic entities lack such emotional appeal, they have to couch their activities in discourses that resemble those one identifies with close friendships, deep family ties, stable peer groups or the everyday interaction with friendly next-door neighbours. In this context, it is no surprise that nearly all nationalist ideologies invoke kinship and friendship metaphors and speak about one's nation as 'our precious mother' or 'our sacred fatherland', while fellow citizens are depicted as 'our brothers and sisters' or 'our comrades and our brethren'. For example, even the communist states which nominally legitimised their rule in terms of proletarian universalism relied heavily on such kinship-based metaphors.

So North Korean publications regularly refer to the 'motherly bosom of our fatherland' and 'the spirit of the motherland' (Ryang 2000: 37, 126), while the Soviets would often speak of the immense 'love of the glorious motherland', 'the brotherly peoples of the Soviet Union' and 'its elder brother, the Russian people' (Berkoff 2012: 205).

Many representatives of nation states and nationalist movements invoke these kinship and friendship-based images deliberately aiming to link their anonymous and instrumentally driven organisations with the inherent warmth and intimacy of face-to-face micro-group interactions. However, much of this process is structural rather than voluntarist in the sense that all durable large-scale social organisations tend to tap into this emotional and moral microcosm in order to justify their existence, as well as to make their daily operations as frictionless as possible. In other words, it is more comfortable to work and live in an environment that projects the imagery of sisterhood and friendship rather than one associated with organisational demands, formal plans and robotic commands. Crucially, the successful mimicking of micro-solidarity also sooths the coercive underbelly of the organisational power.

The fact that the social organisations regularly engage in this process that I call the envelopment of micro-solidarity, does not mean that they embark on a giant brainwashing exercise. Not at all, as much of what happens here does not go against the beliefs of those who are members of these organisations, including the nation state. There is no doubt that, in the contemporary world, the majority of people see their nation states as the only legitimate form of territorial rule and their nationhood as the principal mode of collective identity (Malešević 2013a). Instead, this is a structural phenomenon that has developed over a long period of time. Although nationalism is a modern form of collective subjectivity, the historical conditions that ultimately gave birth to this phenomenon are much older. Hence, the envelopment of micro-solidarity is grounded in the longue durée processes that were present throughout history. Pre-modern social organisations also utilised the language and practices of micro-groups to boost their legitimacy and to mobilise social action. For example, chiefdoms, ancient empires, city states, patrimonial kingdoms, khanates, sultanates and many other traditional forms of polity drew upon kinship-based images to link different mythological, religious and imperial doctrines with the everyday reality of their worlds. For example, populations of Renaissance city states of the Apennine Peninsula such as Venice, Florence, Genoa or Pisa developed a strong sense of territorial attachment and local identification which was in part rooted in the networks of micro-solidarity (Viroli 1997). Furthermore, these city states had unusually high literacy rates, reaching up to one third of the entire male population, which was rather exceptional for a pre-modern world (Burke 1986; Martines 1983). In this context, the social organisations could to some extent infiltrate the everyday life of their inhabitants and generate a degree of loyalty with their city states. Nevertheless, even this unusually high sense of popular attachment for a pre-modern polity requires a lot of contextualisation. As I have argued before, city states, patrimonial kingdoms and other pre-modern polities were still ideologically too hierarchical and deeply stratified while also lacking the organisational capacities that characterises the world of nation states (Malešević 2013a). Nevertheless, occasional reliance on the discourses and practice of micro-solidarity in the traditional world indicates that contemporary nationalist rhetoric draws on the already-existing topoi that resonate well with most individuals. Such appeals to one's close kin and deep friendships have historically had strong resonance as they centre on one's sense of emotional attachment, moral commitment and ontological security. Where the world of nation states differs from their pre-modern counterparts is in its organisational and ideological structure: it is this structural context that successfully, and often indiscernibly, links pockets of micro-solidarity with societywide ideological narratives. In other words, in the traditional, deeply hierarchical, world, peasants could almost never be family members or friends of aristocrats, thus, the discourses of micro-solidarity could not be ideologically framed and deployed outside one's social strata. Hence, in the pre-modern universe of capstone empires and composite kingdoms, such rhetoric was for the most part confined to a very narrow circle of fellow aristocrats. In contrast, the nation states are grounded in the principles that value nominal egalitarianism, the moral equality of its citizens and popular sovereignty, all of which foster an environment that is receptive to the imagery of nations as extended families and co-nationals as brothers, sisters, friends and neighbours. It is these long-term processes that make grounded nationalisms possible.

Conclusion

One of the key criticisms levelled against modernist theories of nationalism is that they are present centric and as such ignore the historical complexities of nation-formation. Such accounts are also deemed to be too rationalist, too structuralist and too materialist to understand the popular and worldwide resonance of nationalism. To address these shortcomings, Anthony D. Smith, John Hutchinson and John Armstrong have articulated what they deem to be a better explanatory model – the ethno-symbolism. In this chapter, I challenged their criticisms by demonstrating that modernism is not inherently incompatible with the longue durée perspective. The chapter identified several modernist accounts that reject the image of the pre-modern world as tabula rasa and which are clearly open to the long-term analysis of nation-formation processes. Furthermore, I identified the blind spots of both ethno-symbolism and the long-run modernism and then developed a framework for an alternative, grounded, longue durée approach that centres on the historical transformation of organisational capacities, ideological penetration and the envelopment of micro-solidarity.

3　Empires and Nation States

Introduction

Until quite recently, most scholars shared the view that empires and nation states do not have much in common. Moreover, the general perception was that an imperial form of political rule was a thing of the past, destined to be replaced by the only rational, legitimate and feasible type of territorial political organisation – the nation state. This early confidence has now been replaced by much more cautious assessments. Over the last decade or so, several influential historians and historical sociologists have questioned this premise, arguing not only that nation states and empires have more in common than previously thought but also that the imperial mode of governance is not dead and buried but remains an ever-present possibility for rulers to pursue now and in the future (Kumar 2017, 2010; Go 2011; Burbank and Cooper 2010; Munkler 2007). Nevertheless, while we now accept that empires and nation states are not mutually exclusive forms of social organisation preordained to replace one another in a strictly evolutionary fashion, it is not completely clear how are they similar and where exactly this resemblance comes from. Some scholars argue that the modern politi-cal, cultural and economic institutions that define a nation state have deep cultural or biological roots. Hence, Smith (2009, 1986) and Hutchinson (2017, 2005) analyse the transition from the pre-modern imperial order to the modern day world of nation states through the prism of cultural continuity: in this view, traditional ethnic identities gradually transform into politicised forms of nationhood. Gat (2012) and van den Berghe (1981) make the case that this long-term continuity between different forms of political and cultural organisation has strong biological roots: they insist that our genetic propensity for survival drives major institutional innovations, including the evolutionary shift from imperial to national modes of governance. In contrast, other scholars emphasise economic, political and military factors as being crucial in making the transition from empire to nation state possible (Halperin 2017; Arrighi 1994; Tilly 1992; Mann 1986, Wallerstein 1974). In this chapter, I briefly articulate an alternative interpretation that explores the similarities and differences between these two types of polity. By zooming in on the three longue durée processes – the cumulative bureaucratisation of coercion, centrifugal ideologisation and the envelopment of micro-solidarity – I aim to identify what exactly makes empires and nation states similar and where this resemblance comes from.

The Two Forms of Polity

Since the end of WWII, the nation state has been gradually institutionalised as the only legitimate form of territorial rule. This idea is clearly stipulated in the UN charter where article 2 (chapter I) reaffirms the notion of 'the sovereign equality of all its Members' and states that no member is allowed to use 'force against the territorial integrity or political independence of any [nation] state' (www.un.org/en/sections/un-charter /chapter-i/index.html). Most other international organisations, from the IMF, World Bank, WTO, OSCE, to ICC or Interpol, to name a few, subscribe to the same principle: political sovereignty and territorial integrity is the sole prerogative of nation states. Although our world still contains city states, traditional kingdoms and even some chiefdoms of sedentary hunter-gatherers, all these entities could survive only by redefining themselves as small nation states or as autonomous regions within existing nation states. Hence, Monaco and Singapore are city states that take their seats in the UN and other international organisations as nation states. Complex and sedentary hunter-gatherer societies such as the Guarani or Yanomami of South America or the Torres Strait Islanders are now relabelled as 'Native Brazilians' or 'Indigenous Australians' and as such integrated within the organisational and ideological framework of their respective nation states: Brazil and Australia. Traditional kingdoms such as Swaziland, Saudi Arabia, Oman or Brunei are all now redefined in international law as nation states.

Nevertheless, what is noticeable is that one type of territorial organisation has not undergone such relabelling – the empire. Unlike city states, city leagues, khanates, sultanates, composite kingdoms or tribal confederacies which have all been incorporated into the nation state project, the empire has largely been excluded. Moreover, the contemporary world has made no legitimate space for the existence of empires. Hence, with the partial exception of Japan, which is still nominally headed by an emperor, no contemporary ruler embraces the imperial title and no state is self-described as an empire.[1]

Even though the remnants of imperial décor were still visible until late 1970s, with Haile Selassie I of Ethiopia, Mohammad Reza Pahlavi of Iran or even Jean-Bédel Bokassa of the Central African Empire insisting on their imperial titles, the age of nominal empires seemed to be at an end. The post-WWII era was often described as the period of decolonisation and political liberation where there was no room for empires. Furthermore, as the nation state was originally conceived to be an entity that stands in direct opposition to the ancient imperial order, its world-wide proliferation was meant to appear at the expense of the old empires. In this context, empire became a synonym for a decaying ancien régime that was destined to be replaced with modern and vibrant nation states.

Hence, while politicians and the general public now perceived empires as 'the prison houses of nations' bent on violent expansion, much of the academic community was resolute that these two forms of territorial organisation are mutually incompatible models of state organisation. The conventional wisdom had it that whereas empires are large entities underpinned by deep inequalities, formal social hierarchies and no sense of cross-class solidarity, the nation state stood for liberté, égalité and fraternité. Although many scholars remained aware of the complexities of individual cases and showed less enthusiasm towards such sharp distinctions, there was still general agreement that imperial orders were destined to be replaced by the world of nation states. This view was just as prevalent among historians who understood empires as the vanishing predecessors of nation states as among social scientists who identified similar institutional trends pointing towards the proliferation of nation-state models throughout the world.[2] For example, a well-known German historian Wolfgang Mommsen (1982: 113), wrote in his highly influential

---

[1] Japan is the only state in the world that has an emperor but even in this case there has been a shift from the traditional designation Mikado (帝) which is closer to the English term 'emperor' towards Tennō (天皇) which stands for 'heavenly sovereign'. The 1947 Japanese constitution makes clear that the emperor is only 'the symbol of the State and of the unity of the people' and has 'no powers related to government'. Another recent exception was ISIS, which explicitly rejected the idea of nation state and installed the Caliph as a head of a theocratic polity, that, just like an empire, was a conquest-oriented entity without fixed borders. However, ISIS was an unrecognised political entity temporarily forged in the context of wars in Syria and Iraq.

[2] This is not to say that there was unanimity on these issues. For example, there is a large literature on neo-colonialism, US imperialism and internal colonialism, most of which was adamant that neo-imperialism was highly compatible with the proliferation of nation states in the era of decolonisation (Chatterjee 2017; Hechter 1977; Nkrumah 1965). However, much of this literature did not question the quasi-evolutionary teleology of the historically inevitable, and what they thought to be highly desirable, transition from empires to nation states.

book *Theories of Imperialism* that 'the age of imperialism is dead and buried'. Other, more conventional, historians stuck with quasi-evolutionary interpretations of the past, where empire was perceived to be just another historical step towards the natural model of state organi-sation – the nation state. Hence, the traditional historiographic views tended to portray the late nineteenth-century unification of Italy and Germany as a result of strong nationalist movements led by Mazzini, Garibaldi, Bismarck and others aspiring to establish a modern nation state. In these interpretations, the shift from empire and city state towards the nation state model was perceived as willed and historically inevitable (Shreeves, 1984). In a similar way the Stanford neo-institutionalist school focused on documenting how the modern organisational models built around the nation-state apparatuses were gradually emulated throughout the world. As Meyer and his collaborators (1997, 1992) insist, the post-WWII world is characterised by ever-increasing standardisation of mod-els of governance and shared values that underpin these models. Meyer identifies a wide range of such isomorphic practices that have proliferated throughout the world: from standardised mass education, population control policies and welfare regimes to the adoption of relatively uniform constitutions, legal systems and demographic records, among many others (Meyer et al. 1997). At the core of this theory is the idea that the global replication of the nation-state structure makes imperial and other models of governance redundant in the modern world.

Nevertheless, this well-established, and largely teleological, narrative has recently been challenged by a number of influential historical sociologists and historians, all of whom claim that empires and nation states have more in common than previously thought. For example, Burbank and Cooper (2010) argue that empires and nation states share several important features, including their dependence on the wider geo-political environments defined by the ongoing economic, political and cultural interaction with their neighbours and the rest of the world, as well as their shared layered sovereignties. Just as empires of the past, so do nation states today exist in an interconnected universe: 'The world did not then – and still does not – consist of billiard-ball states, with impermeable sovereignty bouncing off each other. The history of empires allows us instead to envision sovereignty as shared out, layered, overlapping' (Burbank and Cooper 2010: 17). Similarly, Kumar (2017, 2010) is adamant that empires are not neces-sarily a thing of the past but an organisational form that can be resurrected relatively swiftly in the present and near future. Rather than seeing empires as ancient relics confined to the dustbin of history, Kumar conceives of empires and nation states as organisationally and ideologically viable political projects that remain at the disposal of elites who can pursue either model depending on the changing historical situation. In his own words: 'Empires can be nations writ large; nations empires under another name' (Kumar 2017: 23). Rather that simply assume that an 'age of empire' preceded an 'age of nation states', one should recognise that 'empires have been part of the modern world order as much as, and arguably more than, nation states' (Kumar 2017: 35). Munkler (2007) also sees empires as entities capable of survival and growth in the twenty-first century and beyond. Instead of defining nation states and empires as mutually exclusive phenomena Munkler (2007: 6) argues that they are in fact compatible and can complement each other: 'Since the whole habitable surface of the earth has been organised in the form of states, there remains only a complementary, not an alternative, relation between the two types of border: imperial structures are superimposed on the state order, but they no longer replace it' which occasionally 'makes it difficult to identify an empire'. Hence, instead of being an entity identified with yesteryear, the empire seems to be a present-day reality and also an organisational form that might vigorously re-emerge in the near future. Julian Go (2017, 2011) also argues that national and imperial projects are often highly compatible. His analysis of the British and American polities indicates that they have adopted very similar imperial strategies. Despite their nominal commitment to the principle of nationhood, they have maintained many imperial features that become more visible once the polity is experiencing deep crises and is organisationally weakened. Thus, the key parameters of what differentiates an empire from the nation state seem not to be so certain and straightforward as they once were.

The argument advanced in this chapter follows these new interpretations in the sense that I, too, acknowledge that empires and nation states have more in common than conventional understandings allow. This is not to conflate these two ideal types of polity organisation. Obviously, a nation state as an ideal type stands for a set of principles that clearly clash with those that underpin an imperial order. As I have argued elsewhere, a nation state is nominally conceptualised as 'secularised social organisations with fixed and stable territory and a centralised political authority underpinned by intensive ideological particularism and the promotion of moral egalitarianism, social solidarity and cultural homogeneity among its populace' (Malešević 2013a: 66). Nation states are also defined by their ability to legitimately monopolise the use of violence, education, legislation and taxation on their territories (Malešević 2013a; Elias 2000; Weber 1968; Gellner 1983). In contrast, empires stand for universalist principles, discourage cross-class solidarity and cultural homogeneity and usually do not aspire towards establishing permanent and fixed borders. They are conceived as deeply hierarchical social orders that 'foster a vertical sense of attachment where each stratum maintains its socio-economic and cultural difference' (Malešević 2013a: 35).

Nevertheless, these nominal features do not necessarily translate well into the everyday reality of empires and nation states. For one thing, very few contemporary nation states are culturally homogeneous or built around strict moral egalitarian principles. While this might feature as a strong ideological aspiration, often inscribed in the constitutions of modern states, the actual realties rarely match these ambitions. For example, even the most prosperous and egalitarian polities such as those in Scandinavia still maintain a clear distinction between full citizens entitled to all rights and state provisions and non-citizen immigrants with only some rights, a lesser or no sense of symbolic belonging to the nation and lower status recognition by the majority population. For another thing, many contemporary nation states struggle with establishing a legitimate monopoly on violence, education, legislation and taxation. For example, many African, Latin American and Asian polities do not fully control their territories and, in some instances, have to deal with well-armed warlords or breakaway regions. Even the militarily most powerful state on the planet, the USA, does not possess a full monopoly on the use of violence: its citizens own no less than 300 million firearms (Horsley 2016) and the government has to deal constantly with violent militias, vigilantes, armed religious cults and many other groups. While EU states largely maintain this monopoly on the use of violence, they have relinquished some of their monopoly on taxation and legislation, as the EU Central Bank, the EU Court of Justice and the European Court of Human Rights have substantial powers that can override the courts and taxation policies of the individual member states.

This diversity is just as visible among the imperial orders of the past. Whereas some empires were strictly hierarchical, others allowed for more social mobility. In a similar vein, some empires were ignorant of cultural difference while others developed firm ethnic hierarchies (Kumar 2017; Darwin 2013; Gat 2012; Go 2011; Burbank and Cooper 2010). John Darwin (2013: 160–9) writes about imperial ethnicities that emerge in specific historical contexts where some imperial orders clearly privileged one ethnic group over other, such as the imperial Britishness of white settler colonies vis-à-vis native populations or the Manchu dominance over the Han until the end of the Qing dynasty in 1911. Other scholars distinguish between ancient and modernising empires and argue that, unlike their pre-modern counterparts, eighteenth and nineteenth century empires had much more similarity with nation states (Hall 2017, 1986;

Breuilly 2017; Malešević 2013a; Kumar 2010; Burbank and Cooper 2010). This was particularly visible in terms of how they managed cultural difference and class conflicts: while the ancient empires were less pressed with these issues, the modernising empires had, just as the nation states, to develop effective strategies to deal with popular mobilisation around class and ethnicity.

However, to identify these similarities between empires and nation states does not mean to suggest either that they are almost identical forms of social organisation or that they have very little in common. Instead, the argument is made that these ideal types appear in a variety of empirical guises and as such maintain a substantial degree of difference while also exhibiting some similar features. More specifically, I argue that empires and nation states are different but highly compatible forms of social organisation and as such are prone to transform into each other under the right historical conditions. This means that the transition from empires to nation states is not necessarily a one-way process. Nation states are not destined to replace empires and empires are not necessarily something that belong to the past. Although the historical record indicates that there are many more instances of empires developing into nation states (Wimmer 2018, 2012), there are also notable cases of nation states and republics becoming formal empires: from Napoleon's creation of the French Empire (1804–14), to the Empire of Haiti (1849–59) under Emperor Faustin I to the Mexican Empire under Maximilian I (1864–67), the Central African Empire (1976–79) under Bokassa I or the Brazilian Empire under Dom Pedro I and II (1822–89). Furthermore, as Go (2011) and Mann (2003) argue, being a nominal nation state does not preclude one from attaining imperial features and acting as an empire in the international arena. More importantly, some of the similar features that empires and nation states possess indicate that reversibility and transformation from one into another is an everlasting possibility. So what are these common building blocks of empires and nation states and what exactly makes these two forms of polity different? What are these structural and interactional ingredients that make the transition from empire to nation state possible?

Coercive-Organisational Power and State Formation

As I have argued in the previous two chapters, modern social organisations do not emerge ex nihilo but develop gradually on the organisational, ideological and micro-interactional contours of previous institutional forms. In this context, I identify three key historical processes that have helped shape this long-term transformation: the cumulative bureaucratisation of coercion, centrifugal ideologisation and the envelopment of micro-solidarity (Malešević 2017, 2013a, 2010). The central issue here is the coercive capacity of social organisations and their ability to ideologically penetrate the social order under their control. In the pre-modern world, coercive power was a primary mechanism of social dominance and organisational development. The increase in the organisational capacity to accumulate, store and distribute food, to provide permanent housing, to ensure protection and security were all premised on the enhancement of the coercive potential of the social organisations involved in this process. As Mann (1986) demonstrated convincingly, the emergence of pristine states was paralleled by the expansion of social caging whereby an individual's security and relative prosperity was now permanently tied to the continuous loss of individual liberties. Although Mann focuses on states, the same process affected other social organisations – from private corporations, religious institutions, political parties, to social movements and many other organised collectivities. In all of these cases, the rise of organisational power went hand in hand with an increase in the coercive capability of these organisations. This process can be traced back to 12,000 years ago but it has radically intensified in the last 200 to 250 years. Although throughout history individual organisations have experienced decline and many have disappeared, were destroyed or amalgamated into other entities, coercive-organisational power as such has largely been cumulative in the sense that it has greater infrastructural reach, wider territorial scope and deeper social penetration than ever before (Malešević 2017, 2010). That is why I call this process the cumulative bureaucratisation of coercion.

In this context, the rise of imperial power was deeply wedded to empires' organisational strength. The empires expanded through military might which also had to be underpinned by economic, political and ideological force. Hence, to become and also remain a great empire, it was necessary to develop and maintain a potent coercive-organisational scaffolding. Most empires retained and improved their organisational might through continuous expansion and conquest. For example, both the Roman and Chinese empires were forged in warfare and their incessant organisational growth was highly dependent on their ability to win wars and expand their territory and population. Although the Roman state attracted 'barbarians' with its relative affluence, rule-based order and vibrant civic life, the principal source of the empire's success was its military might. This military capability was in part shaped by the state's ability to recruit large number of soldiers (i.e. at its peak in 211 the army consisted of over 450,000 men), but even more important was the military's highly effective system of organisation. The military was comprised of three type of formations: legions (mostly volunteer heavy infantry force consisting of Roman citizens only serving twenty-five-year terms); auxilia (non-citizens providing support staff but also cavalry, archers and light infantry) and numeri ('barbarians' who usually fought as mercenaries). The legion was the apex of Roman power as it combined strict discipline, professionalism and deep micro-level comradeship with organisational flexibility. Hence, the army was well equipped to fight in constantly changing conditions but was also capable of building roads, bridges, canals, walls, dams and aqueducts. As Burbank and Cooper (2010: 28–34) and Mann (1986: 266–74) point out, the Roman Empire had an almost non-existent civilian bureaucracy but it maintained an enormous military organisational structure built around the offices of a military commander – the praetor. As the empire expanded, praetors were instituted in the newly acquired provinces to collect taxes, mobilise new recruits and develop the infrastructure. In this sense, the military was the state: it consumed up to two thirds of the total state budget (Duncan-Jones 1994).

In a similar fashion, the early Chinese empire was also created and expanded through the might of its coercive-organisational capacity. The unification of the state under the Qin dynasty in 221 BCE was followed by the establishment of a powerful military machine capable of recruiting millions of individuals to fight or to be deployed as the slave workforce. For example, the first emperor's tomb was built by no less than 700,000 prisoners while the army could mobilise up to half a million soldiers to fight the confederation of tribal nomads in the Xiongnu and other regions (Burbank and Cooper 2010: 48–9). Just as in the Roman case, the central point of Chinese power was the military that combined organisational flexibility and discipline with hierarchical centralisation and social cohesion. Qin governance was also defined by its ability to develop solid infrastructure including road networks linking the capital at Xianyang with the conquered provinces and the canals that increased the speed of transport and communication. The empire also introduced new currency, uniform weights and measures, passports and checkpoints to control its population. The coercive capacity of the state was also enhanced by its legal system, focused on severe forms of physical punishment for disobedience including hard labour, mutilation and death. However, unlike its Roman counterpart, the Chinese empire also built a potent system of centralised officialdom. Over the years, this civil service, shaped around a meritocratic system of recruitment through difficult state examinations, became a foundation of the imperial order. Hence, the Chinese empire's rise and longevity remained deeply dependent on its coercive-organisational power including both an effective military and forceful models of internal policing through bureaucracy. As Burbank and Cooper (2010: 57) rightly argue, it is this efficient civilian bureaucratic structure that differentiates the Chinese from the Roman Empire and that partially explains 'why China revived and Rome did not'. Nevertheless, one can go further and argue that the durability and eventual transformation of China from empire into nation state owes a great deal to this coercive-organisational continuity embedded in its uniquely centralised officialdom. This is not to say that the ancient empire and contemporary China are similar polities in any sociologically meaningful way but only that the organisational legacies of previous historical epochs matter. In this context, the ancient bureaucratic structure has served as a foundation for the gradual and multifaceted development of various polities on Chinese soil all the way up to contemporary times.

This reliance on coercion was just as evident in other imperial projects. For example, the secret of the Ottoman Empire and Mameluk Sultanate's military successes was their ability to combine organisational advancements with the proto-ideological justification framed in the Islamic militarist ghazi tradition (Jones 1987; Malešević 2010).[3] Relying on their very effective systems of elite military and civil service recruitment (devşirme and ghulam respectively), these empires created an organisational model which forged skilled, disciplined, highly motivated and completely loyal warrior castes capable of maintaining imperial supremacy over huge territories, including parts of three continents. The Ottoman system of non-hereditary elite recruitment, such as the devşirme and mamluk models, contributed substantially towards the merit-based promotion and the unprecedented loyalty of civil servants and soldiers towards the empire. This and many other organisational developments generated in the imperial period have proved instrumental in the creation of the modern Turkish and Egyptian nation states in the early twentieth century. Although Attaturk's and Nasser's new states were envisaged as diametrically opposed to the old empire, the coercive-organisational legacies of the imperial state served as a backbone of the new republics (Goldschmidt 2004; Anderson 1987). Even though the new states embraced a novel, aggressively secular, nationalist ideology and had smaller territory, their military, police and state apparatuses were mostly built on their Ottoman (and Mameluk) core. In this sense, the transition from the empire towards the nation state was highly (path) dependent on the already-existing organisational scaffolds

---

[3] Kumar (2017: 80–5) is right to question the ghazi thesis as initially articulated by Paul Wittek (1938) who overemphasised the role of religious commitment in empire building. However, one cannot completely discount the significance of ghazi tradition in generating a degree of social cohesion among Ottoman warrior strata.

created by the ancient regime.[4] While the new state has ultimately built much more effective and powerful coercive structures, its very existence was premised on the ability to utilise the remnants of organisational capacity that the old empire produced.

Ideological Penetration and Social Structure

In addition to coercive force, social organisations also require a degree of ideological legitimacy. Whereas in the traditional world, coerciveness was soothed by various forms of proto-ideological justification (mythology, religion, civilising missions, etc.), which usually were aimed at fellow aristocrats, in the modern era, ideological power takes central stage. Conventional narratives emphasise that the French and American revolutions inaugurated a sharp ideological shift whereby political legitimacy was now attained not from the divine authority of monarchs but from the idea of popular sovereignty. More specifically, while pre-modern rulers could utilise mythological, religious or civilisational idioms to justify their right to govern, in modernity, one's right to rule is derived from new ideological principles centred on a much wider sense of participation. Hence, these new ideological doctrines, such as socialism, liberalism, nationalism, republicanism or corporatism, all invoke a sense of popular entitlement: it is the people, or a particular group of people (workers, free individuals, co-nationals, citizens, etc.), that are now seen as having the right to govern. This major structural shift was aided by the rise of literacy, mass education, accessible media, democratisation of political life, expansion of civil society networks, widening of the public sphere and other changes that made ordinary individuals more receptive to, capable of, and engaged with political life.

These ideological changes went hand in hand with the coercive-organisational transformations: the increase in the bureaucratic capacities of states, private corporations, churches and other organisations entailed expansion of ideological mechanisms capable of wide-scale public justification. Hence, I refer to this ongoing process as centrifugal ideologisation: a mass-scale phenomenon centred on the proliferation of ideas, principles and practices able to legitimise particular forms of coercive-organisational power. In the modern age, such ideological drives work towards undercutting existing social divisions by infusing different social strata with doctrines bent on generating a degree of ideological unity.

---

[4] Obviously, in the Egyptian case, the colonial legacy has also contributed to the state's coercive-organisational capacities as Ottoman, French and British rule were instrumental in developing significant elements of the state's organisational infrastructure.

Although it is clear that nation states differ from empires in terms of their principal sources of justification, one should be wary of projecting sharp dichotomies onto the highly complex and multi-faceted historical realities. In other words, while the ideal-type model of a nation state is built around secularised ideological doctrines such as nationalism, liberalism or socialism and ideal-type empires espouse imperial creeds such as the Roman *humanitas*, Confucianism in China or the French *mission civilisatrice*, there are many empirical instances where this doctrinal purity did not materialise. Instead, the political legitimacy of many nation states is still couched in the discourses that emphasise imperial legacies. This is quite obvious with large and powerful states such as the USA, China and Russia where nationalism is often combined with the imperial rhetoric of world leadership and the geo-political dominance (Mann 2012, 2003; Bacevich 2004). However, even smaller nation states such as Turkey, Austria and Portugal invoke the historical legacies of former empires in order to boost their nationalist narratives.

My argument is that, just as with coercive-organisational power, ideological power does not transpire out of nothing but is articulated and developed gradually on the contours of existing ideas and practices. There is no doubt that the French Revolution brought about a very different system of governance legitimised by the novel idea of popular sovereignty. Nevertheless, such a model of rule and its ideological justification were deeply rooted in organisational and value transformations that developed over much longer periods of time. For one thing, the key idea invoked during the Revolution – of the rights of the Third Estate – was articulated in reference to the well-established rights of ordinary citizens to be represented at the Estates General assemblies. The first such assembly was established by Phillip IV in 1302. Although the revolutionaries ultimately managed to profoundly change the meaning of the Third Estate (as visible in the famous 1789 Abbé Sieyès's pamphlet), this ideological transition remained grounded in the historical legacies of medieval parliaments (Kiser and Linton 2002). Furthermore, the central ideas of the French Revolution, including the notions of individual liberty, human rights, social equality and popular sovereignty, were all developed long before any sign of the revolutionary upheaval – these ideas can be traced back to several intellectual movements from the Renaissance and Humanism to the Enlightenment and Romanticism, among others. These strong elements of organisational and ideological continuities were just as visible a century after the Revolution when the French Third Republic (1870–1940) was simultaneously a nation state (at home) and an expanding empire (abroad). The late nineteenth-century French state was built around republican principles that espoused Enlightenment ideas such as the moral equality of all human beings, rule of law, human rights and political equity. Although the republic was deeply polarised with conservatives, the military, the Church and the peasantry opposing the liberal and republican left, most citizens were highly sympathetic to the nationalist ideas. This was particularly visible during the two key political events of this period – the Boulanger crisis (1889) and the Dreyfus affair (1894–1906) – both of which revealed the strength of nationalist sentiment in France. Although republican and nationalist goals were dominant at home, it was imperialism that shaped much of foreign policy. Hence, the second half of the nineteenth century and the beginning of the twentieth century were characterised by unprecedented colonial expansion in Asia, Africa and the Pacific. The French Third Republic acquired and ruled over vast territories and populations in Indochina, North, West and Central Africa, Madagascar, Polynesia and further afield. In this context, the imperial doctrine of mission civilisatrice fed into nationalist ideology, thus generating a peculiar version of imperial nationalism. Hence, rather than the dominant *weltanschauung* of the nation state (nationalism) replacing the leading ideological *topoi* of the imperial state (imperialism), the two have largely merged into a single, although at times deeply contradictory, doctrine. As Kumar (2017: 424) points out, in late nineteenth and early twentieth-century France, imperialism was not stifled by nationalism. On the contrary, 'imperialism was driven by nationalism'. Nevertheless, the imperial expansion was not governed by the economic motives such as profit maximisation or resource extraction as the French mainland saw no tangible economic benefits from the empire. For example, its African colonies such as Niger, Mauritania or Chad were huge territories but largely arid with little resources. Instead, precisely because it was rooted in the nationalist ideology, the French imperial project was driven by the notion of state prestige and the geopolitical ambitions rather than any economic rationality.

The same ideological ambiguity was present in late nineteenth-century Britain which was simultaneously a world-leading empire and a nationalising state. The British state was on the one hand involved in the continuous widening of citizenship rights at home while on the other hand pursuing coercive and ideological expansion abroad. As Marshall (1950) noticed long ago, most inhabitants of Britain acquired civil rights in the eighteenth century, political in the nineteenth and social in the twentieth. For example, while in the early nineteenth century only 3 per cent of the population had the right to vote, by 1885 around 8 million individuals had attained that right. Although this was far from being a smooth and consent-based process, its outcome was a much more cohesive population sympathetic to the nationalist ideas. At the same time, the state was involved in building the most powerful polity in the world, 'this vast empire on which the sun never sets, and whose bounds nature has not yet ascertained' (Kenny 2006: 72). As Hall (2017) argues, late nineteenth century empires were attempting to increase their power through the gradual nationalisation of their core territories – to augment force through greater internal coherence. Nevertheless, this did not come at the expense of imperial conquest. On the contrary, in this period, the British imperial project reached its apex as the empire controlled a vast archipelago of colonies, dominions, protectorates, mandates and other territories throughout the world. At the end of WWI, Britain controlled a quarter of the world's population and a quarter of the world's landmass. Just as in the French case, the British polity successfully combined imperialism with nationalism. However, the link between the two was not straightforward as the imperial project was rooted in the discourse of universality: the British conquest was regularly depicted as a civilising mission undertaken in the name of higher goals. As one of the leading late nineteenth and early twentieth-century British imperial historians, John Adam Cramb (1915: 100), declared: 'Britain conquers, but by the testimony of men of all races who have found refuge within her confines, she conquers less for herself than for humanity.' This link became much more apparent when the empire faced strong military resistance, as was the case during the Second Boer war (1899–1902), or the Indian Rebellion (1857–58). In this context, one could observe how imperialism and nationalism gave birth to jingoism, a fiercely pugnacious doctrine that merged aggressive imperial foreign policy with the exclusionary nationalism at home aided by the bellicose tabloid press. All of this indicates clearly that the long-term ideological transformations do not necessarily develop in an evolutionary fashion whereby national(ist) ideologies simply replace imperial doctrines. Instead there is a great deal of continuity here in the sense that ideological change emerges often on the contours of previous ideas and practices. Hence, while ideological power matters more in the modern era than it did before, its influence is still built on top of the value and organisational transformations that have taken place over much longer periods of time.

The Envelopment of Micro-Solidarity

Nation states and empires cannot exist without organisational and ideological powers. However, these large-scale structural forces are not automatically accepted as given and unproblematic. On the contrary, coercive-organisational control can be, and is often, resisted, while ideological discourses can be challenged and delegitimized. Hence, to be successful, the rulers and administrators of empires and nation states have to integrate organisational and ideological powers with the micro-universe of everyday life. In other words, the longevity and effectiveness of any large-scale social organisation is also determined by its ability to tap into the grassroots and to link this micro-world with its own organisational and ideological aims. This is particularly important as empires and nation states are not the natural forms of social aggregation. As humans are generally wired for life in much smaller groups, any attempt to impose on them a large-scale social organisation is likely to be resisted (Suzman 2017; Malešević 2015; Turner 2007). Daily interactions with the surviving hunter-gatherers indicate that they, as a rule, reject encroachments by civil servants to bring them into the fold of the modern state. Furthermore, social organisations of this size are inevitably formal, anonymous, distant and hierarchical. This contrasts sharply with the microcosm of everyday life of neighbourhoods, friendships, kinships, peer groups, lovers and other small-scale groupings. These groups are defined by intimacy, familiarity, deep emotional and moral attachments, informality, and lack of strict hierarchies. Hence, the key issue for any large-scale social organisation is how to penetrate these grassroots in order to make them compatible with the broader macro-universe of empires and nation states.

It is here that one can encounter the most pronounced difference between the imperial model and the nation state model of social order. While ancient empires largely lacked the organisational and ideological means to successfully infiltrate the micro-world, nation states have proved to be effective in reconciling the public with the private sphere and the personal with the organisational realms. Since most individuals attain a sense of comfort, emotional security and fulfilment from face-to-face interaction developed in intimate settings of small groups, nation states have tapped into this micro-universe by attempting to emulate the language, rituals and everyday practices of such small groups. Unlike ancient empires, which were deeply hierarchical and fostered a sense of vertical solidarity, modern nation states pride themselves on the idea of society-wide fraternity articulated as horizontal solidarity. As Anderson (1991[1983]: 7) noted a long time ago the strength of nationalist appeal is rooted in its rhetoric of comradeship: [nation] 'is imagined as a community, because, regardless of the actual inequality and exploitation that may prevail in each, the nation is always conceived as a deep, horizontal comradeship. Ultimately it is this fraternity that makes it possible.' This has become most apparent in the rise of grounded nationalism as the dominant operative ideology of modernity (Malešević 2006).

It is no accident that most nationalist discourses are framed in language and practices that invoke intimate and close-knit micro groups. For example, Russian nationalists speak about 'Mother Russia' as providing a 'nest' for all its children (Hubbs 1993: xii–xiii). Croatian and Serbian nationalisms are full of the images that invoke family life and kinship: 'our Croat brothers and sisters', 'our Serbian children', 'our sacred fatherland', 'old fireplaces' that members of the Serbian brethren had to leave, and so on (Malešević 2002). French nationalism is also shaped around the idea of fraternité, broadly understood in terms of close kinship and friendships, while American nationalism also utilises idioms and rituals that invoke the intimacy of small-scale groupings: the recital of the Pledge of Allegiance in schools performed in front of one's peers and close friends, singing of the national anthem at sporting and other events accompanied by one's friends and relatives, proudly displaying a national flag on the front porch so as that neighbours could see it, and so on (Duina 2018; O'Leary 2000). Japanese nationalism blends the nation and the family in the idea of Meiji Japan as *kazoku kokka* (family-state) headed by the emperor as the father minzuko (Surak 2012). In Israel military friendships are institutionalised 'as a model for national solidarity' (Kaplan 2018:184). In all of these cases, and many others, nationalism is potent precisely because it is grounded in the networks of genuine micro-solidarity.

This deep level of organisational and ideological penetration, whereby micro-level solidarities become integrated with the macro-level goals of the large-scale organisations, is for the most part, unachievable in the world of early empires. As Hall (1986) made clear, these early social orders were defined by 'capstone' features, meaning that the imperial elites were able to centralise their power but had neither organisational nor ideological means to fully infiltrate the social order they governed. Hence, the early emperors were like capstones in the sense that they sat on top of different societies they could not penetrate. This point ties well with Mann's (1986) distinction between despotic and infrastructural powers where the traditional rulers of large empires were often in possession of great despotic powers (i.e. could order the killing of nearly anybody under their control), but they lacked infrastructural capacities to implement their decisions throughout their realms. In this context, nationalism and other society-wide ideological discourses could only develop and spread with the substantial increase in the organisational capacities of states: standardised weights and measures, unified currencies, developed systems of communication and transport, significantly increased literacy rates, and so on. However, what is also important is that any deeper organisational and ideological penetration was dependent on the ability of the states to link these infrastructural advancements with existing pockets of micro-solidarity.

The conventional sociological interpretations of modernity make much of the supposed distinction between pre-modern and modern forms of social bonds. From Tönnies's *Gemeinschaft* and *Gesellschaft*, Durkheim's mechanical and organic solidarity to Beck's first and second modernity and Giddens's reflexive modernisation, sociologists have emphasised how social ties weaken and change with the expansion of modernity. The conventional narrative has it that, unlike our predecessors who were strongly integrated into their small-scale networks of kinships, clans and tribes, we moderns are highly individualised creatures who pursue our own choices and engage largely in contractual relationships. However, as I have argued before (Malešević 2013a: 196–7), human beings are generally prone towards life in small, face-to-face groupings and, in this context, ever-increasing organisational complexities do not necessarily diminish our predilection towards such micro-groups. On the contrary, such micro-groups thrive and expand in modern conditions not least because modern technology, transport, communication and literacy allow one to maintain such links over much greater space and longer time periods. Therefore, the power of nation states in today's world stems in part from their ability to envelop the universe of micro-solidarity and project these micro-dramas onto the canvas of their large-scale social organisation. In this environment, nationalism and other ideologies succeed mostly when they embrace the language and practices that emulate the micro world.

Capstone empires and nation states represent two very different ideal types, where the former is mostly unable to properly link micro-solidarity with organisational and ideological powers while the latter is largely defined by this very ability. Nevertheless, this difference between the empire and nation state is less pronounced when one compares latter-day imperial projects. As both Darwin (2013) and Breuilly (2017) argue, most modern empires were nationalising states that had to balance their national cores with their non-national peripheries. For example, France and the Netherlands simultaneously pursued nation-building at home and imperial conquest abroad. In this context, the imperial and the national tended often to overlap as imperial expansion reinforced nationalist legitimacy at home. In such an environment, the link between micro-solidarities and organisational power in the metropolitan territory was extended through imperial successes abroad. The late nineteenth and early twentieth-century mass media was a major purveyor of imperial jingoism that successfully framed the colonial conquests as a source of national pride. For example, the media played an important role in justifying the American annexation of Hawaii in 1893: the rebellion against the Hawaiian queen Lili'uokalani was led by newspaper publisher Lorrin Thurston and the US media contributed substantially towards portraying this imperial conquest as a legitimate popular uprising against the monarchy (Bingham 1898).

Nevertheless, this was also a double-edged sword as exhausting imperial wars and defeats could just as much undermine organisational capacity, ideological legitimacy and their links with micro-solidarities at home. The fact that early modern imperial projects, such as those of Portugal and Spain, expanded relatively quickly but then faltered and eventually collapsed has a great deal to do with the historical timing of their growth. Since this wave of imperial expansion largely occurred before the rise of nationalism and the dramatic increase in the coercive-organisational capacities of states, these empires were always prone to imperial overstretch which would undermine their very existence. Furthermore, as these empires emerged before developing a national core, their overseas losses (including military defeats, economic collapse, etc.) tended to severely undermine metropolitan stability and delay the process of ideological and organisational growth and their links with the networks of micro-solidarity.

These modern, nationalising, empires were often just as capable as nation states in weaving the networks of domestic micro-groupings into the broader national/imperial narratives. Moreover, some of these nineteenth-century empires, had more sophisticated organisational scaffolds than many nation states of this period and as such could forge much stronger links between ideology, organisation and micro-solidarities than these nation states. Consequently, major imperial powers such as Britain or France were able to tap into micro-solidarities abroad so that some citizens of their colonial possessions saw themselves first and foremost as British or French. In the British case, as Darwin (2013) shows, it was the dominions dominated by the white Anglo-Saxon populations such as Australia, New Zealand, Canada and South Africa, among others, that were eager to blend the national and the imperial often by relying on the discourse of race. In the French case, the empire was nominally open to full inclusion of indigenous populations who could apply for French citizenship and, in some instances, had symbolic representation in the French Parliament. However, in reality only a very small number were granted citizenship and most elected deputies from overseas were white Frenchmen. Hence, in both of these cases, just as in other nineteenth century imperial states, the national and the imperial were gradually moving towards a collision course as the nationalisation process never included, nor was it intended to encompass, the micro-solidarities of the indigenous populations. In this sense, the centrifugal ideologisation was a very uneven process that largely did not penetrate the indigenous networks of micro-solidarity. Hence, although modern empires and nation states are similar in their organisational, ideological and other structural attributes, they remain different in how widely some of these attributes and processes impact the population under their control. In other words, precisely because nation states are built on the principles of cultural homogeneity and clearly delineated organisational compactness, they cannot accommodate unlimited cultural diversity. Since nationalism is an ideology that posits the nation as a principal unit of human solidarity and political legitimacy, it is bound to eventually clash with the universalist ambitions of the original imperial projects. In this sense, imperial nationalism is an oxymoron with a limited shelf life. Once the cumulative bureaucratisation of coercion and centrifugal ideologisation become fully grounded in the networks of micro-solidarity, the imperial form is bound to give a way to the nation-state model of political organisation. Nevertheless this does not mean that such a process is irreversible. On the contrary, precisely because the unity of micro-solidarity networks depends on the ongoing ideologisation and bureaucratisation, these networks can also crumble and dissipate as soon as the nation state re-embraces an imperial direction of development.

Conclusion

In a world largely dominated by nation states, such as ours, the term empire still evokes deeply negative images associated with aggressive territorial conquests, deep social inequalities, political discrimination, racism and war. Most of all, the popular perception of any imperial order is now firmly embedded with the notion of empires being 'the prison houses of nations'. Nevertheless, when one moves away from such conventional, mostly nationalist, accounts of the past, it is possible to see that empires and nation states have a great deal in common. Hence, to fully understand the historical and sociological relationships between these two ideal types of polity, it is necessary to explore not only their, rather obvious, differences but also their numerous similarities. Furthermore, to make sense of where these similarities (and differences) come from, it is vital to focus on the organisational, ideological and micro-interactional mechanisms that facilitate the transformation from empires to nation states and vice versa. In this chapter, I attempted to explore these complex relationships by zooming in on the three long-term historical processes, that I believe were, and remain, pivotal in the transformation of any polity: the cumulative bureaucratisation of coercion, centrifugal ideologisation and the envelopment of micro-solidarity. While in this chapter my focus was more on the large-scale polities, the next chapter will explore how these imperial and national links operate in the context of smaller states.

4   Nationalisms and Imperialisms

Introduction

Traditional historiographic accounts tend to view nationalism and imperialism as two mutually exclusive phenomena: whereas imperialism is seen as an ideology centred on extending polity's power through the use of coercion, violence and colonisation, nationalism is often identified with the popular aspiration to establish a sovereign and independent nation state. However, a number of influential historical sociologists have challenged these simplified accounts arguing that many forms of late imperialism have been fully compatible with nationalist projects (Breuilly 2017; Chatterjee 2017; Go 2017, 2011; Hall 2017; Kumar 2017, 2010, 2003). Hence, Breuilly (2017) argues that since the modern, nineteenth and early twentieth centuries, empires had much in common with nation states, they were both in a position to utilise nationalist rhetoric to justify their political actions. Go (2017) is also adamant that nation states resemble empires in a sense that they both operate exclusionary and discriminatory systems of rule. While much of this new scholarship focuses on the character of the state, some also explores the ideologies that underpin these state projects. Thus Kumar (2017) sees nationalism and imperialism as quite compatible ideologies by demonstrating how, for much of the late nineteenth century and all the way to the WWI, the two coexisted and often converged into one syncretic ideological doctrine, as was particularly the case in Britain, France and Germany. In a similar vein, Hall (2017) extends this point further by zooming in on traditional capstone empires and modern imperial projects. In his view, the early capstone empires had neither the organisational means nor the interest needed to penetrate the societies under their control. In contrast, nineteenth-century modernising empires managed to increase their power by penetrating their societies and nationalising their polities. In this sense, nationalism and imperialism would often coalesce as the imperial power could be enhanced through 'nationalising one's empire, increasing force through coherence' (Hall and Malešević 2013: 17).

In this chapter, I also question the established historiographic accounts of imperialism and nationalism. However, while other scholars explore how and when imperial projects embrace nationalist idioms and practices, my focus is on the other side of this relationship: how nation states deploy imperial and quasi-imperial designs to boost their nationalist legitimacy at home and power prestige abroad. In this context, I explore the historical dynamics of nationalism and imperialism in the nineteenth and early twentieth-century Balkans. In particular, I compare and contrast the Serbian and Bulgarian nationalist and quasi-imperial projects. I look at how they both utilised discourses and legacies of their respective medieval empires of Tsar Dušan (Serbia) and Simeon the Great (Bulgaria). I also explore the contradictions and paradoxes involved in attempts to reconcile the national and the imperial during the project of nation state formation.

The National and the Imperial Projects: The Clash of Ideologies?

In contemporary political discourse, the term 'empire' is largely used in a pejorative sense. No contemporary rulers employ this term to describe their polities. Instead, this label is mostly deployed to discredit one's foreign policy. Hence, the USA's and Russia's use of force abroad is regularly described as imperial in a sense that it infringes upon the UN charter which explicitly states that its members are not allowed to use force 'against the territorial integrity or political independence of any state'. In sharp contrast, a 'nation state' is nearly universally regarded as a legitimate mode of territorial rule. This view is grounded in the idea that such polities represent a political expression of what is regarded to be the dominant and natural form of group identity – nationhood. Although the international community might object to attempts to carve new nation states on the territories of existing polities, the ideological motivation behind such ambition is likely to be regarded as legitimate. In other words, the powerful states might protest or even intervene against nationalist movements but they would seldom question the central principles underpinning the existence of such movements as their own states are built on the same ideological tenets.

Obviously, this clear-cut distinction between empire and nation state reflects the times we live in, where the nation state is not only the dominant form of state organisation but is also perceived to be the sole legitimate mode of territorial rule (Malešević 2013a). As explained in the previous chapter, this widely shared understanding posits an empire and a nation state as the two mutually exclusive models of polity. While empires are conceived to epitomise the politics of incessant territorial conquest and wars, social hierarchies, exploitation and inequality, the nation state model is perceived to stand for political equality, peaceful resolution of conflicts, individual freedoms and the preservation of national identities (Meyer et al. 1997; Parsons 1951). Nevertheless, this traditional view, which sharply separates these two forms of polity, has recently been questioned by several historical sociologists, historians and political scientists. This new scholarship aims to show how empires and nation states have more in common than the traditional views would allow. For example, Chatterjee (2017: 89) argues that 'empire is imma-nent in the modern nation' as the powerful states, regardless of their nominal designation, maintain 'the imperial prerogative ... [which is] the power to declare the colonial exception'. Munkler (2007: 166–7) too insists that empires and nation states are not mutually exclusive projects as the powerful contemporary nation states regularly utilise imperial policies: both the USA and the EU inevitably borrow from the imperial model. In a similar way, Breuilly (2017), Halperin (2017) and Go (2017, 2011) see these two models of statehood as highly compatible. For example, as Go (2017: 80) argues 'nation and empire are merely two manifestations of the same political form, structured by a core logic of exclusion and subjugation: the empire-state'.

In particular, these studies challenge the conventional quasi-evolutionary understanding whereby the nation state model was destined to replace the imperial orders. Instead, they indicate that the imperial structures are much more durable and resistant, thus leaving a possibility of their periodic re-emergence in the near future. As Burbank and Cooper (2010, 16–17) argue and document, neither empires nor nation states operate as fixed and mutually exclusive entities. Instead, they are char-acterised by sovereignty that is 'shared out, layered, overlapping'. They emphasise that nation states and empires are variable political forms capable of developing 'multiple ways in which incorporation and differ-ence were conjugated'. One strand of new scholarship attempts to show that the imperial model of organisation has never been fully displaced by the nation states. Rather, the imperial order has metamorphosed into novel forms of governance. Thus, some argue that nominal nation states such as the USA, China, Russia, or even the European Union are in fact empires or hybrid forms such as 'nation-empires', 'continental empires', 'empire states', 'incoherent empires' or 'imperial city states' (Halperin 2017; Go 2011; Munkler 2007; Zielonka 2006; Mann 2003). More radical accounts, such as those of Hardt and Negri (2000: 13), claim that the contemporary world is witnessing a transition from conventional nation-state-centred imperialism towards 'empire', which they see as a novel system 'configured ab initio as a dynamic and flexible systemic structure' enveloping the entire globe.

These emerging critiques of the traditional dichotomous views are quite persuasive and illuminating. However, their focus has largely been on the form of the polity and less on the ideological projects that sustain such political orders. In other words, while they tell us a great deal about the structural or economic organisation of the two polity models, they have less to say about the differences and similarities between the ideological doctrines that underpin these projects: imperialism and nationalism. It is mostly in the recent work of Krishan Kumar (2017, 2010, 2003) and particularly John A Hall (2017, 2013), that one can encounter more incisive analysis of the ideological bifurcations that shape the imperial and national projects.

Kumar (2010: 119) argues that 'empires and nation states may in fact best be thought of as alternative political projects, both of which are available for elites to pursue depending on the circumstances of the moment'. Furthermore, Kumar (2017: 35) challenges the conventional historical interpretations that see imperialism as a predecessor of nationalism. Instead, he is resolute that an 'age of nation-states' did not succeed an 'age of empire' but that imperialism and empires 'have been part of the modern world order as much as, and arguably more than, nation-states'. In this context, he compares and contrasts the historical experience of five modern empires – the Ottomans, the Habsburgs, the Romanovs as well as the British and French imperial projects – and shows how in each of them the imperial and the national coexisted and were often dependent on each other. While in the early modernity the national ideas were largely confined to elite minorities, by the end of the nineteenth century nationalism and imperialism regularly strengthened each other. For example, he describes nineteenth-century France as 'the nation writ large' and points out that the rise of nationalism did not stifle French imperialism but in fact the opposite was the case: imperialism was driven by French nationalism (Kumar 2017: 389, 425). Although the British empire was much bigger and developed earlier, it too had to navigate the more universalist imperial doctrine with the rather particularist national idioms. Initially the empire was established as 'protestant, commercial, maritime and free' but it gradually widened its ideological appeal by embracing a particular version of the civilising mission that shifted the focus from religion towards civilisation and enlightenment. Kumar (2017: 337) illustrates this point well in his analysis of the role India played in the British Empire and how British intellectuals understood the empire's role in India. For example, Lord Tennyson believed that without India the empire would be 'some third-rate isle half-lost among her seas' and that India contributes towards making everything 'into one imperial whole'. For Tennyson, Britain's civilising mission was ecumenical in a sense that it 'was to be the teacher of mankind and the metropolis of a world empire'. However, by the end of the nineteenth and early twentieth century, the universalist civilising mission was gradually infused with the discourse of nationalism. From the Boer wars onwards, the political and cultural representatives of the British empire embraced the language of cultural hierarchies where the predominantly white dominions such as Canada, Newfoundland, Australia, New Zeeland and South Africa were often conceptualised as full members of the British imperial nation, whereas the non-white colonies were largely excluded from such membership. The consequence of this hierarchical organisation was the rise of imperial nationalism outside of the British Isles, where the white populations often perceived Britain as their 'imperial fatherland'. How else one could explain the large-scale voluntary participation of populations from the white dominions in the WWI? As Kumar (2017: 359) emphasises, over 2.5 million colonial subjects fought for the British empire in the WWI: 'Canada sent 630,000 troops; Australia – despite rejecting conscription – 415,000, all volunteers; New Zealand sent 130,000 – nearly 20 per cent of the adult male population ... [and] South Africa contributed 195,000 men'. By the early twentieth century, imperialism and nationalism have fully merged.

Hall (2017) shares a view that empires and nation states have more in common than usually thought and he also explores the socio-historical sources of this commonality. For Hall, not all imperial orders are alike and ideological compatibility is only possible in polities that attain a substantial degree of organisational development. More specifically, he distinguishes between the pre-modern, capstone-type, imperial orders and the modernising empires. The central feature of the capstone empires, such as those of ancient China, Egypt or the Roman world, is that the rulers controlled vast territories, populations and resources but had no organisational means to penetrate fully the societies they nominally controlled. By 'capstone' Hall (1986: 52) means a form of imperial state organisation where the 'elite sat atop a series of separate "societies", which it did not wish to penetrate or mobilize; perhaps the key to its behaviour was its fear that horizontal linkages it could not see would get out of control'. Hence such governments were not concerned with 'intensifying social relationships' but primarily with 'seeking to prevent any linkages which might diminish [their] power'. Since capstone imperial orders did not posses the organisational means to penetrate their social order, they had to rely on the local notables, whom they generally distrusted. In such an environment, there was no organisational room to develop societywide ideological doctrine capable of homogenising the social order. Although all pre-modern empires were built around specific proto-ideological doctrines, such as Confucianism in ancient China or the civilising ethics of the late Roman Empire, the capstone character of such polities worked against societywide normative homogenisation. In other words, such imperial orders were defined by deep cultural divides with the small, often court-based, elite partaking in 'high' literate culture and the illiterate peasantry immersed in local, kinship-based, cultural traditions. In this context, imperialism was by and large an ideological project of the elite centre, something that for the most part had no resonance with the rest of society.

In contrast to these capstone systems, the modernising empires of the eighteenth and nineteenth centuries were significantly better integrated. There is no doubt that these were still highly hierarchical orders characterised by deep social inequalities, narrow levels of political representation and the general lack of wider social rights. Nevertheless, these modernising empires were in possession of relatively advanced organisational structures that allowed for greater social penetration. In line with the arguments made by Sombart (1913), Tilly (1992) and Mann (1986), Hall (1988) contends that the intensified inter-state warfare in early modern Europe stimulated the development of autonomous and viable state infrastructures. Moreover, Hall (1988, 1986) argues that the sudden and dramatic rise of Western European empires in the seventeenth, eighteenth and nineteenth centuries owes a great deal to the multi-polarity of the medieval European order where no ruler was strong enough to establish a unified European empire. As the political and ideological powers were split between the Catholic Church in Rome on the one hand, and the numerous small kingdoms on the other hand, this unusual geopolitical environment ultimately stimulated the rise of autonomous towns, and banking and trading centres which later proved highly instrumental in the rise of capitalism, state bureaucracy and civil society. This rather different historical trajectory of Europe and the rest of the world meant that the European imperial dynamics incorporated many organisational elements which were less present in other parts of the world. Hence, the leading eighteenth and nineteenth century empires, such as the British, French, or Dutch, had no resemblance to the capstone model of imperial order. Instead, the rulers of such empires were eager to utilise technological and organisational advances and develop better communication and transport systems. They were also interested in finding ways to incorporate their populations within the state structure. Although these imperial orders intended to retain the existing hierarchical structures, it soon became apparent that further territorial expansion, including the ongoing acquisition of colonies, entailed the simultaneous extension of some citizenship rights to the non-aristocratic groupings. Hence it is no coincidence that the British, French and Dutch colonial expansion abroad often went hand in hand with the gradual concession of religious, political and economic rights to various social strata at home. As these processes unfolded over time large sectors of the population became better integrated into the imperial project. Thus many middle class and even members of lower social strata were employed by the imperial state throughout the globe as administrators, traders, workers, teachers, soldiers, policemen, nurses and so on. Furthermore, with the expansion of citizenship rights, the growth of literacy rates and rise of civil society, imperialism became gradually challenged by other ideological discourses – from liberalism, socialism and anarchism to nationalism.

The rise of nationalism in particular has generally been regarded as the most serious threat to the imperial projects. For example Hiers and Wimmer (2013: 212–13) argue that the proliferation of nationalist movements in the late eighteenth, nineteenth and early twentieth centuries was the main cause of imperial downfall. Analysing the historical experience of the Ottoman, Habsburg, French, British, Portuguese and even Soviet imperial projects, they argue that 'in all cases of imperial collapse nationalist movements played an important, and sometimes, crucial role' and conclude that 'the rise and global proliferation of nationalist movements has been a crucial factor in reshaping the structure of the state system over the past two hundred years'. Nevertheless, Hall, just as Kumar, is more cautious about this relationship between nationalism and imperialism. While accepting the view that from the nineteenth century onward nationalism becomes a dominant ideological matrix for the legitimisation of state rule, he does not see these two ideological doctrines as necessarily being on a collision course. Instead, for Hall, modernising empires differ from their capstone predecessors in a sense that they possess organisational means and ideological know-how to accommodate both imperial creeds and nationalist practices. Such empires differ from their capstone predecessors in two important ways: 1) while the pre-modern empires did not recognise rivals and proclaimed ambition to conquer the whole world, the modernising empires accepted the world of multiple empires; and 2) whereas the capstone orders were culturally heterogeneous and had neither the means nor aspiration to create culturally uniform polities, the nineteenth century empires engaged gradually in the process of cultural homogenisation. As Hall emphasises, while before 'nationalism and imperialism were separated from each other, making any notion of intimacy between them ridiculous', modernising imperial states were different in a sense that they aspired to become nation states and in this process 'seeking, in different degrees, to homogenise different peoples into a singular identity' (Hall 2013: 227). This process in part reflected the dominant ideological shifts in the world but also, for Hall, the fact that the imperial rulers realised that they could increase power by nationalising their empires, 'increasing force through coherence' (Hall and Malešević 2013: 17). In this way, the imperial polities could, on the one hand, stifle the rise of competing nationalist and other social movements and, on the other hand, they could also attain a greater degree of political legitimacy.

However, this attempt to nationalise the empire, as both Kumar and Hall recognise, was neither smooth nor uncontested. Rather, all modernising empires were stretched between the ambition to preserve their territorial conquests and increase the cultural homogeneity of their populations. In this context Hall (2013: 229) differentiates between the traditional agrarian empires and the overseas trading polities, arguing that the former were able to nationalise deeper and faster than the latter. Thus, unlike the Ottomans, Romanovs and Habsburgs, who all expanded as composite imperial orders directly incorporating diverse populations and their territories within the empire itself, the British and French maintained geographical and political distinctions between the inner core territories and the overseas possessions. This distinct historical legacy was critical for any attempt to model the imperial order. Thus, while the French, British and Dutch polities could embark on the gradual nationalisation of their core territories, this process was beset with enormous organisational difficulties and ideological tension in the agrarian composite empires. For example, the Ottoman and Habsburg attempts to nationalise the empire instantly generated a nationalist backlash from movements representing the cultural diversity of the empire. In this situation, nationalisation from the centre often tended to create 'national movements where none existed before'(Hall 2013: 230), which ultimately weakened the social cohesion of the empire and threatened the very existence of such polities.[1] In contrast, the British or French empires could pursue nationalisation at home while still maintaining imperial possessions abroad. Although this situation was also beset with tensions and periodic conflicts (such were the cases of Ireland and Algeria, to name

---

[1] As Stergar and Scheer (2018) show, nationalist movements within Austro-Hungary have often benefited from the unintended consequences of Habsburg bureaucratic classification. The imperial state was often responsible for the creation, promotion and perpetuation of the nation-centred categories as it attempted to simplify governance and communication within the empire.

a few), this model lasted until the mid-twentieth century. Hence for Hall, the modernising oversees trading empires were quite capable of combining imperialism and nationalism.

Both Kumar and Hall offer a nuanced understanding of the multifaceted relationship between the imperial and the national. They show convincingly how and why modernising empires can utilise nationalist ideas and practices. However, I would argue that this perspective can be extended further to explore the other side of this complex relationship. In other words, my aim here is to show that the imperial states are not the only ones trapped in this ideological ambiguity of national and imperial. I would argue that the elements of this ideological cacophony were just as present in some polities traditionally seen as the epitome of a small nation state. Hence, in this chapter, I analyse how the nineteenth and early twentieth-century Balkan states combined nationalism and imperialism to increase their political legitimacy and their international prestige. As this was not a uniform process across the region, I zoom in on the different experiences of Bulgaria and Serbia.

Nationalism and Imperialism in the Balkans

Scholars of nationalism regularly identify the Balkans, together with Latin America, as the cradle of early nationalist movements (Mouzelis 2007; Anderson 1991[1983]; Minogue 1996; Kedourie 1960). For example, Wilson (1970: 28) describes the First Serbian Uprising (1804) as 'the first of the great nationalistic movements of the nineteenth century', while Minogue (1996: 120) insists that in the Greek case 'nationalism long precedes the coming of industrialism'. In a similar fashion, Anderson (1991[1983]: 49–55) argues that nationalism originated in the New World as 'the Creole pioneers' resisted the European imperial order. However, more recent scholarship is highly sceptical of such assessments (Malešević 2013b, 2012; Biondich 2011; Roudometoff 2001; Centeno 2002).[2] For example, Centeno (2002: 25) argues that the early nineteenth-century Latin American 'wars of independence' had little to do with nationalism and much more with imperial decline: 'the wars of independence produced fragments of empire, but not new states. There was little economic or political logic to the frontiers as institutionalised in the 1820s ... the new countries were essentially mini-empires with all the weaknesses of such political entities' (Centeno 2002: 25). In a similar way, I have tried to show how the early nineteenth-century Balkan uprisings were not driven by coherent nationalist agendas but emerged

---

[2] This is elaborated more extensively in Chapters 7 and 8.

as an unintended consequence of pronounced social unrests coupled with wider geo-political changes (Malešević 2012 and Chapter 7 here). The central aim of this new scholarship is to show that one should not take pronouncements of nineteenth-century national ideologues, and of political and cultural elites, at face value and simply assume that they reflect popular sentiments. Instead, by looking at the organisational dynamics and the level of societywide ideological penetration of nationalist ideas and practices, one can demonstrate that this ideology develops quite late in both regions. Most Latin American countries, to use Centeno's (2002) description, remained mini-empires in a sense that only a small number of people, descendants of white settlers residing in large cities, identified with the new states.

Despite their different colonial history, the nineteenth and early twentieth-century Balkans exhibited a similar pattern of deep divide between the minority – the largely urban population – who were the principal proponents of nationalist ideas and the large, mostly peasant, majority generally indifferent towards nationalism. In this context, the conventional narratives of the popular revolts against the decaying imperial order bear no resemblance to the actual historical reality. Rather than seeing the emergence of independent Serbia, Bulgaria or Greece as the product of strong nationalist movements rebelling against the Ottomans, the evidence points towards the conclusion that such movements were weak and marginal and that nationalism largely developed after independence (Malešević 2012; Roudometoff 2001). Moreover, in these conventional narratives, nationalism and imperialism are ordinarily depicted as mutually exclusive ideological projects.

Hence, the traditional historiography is almost exclusively focused on contrasting Serbian and Bulgarian nationalisms with the Ottoman, and later also Habsburg, imperial creeds. Nevertheless, Hall's (2013) and Kumar's (2017) arguments about the interdependence of imperialism and nationalism in this period resonate quite well in the context of small Balkan polities too. This is not to say that the imperial and nationalist discourses deployed in nineteenth-century Britain or France are similar in any way to those used in Bulgaria or Serbia. Obviously the imperial powers, as Hall (2013) rightly argues, were eager to nationalise their polities in order 'to increase force through coherence'. In contrast, new nation states such as Serbia and Bulgaria were built around emerging international principles that delegitimised the Ottoman's imperial dominance over their territories. In some respects, while the embrace of nationalism by the great imperial powers was a reluctant strategy for their long-term survival, the reliance on nationalist idioms was the cornerstone of Serbia's and Bulgaria's existence. However, the historical reality has proved to be much messier. Although both Bulgaria's and Serbia's political elites invested enormous economic, political and ideological resources to build their polities as fully fledged nation states, they also drew extensively on imperial rhetoric and practice. Hence, rather than incessantly opposing the imperial model of governance, the new states often blended the nationalist with imperial discourses and practices. For one thing, both states strongly emphasised their deep historical roots where past imperial legacies were often invoked to legitimise their new polities. For another, the new Balkan rulers attempted to model their states on the existing European polities, many of which remained deeply imperial in their structure and organisation.

Bulgaria

In the Bulgarian case this legacy encompasses the early medieval states which were regularly depicted as the cradle of Bulgarian culture. The focal point is on the First and Second Bulgarian Empires, which are understood to provide the foundation for modern-day Bulgaria. Although the First Bulgarian Empire (seventh to eleventh century) was established by the non-Slavic Bulgar tribes, it gradually incorporated various local groups, eventually becoming a slavicised polity. Nineteenth-century dominant discourses centred on the 'unbroken continuity' between the First and Second Empires and contemporary Bulgaria. This rhetoric was focused in particular on the expansion of the state's territory under several notable rulers (including Krum, Boris I, Simeon the Great and Ivan Assen II, among others), the Christianisation of the population, the development of the first written codes of law, the establishment of the semi-autonomous Bulgarian Eastern Orthodox Church and adoption of the Cyrillic alphabet (Fine 1991: 94–201). In this narrative the reign of Simeon the Great (893 to 927) was accorded a special place. Many of the nineteenth-century and even some early twentieth-century state formation discourses were framed as attempts to resurrect Simeon's empire under the modern guise. In this period, Simeon the Great was celebrated as the ruler who defeated the mighty Byzantine Empire and the always-threatening Magyars and Serbs. Under his rule, the Bulgarian state attained the greatest territorial expansion in its history. Moreover, this period has also been generally regarded as the era of cultural advancement and economic growth. Emphasis was regularly placed on gaining independence for the Bulgarian Orthodox Church and Simeon's support for the cultural activities, such as the translations of Christian literature in Slavic idioms (with the newly created Cyrillic script as well as the slightly older Glagolic script). For example, prominent intellectuals, politicians and military leaders were inspired by the idea of reviving the glories of the medieval empire with such slogans as 'back to Simeon the Great' (Daskalov 2005: 230). During the early and mid-nineteenth century, when Bulgaria was still part of the Ottoman empire, such references to the golden age of Tsar Simeon were for the most part confined to a very small circle of intellectuals, political activists and other professionals, many of whom were educated abroad. Their intention was to invoke the legacy of the medieval empire in order to justify establishment of an independent state. Initially, there was no clear blueprint what the new polity was to look like, with some advocating a pan-Slavic entity under the protectorate of the Romanovs, others envisaging a quasi-federal Orthodox Christian Balkan empire, and yet others advocating the creation of a sovereign Bulgarian state (Roudometoff 2001). Nevertheless, the main focus was on delegitimising the Ottoman rulers while simultaneously justifying the need for new Balkan territorial order. In this context, references to the medieval Christian and Slavic empire were used to emphasise the cultural difference vis-à-vis the Ottoman Muslim and non-Slavic empire. Hence, rather than calling upon the principles of 'national freedom', as the latter-day nationalist historiographies tend to dramatically overplay, the early activists often used the imperial legacy of the past to challenge the imperial rule of the present.

With the establishment of a semi-independent Bulgaria in 1878, the medieval imperial legacy was largely deployed to uphold the nationalist project. Hence, the political, military and cultural elites constructed, institutionalised and reproduced the narratives of ancient glories in the educational system, mass media and public sphere in order to make the majority peasant population into nationally conscious Bulgarians. This process was intensified after Bulgaria gained full independence in 1908 and reached its peak during the Balkan wars of 1912–13. During this period, Bulgarian nationalists largely focused on the legacy of the 1878 Treaty of San Stefano. Under this preliminary agreement between Russian and Ottoman governments, Bulgaria was recognised as an autonomous principality encompassing large territory in the Balkans. However, the 1878 Berlin Treaty quickly revised these territorial gains and made the new Bulgarian polity much smaller. This decision, made by the Great Powers, infuriated generations of Bulgarian nationalists who continued to hail the San Stefano agreement as the only fair solution to the Bulgarian national question, while perceiving the Berlin Treaty as deeply unjust towards the Bulgarians. As Hranova (2011) and Dimitrova and Kaytchev (1998) demonstrate, the education system was highly instrumental in voicing this deep discontent. Late nineteenth and early twentieth-century school textbooks lament how 'unfair' the Berlin Treaty was, like 'a knife which cut up the Fatherland into five pieces' (Bobchev 1881: 289 in Dimotrova and Kaytchev 1998: 54). This narrative emphasises the moral failings of the Great Powers, insisting that their unjust decision partitioned the Bulgarian nation thus 'lacerating living parts off the people's body' (Dimitrova 2003: 58). Leading textbook writers such as Nikola Stanev were adamant that both the Berlin Treaty and the Second Balkan War were unnatural as they did not allow for the proper unification of the entire nation. Instead, the outcome of these events, in his view, was 'the figure of Motherland crying for scattered children (Thrace, Macedonia, Dobrudzha)' (Dimitrova 2003: 58). Although most scholars tend to focus on the nationalist content of such narratives, what is equally important is the parallel invocation of medieval imperial legacies. For example, a number of highly influential novels and popular books published in the late nineteenth and early twentieth century make explicit links between modern Bulgaria in its 'natural' San Stefano borders with its medieval counterparts. Hence, geography and history textbooks tended to reproduce images of Greater Bulgaria that incorporate the medieval and the San Stefano treaty maps while making a direct link between the ancient and contemporary rulers (Hranova 2011: 37). One such textbook proclaims King Simeon the Great as being motivated by exactly the same ambition that drove contemporary nationalist Bulgarians – to unite the nation 'on three seas':

Now the whole Bulgarian nation, which inhabits almost the whole Balkan Peninsula, was united for the first time in one state, under the rule of one king's will [Simeon I]; now it made up one whole, towards which all our kings aspired and towards which we, too, aspire now. (Ganchev 1888: 24 in Hranova 2011: 37–8)

In a similar way, novels of the early twentieth century tended to depict medieval rulers as contemporaries motivated by the same goals of national unification. For example, the highly popular writer Fani Popova-Mutafova's novel *Ivan Assen II* (1936) was set in the thirteenth century where the main protagonist, emperor Ivan Assen II, is portrayed as a nationally conscious Bulgarian bent on liberating his homeland:

God Himself had marked the boundaries of this blessed land: the three seas and the wide white river ... from the throne of Holy Sofia, one will would guide the flowering of the great kingdom: the will of the Bulgarian king ... And there was no one other than the Bulgarian king who could unite, rally around his throne, weld into one, the rebellious, eternally warring nations ... (Popova-Mutafova 1938: 20–21 in Hranova 2011: 37)

The same idea of 'unbroken continuity' with the imperial past was echoed by historians such as Yordan Venedikov whose 1918 book was written on this very premise: 'By a strange coincidence imposed by the inexorable laws of international life, today we are fighting in the same places, against almost the same enemies, and for the same goals for which our ancestors fought under the House of Assen ...' (Venedikov 1918: 1 in Hranova 2011: 38).

Most of these narratives follow a standard nationalist template where there is no distinction between medieval imperial polities and contemporary nation states. In these popular accounts, emperors such as Simeon the Great or Ivan Assen II do not differ much from modern nationalist figures. Thus, instead of acknowledging sharp feudal hierarchies where such overlords had no interest in peasant masses, the novels and textbooks present them as modern individuals driven by an ideology of nationalism. Nevertheless, while nationalism is the driving force of these historical portrayals, what is also important, but rarely acknowledged, is the centrality of imperial legacy in these narratives. Political sovereignty and territorial unification are not deduced only from the popular will of the Bulgarian populace but also from historically rooted claims of previous imperial glory. Hence, when various nationalists invoke the indivisibility of Bulgaria 'on three seas', they regularly invoke the imperial legacy of the 'three ancient provinces' – Moesia, Thrace and Macedonia.

In addition, persistent references to the medieval empire were also used to depict the new independent polity as being an equal among the well-established European states. In this context, and especially in the early years, the focus was not so much on creating a nation state as on providing a structural framework for the existence of an independent and viable polity. Hence, to achieve international recognition and support from the Great Powers, semi-independent Bulgaria accepted Alexander of Battenberg as its first legitimate ruler. This practice, a quite common feature of late nineteenth century Balkans, of appointing a foreign aristocrat as a head of the new state had very little to do with nationalist ideology and was much closer to the imperial conventions of the ancien régime. When Alexander abdicated in 1887, he was replaced by another foreign-born aristocrat, Ferdinand Maximilian Karl Leopold Maria of Saxe-Coburg and Gotha, who remained in power until 1918. To enhance his weak legitimacy, Ferdinand I imitated Simeon I and was declared 'tsar' (emperor) in 1908. By taking the title 'Tsar of the Bulgarians', which was traditionally associated with Simeon I, Ferdinand aimed to enhance his claim to the Bulgarian throne. Since the new ruler maintained his Catholic religion, the Bulgarian Orthodox Church was deeply opposed to Ferdinand's ascent to the throne. Hence, by imitating Simeon

I, Ferdinand was hoping to appease the church leaders. Persistent references to old imperial legacies were particularly pronounced during the 1912–13 Balkan wars when Ferdinand made repeated references to Bulgaria as the seventh Great Power in Europe. During the First Balkan War (1912), when Bulgaria fought the Ottoman Empire, Ferdinand often framed his country's war aims in terms of the re-creation of the new empire ('new Byzantium') and defined the war effort as 'a just, great and sacred struggle of the Cross against the Crescent' (Aronson 1986: 86–7). As Crampton (2007: 149) notes, Ferdinand 'was to dream in 1912 of a triumphal coronation in Constantinople' where he imagined himself as an heir to Byzantine emperors.

Furthermore, in order to boost its international status, the new state adopted models of political and economic organisation from the Western European polities. In this process, it introduced many imperial features into its state structure: from the military to foreign affairs to education and civil service. For example, its 1879 Tarnovo constitution was largely modelled on the 1831 monarchist Belgian constitution. Since Ferdinand tightly controlled the ministries of foreign affairs and war, he was in a position to imprint imperial clout on the military and foreign affairs offices (Crampton 2007: 149). The imperial imagery was also present in the mass media, which often glorified the new state and its rulers as modern day Byzantines.

Serbia

Serbia gained independence from the Ottoman rule much earlier than Bulgaria and in this sense is often perceived as the pioneer of early nationalism. For example, the First Serbian Uprising (1804–13) has traditionally been interpreted as one of the earliest cases of a very successful nationalist movement. However, as I argue in Chapter 7, this and the subsequent early-nineteenth-century Serbian uprisings were mostly social rebellions focused on local concerns that eventually tapped into the broader geo-political transformations of the region (see also Malešević 2012). Hence, neither the leaders of these rebellions nor the ordinary population involved were motivated significantly by nationalist ideology. While the majority of the population consisted of illiterate peasants who had no conception of what the nation was, leaders such as Đorđe Petrović-Karađorđe and particularly Miloš Obrenović were largely motivated by personal ambitions that involved political control and the possibility of expanding their pork trade business with the Austrians (Malešević 2012; Meriage 1977). Obviously, the pronounced religious differences with the Ottoman rulers played an important role in mobilising the peasantry to resist the local janissaries, but in the early nineteenth century such differences still did not have any nationalist resonance. Even the leaders of these uprisings were insisting that they fought renegade ayans and janissaries aiming to 'restore the order on behalf of the Sultan' in Istanbul (Roudometoff 2001: 231). When Obrenović became the head of the Principality of Serbia in 1830 he continued to dress as an Ottoman aristocrat (Pavlowitch 1981). Hence, it seems that the imperial ethos still dominated early nineteenth-century Serbian politics.

Although nationalist ideas gained influence once Serbia became a fully independent polity in 1867, this did not mean that imperial rhetoric disappeared. On the contrary, just as in the Bulgarian case, imperial discourses and practices were deployed extensively to increase domestic and international legitimacy. In this context, just as with their Bulgarian counterparts, Serbian rulers invoked the legacies of medieval Serbian empires. Hence, mass media, the educational system, and the public sphere were all centred on glorifying the early polities of Serbs stretching from the nineth-century First Serbian Principality under the Vlastimirović dynasty to the tenth and eleventh-century grand principality of Raška under the Vukanović dynasty, which was followed by the kingdom of Serbia under the Nemanjić dynasty established in 1217. The Nemanjićs were particularly praised for founding an independent Serbian Orthodox Church in 1219 when King Stefan's brother Rastko (Sava) was ordained as the first Archbishop. Nevertheless, most of the focus on the late nineteenth century has been firmly on the legacies of the Serbian Empire under Tsar Stefan Uroš IV Dušan (1346–55). This emperor, often called Dušan the Mighty, has been credited as the ruler who created a large empire that incorporated much of the present-day Balkan Peninsula. He was generally perceived as one of the most powerful European rulers of his time, capable, just as Simeon the Great, of challenging the power and legitimacy of the Byzantine Empire. Dušan was also celebrated as a ruler who implemented the first constitutional programme for the empire (i.e. the Dušan code), which consisted of a complex set of laws that regulated most segments of life in the empire. He also supported the Serbian Orthodox Church, which during his rule acquired a Patriarchate, and promoted the cultural and economic development most notable for building many large monasteries (Fine 1991). This image of the powerful and enlightened ruler has been reproduced through the folk poetry that was very popular in Serbia during the later Ottoman period. However, with the establishment of an independent Serbian state in the mid-nineteenth century, Dušan's empire acquired a special place in the public sphere. Hence, the focus in this period was firmly on celebrating the medieval glories and attempting to formulate projects which in one way or another were devised as a resurrection of Dušan's empire.

Early plans involved maps of a Greater Serbian state that would encompass all lands where Serbs were assumed to constitute the majority of the population: Franjo Zach's plan from 1843 and Ilija Garašanin's Načertanije of 1844. Serbia's interior minister, and later Prime Minister, Garašanin's plan was particularly influential as its stated aim was not to 'limit Serbia to her present borders, but [to] endeavour to absorb all the Serbian people around her' (Cohen and Riesman 1996: 3). Although this clearly was an idea driven by nationalist aspiration, the actual reality of mid and late nineteenth-century Serbia was much more complex as it blended this nationalism with strong imperial idioms. Just as in the Bulgarian case, the emphasis was on legitimising the very existence of an independent state. In this context, the medieval imperial legacy was deployed to challenge the Ottoman's, and to some extent later also the Habsburg's, right to rule Serbian lands. Similarly to the Bulgarian new rulers, the Serbian political elite made much of the Christian Orthodox and Slavic roots of their imperial past. Hence, rather than relying solely on revolutionary nationalist rhetoric and practice, which could have been challenged by the still-imperial Great Powers, the rulers were intent on demonstrating unbroken continuity between Dušan's empire and the new state. Thus, both the Serbian and Bulgarian governments were initially keen to downplay nationalist rhetoric and accentuate their imperial heritage.

Although the two states shared much in terms of external legitimacy, there were some noticeable differences in how political legitimacy was attained domestically. For one thing, unlike Bulgaria which became ruled by a foreign monarch, an independent Serbia was governed by local rulers. This difference originates in the fact that Serbia's road towards independence started much earlier and was shaped by several successful uprisings, which forced the Ottomans to gradually negotiate more and more autonomy for Serbia's new rulers. Although Karađorđe and Obrenović were initially envisaged as temporary leaders in charge of autonomous, but still Ottoman, provinces, they eventually established themselves as the lawful rulers. For another thing, as Serbia did not have its own aristocrats, most of whom were killed during the Ottoman period, the new rulers created their own royal, and mutually competing, dynasties. Hence, the head of the First Serbian Uprising, Đorđe Petrović-Kara đorđe, became 'Grand Leader of Serbia' (*Veliki Vožd*), and his descendants embraced royal titles (princes and kings). Nevertheless, their right to rule was consistently challenged by the progeny of Miloš Obrenović, who led the Second Serbian Uprising and on that basis also became the

Grand Leader of Serbia. Obrenović, who was responsible for Karađorđe's death, was later enthroned as the first prince of Serbia. The fact that both of these newly established royal houses stemmed from commoners and, as such, could have been perceived as deeply illegitimate fostered very different internal dynamics in Serbia when compared to Bulgaria. While in the Bulgarian situation, internal legitimacy was tied in part to the legacy of medieval rulers and in part to 'imported' European nobility, in Serbia both dynasties were engaged in fierce conflict whereby the two competing dynasties put enormous effort to delegitimise each other (see Chapter 8). In this context, the representatives of both dynasties were eager to prove their imperial credentials by invoking imagined and fabricated links with Serbian medieval nobility while simultaneously denouncing their competitors. Thus, imperial discourse and the corresponding rituals became a cornerstone of the state's legitimation practices.

However, this is not to say that nationalism was irrelevant as a mode of political communication and rule justification. On the contrary, precisely because Serbia had such weak imperial foundations, nationalism was regularly deployed to sustain the competing claims to rule. Rather than acting as inherent ideological enemies, in late nineteenth-century Serbia, imperialism and nationalism were often best of friends. In order to enhance their domestic and international legitimacy, the two competing royal houses often combined imperial and nationalist rhetoric. Hence, both royal houses invested heavily in establishing their aristocratic origins while also attempting to utilise nationalist ideology to gain popular support domestically. In this context, both Karađorđevićs and Obrenovićs courted European royals and had their sons and daughters married to members of European royal families. Once independence was granted, the focus was on the Habsburgs and the two royal houses built alliances with the Austrian rulers. Later, they shifted their diplomatic gaze towards other European courts: Russia, France, Germany and Britain. The tendency was for one royal house to attain support from one of the Great Powers. For example, Karađorđevićs were often supported by Russia and France while Obrenovićs attained support from Austria and Germany. The two dynasties also used royal pageantry, including coats of arms and flags, both of which deliberately incorporated imperial symbols of Tsar Dušan: yellow flags with the red two-headed eagle. Both dynasties were also eager to prove that they possessed genuine aristocratic heritage. For example, Karađorđevićs traced the origins of their dynasty to the Montenegrin Vasojevići clan, who themselves claimed to be descendants of the Nemanjić dynasty (thus including Dušan the Mighty). These imperial trappings were just as important domestically to show that each dynasty had a legitimate claim to rule while also delegitimising the competing dynasty.

Nevertheless, to strengthen their mutually exclusive claims, the two royal houses also relied on nationalism. However, as the overwhelming majority of the population was illiterate and tended to identify largely in religious or local, kinship-based, terms, the focus was on creating institutions that would transform peasants into Serbs and in this process foster a wider support base for the (national) royal family. Hence, when in power, each royal household supported the establishment of educational institutions, mass media and cultural organisations centred on the glorification of nationhood. From the mid-nineteenth century onwards, the state fostered publication of primary and secondary school textbooks that promoted fiercely nationalist narratives (Roudometoff 2001: 127; Jelavich 1989: 47–75). The ministries for culture also sponsored mass media devoted to propagating nationalist and monarchist causes. Furthermore, in this period, the government founded key national institutions such as the National Library (1832), the National Museum (1844), the Serbian National Theatre (1861) and the Serbian Royal Academy of Sciences (1886) (see Chapters 7 and 8).

Although Bulgaria and other independent Balkan states went through similar processes of nation-state building, the Serbian case was different in a sense that nationalism was often deployed as a political strategy to enhance one dynasty's right to rule while simultaneously delegitimising hostile competitors (see Chapter 8). The history of late nineteenth and early twentieth-century Serbia was characterised by excessive violence between the two royal households with numerous assassinations, coups and forced abdications. This conflict at the top also spread to the military and political establishments, which gradually became involved in protracted struggles over legitimacy. In this context, nationalism developed as a strategy to attain popular support at home. The decline of the Ottoman Empire provided an opportunity for the rulers to augment their legitimacy through the rise of expansionist nationalism. In this novel historical environment, traditional imperial claims were supplemented with new imperial forms of nationalism. In other words, rulers advocated territorial conquests as means to realise nationalist goals. Hence, military victories in the Balkan wars (1912–13) acted as quick enhancers of political legitimacy. By dramatically expanding the territory and population of Serbia in 1913, the Karađorđevićs ultimately prevailed over the Obrenovićs. Since the Serbian state doubled in size and acquired over 1.2 million new inhabitants, the imperial nationalism was judged to be a way forward for the new state.

Nationalising Empires and Imperialising Nation states

Both conventional historiography and mainstream historical sociology make much of the distinction between empires and nation states. In this dominant view, empires stand for deep social inequalities, territorial conquests and supremacy of one ethnic group over the others. In contrast, nation states are thought to convey a social order defined in principle by political equality, cultural homogeneity and popular sovereignty. In this understanding, ideological projects that underpin these two models of polity organisation are judged to be mutually exclusive: whereas imperialism denotes an ambition to extend state power through violence and colonisation, nationalism is associated with popular self-rule, autonomy, independence and the preservation of cultural authenticity.

There is no doubt that as ideal-types, empires and nation states represent very different models of polity organisation. Nevertheless as Hall (2017, 2013, 2011) and Kumar (2017, 2010) rightly emphasise, no polity is a static entity but rather something that is continuously shaped by broader geopolitical changes on the one hand, and by the vagaries of domestic politics on the other. In this sense, nineteenth century empires, such as those of Britain, France and Germany, differed profoundly from their ancient, capstone counterparts such as the Roman or Chinese ones. While traditional imperial orders could manage cultural differences through excessive violence or plain ignorance, modernising empires had no other choice but to respond to changing international and domestic conditions. As Hall (2011: 20–2) makes clear, the combination of the global struggle for territory, resources and state prestige abroad together with the rising nationalist movements at home forced imperial rulers to nationalise their empires. The general hope was that national homogenisation would stop the domestic centrifugal forces, prevent secessionism, strengthen the empire and ultimately prolong its life. However, the historical record indicates that once 'nationalism and imperialism were joined together in a powerful mixture' (p. 20) the path was set towards further expansion and violence. For Hall, World War I was the outcome of this deadly cocktail: nationalising homogenisation combined with imperial ambition. What Hall's and Kumar's analyses show is that in a rapidly nationalising late-nineteenth-century world, imperial rulers could do little else than attempt to nationalise their empires.

This argument is potent and persuasive but it does not fully address the other side of this relationship: how nation states embraced the imperial rhetoric and sought to boost their political legitimacy at home and abroad. It is true that the late nineteenth and early twentieth centuries were characterised by blurred boundaries of imperialism and nationalism.

However, it was not only a case of nationalising empires: this process was just as present on the other side of this dichotomy, with some nation states embracing imperial garb. The Balkan polities are usually perceived to epitomise the example of a typical small nation state driven by popular nationalisms. In this understanding, Serbia, Greece, Bulgaria and other states were often seen as beacons of early nationalism standing against the imperialist ambitions of the Great Powers. Nevertheless, one should question such assumptions. Not only was popular nationalism very weak until well into the twentieth century, but these states also cherished their own imperial projects. Hence, rather than resisting imperialism and pursuing nationalism, the Bulgarian and Serbian new rulers regularly combined the two ideological projects in order to enhance their political legitimacy. While the Great Powers attempted to nationalise their empires in order, as Hall stresses, 'to increase force through coherence', the Balkan polities were eager to imperialise their nation states. Despite the different means and strategies deployed, they embraced imperialism for similar reasons that compelled the Great Powers to adopt nationalism: to increase their power. Furthermore the embrace of imperial doctrine was not just confined to proclamations, rituals, rhetoric, imagery and pageantry. Rather, with the 1912–13 Balkan wars, Serbia and Bulgaria both became involved in the quasi-imperial conquest for territory previously controlled by the Ottoman Empire. In this context, the two governments combined imperialism with nationalism to justify their spoils of war. While nationalist arguments were regularly deployed to legitimise inclusion of fellow ethnic brethren living outside the boundaries of the homeland, imperialist doctrine was often invoked to validate the right to expand one's territory.

The experience of these two small Balkan states indicates that conventional historical analyses that differentiate sharply between different forms of polity organisation and the corresponding ideological matrices cannot account properly for the complex and often contradictory social reality. The late nineteenth century was a world abundant in what we would perhaps consider strange types of polities: imperialising nation states and nationalising empires. Hence, rather than taking for granted that nation states and empires have nothing in common and that nationalism and imperialism are always enemies, it is crucial to understand that historical reality is full of hybrid ideological and organisational forms. There is much more to nationalism and imperialism than our history textbooks have taught us.

5 What Makes a Small Nation?

Introduction

Nineteenth and early twentieth-century Irish and Balkan nationalisms have often been interpreted as having much in common. For one thing, they were understood to be a similar form of popular resistance against what was perceived to be illegitimate imperial rule. For another, they were identified as having a predominantly ethnic character where the focus was on the cultural as opposed to the political sense of group identification. In other words, the Irish nationalist spotlight on religion and language seemed to resemble the Balkan and East European nationalist experiences much more than that of their West European neighbours (Barry et al. 2016; Hroch 2015, 1985; Biagini 2007; Todorova 2007). Finally, Balkan and Irish nationalisms are generally perceived to be typical examples of small-nation projects fending off the presence of dominant large nations. In the words of leading Czech historian Miroslav Hroch (1985: 9), who was instrumental in developing this comparative field of study, small nations 'are those which were in subjection to a ruling nation for such a long period that the relation of subjection took on a structural character for both parties'.[1] Over the last two decades, this field of research has expanded substantially with many specialised comparative analyses of small nations ranging from state formation and political economy (Campbell and Hall 2017; Cornell 2014), to performance, theatre and cinema of small nations (Blandford 2013; Hjort 2007), to viability of small nations in a globalised world (Hannertz and Gingrich 2017; Jones 2014; Bodley 2013). Some of the more historical studies written in such a comparative 'small nation' vein, have made direct links

---

[1] In this context Hroch's (1985) initial focus was on the historical dynamics of nation-formation in seven European 'small nations': Czechs, Slovaks, Norwegians, Finns, Flemish, Estonians and Lithuanians. In his later works, he also devotes a great deal of attention to other 'small nations' including Irish, Serbs, Croats, Bulgarians, Catalans, Basques, Icelanders, Macedonians and others (Hroch 2015, 2009).

between late nineteenth century and early twentieth-century Ireland and the Balkans (Barry et al. 2016; Keown 2016; Hroch 2015). For example, a recent comparative study of 'small nations' in World War I emphasises the commonalities between Ireland and the Balkan small nations. In this interpretation, the early twentieth-century Balkan states were seen to be quite similar to Ireland in the sense that they were all 'small nations' dealing with the violent legacies of empires. Hence, the authors describe Ireland as a small nation, 'which was not yet a state [and] was poised precariously during World War I between the maintenance of the Union Britain and the opposition to the War' (Barry et al. 2016: 11). The same small nation idea is also attributed to the Balkans as they allegedly 'typify the drive of small nations to liberate themselves from imperial powers through violence. They demonstrate the difficulties of achieving self-determination in a region occupied by competing imperial powers and emerging states' (Barry et al. 2016: 7). Hence, in this now well-established interpretation, small nations are characterised by a long history of foreign rule that ultimately generates a particular relation of subjugation and interdependence.

In this chapter, I aim to problematise and deconstruct the idea of a 'small nation'. I argue that rather than being a simple descriptive category denoting the size of a particular nation, this idiom has historically played a potent ideological role. By comparing and contrasting the different uses of this notion in nineteenth and early twentieth-century Ireland and the Balkans, I attempt to show how the concept of a 'small nation' was deployed to serve different ideological goals. Hence, rather than simply assuming that categories such as a small and a big nation are innocent geographical descriptions, it is paramount to historically contextualise such idioms in order to provide a sociological explanation of their social and political meanings.

First of the Small Nations

There is no doubt that Irish and Balkan nationalisms have some common features. It is true that these nationalisms have historically been framed in terms of resistance to imperial powers: the British, the Ottomans, and the Habsburgs respectively. Nevertheless, as Smith (1973: 10) noted long ago, all nationalist ideologies subscribe to a standard and similar set of key principles including the view that the world is naturally divided into nations, that the loyalty to one's nation overrides other loyalties, that not identifying with one's nation is a source of moral failing and that nations can be fully realised and liberated only when they attain political independence and sovereign statehood which in itself is seen as contributing to securing global peace. The Irish, just as the Bulgarian, Serbian, Greek and other Balkan nationalist movements, were all driven by these principles. For example, the pledge circulated during the 1918 conscription crisis in Ireland proclaims that 'Ireland is a distinct nation with a just right to Sovereign Independence. This right has been asserted in every generation, has never been condemned and never allowed to lapse' (Augustejin 2002). In a very similar vein the Bulgarian declaration of independence (1908) invokes 'the brave heroic Bulgarians' who 'broke the chains which had tied Bulgaria, once so great and glorious, as a slave for so many centuries'. The declaration also makes reference to past generations as 'the Bulgarian people, preserving the memory of those who toiled for their liberty and inspired by their tradition, have worked without rest for the progress of their beautiful land', and have ultimately achieved an independent 'state that can become an equal member among the family of civilized nations' (Strupp 1911). While it is obvious that these two documents exhibit a great deal of similarity, such discourses are far from being unique to Ireland and the Balkans. In fact, all nationalisms that emerge in the context of crumbling imperial orders tend to adopt the language of popular legitimacy which empires inevitably lack. In fact, nationalism is first and foremost an ideology that rests on the popularly shared perceptions that posit the nation as the principal unit of human solidarity and political legitimacy (Malešević 2013a). In this context, there is nothing peculiar to Irish and Balkan nationalisms as they resemble most other anti-imperial and post-imperial nationalisms. The anti-imperial and nationalist rhetoric present in the nineteenth century Balkans and Ireland is very similar to the nationalist discourses one could encounter in Norway, Poland, Italy, Mexico, Haiti, Bolivia, Columbia and many other nationalist movements throughout the world. Even the former imperial states such as Portugal, Belgium or Denmark have appropriated the discourse of popular sovereignty and have grounded their political legitimacy in nationalist terms (Rothermund 2015; Østergaard 2006).

It is also true that ethnic markers such as religion and language have played a prominent role in both the Balkan and Irish nationalist movements: Catholicism and Gaelic cultural revival have underpinned much of Irish late nineteenth-century nationalism, as have the Easter Orthodox denominations and the national vernaculars in the Balkans. However, these shared commonalities are far from being unique to these two regions as many nationalisms have utilised various cultural symbols to mobilise a degree of public support. Furthermore, the reliance on ethnic markers does not in itself attest that these nationalist projects were inevitable or exclusively ethnic in nature. Thus, to characterise the Balkan and

Irish cases as being distinct and similar in terms of their overemphasis on ethnic over civic markers of group identity is equally problematic.

For one thing, this sharp distinction between civic and ethnic forms of nationalism has been extensively criticised by many scholars of nationalism. For example, Yack (1999), Brubaker (2015, 2004, 1998), Smith (1998) and Kymlicka (1999), among others, have questioned this simplified dichotomy for years, arguing that this very typology was often deployed in a crude ethnocentric way to label other nationalisms as ethnic (i.e. irrational, nativist, inherited) and one's own as civic (voluntary, rational, consensual). As Kymlicka (1999: 24) emphasises 'this non-cultural conception of national membership is often said to be what distinguishes the 'civic' or 'constitutional' nationalism of the United States from illiberal 'ethnic nationalism' but this is 'mistaken' not least because immigrants to the USA 'must not only pledge allegiance to democratic principles' but have to also 'learn the language and history of the new society'. In a similar way, Yack (1996: 193)argues that 'purely civic nationalism' is a myth as no nation state in the world developed and exists as an entity rooted solely in the 'mutual association' based only 'on consciously chosen principles'. In fact, states such as France or the USA, both often identified as primary examples of civic nationhood, were forged around specific cultural categories and still remain culturally hierarchical polities. It is quite clear now that most nationalisms are composed of ethnic and civic components and that the civic nationalisms, such as the French or American, can be just as exclusive and xenophobic as the ethnic ones (Lieven 2012; Kreuzer 2006; Mees 2003). Hence, depicting Irish, Serbian or Greek nationalisms as having solely ethnic features is conceptually problematic and empirically wrong. In these cases, too, the dominant nationalist movements have utilised both the ethnic as well as the civic markers to mobilise public support. Hence, this standard and stereotypical association of ethnic nationalisms with the Balkans and Irish nationalisms does not seem to hold as this alleged similarity is rather superficial.

The third, and most promising, point of resemblance is the notion of small nations. In some respects, this seems obvious as Serbia, Greece, Croatia, Albania, Bulgaria and other Balkan states are, just as Ireland, small in terms of their territory, population size and international influence. Yet this category, I would argue, is much more controversial than it initially seems and also one that clearly differentiates the trajectory of Irish nationalism from its Balkan counterparts.

In historical terms, Irish nationalism has often been depicted as a political and cultural project of a small nation. At the end of the nineteenth and beginning of the twentieth centuries, Irish nationalists were keen to stress the similarity of popular aspirations and legitimacy of claims for independence among many small nations in Europe. The focus here was clearly on the colonial status of such entities living under 'the yoke' of various imperial powers – from the Ottomans in the Balkans, Habsburgs in the Central Europe, Romanovs in Russia and Eastern Europe to the presence of the British Empire in Ireland. In this context, Ireland was regularly compared to Finland, Bohemia/Czechoslovakia, Norway and the Baltic states in order to advance the cause of independence. For example, one of Sinn Féin's election songs invoked this issue in a European context and emphasised the alleged injustice that Ireland faces:

> The Spaniards, Bulgars, Swedes and Danes
> Have claims less high than we,
> Yet suffer they no foeman's chains –
> Those nations can be free,   (Laffan 1999: 265)

The cause of Ireland's independence was often framed in comparative terms where the successes of other independence movements in Europe were often utilised to signal what was perceived to be the inevitable trend – the independence of small nations. The emerging new paradigm of this period was the notion of national self-determination which included the right of small nations to determine their own future. These ideas were formulated throughout the political spectrum ranging from Lenin's April Theses in 1917 to President Woodrow Wilson's January 1918 US Congress speech where he used the example of Belgium and Poland to make a point about the centrality of self-determination. Wilson insisted that Belgian independence 'must be ... restored, without any attempt to limit the sovereignty which she enjoys in common with all other free nations' and that 'an independent Polish state should be erected which should include the territories inhabited by indisputably Polish populations' (Halsall 1997).

However, the relative failure of the 1916 Easter Rising, coupled with the tighter British grip on Ireland in the wake of intensified WWI operations, lead towards disillusionment with such Europe-wide comparisons. Hence, de Valera was bitterly disappointed with the proposed plans for the League of Nations, and also President Wilson's attitude towards Ireland whose representatives were excluded from the Peace conference in 1918 on the grounds that the Peace conference only discussed territories of defeated empires. In this context, de Valera responded in the following way: 'I need only say that the narrowing down of and limitation at the Peace conference to only such matters as affected territories belonging to defeated empires was altogether out of accord with war aims of

America as enunciated by the President and the professions of Entente statesmen during the war' (Sisson 2014: 2488). The same disappointment was voiced by Arthur Griffith who now shifted the focus towards Irish exceptionalism and was adamant that 'the right of the Irish to political independence never was, is not, and never can be dependent on the admission of equal rights in all other peoples. It is based on no theory of, and dependent in nowise for its existence or justification on, the 'Rights of Man' (Quinlan, 2005: 73).

With the end of WWI, with Ireland not having been granted independence while many other states of similar size enjoyed full sovereignty, the small-nation argument was reformulated to emphasise the double standards of Great Power politics. In particular, Irish nationalists were regularly pinpointing what they understood to be a hypocrisy of the British government which justified its involvement in WWI as a fight for 'the freedom of small nations' but that same principle was never later applied to Ireland. Hence, Sinn Fein's pamphlets published in this period made abundantly clear that Ireland was well ahead in terms of population and territory size, revenue per capita and the longer history of resistance to colonial rule than most of the states that were granted independence at Versailles. In the nationalist discourse of its time, Ireland was deemed to be 'First of the Small Nations' whose representatives were unfairly excluded from the Versailles talks and whose right to self-determination was unjustly ignored.

The same small nation discourse was also present during the establishment of the Free State. However, what before independence was a moral yardstick to build a legitimate demand for sovereign statehood was now gradually transformed into a claim for moral leadership among the 'small nations' of Europe and the wider world. Hence, in the 1922 Dáil Éireann Report on Foreign Affairs one can encounter the following statement:

No country ever started its international career with better prospects than were ours after the war, for our soldiers had won us warm friends everywhere, and we had no enemies to speak of throughout the Continent of Europe. Ireland had every reason to expect rapidly *to become recognised as the First of the Small Nations*. (www.difp.ie/docs/1922/Foreign-Policy-General/277.htm, italics mine)

The idea of a small nation appears regularly in the 1920s, 30s, 40s and 50s when this idiom was often articulated more widely to symbolise a relatively unique moral position of small countries in the changing world as well as to link Ireland with other postcolonial societies. For example, the Labour party leader, Thomas Johnson, expressed the view in parliament that the Free State has a unique position in the world as a small nation that can play an important part in 'in the formation of world opinion in regard to human progress' (Keown 2016: 148). In a very similar way, in his letter to the League of Nations, Irish diplomat Bolton Waller argued that 'if Ireland is to stand high in the eyes of the world it must be by intellectual and moral attainments, by the achievements in the spiritual rather than physical realm' (Keown 2016: 148). During this period, Irish political and cultural elites regularly drew parallels with the other 'small nations' that had attained independence from their larger neighbours, such as Finland, Norway, Belgium and Holland. In this context, de Valera opposed Nazi Germany not on the basis of its extremist ideology but primarily because the German military trampled on the sovereignty of small nations: 'it would be unworthy of the small Irish nation not to protest against the cruel wrong perpetuated on Holland and Belgium' (Lee 1985: 263). The small-nation paradigm gained in significance after WWII and the wave of decolonisation that swamped Africa, Asia and other parts of the former European imperial possessions. In this environment, Ireland's struggle for independence was often perceived as an example to be emulated by the various decolonising movements throughout the world. Here again the focus was on the small-nation idea.

This interpretation was reinforced by US President JF Kennedy's 1963 speech in the Irish parliament where he proclaimed that Ireland maintains a unique position in the world as 'the first of the small nations'. More specifically, he stated:

Ireland is clad in cause of national and human liberty with peace. To the extent that the peace is disturbed by conflict between the former colonial powers and the new and developing nations, Ireland's role is unique. For every new nation knows that Ireland was the first of the small nations in the twentieth century to win its struggle for independence and that the Irish have traditionally send their doctors and technicians and soldiers and priests to help other lands to keep their liberty alive. (Sachs 2013)

The same concept was later deployed to elucidate the collapse of communism in Eastern Europe with the proliferation of relatively small independent nation states from Lithuania, Latvia and Estonia to Georgia, Armenia and Moldova. Here again the discourse of small nation was used to make a case that, just as Ireland, these new polities are geopolitically viable and can prosper in the new world order. The presence of so many smaller polities in Europe has further contributed towards the idea, which become popular in Ireland, that the Irish example can be emulated elsewhere.

During the Celtic Tiger era, the small-nation discourse was reformulated yet again to demonstrate how size of the nation state is not detrimental to its economic development. Hence, Irish economic success was understood to parallel the previous success stories of small-tiger economies such as Singapore, Taiwan and Hong Kong. The assumption shared initially among economic and political elites, and later also by the Irish public at large, was that small nations such as Ireland are capable of unparalleled economic success in a globalised world (Campbell and Hall 2017). Most recently, the small-nation discourse was deployed by politicians to indicate how the enormous challenges of post-2008 recovery can be overcome by the strong will of the small nation. Hence, in one of his 2012 speeches, Taoiseach Enda Kenny emphasises that 'in the long history of our small nation there has never been such an unprecedented challenge nor such an extraordinary opportunity' and that the Irish citizens find themselves 'at a time in this country when we are securing our recovery, and Ireland has reclaimed its place in the world' (Kenny 2015).

The Greater Balkans

There is a great deal of continuity within Irish nationalist narratives in their emphasis on smallness. Regardless of whether a proponent of Irish nationalist cause comes from a conservative, liberal or socialist background, the tendency is to depict Ireland as a small nation. Although the particular emphasis in the discourse of small nation has changed through time – shifting from the moral and political issues towards more economic and cultural concerns – the discourse itself has largely remained unchanged. Some Irish nationalists remained preoccupied with the prompt unification of the island while others have been more gradualist or largely unconcerned with this issue. However, none of them has conceived of Ireland as a polity that could or should espouse expansionism. In other words no strain of Irish nationalism has ever flirted seriously with the idea of territorial expansion beyond the island of Ireland. This stands in a sharp contrast to the dominant discourses of many nineteenth and early twentieth-century Balkan nationalisms, most of which emphasised the territorial greatness of their respective nations. Thus, the leading Greek, Serbian, Bulgarian, Romanian, Albanian and Croatian nationalist movements tended to focus not on the small size of their nations but on the past glories of the ancient and medieval polities that dominated this part of the world. While Irish nationalism was framed around the question of territorial unification of the entire island, the Balkan nationalisms centred on the large-scale territorial expansions along the line of clearly articulated nationalist blueprints: Greater Greece (*Megáli Idéa*), Greater Serbia (*Velika Srbija*), Greater Bulgaria (*Velika i Obedinena Bulgariia*), Greater Romania (*România*

Mare), Greater Croatia (*Velika Hrvatska*), Greater Albania (*Shqipëria Etnike*) and so on.

The Greek nationalist movements have historically been focused on recapturing all of what they considered to be the ethnic Greek inhabited areas, including those territories that belonged to the Byzantine Empire and the Ottoman Empire. The Megáli Idéa (meaning 'great idea'), fully formulated in the early nineteenth century, became a guiding principle of Greece's foreign policy throughout much of the nineteenth and early twentieth century. Drawing on the ideas of the ancient geographer Strabo and other scholars and political leaders, prime minister of Greece Ioannis Koléttis developed this concept to act as a driving ambition for future Greek leaders. The Megáli Idéa was conceived as a long-term project that combined political, military and cultural aims. The focus was on developing military capacity in order to recapture various territories (from Thrace, Macedonia and Epirus to Crete and Cyprus as well as the lands from the Ionian Sea to Asia Minor and Black Sea) and make Constantinople (Istanbul) its true capital. Furthermore, the Great Idea also involved ambition to establish an extensive educational and propagandistic cultural programme to forge a strong sense of Greek identity among the citizens of what were to be the newly conquered lands. The plan was to create a new, enlarged, state – 'Greece of Two Continents and Five Seas'.[2] As Koléttis proclaimed in the Greek parliament in 1844: 'The Kingdom of Greece is not Greece. Greece constitutes only one part, the smallest and poorest. A Greek is not only a man who lives within this kingdom but also one who lives in any land associated with Greek history or the Greek race. There are two main centres of Hellenism: Athens, the capital of the Greek Kingdom, and Constantinople, the dream and hope of all Greeks' (Brewer 2012). Guided by this Megáli Idéa, Greece continued to expand its territory until the defeat in the 1922 war and the agreed 'exchange of population' with Turkey in 1923.

A very similar model of territorial expansion was constructed by Serbian intellectuals, politicians and military leaders. Serbian nationalist ambitions, articulated in the notions of Velika Srbija (Greater Serbia), centred on recreating the greatness of the tsar Dušan's (1308–1355) medieval Serbian empire by expanding the state's borders towards regions where the Serb population lives – from Croatia, Bosnia and Herzegovina to Macedonia, parts of Albania and further afield. Just as with the Greek case, this expansionist project was formulated early during the nineteenth century and was fully developed in 1844 in the secret

---

[2] Hence, Europe and Asia with the Ionian, Aegean, Marmara, Black and Libyan seas.

political programme, Načertanije *[Начертаније]*, drafted by the Serbian minister Ilija Garašanin. This document drew on already-existing plans sketched earlier by Polish intellectuals Adam Czartoryski and Franjo Zach and envisaged different strategies for conquering territories inhabited by Serbs and also assimilating the non-Serbian populations that lived on some of these lands. Hence, just as Koléttis, Garašanin believed that the present Principality of Serbia does not represent the whole of Serbia and for that reason he was adamant that Serbia requires an expansionist programme: 'A plan must be constructed which does not limit Serbia to her present borders, but endeavours to absorb all the Serbian people around her' (Cohen and Riesman 1996: 3). In addition to the military and political goals of capturing territories in Bosnia and Herzegovina, Montenegro, Northern Albania and further afield, this plan also provided suggestions on the best ways to assimilate Croats and Bosnian Muslims who were deemed to be Serbs of Catholic and Islamic faith respectively. By the early twentieth century, this expansionist project, rooted in the idea of uniting all Serbs into one single Serbian state, become a guiding principle that underpinned much of the foreign and domestic policy. Hence, as with Greece, Serbia continued its territorial expansion for much of this period. In fact, as discussed in Chapter 8, Serbia has experienced an unprecedented rise and territorial enlargement until well into twentieth century.

The Bulgarian nationalists developed rather similar ideological blueprints to that of Greek and Serbian nationalists. The central aspiration here was to bring to life Greater Bulgaria that would, on the one hand, invoke the legacy of the medieval Bulgarian Empire under Simeon the Great (893–927) and, on the other hand, would include territories of Macedonia, Thrace and Moesia as stipulated in the 1878 Treaty of San Stefano. This nationalist ideal was seriously undermined by the 1878 Treaty of Berlin which revised the San Stefano agreement and created a much smaller Bulgarian state. This was a pivotal moment in galvanising Bulgarian nationalists who envisaged implementation of the San Stefano agreement in order to establish a much greater state – 'Bulgaria on three seas'. At the end of the nineteenth and early twentieth century, the foreign policy was largely built around the key principle of attaining a Greater and Unified Bulgaria (Velika i Obedinena Bulgariia). This nationalist goal gained further momentum with the 1885 unification of the Principality of Bulgaria and Eastern Rumelia and the Bulgarian unexpected victory in the 1885 Serbo-Bulgarian war. Emboldened by these early successes, the Bulgarian governments embarked on two Balkan wars (1912–13) and were also involved in WWI. These wars have traditionally been regarded as the 'wars of national unification'. For example, a school textbook used before the end of WWI describes these conflicts in the following way: 'The Bulgarians participated in the European war, defeated their enemies, and liberated Macedonia, the Morava lands and Dobrudzha. In this way they restored the great and whole Bulgaria' (Hranova 2011: 33). However, with the defeat of the Bulgarian military forces in the second Balkan war and WWI, the original idea of restoring an enlarged state along the lines proposed at San Stefano was severely compromised. In this context, Bulgarian nationalists refocused their attention towards Macedonia, whose population they have always regarded as a fully fledged part of the Bulgarian nation.

Although the Romanian nationalist project shares many similarities with other Balkan states, it differs in the sense that the 1918–40 Kingdom of Romania was in fact a realisation of 'Greater Romania' ideal. Hence, the notion of România Mare is now largely associated with the restoration of these pre-WWII borders. Romanian nationalists aspired to unite all Romanian speakers into a single polity that would incorporate a range of what they regarded to be 'the lost territories', including northern Bukovina, Bessarabia and other territories that are today part of Moldova. Nevertheless, until 1918, Romanian nationalists were inspired by the same goals as other nationalists in the Balkans. Hence, the unification of Moldavian and Wallachian principalities in 1859 leading toward the establishment of Romanian state, which gained independence from the Ottomans and became a kingdom in 1881, was seen then as a first step towards the creation of the Greater Romania. This idea developed fully in the early twentieth century when the Romanian cultural and political elites articulated a notion of enlarged state that was rooted in the legacies of traditional rulers such as Michael the Brave (1558–1601) and Stephen the Great (c 1440–1504) and which would include Transylvania, Bukovina, Bessarabia and other territories. When Entente powers promised territorial compensation for Romanian participation in WWI in 1916, King Ferdinand's speech echoed other Balkan leaders in invoking importance of territorial greatness:

Rumanians! ... [this war] has brought the day which has been awaited for centuries by the national conscience, by the founders of the Rumanian State, by those who united the principalities in the war of independence, by those responsible for the national renaissance. It is the day of the union of all branches of our nation. Today we are able to complete the task of our forefathers and to establish forever that which Michael the Great was only able to establish for a moment, namely, a Rumanian union on both slopes of the Carpathians. (www.firstworldwar.com/source/romania_ferdinandproc1 .htm)

With Romania's government siding with the Axis powers in 1940, and thus losing substantial parts of its territories to the Soviet Union and Bulgaria, the idea of România Mare regained its importance among Romanian nationalists.

Croatian nationalists also envisaged the establishment of a Greater Croatia based on a blueprint inspired by the medieval kingdom of King Tomislav (died 928) which would integrate Bosnia and Herzegovina and parts of Serbia and Montenegro. The early proponent of this idea was the Habsburg writer and diplomat Pavao Ritter Vitezović (1652–1713) who argued that all Slavs were Croats and that in this context Croatia should extend from Adriatic to the Black sea and the Baltics (Fine 1994; Banac 1986). The rise of Hungarian nationalism, together with its aggressive Magyarisation policies within its part of the Habsburg empire in the early nineteenth century, fostered the development of Croatian nationalism. Initially, the leading Croatian intellectuals and political leaders embraced a pan-Slavic idea of Illyrianism in order to counter a Hungarian hegemonic project. Hence, in 1832, Croatian Count Janko Drašković published a pamphlet that proposed the establishment of a 'Great Illyria' as a political entity composed of all South Slav provinces of the Habsburg Empire (Despalatović 1975). Nevertheless, the more radical strands of Croatian nationalism rejected the idea of South Slav unity and instead became the leading proponents of Greater Croatia. The principal ideologues of this project were the leaders of the Croatian Party of Rights, Ante Starčević and Eugen Kvaternik, who envisaged a united Croatia that included territories of the present day Croatia as well as the whole of Bosnia and Herzegovina and parts of Serbia, Montenegro and Slovenia. Starčević deemed all South Slavs to be Croats. With the collapse of monarchist Yugoslavia in 1941, the Nazi German forces dismembered the old Yugoslav state and allowed for the creation of a puppet 'Independent State of Croatia' governed by the extreme right-wing nationalist group Ustashas led by Ante Pavelić. This puppet state was presented by its rulers as a realisation of the 'thousand year old dream' of an independent Greater Croatia. However, the state was largely controlled by the German and Italian authorities and did not include many parts of the present day Croatia.

Although Albanian nationalist movements developed later and could not invoke medieval roots (apart from rather spurious links with the ancient Illyrians), they too advocated pan-Albanian ethnic unification through the prism of 'Ethnic Albania' – Shqipëria Etnike. The notion of all Albanian speakers living in a single polity was fully articulated by the League for the Defence of the Rights of the Albanian Nation, better known as the League of Prizren, which was established in 1878 in

Prizren, Kosovo. The League delegates were adamant to resist Serbian and Greek attempts to seize what they regarded to be Albanian territories. Hence, the national programme was formulated emphasising that the principal national goal is 'the unification of all territories populated by Albanians into a single province' and it is necessary to fight 'to the last drop of blood against any annexation of Albanian territories' (Iskenderov 2015). Key early ideologues of Albanian nationalisms, such as the Frashëri brothers (Abdyl, Sami and Naim) and Pashko Vaso Shkodrani, were largely reformists deeply influenced by the European intellectual debates about popular sovereignty. In this context, Shkodrani wrote poems that were centred on reconciling clan and religious divisions among Albanians. In one of his best known poems he proclaims:

> Wake, Albanian, from your slumber,
> Let us, brothers, swear in common
> And not look to church or mosque,
> The Albanian's faith is Albanianism.   (Endresen 2013)

The Prizren League focused on uniting all Albanians within the single province of the Ottoman Empire. With the establishment of an independent Albania in 1912, the emphasis has shifted towards the unification of all regions with an Albanian-speaking majority within a single state. The Albanian nationalists envisaged a state consisting of Albania proper, Kosovo, western Macedonia, parts of southern Montenegro, northwestern Greece and southern Serbia. The Italian occupation in 1939 was highly instrumental in fostering the idea of the Greater Albania. The Italian fascist regime established a protectorate of Albania which included annexed territories from neighbouring states Kosovo, Western Macedonia and a substantial part of Greece (Chameria). Although the Italian military was fully in charge here, the nominal rule was in the hands of the Albanian Fascist Party led by the prime minister Shefqet Verlaci. In this context, many Albanian nationalists supported this arrangement as they perceived it to be a realisation of the Greater Albania project. The ultimate defeat of Germany and Italy ended this project but the idea of Shqipëria Etnike is still part of the everyday nationalist discourse.

While these expansionist nationalist projects dominated the late nineteenth and early twentieth-century politics and intellectual debates, they remained present and influential throughout much of the twentieth century and are still discussed in the public sphere. The 1912–13 Balkan wars and the two world wars kept these blueprints alive as the borders of the Balkan states continued to shift until 1945. Although the Cold War stabilised existing borders for decades, these expansionist nationalist ideologies remained visible throughout the region. Despite nominal commitment to communist universalism, the policies of the state-socialist Balkan states did not significantly differ from anti-communist Greece or Turkey: they all espoused firm nationcentric ideologies in education, mass media, foreign policy and many other fields. With the collapse of communism and disintegration of Yugoslavia, expansionist nationalism became even more prominent in the public eye as post-Yugoslav wars were in part waged to realise such ideological blueprints. Actual, or in other cases, expected, membership in the EU has dented some of these ideas but they have not gone away. While partially accepting the label of a small nation, dominant nationalist discourses in the Balkans are still, unlike Irish nationalism, strongly wedded to the notion of national greatness.

When Did Ireland Become a Small Nation?

Why was the idea of the small nation so appealing to Irish nationalists and not to their counterparts in the Balkans? Where do these two diametrically opposed views of nationhood come from? One could argue that the difference comes from the geographical limits whereby Irish nationalism inevitably encounters the finite borders of an island whereas the territories of the Balkan nationalist ambitions are substantially less limited. However, geographical restrictions were not an obstacle for the rise of expansionist nationalist and imperial projects in many other cases (including Denmark, Japan and Britain), while Greek nationalism was also able to overcome the territorial spread into thousands of small islands. Although geography plays a role in this process, it is difficult to see it as being the main reason for such contrasting visions of a nation. To avoid simple geographical determinism, it is necessary to explore other reasons for this difference.

Another possible interpretation would focus on the different historical legacies of the two regions: while nineteenth-century nationalism in the Balkan states could draw upon the powerful and unified medieval kingdoms as the alleged cradles of nationhood, Irish medieval history was characterised by less centralised and more patchy clan-based chiefdoms often at war with each other. Nevertheless, this argument could not account for the expansionist narratives of Albanian nationalism which could not invoke the memories of medieval statehood. Moreover, the Greek nationalist narrative was not built around a particular medieval kingdom but continued to be deeply split between those who envisaged an enlarged Greece on the blueprint of Byzantine Empire (conservatives) and those eager to resurrect the philosophical traditions and territories of the ancient Hellenic world (liberals) (Smith 1986). As all nationalisms draw upon the mythology of the glorious past, Irish nationalism could just as easily create a narrative of greatness on the basis of the military and political success in the pre-modern era: from the legendary kingship of Tara to the mythologies associated with the High Kings of Ireland to the glorification of Brain Boru as 'the heroic Irish unifier'. The expansionist version of Irish nationalism could have also been built on the claims that all people of Gaelic descent are part of the Greater Irish nation. However, this never happened.

One could also pinpoint the extremely competitive and culturally highly diverse world of the Balkans often steeped in violent conflicts triggering exclusivist nationalism. This would contrast with Ireland where conflicts were allegedly more sporadic and focused largely on the Catholic-Protestant power struggle. However, this stereotypical view of both regions has been challenged by scholars who now emphasise that, for much of its history, the Balkan region was not particularly violent, with the actual death tolls being significantly lower than in many other parts of Europe. It is only in the wake of the 1912–13 Balkan wars that this region became associated with violent nationalism (see Chapter 7). In a similar vein, students of Irish history highlight the complexity and changing dynamics of group relations on the island where violence often transpired outside and across religious divides (Bew 2016; Bourke 2016; Mulholland 2016).

Another line of argument could zoom in on the different role these small nations have played in nineteenth and early twentieth-century imperial clashes. In this context, political and national conflicts in Ireland could be viewed as a relatively marginal issue taking place at the Atlantic edge of the vast British Empire focused on global dominance. Although, historically, Ireland was interesting to other imperial powers such as France and Spain, by the mid to late nineteenth century Britain was a sole world power involved in Ireland's affairs (Crosbie 2011; Kenny 2006). In contrast, the Balkans were often seen as the geopolitical battleground for several world-leading Empires with the Ottomans, Habsburgs and Romanovs all fighting for control of the strategically important region. With the gradual decline of the Ottoman empire, this geopolitical struggle only intensified as the Habsburgs and Romanovs fought fiercely over control of the Balkans while other European imperial powers, including the British, French and German, also extended their influence in the region. These different geopolitical contexts could be viewed as triggering different types of nationalisms in Ireland and the Balkans: one more insular and the other more expansionist. However, this line of argument is framed in a wrong way. Rather than emphasising Ireland's marginality and the Balkans' centrality in world politics, it is the other way around that will lead us towards the more accurate explanation. The nationalist rhetoric of the small nation often hides the level of Ireland's importance in the nineteenth and early twentieth century world while overemphasising the significance of the Balkans.

This historical idea of Irish smallness was largely built around the continuous comparison with Britain. In this context, Ireland does appear as a much smaller and less significant entity in almost every respect: the size of territory, population, natural resources, industry, technology, science, military might, economy and so on. However, considering that for much of nineteenth and early twentieth century, Britain was the largest and most powerful Empire in the world, such de-contextualised comparison with Ireland is analytically futile. The truth is that, in this period, Ireland was not a small nation. Instead, pre-famine, the island boasted a very large and highly dense population that by 1840s reached 8.5 million people (Boylan 2016: 405). With this many people, Ireland was far ahead of Belgium (4 million), the Netherlands (3 million), Sweden (3 million), Norway, Denmark and Finland (each less than 1.5 million), Portugal (3.7 million) and many other European states. At the time, Ireland's population size was much closer to some of Europe's largest states such as Spain (14 million), England (15.9 million) and Austria (16.7 million) than the other 'small nations'. At the same time, the populations of the Balkan nations were very small, ranging from 1.5 million in Croatia, 1 million in Bulgaria to 0.8 million each in Greece and Serbia and 0.2 million in Albania (Rothenbacher 2002).

Furthermore, unlike the Balkans and many central European polities, Ireland was well integrated into the world economy and global cultural developments while many Irishmen (and some women) played a significant role in the spread of the British Empire throughout the world (Bender 2016; Crosbie 2011; Kenny 2006). The Irish population was an integral part of the imperial project with settlers, traders, administrators and soldiers from Ireland acting on behalf of the British Empire from New Zealand and Australia to Africa, India and further afield. In Carey's (2011: 124) apt words: 'the Irish were practical imperialists – cheap, adaptable, willing to travel, hold a gun, beat a drum, preach a sermon, and generally serve in many useful positions along the colonial frontier'. For example, between 1825 and 1850, almost half the European soldiers of the East India Company's Bengal army were from Ireland, and many of them were Catholic (Bender 2016: 347). In mid nineteenth century, the British military forces had a huge number of Irish soldiers: while Irish comprised 'some 32.2 per cent of the population of the United

Kingdom, there were more Irishmen than Englishmen in the British Army' (Spiers 1996: 335–6).

Being an integral part of the British imperial project meant also that the Irish Catholic clergy was highly instrumental in promoting a particular version of the civilising mission on behalf of the Empire. Initially, the Church was involved in missionary activities to Irish diaspora, but over time its principal task was the conversion of non-Christian populations in the colonies. At the beginning of twentieth century, Irish Catholic missions spread throughout Asia and Africa where the colonial missionary movement 'provided a rapidly mobilised workforce for the construction of churches, schools, and other religious institutions throughout the colonies' (Bender 2016: 353).

Since Irish ports were crucial in the Atlantic trade routes, its population had access to the imperial markets of Britain. At the beginning of nineteenth century, Dublin was the second largest city on the British isles and also the sixth largest city in Europe. By the end of nineteenth century, Dublin, Belfast and Cork were important centres of trade, industry and manufacturing. For example, during the second half of the nineteenth century, the Belfast linen industry tripled in size as a result of the American civil war and the increased demand for products made from linen. During this period, both Belfast and Cork were major ship-building centres within the United Kingdom. By the 1880s, Belfast experienced a substantial increase in foreign investment led by Edward Harland and consequently expanded its industries to become one of the world-leading centres of ship building (Johnston 2017: 8). Belfast was also an important centre for banking and financial services. In addition to Belfast, other major Irish cities were also more industrialised than most parts of central and Eastern Europe. The industries that dominated at that time were quite diverse, ranging from sugar-baking, dye-works, whiskey distillation and brewing to framing, agriculture and textile and clothing production. Even after a dramatic decline in population size with the onset of the Great Famine and large-scale emigration, Ireland remained an important part of world trade, shipping and textiles.[3]

Moreover, with the unprecedented levels of emigration to North America, Australia, Britain and other parts of the world, the Irish population was soon involved in forging a global nationalist movement, centred

[3] Ireland experienced several large-scale famines during the eighteenth and nineteenth centuries. For example, the famine of 1740–41 was particularly devastating, resulting in the deaths of up to 16 per cent of the entire population. However, the most destructive was the Great Famine of 1845–52 when close to one million people died from hunger or disease and another million emigrated abroad. This deadly event resulted in up to 25 per cent population decline in Ireland (Boylan 2016).

on anti-imperial activities, which ultimately had a decisive influence on British and thus also world politics. If not for the presence of millions of Irish emigrants in North America, influential organisations such as Clan na Gael and the Fenian Brotherhood would not have emerged and would not affect political life in the British isles. In this context, the Great Famine, together with, sixteenth and seventeenth century English colonisation involving plantations and land dispossessions, become powerful nationalist symbols of suffering associated with the British empire. In this context, the idea of a small nation developed as a strategic narrative utilised to delegitimise the powerful British empire. Hence, to claim the mantel of victim, it was essential to represent Ireland as a small country suffering under the yoke of its omnipotent and ruthless neighbour. For much of this period, and well into the twentieth century, Irish nationalism relied on the notion of smallness to justify its political ambitions. In this narrative, Irishness and Britishness were depicted as a mutually exclusive phenomena: where Britain was the beacon of industrialisation, Ireland was associated with domesticity and nature; where Britain stood for rationalism and utilitarian principles, Ireland was conceptualised as a heartland of spirituality and collective sacrifice; and where Britain was seen as a world empire centred on conquest and domination, Ireland symbolised a small nation struggling for its survival and independence. Thus Ireland was not always a small nation. Instead, for much of its recent history, it left a significant mark in the political, economic and social affairs of the British Empire, and thus the world. Ireland become small not through its geography or, declined population size but principally through the particular re-articulation of Irish nationalist narrative.

Small and Great Nations

In contrast, the Balkan nationalist projects developed later and also started off from the much weaker organisational and ideological base. At the beginning of nineteenth century, most Balkan populations were still ruled by the Ottomans, who by this time largely lagged behind the West in terms of economic development. Although once a superior military and organisational power, by the early nineteenth century, the Ottoman Empire was significantly weakened and unable to prevent the ever-growing political autonomy of the Balkan polities. Hence, by the time of the Treaty of Berlin (1878), most Balkan states gained full independence and embarked on the project of state and nation building. However, the new polities had no administrative apparatuses, industries, viable transport and communication networks, educational systems, media or publishing services. Most of these new states did not have national banks, currency system or even a town with more than 30,000 people until the second half of nineteenth century. Literacy levels were also abysmal and the overwhelming majority of the population consisted of an impoverished peasantry focused on everyday survival (see Chapter 7). In other words, the Balkan region lacked organisation capacity, ideological penetration and the envelopment of micro-solidarity that characterises bounded nationalisms.

Nevertheless, with intense, speedy, but highly uneven, modernisation centred on state formation and nation-building, this all changed relatively quickly. Hence, by the early twentieth century, new states had built large capital cities and continued with urbanisation and industrialisation programmes. They all also established quite a large civil service. For example, while in 1814 Serbia had only 24 civil servants, by 1902, 22 per cent of all Belgrade households were civil servants and their families (Stokes 1976: 4; Roudometof 2001: 113). The new polities have also invested heavily in the two pillars decisive for the transformation of ordinary population into nationally conscious Serbs, Bulgarians and Greeks: the educational system and the mass media. For example, between 1879 and 1911, the Bulgarian budget for education grew by an astounding 650 per cent (Roudometof 2001). The governments also supported and financed newspapers and other media so, by early in the twentieth century, Serbia, Greece and Bulgaria had large numbers of daily and weekly papers many of which were eager to intensely pursue nationalist agendas. Likewise, new transport and communication networks were built throughout the Balkans. For example, between 1885 and 1912, the length of railway lines increased by staggering 841 per cent in Bulgaria and 613 per cent in Greece (Stoianovitch 1994; Mirković 1958). The long-term consequence of these policies saw an increase in coercive organisational and ideological power, thus contributing towards the development of grounded nationalisms. However, the uneven character of modernisation proved to be an obstacle for the integration of wider sectors of the population. Hence, pockets of micro-solidarity were not fully amalgamated into the broader nationalist narratives (see Chapters 7 and 8).

These significant structural changes and investments were possible because the Balkan states, unlike Ireland, have become fully independent entities where government could use state budgets and foreign loans to finance expensive nation-building exercises. Nevertheless, despite these impressive improvements, the region continued to lag behind Western Europe, which was particularly evident after WWI. Saddled with huge foreign loans used to prop up state building projects (and very large militaries), the Balkan polities become even more marginal in European and world affairs early in the twentieth century. With the collapse of the Ottoman Empire and the changed geo-political priorities of the Great Powers, the Balkan region was, yet again, confined to the periphery of European politics and economy. While there was more Western attention on the Balkan region during the 1912–13 Balkan wars and WWI, with the end of these wars the attention of the Western mass media and politicians has largely shifted away from the region.

In contrast, and around the same time, Irish nationalism gained world-wide prominence. The late nineteenth and early twentieth century was a defining period for Ireland. This was an era of political turbulence, economic development and cultural expansion where Irishness acquired global visibility and influence. The political wrangling with Britain, from the Home Rule debates to the Easter Rising, all had global ramifications spreading to the British colonies, the English-speaking countries hosting large Irish diaspora such as the United States, Australia and Canada, as well as to many other regions where political movements were inspired by Irish political events. Thus, the 1916 Easter Rising had a direct impact on similar revolutionary attempts from India, Indochina, East Africa and Egypt to the African American movements in the USA and Irish diaspora in Australia and North America. For example, one strand of the Indian independence movement, led by Surya Sen in Bengal, was deeply influenced by the Easter Rising episode. Hence, Sen's Indian Republican Army staged a copycat uprising by taking over the post office in Chittagong (now Bangladesh) on Good Friday 1930 (Chandra 1989). The 1916 Rising also had strong ramifications in the USA. The event was extensively reported in all important American newspapers with *The New York Times* covering the Rising on its front page for a full two weeks. These violent events also had direct global resonance as the killings of Easter Rising leaders drew large protests in many cities, including 20,000 protesters in New York (Naughton 2016).

In addition, as Joe Lee (2008) demonstrated, by the beginning of the twentieth century, Ireland experienced rapid economic and political modernisation where high rates of emigration generated a new economy centred on tenant farmers engaged in a market-focused agriculture. This period also witnessed unprecedented cultural successes resulting in literature and the arts that ultimately gained world fame (from Yeats and Joyce to Stoker and Wilde). None of these developments would suggest that Ireland was a small nation in any way. Yet the idiom of smallness continued to dominate Irish public discourse. In direct contrast, the Balkan nation states experienced limited economic growth, modest political influence and rather negligible cultural success in the world at this time yet their leading representatives were all involved in developing and promoting the idea of a great nation. So why was Irish nationalism steeped in the idea of 'small nation' while Balkan nationalisms, which objectively represented smaller and less influential entities, were obsessed with the notion of 'great nation'?

This paradox owes much to the different structural conditions of Ireland and the Balkans in the nineteenth and early twentieth centuries. These nationalisms emerged in very different historical contexts and as such had to articulate quite different interpretations of nationhood. In order to legitimise their claims for independence and to mobilise wider public support, at home and abroad, Irish nationalists had to depict Ireland as a small and innocent victim of the most powerful and still-rising world Empire. Such a discourse had to portray Ireland as the exact opposite of Britain: so if Britain is big and powerful, Ireland had to be small and weak; if Britain was defined by imperial expansionism, Ireland was to be seen upholding the right of the small nations in the world; if Britain cherished the past military glories, Ireland had to celebrate non-military national traditions and so on. To gain a degree of global sympathy and public support at home and in its large diaspora abroad, Irish nationalists could not successfully utilise the image of national greatness. Even when independence was achieved in 1921, the new state elite maintained this discourse of smallness. This strategy reflected in part the continued struggle for full sovereignty, which was not achieved until 1949, and in part an attempt to position the new state in the hostile global order of the Cold War.

Furthermore, at the end of the nineteenth and beginning of the twentieth century, the two regions differed substantially in their levels of stateness and nation-ness. By the early twentieth century, Irish nationalism was already well grounded in the public and private realms throughout the island of Ireland. For example, the literacy rates and the primary school attendance rates were very high when compared to many other regions in Europe. Hence, by 1911, most Irish citizens were literate – 91.7 per cent of population were literate with Dublin city reaching 96.2 per cent literacy rate while 70.7 per cent of children attended National schools regularly (www.cso.ie/en/releasesandpublications/ep/p -1916/1916irl/introduction/). Ireland also had a very vibrant public culture, publishing industry and mass media. The Catholic Church had enormous influence. Its institutions were involved in nearly every aspect of life – from religious sacraments and education to all key personal events thus reinforcing the cultural difference of the Irish population and indirectly contributing towards the nationalisation of ordinary people and the greater ground-ness of Irish nationalism. Compared to the Balkans, Ireland possessed more organisational capacity and higher ideological penetration. These structural developments have all contributed substantially towards making the Irish population highly receptive to nationalist ideas at the beginning of the twentieth century. Thus, having a more 'nationalised' population there was less need to utilise the violent mythological past and excessive territorial projects to mobilise mass-scale support for the nationalist cause. The focus here was less on the nation-building and much more on the capture of the (independent) state. In this context, any serious attempt to invoke the idea of expansionist nationalism through the images of the 'great nation' would only undermine the Irish nationalist project. However, while Irish nationalism was better grounded than that in the Balkans, it too was riddled by deep social and class divides and, as such, lacked a greater integration of micro-level solidarities with societywide nationalist narratives (see Chapter 6).

In contrast, the Balkan states found themselves in the situation whereby they acquired independent statehood before the majority of the population could identify first and foremost as the members of their respective nations (see Chapters 7, 8 and 9). Fully fledged nationalisms presuppose the existence of state-wide educational systems capable of inculcating specific nationcentric discourses, national mass media helping reinforce and maintain the national public sphere and relatively high literacy rates that would allow citizens to consume nationcentric discourses in everyday interaction. While these and other ideological and organisational infrastructures were largely present in Ireland, they, for the most part, were still lacking in the early twentieth-century Balkans. For example, most Balkan states had extremely low literacy rates well into the twentieth century. In 1900, only 29.5 per cent of the Bulgarian population was literate, while this figure was even lower for Serbian citizens with a rather abysmal 17 per cent literacy rate in 1900 (Daskalova 2010: 161; Ekmecic 1991: 333). Even in 1930, only around 43 per cent of Romanian adults were illiterate (Brucan 1993). Consequently, the Balkan nation states also lagged behind in terms of mass media consumption, educational participation and the development of the shared public sphere. Thus, to transform their citizens into loyal and enthusiastic Greeks, Serbs, Bulgarians, Romanians or Albanians, it was necessary to create these organisational and ideological scaffolds almost from scratch. In this context, the mythology of past (and future) national greatness was deployed to instil a sense of nationhood among people who still identified more in local, clan, family or religious than national terms. Hence, the pseudo-utopian projects of the Greater Greece, Greater Serbia or Greater Bulgaria were often used as quasi-pedagogical tools to socialise the peasantry into nationally conscious Greeks, Serbs or Bulgarians. By invoking the imagery of the mythical glorious past where one's predecessors were depicted as mighty emperors who ruled vast territories, nationalist narratives played well into the status insecurities of ordinary individuals. As the Balkan states often found themselves at the bottom of European status hierarchies, nationalist megalomania was often employed as a substitute to compensate for the objective smallness, economic underdevelopment and global political insignificance of these nation states. Such grand maximalist projections were, thus, often used to mask the ever-increasing sense of geopolitical irrelevance. This was still a poorly grounded nationalism that lacked a society-wide appeal.

Conclusion

When, in 1985, Hroch inaugurated the comparative study of 'small nations' he inadvertently contributed towards naturalising and normalising a concept that is profoundly ideological. The underlining assumption of this approach, where nationhood is understood through the prism of inherent smallness (or greatness), is deeply problematic and misleading. As I have tried to show in this chapter, the label 'small nation' has less to do with the size of one's territory or population and much more with specific ideological vistas, geopolitical ambitions and economic projections or military strategies. Hence, rather than treating this concept as a simple and innocent geographical description, it is paramount to deconstruct and historicise its sociological underpinnings and its political uses. Since nationhood is a contingent historical product of the long term structural processes, it often relies on very different organisational and ideological ingredients to develop and expand. In this context, the framing of the national project and labelling one's nation as a being small or great had less to do with the actual size and much more with the ideological message that needed to be sent. Hence, although Ireland has historically been much more influential in world affairs than its Balkan counterparts, Irish nationalists regularly deployed the notion of smallness as a potent ideological chip. In contrast, nationalists in the Balkans tended to amplify their historical and political significance through the idea of national greatness. These different strategies stem in part from different structural contexts: while in the Irish case the focus was on attaining ownership of the state, in the Balkan case the emphasis was on forging the nation. While these were clearly two very different nationalist strategies, they also show a degree of similarity in the sense that they both were engaged in articulating a moral argument to justify one's claim for independent and politically sovereign nationhood. In this context, the rhetoric of a 'small nation' should never simply be read as a politically innocuous and objective statement of fact but as a particular strategy to make the nationalist case more legitimate and popular while simultaneously delegitimising the political claims of one's adversary. These two cases demonstrate how nationalist projects can acquire very different forms while still pursuing similar aims and ambitions. Whether nationalism speaks in the language of smallness or greatness, its target is still the same: the idea that nationhood matters more than other forms of group attachments and that every nation should have a state of its own.

6   Nationalisms and Statehood in Ireland

Introduction

Many traditional historical and literary studies of Irish nationalism insist on its unique characteristics. Some focus on the unusual mixture of ethnic and civic ideas that have historically underpinned nationalist narratives and practices in Ireland. Others point out the uncommon tendency for Irish nationalism to incorporate both the left and the right of the political spectrum. Many emphasise the distinct colonial legacy, unusual geographic position, religious specificity, exceptionally rich and advanced cultural heritage or the distinctive cult of violence. For example, Terry Eagleton insists that the 'Irish have a keener sense of their history than other nations'; that 'the Irish were the first nation to recognise the potential of the popular movement for the goal of political reform' and that Ireland is 'the first modern post-colonial society' (Eagleton 1999: 99, 102,163). Nevertheless, this general obsession with Irish exceptionalism is most often linked to the island's political split between North and South. In fact an overwhelming number of studies written on Irish nationhood understand nationalism through a very narrow prism – as an aspiration to national unification.[1]

Furthermore, many such analyses tend to view Irish nationalism as an ideology in decline. The argument hinges on the belief that as the question of unification becomes less pertinent in social and political discourse, nationalism is bound to weaken. More specifically, they contend that as the world becomes ever more globalised and integrated and as the Republic and Northern Ireland experience further development, both Irish and British/Unionist nationalisms are destined to wane (Kearney 2002). Even the recent de-globalisation trends exemplified by Brexit, Trumpism and the Europe-wide rise of populist and far-right movements

---

[1] For good criticisms of these traditional approaches to Irish nationalism see English (2007), Foster (1988) and Lee (1985).

have not significantly dented the view, entrenched among many scholars, that Irish nationalism is in permanent decline (O'Brien 2017, 2009). Hence, when comparing contemporary Ireland with its 1950s counterpart, it seems palpable to most analysts that the nationalism of the 1950s was much stronger and more widespread than the one experienced today.

However, this chapter challenges both of these assumptions. I argue that despite some superficial differences, Irish nationalism is not unique. In all significant sociological respects, Irish nationalism is very similar to other nationalisms in Europe and other parts of the world. Irish nationalist ideologies and movements have originated and developed in a similar historical period and under similar structural conditions as other European nationalisms. Instead of approaching Irish nationalism as a distinct species, its emergence and development makes sociological sense only when viewed as a part of the broader pan-European and ultimately world processes.

Secondly, I contest the idea that nationalism in Ireland is experiencing a gradual decline. On the contrary, this chapter makes the case that, as nationalism requires the presence of strong organisational and ideological scaffoldings and well-established cross-class ties of solidarity, the existence of strong nationalism entails intensive social development. Hence, despite the veneer of sturdy nationalist identities, post-Independence Ireland lacked the organisational and ideological capacity for the development of deep societywide nationalism. Consequently, nationalist ideology and practice has actually intensified over the last several decades and today's nationalism is much more powerful and socially grounded than the one present in de Valera's era.

The Rise of Nationalisms

We live in a world where everybody is expected to possess a distinct nationality. Moreover, there is a general perception that it is normal and natural to feel a strong sense of attachment to one's nation. To be proud of being French, Norwegian, Greek or Irish is usually seen as a noble virtue while being alienated from one's nation is likely to be understood by many as a moral failing. More specifically, in our world, it is virtually impossible to opt out from nationhood: one can change nationalities, have multiple passports, become highly proficient in several languages and distinct cultural practices, or convert to the religion of the majority nation but having no nation is simply not an available option.

Furthermore, we inhabit a world where nationhood is deemed to be the principal locus of one's identity, solidarity and political legitimacy. Hence, it is widely believed today that no nation should rule or dominate another nation; that all nations should have a state of their own; that divided members of a nation should live under a single political roof; that each member of a particular nation should demonstrate solidarity with their co-nationals; and that in some important respects national allegiance should supersede most other allegiances. In this context, it seems obvious to support the idea that Palestinians, Kurds, Catalans, Chechens, Basques and other 'state-less' nations should have a sovereign state of their own, or that 'partitioned' nations such as the Irish, Koreans, or Chinese should live in a single nation state.

Although individuals and organised groups might differ sharply in their views on how the rights of self-determination are to be achieved and who has historical or political entitlements to a particular territory, there is near-universal agreement that all nations should be free, independent and self-governing and that shared nationhood is the principal source of a state's political legitimacy.

This contemporary tendency to see nationhood as a normal, natural and ubiquitous form of group identity and solidarity obscures the fact that, for much of our history, human beings were nationless as they inhabited entities that were either much smaller or much larger than nation states: from foraging bands, chiefdoms, city-states, city leagues, composite kingdoms, confederate tribal alliances to various forms of imperial orders. More importantly, the historical predecessors of nation states had no organisational mechanisms nor ideological need to foster greater cultural or political homogeneity among the inhabitants. The pre-modern forms of social order were either very small, less stratified, decentralised and disorganised, such as the hunting and gathering bands, or they consisted of huge, highly hierarchical and centralised entities characterised by pronounced cultural diversity, as was the case with empires. The inhabitants of these social orders did not and could not conceptualise the world in terms of nationalist principles of political sovereignty, cultural homogeneity and the equal moral worth of all its members. Instead, they tended to identify with, and their rulers would justify their position in relation to, belief systems that were either highly localised (i.e. totemic kinship, clan and tribe-based solidarities) or they would embrace universalist creeds (i.e. mythology, religion or a particular imperial doctrine). In other words, for 99.99 per cent of our existence on this planet, we have lived in entities that bear no resemblance to the nation state and our dominant belief systems had no room for comprehending the world in nationalist terms. Expressing a deep feeling of solidarity and attachment with someone who was not a family or clan member, a trusted neighbour, a companion aristocrat or a personally well-known fellow adherent of the same religious tradition would make no sense in sociological terms before the age of nationalism. No pre-modern peasant or aristocrat would ever be willing to sacrifice their lives for such an abstract, and in their world incomprehensible, concept that is a nation. Despite latter-day nationalist historiography, neither Brian Bóruma, Turlough O'Brien or any other kings of 'Irish provinces' could possibly envisage Ireland as a sovereign, culturally homogenous and politically unified nation. For nationhood to become a central category of one's identity, solidarity and legitimacy, it was necessary for Europe and then the rest of the world to undergo dramatic and unprecedented structural transformations.

There is neither nationhood nor nationalism without large-scale organisational changes and these are brought about with the onset of modernity. The emergence and gradual proliferation of ideas that constitute nationalism, such as popular sovereignty, cultural authenticity, self-rule and economic independence, owe a great deal to revolutionary upheavals. These include such gigantic social transformations as industrialisation and technological and scientific advancement, the expansion of capitalism and organisational principles of the division of labour, the centralisation of state power, the development of constitutionalism and parliamentarism, the advancement of state-wide systems of transport and communication, the establishment of state monopolies on the legitimate use of force, taxation and legislation, the standardisation of vernacular languages, the establishment of society-wide educational systems, the dramatic increase in literacy rates, the formation of a substantial degree of cultural and linguistic uniformity, the expansion of institutions of 'high culture', the standardisation of chronological measures of time, and the large scale production and consumption of mass media (Mann 1993, 1986; Breuilly 1993; Anderson 1991[1983]; Gellner 1983). These structural transformations were the product of historical contingencies, changing geo-political environments and economic bifurcations, all of which have helped generate the development and expansion of diverse ideological worldviews. The immanent success of science and technology fostered a steady decline of the theological interpretations of past, present and future, whereas the rise of Enlightenment, Romanticism and other intellectual movements contributed to the growth of diverse ideological articulations of one's social reality. It is no accident that all major contemporary secular ideological discourses – from liberalism, socialism, conservatism, anarchism to nationalism – originated in the wake of the French and American revolutions. The fact that nationalism established itself as the most popular and dominant ideological discourse of the modern age had a great deal to do with its rhetoric and practice of popular rule and its ability to successfully penetrate the micro universe of family, friendship and locality by embedding these feelings of micro-solidarity into a wider nationalist narrative (Malešević 2013a). The key issue here is that despite its loudly proclaimed worship of authenticity, difference and particularity, nationalism was and remains a universalist, modern, doctrine that advocates the same principles throughout the globe.

Even though all nationalist doctrines strongly insist on the unique and irreplaceable qualities of their nation, this discourse is itself a product of the almost-identical structural and organisational processes that came about with the inception of modernity and which have affected most of the world. The nationalist call for the preservation of distinctive and unique features of one's nation is a direct offshoot of the huge structural changes which provided social conditions for the emergence of nationalist movements in Europe and the Americas. Furthermore, as Gellner (1983: 124) shows, all nationalist creeds are rooted in a deep paradox: they claim 'to defend folk culture while in fact [they are] forging a high culture'; nationalism 'claims to protect an old folk society while in fact helping to build up an anonymous mass society [...] It preaches and defends cultural diversity, when in fact it imposes homogeneity both inside and, to a lesser extent, between political units.' In other words, in an important sociological sense, all nationalist movements and ideologies are alike as they all arise under similar structural conditions and they all utilise almost identical rhetoric.

How Unique Is Irish Nationalism?

Hence, when viewed from this broader historical horizon there is nothing substantially unique in Irish nationalism. Irish nationalist movements developed and spread at the same time and often in a very similar way to their European counterparts. The first proto-nationalist ideas were articulated by the representatives of cultural elites. Henry Grattan, Wolfe Tone, Robert Emmet, Thomas Davis, Terence McManus, Daniel O'Connell and others lead organisations (i.e. United Irishmen, Irish Republican Brotherhood, Young Ireland, etc.) that advocated exactly the same principles as their European and American colleagues. Moreover, they often imitated their rhetoric, strategies and tactics in the political activism of their day. They initiated the establishment of secret societies, which were a highly popular form of elite cultural and political activism in nineteenth-century Europe and Irish secret societies were very similar to their German, Italian, French, Spanish, Portuguese and Greek counterparts (i.e. Burschenschaft, Carbonari, Philiki Hetairia, Carbonária, etc.). In many instances, the leading cultural and later political nationalists were part of broader networks of nationalist ideologues, intellectuals, artists and activists. For example, the Grimm brothers and

Goethe were connected with nationalist intellectuals throughout the European continent and these well-established networks included a number of Irish intellectuals such as the grammarian John O'Donovan who became a member of the Prussian Academy on Goethe's recommendation (Leerssen 2008).

Enlightenment and Romanticism-inspired movements such as Young Ireland were directly modelled on their European counterparts such as Mazzini's Young Italy, Young Germany, Young Switzerland and later influenced further copycats such as the Young Poland, Young Turks, or Young Bosnia. The establishment of the first nationalist newspapers and periodicals, choral societies, and folklore associations has followed exactly the same pan-European processes clearly visible in Germany, France or Italy. The romanticist poetry, prose and cultural activities of W.B. Yeats, Lady Gregory and John Synge, the gothic novels of Bram Stoker and the painting of Jack Yeats and Paul Henry were an integral part of the pan-European cultural nationalist aspirations spearheaded by the early ambitions of Goethe, Lord Byron and Walter Scott that celebrated the authenticity, the diversity and the legitimate objectives for independence among the 'small nations' of Europe from the Balkans to Ireland. The mythology of Celtic Ireland, that underpins much of Irish nationalism, had direct echoes in the French nationalist myths of Gaulish and Frankish origin or the German nationalist mythology of the Teutonic knights.

From its organisational inception in the late eighteenth and early nineteenth century, nationalism has always been and remains a global movement and ideology. In this case, just as in other European and American cases, the emergence and expansion of nationalism was grounded in deep structural transformations. The fact that Ireland was economically less developed than France or Germany does not suggest that Irish nationalism was profoundly different from its European counterparts. It only means that in some forms of nationalist experience, Ireland lagged behind and was a late developer.

However, in other aspects, Irish nationalism was at the forefront of large-scale changes. For example, much of Ireland was dominated by rural dwellings and kinship-based localism well into the second half of the twentieth century, and the country's overall industrial output was very slow to develop. Nevertheless, the island's main cities Belfast and Dublin were global pioneers of industrialism and mass production in ship building, textiles and commerce. In a similar fashion, for much of the nineteenth and early twentieth century, the country lacked decent roads and reliable transport systems. And yet, at the same time, Ireland was 'one of the first European countries to rail-roadise'. The island had '65 miles of track in 1845, 1,000 in 1857, 2,000 in 1872 and, with 3,500 by 1914, boasted one of the densest networks in the world' (Lee 2008: 13). The standardisation of the Irish vernacular was extremely slow and patchy with the official codification of language being finalised only in the 1950s (Watson 2003: 29; Garvin 2003: 88). Nevertheless, Irish society was also characterised by high literacy rates in English: in the 1850s more than half the population was literate and by 1911 this had risen to almost 90 per cent (Lee 2008: 13). In line with most of Western Europe, Ireland had well-developed networks of mass communication with ever expanding news outlets. For example, in 1853 there were 109 newspapers and periodicals in circulation and by 1913 this number had more than doubled to 230. Some newspapers had exceptionally high circulation, with the sales of the Irish World in the region of 20,000 and Parnell's United Ireland reaching a staggering 100,000 in the 1880s. Furthermore, the key vehicle of nationalist socialisation, the educational system, was firmly established in the early nineteenth century and by 1850 included 4500 schools and over half a million pupils with these numbers doubling by 1914 (Lee 2008: 13, 27, 96). All these figures indicate that the emergence and expansion of nationalism was rooted in the dramatic structural transformation and the gradual modernisation of Irish social and political space. Just as in other parts of Europe and the Americas, nationalist ideology was articulated and initiated by cultural and political elites and its popular expansion remained dependent on large-scale structural transformations. In the late nineteenth century, the principal bearers of the nationalist torch were the ever-expanding professional middle strata (solicitors, doctors, clergy, artists and teachers) but is only in the twentieth century that nationalism became a fully fledged ideology that motivated the action of the majority of the Irish population.

The Puny Leviathan

There is a pronounced tendency to associate the strength of nationalism with unbridled outbursts of animosity towards others, the loud proclamations of one's national pride and the view that any significant self-criticism of the nation is a form of moral treason. Hence, the omnipotence of nationalism is regularly linked to violent activities including warfare, revolutions, genocides, terrorism or the organised intimidation of non-nationals and disloyal co-nationals. When one thinks of contemporary manifestations of nationalism, the inclination is to look at radical movements on the far right or the far left of the political spectrum: PKK, ETA, Jobbik, Golden Dawn, Tamil Tigers or Óglaigh na hÉireann.

Nevertheless, one should not conflate political radicalism with strength. Although extreme political organisations can occasionally stir up collective emotions and create intensive nationalist frenzy, such heightened emotional states cannot be maintained for a long time. As Durkheim (1976) demonstrated so convincingly, collective effervescence is a highly intense but rare and temporary phenomenon that simply cannot last. Nationalist euphoria generated by radical organisations is usually very visible and intensive but that in itself is not a particularly reliable indicator of its strength. On the contrary, hostile defensiveness, rampant intolerance and constant accusations are often reliable signals of one's insecurity, fragility and the lack of a firm and stable foundation. It is weak not strong nationalisms that are noisy and brazen. Well established, taken-for-granted, nationalisms do not require relentless and instant mobilisation. Thus, it is the habitual, banal, practices that are much more important for the reproduction and expansion of nationalism than aggressive posturing. This habitual nationalism is much more muted, less visible and characterised by ordinary routine activities. Billig (1995) emphasised the centrality of banal practices as being vital for the everyday maintenance and strengthening of nationalism. These include mundane activities such as the routine use of the plural personal pronouns ('we', 'us') in the mass media and political speeches that simply assume one's membership in a specific nation, the consumption of nationally focused and geographically demarcated TV weather reports, or the passing by of unnoticed national flags hanging on state institutions. In all of these cases, banal nationalism is reproduced habitually and, for the most part, unconsciously, thus helping to preserve nationcentric understandings of social reality.

However, what is missing in Billig's account is the in-depth focus on the role of coercive organisational powers as such habitual reproduction entails the presence of robust organisational and ideological scaffoldings (Malešević 2013a and Chapter 9). The strength of a particular nationalism is often determined by its organisational capacity and infrastructural reach and its ability to provide potent ideological glue capable of projecting, and at times forging, unity and cultural homogeneity for the entire society. In other words, the persistence and growth of nationalism is heavily influenced by large-scale structural transformations. These include ever-expanding state centralisation and its capacity to permeate civil society by controlling its external borders, successfully policing its territory, taxing income at source, collecting and utilising personal data, enforcing the use of identity documentation (birth certificates, passports, driving licences, etc.) and providing welfare provisions among others (Mann 2012, 1993). These organisational advancements regularly accompany and stimulate expansion of social devices for ideology creation and dissemination: standardised educational systems with near universal literacy, mass media, legislative structures and the rich repertoire of civil society networks. The incessant growth of these organisational and ideological powers is decisive for the continuous attempt to establish and structurally embody nationhood as the dominant category and practice of everyday life.

In this context, Irish nationalism had a similar trajectory to other European nationalisms. There is a general perception that in the 1930s, 40s and 50s Ireland was a hotbed of rampant nationalism and that the Celtic tiger era and its aftermath represent the time when nationalism went into a gradual but certain decline. This is not the case. On the contrary, Irish nationalism is significantly more dominant and influential today than it was in the early and mid twentieth century. De Valera's years of rule are generally seen as being characterised by fierce nationalist indoctrination, which was bolstered with rhetoric and practice that strongly exalted the Gaelic revival, Roman Catholicism and anti-monarchist republicanism as the bulwarks against the British legacies. Moreover, for much of this period, a majority of Irish political organisations and civil society groupings seemed to be united in the view that Northern Ireland should and eventually would became unified with the rest of the Republic.

There is no doubt that nationalist discourses were widespread throughout society and were institutionalised in the educational system, courts, police, military, mass media and the public service, among others. Mid-twentieth century Ireland was certainly dominated by an excessive nationalist rhetoric which envisaged entire Ireland as a cosy village community populated by a frugal people. As colourfully described in de Valera's 1943 speech, Ireland was to become an entity 'whose countryside would be bright with cosy homesteads, whose fields and villages would be joyous with the sounds of industry, with the romping of sturdy children, the contest of athletic youths and the laughter of comely maidens, whose firesides would be forums for the wisdom of serene old age' (Keogh 1994: 33–4). This nationalist ideal was also codified in the 1937 Constitution that emphasised the unique character of Irishness: 'The Irish nation herby affirms its inalienable, indefeasible, and sovereign right to choose its own form of government . . . and to develop its life . . . in accordance with its own genius and traditions' (English 2007: 329).

However, the fact that the nationalist idiom was so prevalent, and occasionally expressed in aggressive outburst, is not in itself a reliable indicator of its strength. In fact, the loud proclamations and incessant glorification of the mythological Celtic past, the purity of Irish language and traditional practices can be equally seen as a sign of insecurity and weakness, as an attempt to rescind all the ambiguities and contradictions deeply present in the nationalist project. More importantly, post-independence Ireland lacked the organisational and infrastructural capacity required to make nationalism structurally grounded in the everyday life of its population. De Valera's state apparatus was generally weak and underdeveloped. Although the Irish state inherited a solid civil service and a stable parliamentary system, the state's ability to penetrate civil society remained feeble until the late 1970s. As Garvin (2003: 83) convincingly demonstrates, post-independence Ireland 'constituted a very strong society but rather weak state'. The new polity had great difficulty in establishing a monopoly on the legitimate use of violence, taxation and legislation. The educational institutions overemphasised the teaching of arts and theology over science and technology and the long-term outcome of this policy was a constant shortage of technical and scientific expertise. Ireland's infrastructure was particularly weak and successive governments were ill disposed towards developing better transport and communication networks. Moreover, in the 1940s, 50s and early 60s there was strong opposition towards building motorways and bypasses, establishing airline systems, and introducing telephones, radios and TVs since they were generally seen either as an unnecessary luxury or as something that might undermine the vested interest of local businesses. For example, small town shopkeepers were crucial in preventing the building of bypasses and motorway across the country as they feared the loss of 'passing trade' (Garvin 2003: 102).

The dominance of the insular world-views that characterised the post-independence 'Éire' was also reflected in the general animosity towards foreign investment, secular higher education and industrialisation. The introduction of heavy-handed censorship stifled the wider proliferation of what Gellner (1983) calls a 'high culture', a standardised and society-wide idiom of shared aspiration and communication – one of the key prerequisites for a successful nationalist project. The partial consequence of this policy was the chronic underdevelopment of cultural and artistic institutions outside Dublin and Cork. An overwhelming majority of the population remained focused on their locality and kinship-based networks with familialism, nepotism, clientelism and patronage networks dominating political, economic and cultural life (Coakley and Gallaher 2009). Even the educational system, a backbone of nationalist socialisation, remained patchy, not fully standardised and was firmly monopolised by the Church, not the nationalising state. The two pillars of the de Valera era of nationalist narrative were Catholicism and Gaelicisation, but whereas the former remained split between its normative universalism and everyday parochialism, the latter was not particularly successful. Despite the symbolic significance of Catholicism for Irish nationalist narrative, in the early post-independence period 'the Church was actually rather provincial, even localist and very decentralised ... Religious orders had autonomy from Irish episcopate, holding their authority from their centres in Rome or elsewhere' (Garvin 2003: 160). Similarly, the project of linguistic revival and Gaelicisation of wider cultural practices had almost the exact opposite effect of what was intended, as the number of fluent speakers of the, belatedly standardised, Irish language plummeted in the new Republic. Whereas in the early nineteenth century, more than 3 million people used some version of Gealic as their primary means of communication, by the beginning of the twenty-first century only 72,000 individuals declared in the census that they used Irish as a daily language outside education (Wolf 2014; 2006 census).[2] With the partial exception of the Gaelic Athletic Association (GAA), the Gaelicisation project was largely a failure. Furthermore, despite the popularly shared rhetoric of cultural nationalism, the majority of the population continued to distrust state officials and often engaged in excessive anti-state diatribes. Hence, de Valera's Ireland was nominally saturated with intense nationalist chatter but this nationalism was weak. It lacked a stable, secure and developed organisational and ideological grounding.

The Organisational Capacity and Nationhood

In contrast to its post-independence incarnation associated with poverty, insularity and nationalism, contemporary Ireland is often depicted as being the hub of modern global trends. These include full integration in the European and World political structures (EU, CE, UN, WTO), its highly globalised economy that attracts the leading multinational corporations and its cultural openness to international influences in art, science, technology and education, among others. Even though the country was heavily affected by the 2008 economic recession, it remains wide open to international influences. For example, between 2009 and 2013, over '€125 billion (61 per cent of GDP) of foreign direct investment (FDI) flowed into Ireland' (Haugh 2016). With its English-speaking, educated and young workforce together with very low taxation policies, Dublin and other Irish cities have proved attractive for international corporations. Hence, Google, Facebook, Twitter, Airbnb, LinkedIn

---

[2] The failure of linguistic Gaelicisation is perfectly exemplified by the case of Timothy Corcoran, UCD Professor who was the principal ideologue behind the idea of making Irish a compulsory subject in the primary and secondary education, but who himself never learned Irish.

and other social media companies have moved their European head-quarters to Ireland. In addition, Ireland's economy has also expanded in other sectors that draw international investments – the financial services, pharmaceuticals and medical devices. For example 'eight of the top 10 global pharmaceutical companies have a significant presence in Ireland centred on Cork, while half of the world's top 50 banks and top 20 insurance companies operate out of the International Financial Services Centre in Dublin' (Haugh 2016).

However, despite these intense globalising effects, Irish citizens, just like the rest of Europe, remain deeply committed to ideas and practices of nationhood. As various surveys show, the populations of European states are more attached to their nations today than at any other time in history and the sense of belonging to one's nation has been increasing constantly over the past three decades. For example, the longitudinal Eurobarometer survey indicates that in the period between 1983 and 2005, support for the statement that one is very proud or quite proud of being Irish has increased from 89 to 98 per cent of Republic's population (Antonsich 2009: 286). Nevertheless, the real strength of nationalism is better gauged by looking at the changing organisational and ideological armature of the nation state.

Over the past three decades, the organisational powers of the Irish state have increased dramatically. The development of industry, education, transport, communications, science and technology created conditions for the expansion of state capacity and the deeper ideological penetration of nationalist ideas and practices. Whereas in the 1940s and 50s, the Irish state was extremely weak to the point that the prime minister Sean Lemmas declared in 1959 that not only was the economy weak but also the state itself was on the brink of collapse, pointing that something 'has got to be done now … If we fail everything else goes with it and all the hopes of the past will have been falsified' (Lee 2008: 373). For example, while in 1950s the average growth in Europe was up to 8 per cent, in Ireland it was less than 1 per cent (McLaughlin 2002: 232). In contrast, during the Celtic tiger period, Ireland experienced unprecedented economic expansion which positioned the country as one of the leading European states in terms of GDP increase per capita (Hennigan 2012). This staggering economic rise was also reflected in the substantial increase in the infrastructural capacities of the state. There has been continuous investment into new transport and communication networks, education, health, and other service provisions, and the state also increased its capacity to collect revenue. For example, capital expenditure ranged from 2.5 per cent to as much as 6 per cent of GNP between 1995 and 2008 (Scott and Bedogni 2017). Furthermore, the state substantially increased investment in transport – from 0.5 per cent in 1950s to 1.44 per cent from 1999 to 2011. The value of capital generated in land transport was €3.5 billion in 2008 (Jenkinson et al. 2017).

Although Ireland was affected hard by the 2008 recession, the economic crisis did not have a profound long-term impact on its organisational strength. In fact, by 2015, the economy had largely recovered and the state continued with further investments in service provisions and infrastructure. So while there were no motorways in Ireland until 1983, by 2017 Ireland had around 1000 km of motorways. 'With 20.9 kms per 1000 inhabitants Ireland has the 5th highest density in the EU and is significantly above the EU28 average of 9.5kms. Ireland can also be seen to have over three times the level of the UK (6.5 kms per 1000 inhabitants)' (Jenkinson et al. 2017: 18–19). The same trend is visible in other areas of infrastructure and service provisions. For example, the Irish educational system has experienced exceptional development over the last sixty years: while in the late 1950s only a small section of the population would continue with secondary-level education, with a 'huge dropout rate of almost 90 per cent after primary school', and only a few thousand individuals attending college, in 2015, there were 173,649 individuals in full-time, third-level education with almost 50 per cent of secondary students continuing from secondary to tertiary education. In 2014, as many as 34.3 per cent of adults had a third level education while 71.7 per cent had attained secondary level education or above (CSO 2015). The Irish state has also been very effective in collecting revenue. For example, in 2015 government tax revenues were increased by 10.5 per cent compared to 2014, amounting to €45.6bn and the similar trend continued in 2016 (Duffy 2017).

The contemporary Irish nation state is much more centralised, and more able to police its territory, supervise its borders, tax its citizens, implement its laws and provide controlled welfare provisions than ever before. Moreover, the existing state apparatus can easily and quickly collect and utilise vast amounts of personal information on all its citizens: it has highly digitalised systems of control including the ever-expanding surveillance devices (i.e. CCTV cameras, alarms, computer and phone supervision), it enforces the use of identity documentation such as birth certificates, biometric passports, ID age cards, driving licences and welfare cards that 1950s state administrators could not even dream of. For example, while in the 1950s an overwhelming majority of Irish citizens did not have passports, driving licences or ID cards of any kind, today almost every single citizen possesses one of these documents. Furthermore, the state continues to increase its controlling capacity in this area as it has introduced biometric Public Service Cards that are likely to become a compulsory requirement for anybody applying for or renewing their passports or driving licences and even for those who sit the driver theory test (Akl 2017).

The education system, with the standardised curriculum and uniform assessments (such as the Junior and Leaving cycle certificate exams), is controlled and regulated now by the state much more than the Catholic Church. While in the 1950s the Church resisted and quickly delegitimised any government interference in the primary and secondary education, today most Catholic orders that still run schools have expressed a wish for greater involvement by the state in the educational system. The full literacy and the large-scale presence of national mass media with all-state coverage have helped reinforce the shared perceptions of an imagined community embedded in the concept of 'deep horizontal comradeship' (Anderson 1991[1983]). Although the population of Ireland had already attained a high literacy rate in the second half of nineteenth century with only 8.3 per cent illiterate in 1911 (CSO 2017), before independence, most individuals remained attached to their locality and tended to be informed by the local newspapers. With the increased organisational capacities of the state, one could also witness increased visibility and circulation of national newspapers, radio and later television as well. The gradual dominance of high-circulation national over local and regional newspapers, and the exceptionally high viewing figures of RTE news and information programmes, indicate how grounded national understandings of everyday events have become. For example RTE's Six One news is watched regularly by the majority of the population as they receive no less than '500,000 tuning in each evening' (Hade 2015). The proliferation of independent media outlets, as well as the expansion of social media, have not really dented the nation-centric production and reception of social reality in Ireland.

Reproducing Irishness

There is no doubt that the strength of Irish nationalism stems in large part from the ever-increasing organisational capacity of the Irish state. Nevertheless, the state apparatus is not the only vehicle for the creation and reproduction of Irishness. The nation-centric understanding of social reality is also generated and sustained by civil society, family, friendship networks and other non-state realms of social interaction. Over the last fifty years or so, one could witness a substantial expansion of the civil society sphere in Ireland, much of which has contributed substantially towards the grounding of nationalism in everyday life. The number of NGOs has expanded dramatically since the 1950s. For example, while there were only 70 registered non-profit voluntary and community organisations in 1950s Ireland, by 1999 this number had increased to 3,571 and by 2010 there were 4,934 such organisations. The economic strength of these organisations is reflected in their income and assets which in 2009 amounted to €5.75bn and €3.4bn respectively (www.wheel.ie/policy /facts-and-statistics). Most of these non-profit organisations include local development associations as well as community-based organisations and charities. However, the civil society sector in Ireland is much wider and encompasses a variety of non-state groups, movements and organisations – from religious institutions, consumer protection societies, human rights organisations, to political pressure groups, sporting associations, environmental, gender based, immigrant and other associations. While in the 1950s, there were only a handful of such groups, today Ireland boasts an extremely vibrant civil society which is characterised by high levels of engagement and volunteering. According to data from the National Committee on Volunteering (2002), Ireland ranks high in terms of levels of volunteering which has continuously been above 33 per cent, similar to other well-developed states such as Germany, Denmark or Canada (Tovey and Share 2003: 125).

Civil society groups are traditionally perceived as a vital social mechanism for counterbalancing state power and, as such, protecting different group interests as well as maintaining and enhancing individual freedoms (Gellner 1994). However, since most civil society associations operate within the existing national institutions and dominant nation-centric discourses, they regularly tend to reinforce such discourses in order to justify their own role. For example, leading humanitarian NGOs in Ireland, such as Trócaire, the Society of St. Vincent de Paul or the Religious Sisters of Charity, are all established on general principles advocating values of Christian universalism. Yet as they operate in the world of nation states, they too have adopted the particularist language that reproduces the nation-centric understanding of social reality. Hence, the Society of St. Vincent de Paul (SVP) is nominally described as 'an international Christian voluntary membership organisation' that was founded in Paris in 1833 and is open to all who share its universalist ethos. However, much of their activities and success is framed in national terms. Thus, on their website, SVP emphasises how 'during its history it has helped people in need through a Famine, a Civil War, a War of Independence, two World Wars and several economic recessions' (www .svp.ie/). What is noticeable here is that the nation-centric view of social reality has been so internalised that there is no need to clarify that all these momentous historical events mentioned refer to Irish history and Irish people only. This self-description of the organisation is focused on demonstrating how its activities have always been in tune with the needs of 'the people', where 'the people' clearly stands for the Irish national collective involved in the shared trans-historic and trans-class community overcoming enormous historical obstacles – from the Great Famine to Civil War, a War of Independence to more recent economic recessions. Similarly, Trócaire, a humanitarian organisation focused on oversees aid, espouses universalist values ranging from equality, poverty reduction, women's empowerment and human rights while also framing their activities in national terms. Hence, the organisation highlights its internationalism while also stating clearly that it 'was established . . . as a way for Irish people to donate to development and emergency relief overseas' (www .trocaire.org/). Here again, the international activities are firmly grounded in one's nationhood. Although Trócaire is driven by humanitarian internationalism, its raison d'être is to provide the channel for the Irish people (not others) to express their altruism. By associating the organisation with the Irish people, Trócaire contributes to re-affirmation of Irishness as something wedded to altruism, thus raising the social status of the Irish nation state in the world. The Sisters of Charity are just as grounded in the nation-centric discourses. For instance their contribution to addressing the problems of immigration are understood in terms of assimilation into the existing nation state structure: 'Our Sisters also work to integrate asylum seekers, refugees and immigrants in the local area. Part of their work is welcoming people to local parishes and liaising with schools on integrating pupils and their families' (http: //religioussistersofcharity.ie/what-we-do/immigrant-support/).

The expanded civil society groupings have widened the debate on key social, political, economic and cultural issues in Ireland. However, this process has not undermined the dominant nation-centric understandings of social reality. On the contrary, the proliferation of civil society organisations has largely fostered the expansion and ground-ness of nationalism in everyday life. This strength of contemporary Irish nationalism is well illustrated in its habitual reproduction. Unlike the 1940s and 50s, when nationalism was insecure and weakly grounded in everyday life of highly localised kinship-based solidarities, today's nationalism is well established and constantly reproduced in everyday practices. In other words, while before micro-level attachments were largely disconnected from the wider nationalist narrative, contemporary Irish society is characterised by a well-integrated, society-wide, grounded nationalism.

This is visible in a variety of everyday practices, such as active mass public support for Irish national teams in various sporting competitions: from the Football World and European cups, Olympics to Six Nation

Rugby or GAA International Rules games. In this context, the participation of the Irish national team in the 1990 world football cup in Italy has generally been identified as a pivotal moment in the transformation of Irish national identity (Cronin 1999). This was not only the first time an Irish national football team qualified for the world cup finals, but the team was extremely successful, reaching the quarter-finals and only losing to the eventual world cup winners – Italy. This success had enormous impact on the ordinary population as it created a Durkhemian moment of nationalist collective effervescence. More significantly, it reflected how grounded Irish nationalism has become: long-term historical development resulting ultimately in the coalescence of increased organisational capacity, ideological penetration and the envelopment of micro-solidarities. As Dorney (2012) describes:

For three weeks the nation experienced something close to mass hysteria. I can recall, as a nine-year-old, people literally weeping with emotion after the penalty shootout against Romania. All that night car horns blared out from tricolour-laden cars. Eamon Dunphy, who had dared to criticize the team was all but burned in effigy. Half a million people came out onto the streets of Dublin to welcome the team home after the defeat against Italy.

This emotional intensity associated with the symbolic success in the international sporting arena was repeated at the 1994 football world cup in the USA as well as during the 1996 Atlanta Olympics, both of which were considered to be highly successful events for the Irish team. For example, Michelle Smyth's three gold medals and one bronze at the 1996 Olympics generated a popular sense of euphoria. As one commentator describes:

Her home-coming was euphoric also. I suppose at the time when the American swimmer [Janet Evans] made the ill-tempered comments, I think it was almost classified as a national affront. I think there was a sense of great national pride, something we never experienced. The number of successes over such a short period was something we had never experienced at international or Olympic level. I think everybody at the time took great pride in her achievements. (Watterson 2016)

Although the Irish international sporting successes were celebrated long before the 1990s, the scale, intensity and character of these celebrations indicate that there was a substantial change in how nationalism penetrated everyday life. While before the nationalist discourse was more insular and focused on the questions of Ireland's reunification only, the contemporary nationalist discourses have become more status conscious and centred on enhancing Ireland's prestige in the global arena. All of this was a product of increased organisational, ideological and micro-interactional powers. This change is visible not only in the sporting competitions but also in the arts, music, cuisine, tourism and many other spheres of social life.

With the unprecedented economic growth experienced during the Celtic tiger years (mid-1990s to mid-2000s), Irish nationalism reflected this rising sense of national confidence. For example, during this period, the Irish public wholeheartedly embraced successful sports that have traditionally been regarded as the antithesis of what it means to be Irish such as rugby, soccer, golf and more recently even cricket. Hence, international successes in the rugby and golf competitions (i.e. Six Nations, World cup, the Masters, US Open, Ryder cup, etc.) have gradually attracted a large following in Ireland and have also become an important source of national pride. Even the bastion of traditional insular nationalism, the GAA, set up in 1884 to promote 'indigenous' sports such as hurling, camogie, Gaelic football, handball and rounders, underwent significant transformation in this period. In 2001, the GAA congress voted to abolish the rule that prohibited members of British security forces to play hurling and Gaelic football. The GAA also relaxed other rules including those prohibiting the play of non-GAA sports on its stadiums. At the same time, GAA representatives started engaging in the greater internationalisation of its sports, which was reflected in GAA sporting competitions now taking place in thirty-two countries all over the world. In addition, the GAA and the Australian Football League have established the International Rules Football competition that now takes place annually. The golfing competitions, once firmly associated with the upper class colonial representatives, have also become very popular. The international success of Irish golfers such as Rory McIlroy, Padraig Harrington, Darren Clarke and Graeme McDowell, among others, has contributed further to the incorporation of golf into the Irish national narrative. In all these cases, international sporting accomplishments have been utilised as a mechanism for national self-promotion.

The transformation and proliferation of grounded nationalisms in Ireland has also been visible in the domain of arts. While in De Valera's Ireland there was little or no support for creative and critical non-traditional artists, contemporary Irish society is much more appreciative of artists and especially those who attain international recognition. Hence, while Irish Nobel laureates and other internationally recognised writers such as Samuel Beckett, James Joyce, George Bernard Shaw and Edna O'Brien, among others, were largely ignored in 1950s Ireland as their works were often deemed to be sacrilegious, the successful writers are now seen as being integral to the national project. In fact, much of contemporary Irish nationalism is rooted in the belief that Irish literary culture has made an enormous contribution to world literature. The popular mass media often make reference to the world-wide impact of Irish writers: 'Ireland has produced some of the greatest authors and writers in literature throughout the 19th century and 20th century as well as some incredible modern Irish authors' (Kozupski 2017). The international success of Joyce, Becket, O'Brien, but also Oscar Wilde, Seamus Heaney, W.B. Yeats, John Kavanagh, Emma Donohue and others have been regularly identified a source of national pride: 'We are a nation of a rich literary past and are continuing to churn out some world class writers' (www.buybooks.ie/blog/irish-literary-legends/), or 'While "world domination" might be overstating the matter somewhat, clearly, when it comes to the short story, the claim that Irish writers rank as (being among) the best in the world is a claim with solid foundation ... while Ireland produces fantastic short story writers it also produces world-class novelists, playwrights, poets. We ... are simply very good at writing' (James 2014).

The habitual reproduction and grounding of nationalist topoi is even more visible in the popular glorification of Irish successes in the global film and music industry. The print and digital media regularly report on the activities of Irish actors in Hollywood blockbusters and British films. The major award-winning ceremonies are covered extensively with the emphasis firmly on Irish actors and their success. Most media outlets provide extensive weekly information on the whereabouts of Pierce Brosnan, Saoirse Ronan, Brendan Gleeson, Liam Neeson, Colin Farrell, Ruth Negga and other Irish-born Hollywood successes. Even other successful actors who are not born in Ireland are regularly claimed for the national pantheon. For example, one can frequently encounter the typical justifications for this inclusion: 'Although born in Germany, Michael Fassbender's mother is Irish, and he was raised in Killarney, County Kerry. Over the past decade, Fassbender has become one of Ireland's best-known actors', or 'while she wasn't born in Ireland, prolific actress, producer and director Olivia Wilde holds an Irish passport. Her father is the Irish journalist Andrew Myles Cockburn, and she spent her childhood summers in Ardmore, County Waterford' (Phelan 2017).

Everyday Irish nationalism is also reproduced through the celebration of Irish pop and rock bands such as U2, Westlife, Boyzone, Girls Aloud, Thin Lizzy, the Corrs, the Pogues, the Cranberries and so on. Radio and TV programmes devote great deal of attention to these bands, constantly invoking their world-wide recognition and fame: 'For an island with a relatively small population, Ireland has always punched way above its weight when it comes to musical output' (Dome 2016), or 'For a small country Ireland has made and continues to make a huge impact on modern music' (http://irishrockers.com/IrishRockHistory.php). The popular commentators highlight the global influence and popularity of Irish rock and pop bands. For example, U2 are regularly described as 'giants of the world rock', or as 'one of the most successful bands in the world since the Beatles' who 'dominate the music world' http: //irishrockers.com/IrishRockHistory .php). In similar ways, the former pop boy bands such as Westlife and Boyzone are depicted as the most successful boy bands in the world. Some individual signers such as Enya, Sinead O'Connor, Hozier and van Morrison, among others, have also attained universal recognition among the Irish population and their international achievements have been celebrated and used as a source of national pride. Successful participation in pop music competitions has also contributed to the increased sense of national confidence. For example, the series of Eurovision song contest wins in the 1990s (92, 93, 94 and 96) was often described as a major boost to Irish national identity (Ó Giolláin 2017; Wulff 2008).

Irish folk and traditional music and dancing have also experienced significant revival. Here too the focus has shifted from the insularity of local songs and dances towards branding of 'Irish traditional music' and 'Irish dance' as a global, standardised and uniform product to be exported to the rest of the world. In this respect, Michael Flatley's *Riverdance* theatrical show launched in 1995 inaugurated the proliferation of this performative genre that received global recognition and in this process also helped popularise 'traditional' Irish singing and dancing. As Sherlock (1999) shows, the *Riverdance* performance appealed to numerous global Irish diaspora which responded to 'resonances of homeland and nostalgic memories of community [and] the feelings of … nationalist belonging'. Leading Irish journalist Fintan O'Toole (1997) captured well the popular feelings that *Riverdance* invoked: 'it become customary to talk of *Riverdance* as an act of reclamation, a taking back for popular entertainment of a form that had been prettified and stultified'.

The *Riverdance* phenomenon was also a catalyst of an important social change that was reflected in the sudden expansion of Irish step dancing competitions for children. These competitions, ranging from local and national to world championships, are now highly standardised events that involve specifically designed dresses, shoes, hairstyles (with elaborate wigs), makeup and other equipment. The global expansion of this codified version of step dancing has been particularly influential in enhancing the prestige of everyday Irishness in the world. While before, Irish step dancing was firmly associated with insular nationalism of the Catholic majority, in twenty-first-century Ireland, this form of dancing has become a global cultural product performed by millions of children throughout the world and consumed by wide global audiences. A dance that was originally created by Gaelic League representatives in 1893 and was traditionally seen as a form of Catholic nationalist protest to the British occupation (Hobsbawm 1990) has metamorphosed into a global hip phenomenon.[3] Although its form and the idiom of expression have changed, Irish step dancing still remains a highly potent nationalist symbol. In fact, its transformation into a global sensation has substantially increased its status value, thus further enhancing its nationalist resonance.

The gradual rise of grounded nationalism is also visible in the changed character of national commemorations. For example, St. Patrick's Day parades have become much more prominent and more significant in Ireland as they have attained a degree of global recognition. Organised celebrations of St. Patrick's Day, together with the accompanying parades, were invented in the eighteenth-century USA and it was not until well into the twentieth century that this ritual has gained root in Ireland (Cronin & Adair, 2006: xxiii).[4] More importantly, the central ideological message and the organisation of the parades have experienced substantial change over the years: whereas before, parades were seen as events glorifying Catholic heritage and republican principles that underpinned the new independent Irish state, today St. Patrick's Day parades tend to involve immigrants and other minority groups and are, as such, are conceptualised as events that celebrate multiculturalism. Furthermore, contemporary parades are also globally associated with fun, entertainment, drinking and consumerism. This significant ideological shift is often interpreted as a sign that the nationalist component of St. Patrick's Day celebrations has dramatically declined or completely disappeared. Nevertheless, as Schuldt (2017) shows the global recognition and acceptance of this holiday has in fact strengthened rather than weakened Irish nationalism. This national holiday has become a global phenomenon with over sixty world landmarks, from the Sidney Opera House to the Eiffel Tower, being illuminated green to celebrate this day. In this way St. Patrick's Day has become 'a unique national signifier, and a key component in the consumption of Irish 'national identity' thus making Irish nationalism 'one of the strongest, if not the strongest, variants of nationalism in the contemporary world' (Schuldt 2017: 2).

The 1916 Easter Rising celebrations have also undergone important transformation. In de Valera's Ireland, this event was a cornerstone of republican Catholic nationalist narrative linking Irish independence with

---

[3] 'Two of its [Gaelic League] members decided to add a social dimension to the League's Irish language classes after attending Scottish "ceillithe" nights. The London branch held the first social dance event, called a ceili in 1897' (Smith 2013).

[4] The first state-sponsored St. Patrick's Day parade took place in Dublin only in 1931.

the martyrdom of 1916 revolutionaries. The event was traditionally commemorated with the official military parade on Easter Sunday, a wreath-laying ceremony in the cemetery at Arbour Hill and the series of political speeches celebrating the 1916 martyrs. Although recent commemorations have tended to maintain the same ritual patterns, including the military parade, wreath laying and political speeches, the content of the key ideological messages has changed.[5] The new commemorations have become much more inclusive and focused on the present rather than the past. The end of violent conflict in Northern Ireland, together with economic prosperity in the South, have shifted the celebratory narrative towards the achievements of the Republic. In this context, the celebrations emphasised reconciliation and inclusivity in terms of religion, gender and class. This has been particularly pronounced during the centenary celebrations in 2016, when the Easter Rising was re-interpreted as an event associated with religious tolerance, gender inclusivity, egalitarianism and a sense of universal justice. For example, the president of Ireland, Michael D. Higgins's speeches emphasise all these elements. Hence, he depicts the Rising as a non-sectarian event centred on fighting 'the destructive consequences of imperialism' but also as an event defined by 'the ethical appeal of egalitarianism' and something that was fully in tune with 'the other progressive movements then under way, such as the movement for women's rights, socialism and cultural nationalism'. The speech also highlights the central role played by women:

One of the most remarkable legacies of the Irish Citizen Army for us today is, I believe, the place it carved out for women, both among its ranks and in its vision for the Ireland of the future. It is well known that, during the Rising, Citizen Army officer Dr Kathleen Lynn was second in command at City Hall, while Constance Markievicz and Margaret Skinnider played an important combatant role at St. Stephen's Green.

The speech concludes with the line from the Proclamation of Independence that the president sees as having been 'most meaningful to us today': 'The Republic guarantees religious and civil liberty, equal rights and equal opportunities to all its citizens' (Higgins 2016). At first glance, this narrative of inclusivity, equality and justice might seem to indicate that nationalism has been downgraded or even displaced in the 2016 celebrations. However, this discursive shift indicates only that Irish nationalism has transformed over the years by successfully incorporating what are today regarded to be the universalist topoi such as human rights, gender equality, religious tolerance, environmental protection and social justice. Thus, by appropriating

---

[5] The military parade was abolished during 'the Troubles' but was reintroduced in 2006.

the language of inclusivity and tolerance, Irish nationalism enhances its global prestige and appeal. The universalist, egalitarian and peace-oriented rhetoric displayed in the president's speech is so poignant that it precludes a listener from comprehending that what is celebrated here is in fact a violent event which, at the time, was deemed to be sectarian, illegal, irresponsible and initially had little or no support among the population of Ireland. Nevertheless, since the 1916 Rising fostered the establishment of the Republic and has in one way or another been one of its foundational myths, it is necessary for any Irish president to provide a justification for this event. In this context, the discourse of inclusivity provides a much more potent source of legitimation.

With the ever-rising prestige of Irishness in the wider world, its traditional and stereotypical symbols have become sought-after consumerist items. Thus, the Irish tricolour, shamrock, Claddagh rings, Celtic crosses, harps, green jerseys and other images are now produced on a massive scale and sold all over the globe. For example, jewellers have developed a wide and elaborate range of 'Celtic designs' including the following styles: Book of Kells, Celtic cross, Celtic knot, Celtic tree of life, Celtic warrior shield, Claddagh, Connemara marble, Irish gold, Irish harp, Mo Anam Cara, Trinity knot, etc. (www.myirishjeweler.com/eu /celtic-earrings/?&dFR[type][0]=Earring). These consumerist items, together with other artefacts perceived as distinctly Irish (from Guinness beer and whiskey to Irish stew, leprechauns, St. Brigid's crosses or green post-boxes), have proliferated throughout the world. Although some scholars such as Bauman (2006) or Beck (2006) see consumerism as being ultimately corrosive to the nationalist projects, as allegedly its atomising individualism undermines nation states and communitarian ideologies, this really is not the case. The Irish case illustrates what I have argued before (Malešević 2013a), namely that consumerism has always been an integral part of the nationalist experience: the mass production, mass circulation and mass consumption of products imprinted with nation-centric images contributes substantially towards the continuous reproduction of nationhood and nationalisms. The popular reception of nationalist ideologies entails visibility and the everyday use of national symbols imprinted in various objects. With the development of the state and capitalism and their organisational capacities, such products have become even more accessible to ordinary individuals. More recently, many nation states and other organisations have embraced and lavishly funded the so-called nation-branding projects. As Aronczyk (2013: 1) shows, there is a whole industry dedicated to developing a unique brand for specific nation states. Government representatives employ public relations advisors and branding consultants who deploy their standard marketing and advertising tools and techniques 'to help nations articulate more coherent and cohesive identities, attract foreign capital, and maintain citizen loyalty'. In this context, tourism plays an important part as branding regularly involves promotion of idealised tourist destinations and packaged cultural heritage. In the Irish case, these branded objects range from medieval castles (Ashford, Bunratty, Blarney, Cahir, etc.) to the cottage landscapes of Connemara and Cliffs of Moher to Celtic themed destinations and events, the Book of Kells and so on. As Edensor (2008, 2002) demonstrates, tourism involves choreographed, staged and regulated performances that have become central to the reproduction of nationhood today. Hence, Irish nationalism is not an exception but something that reflects world-wide trends. In all these instances, nation-centric images and practices are normalised, naturalised, routinized and taken for granted. Just as with other nationalisms, Irish nationalism has gained strength by becoming habitually grounded in everyday life.

Conclusion

The general propensity of all nationalist discourses is to see their nation as unique and irreplaceable. Some nationalists explicitly insist on the inherent superiority of their nation vis-à-vis the others but, in most cases, such arguments are made indirectly by insisting on one's distinctiveness and peculiar features. So one can often come across this type of reasoning: We might not be the wealthiest, the most powerful, or the most advanced nation but we possess other special characteristics that other nations lack – glorious past, moral purity, remarkable sense of national solidarity, political maturity, exceptional heroism, extraordinary sense of social justice, unique affinity to liberty, unmatched presence of fair play and civility or the distinct ability to survive and thrive in difficult circumstances. For if this was not the case there would be no sensible social justification for the existence of separate nations and their political roofs – the nation states.

Irish nationalism is not particularly different in this respect. Despite the perceptions of many analysts that Irish nation-formation is historically unique and that contemporary Irish nationalism stands out from its European counterparts, there is nothing substantially different in nationalist rhetoric and practice in Ireland. Irish nationalism originated, developed and expanded and continues to be reproduced in line with the same processes present in other modern societies. Furthermore, just as in the rest of the world, nationalism in Ireland is not on the wane. On the contrary, as organisational and ideological structures constantly develop, they provide social and institutional mechanisms for the expansion of nationalism. The fact that much of this nationalism is muted, banal and routine has misled many to confuse invisibility with insignificance. However nationalisms are strongest when they become inconspicuousness, when nationhood is universally perceived to be normal, natural and ubiquitous. Irish nationalism is no exception.

7   Nationalisms and Wars in the Balkans

Introduction

There is nothing inherently aggressive in nationalist ideology. Most nationalist organisations have managed to operate for decades without any reliance on violence. For example, the Quebecois, Flemish, Catalan, Scottish and Veneto nationalist movements, among many others, have largely pursued their political agendas through peaceful means including elections, legitimate protests and public campaigns. However, in some instances, the nationalist aspirations have been underpinned by the excessive use of violence ranging from violent demonstrations over terrorism and insurgency such as in the casas of the ETA, IRA, PKK, to the all-out civil war as exemplified by Tamil Tigers (LTTE), KLA or the Chechen independence movement. In this context the commentators differentiate clearly between what Mark Beissinger (1998) calls 'nationalisms that bark and nationalisms that bite'. There is no doubt that the Balkan region has traditionally been associated with the biting type of nationalism. The popular perceptions of the Balkans are of a region prone to rampant nationalism and incessant violence. Such a stance was already present in the early nineteenth century when the image of the Balkans gradually replaced that of the Ottoman Empire as the 'uncivilised', underdeveloped and chaotic Other. While the wars of independence against the crumbling 'sick man of Europe' were generally greeted with enthusiasm in the West, attempts by the newly independent Balkan states to establish genuine autonomy from the Great Powers at the end of the nineteenth and early twentieth centuries provoked profound animosity in the major European capitals. This view was already present before the first Balkan War (1912) but was particularly pronounced during and after the second Balkan war (1913). The Balkan region was usually depicted as the hotbed of intrinsic violence. For example, the British Evening Post's depiction of Serbia following the assassination of King Aleksandar Obrenović in 1903 illustrates this well:

> Servia, the land of assassinations, abdications, pronunciamientos, and coups de etat, has surpassed itself and caused all previous achievements to pale into insignificance beside the tragedy enacted between midnight and the small hours of this morning at Belgrade. A central Asian khanate, a not European city, would be a fitting theatre for such ruthless and accurately planed regicide. (EP 1903: 13)

These stereotypical Western perceptions of the region were often shared by the educated classes in the Balkans. Hence, some of the more prominent Balkan intellectuals embraced these Orientalist themes and wrote about the region in a very similar terms, indicating its unique 'Balkan mentality', 'violent nature', rampant ethnocentrism and 'barbarism' (Dvorniković 1939; Cvijić 1922). Although contemporary commentators now avoid using such crude descriptions, the region is still associated with what many regard to be ubiquitous violence and entrenched nationalisms. For some analysts, it is this prevalence of aggressive nationalism that is one of the principal causes for the economic and political 'backwardness' of the Balkans (Berend 2003; Gerolymatos 2002; Kennan 1993). For example, in his 1993 introduction to the reprinted Carnegie Endowment report on the Balkan Wars of 1912–13, George Kennan directly links the violent conflicts in the region at the beginning and at the end of the twentieth century arguing that the lack of development in the Balkans was not rooted in religious differences but in 'aggressive nationalism ... [which] manifested itself on the field of battle, drew on deeper traits of character inherited, presumably, from the distant tribal past ... and so it remains today' (Kennan 1993: 4–6).

Much of contemporary scholarship on the Balkans has rightly critiqued and dismantled this nebulous 'ancient hatreds' idea (Jović 2001; Oberschall 2000; Cohen 1993). However it is necessary to go a bit further and try to tackle the complexities of the Balkan case by zooming in on the relationship between war and nation-state making processes. Such an analysis would challenge not only the notion of 'ancient hatreds' but would in fact indicate the opposite – that the Balkans have historically experienced less nationalism and less violence than many other parts of Europe. Hence, in this chapter, I argue that it was the absence of coherent, popular and grounded nationalist ideologies and protracted interstate warfare that have often proved to be a crucial hindrance for intensive social development in south east Europe. The core argument combines theoretical and empirical aspects. The first section engages with the bellicist tradition in historical sociology that sees the state as a direct product of warfare and questions the blanket proposition that 'wars make states' in the context of Balkan history. I argue that the conventional bellicist argument requires a serious qualification as it seems unable to explain the persistent weakness of the state in the nineteenth and early twentieth-century Balkans. The second section focuses on the relationship between organised violence, state formation and nationalism. My aim here is to rehabilitate the modernist theories of nationalism which are often criticised for not being able to account for the alleged emergence of nationalist aspirations in the early nineteenth-century Balkans. In contrast to the mainstream Balkan historiography, I argue that there was very little, if any, nationalism in south east Europe for much of the nineteenth century and, for large sections of the population, nationalism was still a marginal ideology well into the twentieth century.

South East Europe and the Bellicist Historical Sociology

The idea that wars make states has a long tradition in social sciences, expressed by numerous theorists: from Gumplowitz (1899), Ratzenhofer (1881), Ward (1913), Oppenheimer (1926), Hintze (1908[1975]) and Rüstow (1950[1980]) to the more recent theories of Carneiro (1970), Downing (1992), Ertman (1997), Centeno (2002) and Gat (2006). This bellicist historical sociology gained momentum with Tilly's (1975, 1985, 1992) sophisticated reformulation which emphasised the broader geopolitical context in the changing character of the imperial interstate warfare in early modern Europe. For Tilly, protracted wars were the principal catalyst of state transformation as they ultimately enabled the development of the omnipotent bureaucratic apparatuses, effective revenue systems, state-wide juridical control, integrated regional administration and substantially better financial infrastructure. Furthermore, the constant war making increased demand for greater military and economic mobilisation of ordinary people whose material resources and military participation became decisive for the long-term survival of warring states. The unintended consequence of these changes were gradual but steady payoffs that the state rulers had to make to their subjects, including wider citizenship rights, expanding parliamentary systems, religious freedoms and social protection, all of which also encouraged the development of civil societies.

The Western European multi-polar order prevented the emergence of a single empire, thus creating a semi-anarchic environment where rulers were gradually forced to rely on broader sectors of the population under their control. Hence, to effectively fight external threats, the rulers often embarked on pre-emptive wars while simultaneously trying to neutralise domestic forms of violence. To finance ever-more-costly warfare in the context of rapid military transformations (with the invention and mass manufacturing of more destructive weaponry and dramatic improvements in transport and communication systems), rulers had to constantly increase resource extraction and introduce universal conscription in the territories under their control. As Tilly (1985: 172) emphasises, this process was highly contingent on states emerging as a corollary of war making, extraction of resources and capital accumulation. In other words, to extract money, people and material, it was necessary to subdue and disarm internal rivals and defeat external foes. In this process, state rulers operated in a similar way to gangs who offer security in exchange for regular financial payment. That is, the state developed as an institutionalised and legitimised large-scale protection racket:

Governments' provision of protection ... often qualifies as racketeering. To the extent that the threats against which a given government protects its citizens are imaginary or are consequences of its own activities, the government has organised protection racket. Since governments themselves commonly simulate, stimulate, or even fabricate threats of external war and since the repressive and extractive activities of government often constitute the largest current threats to the livelihoods of their own citizens, many governments operate essentially the same ways as racketeers. (Tilly 1985: 171)

Therefore, the bellicist tradition argues that the modern, centralised, nation states were a direct by-product of the intensification in Western European war making from the sixteenth century onwards.

This bellicist interpretation has provoked a great deal of attention: it has been applied to various parts of the world with a focus on the structural differences between Western Europe and the rest of the world. For example, Lustick (1997) interprets state instability in the Middle East through the prism of earlier state development in Europe whereby better-organised and more powerful European states colonised the region and in this way averted the emergence of 'state-building wars' in the Middle East. Barnett (1992) provides a comparative analysis of Israel and Egypt, arguing that the relationship between war and state making is highly dependent on the different strategies of state building pursued by the rulers in the two countries. In contrast, Tin-Bor Hui (2005) pinpoints striking similarities between China in the Spring and Autumn and Warring States periods (656–221 BCE) with early modern Europe: whereas both regions experienced the proliferation of warfare, development of centralised bureaucracy and expansion of trade, they nevertheless eventually experienced different outcomes. Taylor and Botea (2008) contrast the impact of war on state development in Vietnam and Afghanistan, arguing that the relative ethnic homogeneity was a decisive factor contributing to state-making war in Vietnam and state-destroying war in Afghanistan. Centeno (2002) and Herbst (2000) have compared the experience of state formation in early modern Western Europe with that of Latin America and Africa respectively, pointing to different organisational trajectories in these two continents where, in contrast to West European protracted wars and strong states, sporadic and limited warfare generated weak and internally polarised states.

The general tendency among the scholars is either to endorse or disprove the 'war makes states' thesis. Some authors such Thies (2007), Ayoob (1995) and Herbst (2000) side with Tilly in the argument that the proliferation of protracted interstate warfare is conducive to development of pervasive state apparatuses in other parts of the world such as the Middle East, Africa, or South Asia. Others, such as Leander (2004), Reno (2003) and Kaldor (2001), have tended to be much more critical of this assumption, arguing that the historical context has significantly changed: in the post-WWII international system, all attempts at unilateral border change are quickly delegitimised, which creates a situation where interstate warfare is on the wane while intra-state (civil) wars – conflicts that destroy state capacity – proliferate.

The Balkan case remains something of a puzzle as it does not easily fit into either of the two competing perspectives. At first glance, it might seem that the south east European experience quickly refutes the bellicist thesis as the common perception of the region is one of relentless civil warfare and weak states. However, careful historical sociological analysis shows otherwise: for much of its history the Balkans have not experienced more violence than other parts of Europe. The rulers of the medieval kingdoms of Serbia, Croatia, Bosnia and Bulgaria waged frequent wars with the Byzantine Empire and between each other but in terms of intensity, human casualties and their organisational features, these wars were no different to other medieval conflicts fought in the same period throughout the European continent (Nicholson 2004; Keen 1999; Fine 1994). Just as nearly all wars in the feudal age, these conflicts were essentially small-scale, low-casualty ritualistic affairs with very few proper and lasting battlefields. The majority of these conflicts were fought by small and quite expensive armies of aristocrats who tended to avoid direct battles and were mostly focused on the plundering and sieges of large castles. Once the Ottoman Empire conquered much of south east Europe, the entire region was successfully pacified for centuries. While some areas in the Balkans were sites of inter-imperial wars between Ottomans, Habsburgs, Venetians and the Russian Empire for much of the sixteenth to eighteenth centuries, this region has nevertheless experienced substantially less organised violence than other parts of Europe.[1] With the gradual weakening of the Ottoman Empire in the early nineteenth century, the Balkans became a zone of interest for the Great Powers whose political and cultural elite encouraged violent resistance to the Ottoman rule. From Chateaubriand and Flaubert to Lord Byron, Shelley and Goethe, south east Europe and Greece in particular were suddenly rediscovered as the exotic cradle of European civilisation (Todorova 1997: 89–115).[2] It is only in this period that one can witness the acceleration of organised violence in the region. Nevertheless, this is hardly unique for the Balkans as the scientific, technological and organisational developments have made nineteenth century warfare much more deadly all over the world: for example, whereas the global war casualties for the combined sixteenth and seventeenth centuries amounted to less than 8 million this figure of war deaths jumps to over 19 million for the nineteenth century alone (Eckhardt 1992: 272–3).

In this context, organised violence in the Balkans appears miniscule when compared to the intensity and scale of destruction and human casualties resulting from wars, revolutions, uprisings and industrial conflicts in the large and powerful European states. For example, whereas the French and British polities were fighting wars, colonising the globe and dealing violently with various revolutions and numerous uprisings throughout the nineteenth century – with Britain involved in more than sixty major wars – during the same period, south east Europe experienced only six violent conflicts and five major (peasant) rebellions (Clodfelter 1992). Furthermore, while at the beginning of the nineteenth century much of Europe was engulfed in the extremely destructive Napoleonic Wars with casualties totalling close to 6 million, the Balkan uprisings of the same period amounted to merely a few thousand casualties (Biondich 2011; Clodfelter 1992: 322). With a clear exception of the Greek War of

---

[1] The only substantial conflicts occurred in the late seventeenth and early-to-mid eighteenth centuries. These include the Ottoman-Venetian wars over Peloponnesus, Austrian-Ottoman wars in the 1710s and 1730s in Bosnia and Serbia and Russian-Ottoman wars that concluded with the Treaty of Kuchuk Kaynarca (1774) (Zarinebaf, Bennet and Davies 2005)

[2] However, this sudden obsession with the Balkans was not very deep: 'They loved the Greece of their dreams; the land, the language, the antiquities, but not the people. If only, they thought, the people could be more like the British scholars and gentlemen; or failing that, as too much to be hoped, if only they were more like their own ancestors; or better still, if only they were not there at all' (Woodhouse 1969: 38–9).

Independence (1821–9), all the nineteenth century Balkan wars and uprisings were small-scale conflicts involving several thousand casualties.

Nonetheless, the Greek War of Independence was far from being a domestic Balkan affair. It was fostered and supported by the Great Powers and it was their military, economic and political involvement that sealed the 'Greek' victory as not many Greek soldier took part in the major battles (such as that of Navarino, 1827) that decided the fate of the war. The large casualty rate was primarily a product of the highly disorganised infighting among the supposedly unified and 'nationally conscious' Greeks and the civilian massacres by various brigand forces (Roudometof 2001; Mazower 2000).

Early twentieth-century warfare was significantly more destructive with the two Balkan wars (1912 and 1913), World War I and the Greco-Turkish war of 1919–22 defining the character of organised violence in south east Europe for this period. The 1912–13 Balkan wars were particularly important as their scale, intensity and outcome had a profound impact on the perception of the region in the West. Although the massacres of the Greek War of Independence dented the until-then popular view of the Balkans as a land of 'noble savage Christians' who needed to be saved from the 'Turkish yoke' and brought back to their ancient Greek heritage, it was really the unexpected context of the Balkan wars that completely changed popular perceptions of the region in the West. As Todorova (1997: 122–39) convincingly argues, and demonstrates, 'violence as the leitmotiv of the Balkans was, strictly speaking, a post-Balkan wars phenomenon'. Whereas the start of the First Balkan War was still largely interpreted in the Western media through the prism of liberation from the Ottomans (as it involved organised alliance of the small Balkan states against the Ottoman Empire), the swift and comprehensive military victory of the Balkan League changed this perception. For example, the Commission set up by the Carnegie Endowment for International Peace to identify the causes of the two Balkan wars differentiated strongly between the two wars: the first conflict was depicted as 'the supreme protest against violence … the protest of the weak against the strong … and for this reason it was glorious and popular throughout the civilised world', whereas the second conflict was defined as a rapacious war where 'both victor and vanquished lost morally and materially' (Todorova 1997: 4).

The outbreak of the Second Balkan War with the former allies now fighting each other over the former Ottoman possessions provoked outrage in the capitals of the Great Powers. The fact that, for the first time in modern history, the political elites of the small Balkan polities were in the position to pursue their own geo-political interests and in this process largely ignore the wishes of the Great Powers infuriated the political establishment in the major European capitals. In addition, the unprecedented scale of the conflict came as a shock to most external observers. The armies of the Balkan states were well equipped with modern weaponry, well trained in the most recent military doctrines and strategies, relying heavily 'on the ideas of the French Colonel Louis de Grandmaison to carry out the attack quickly and in force', and were able to mobilise hundreds of thousands of soldiers (Hall 2000: 15–18). The direct consequence of this speedy, comprehensively organised, well equipped and thoroughly armed mass mobilisation was mass destruction on a scale not seen before in this part of the world. The total casualties of the two Balkan wars amounted to over 150,000 people (Eckhardt 1988; Singer 1972); the losing sides (Ottoman in the first and Bulgarian in the second) had substantial territorial losses while the winners (Serbia, Greece, Montenegro and Romania) had, in most instances, more than doubled their pre-war territories (i.e. Serbia by 81 per cent Greece by 64 per cent, Montenegro by 62 per cent (Biondich 2011: 78).

This particular outcome shocked the political and cultural elites of major European states. The highly violent struggle for territory, which was now justified in explicit nationalist terms, reinforced the perception that the Balkan region is an eternal epicentre of aggressive nationalism. This attitude was already present in the first academic analysis of the two Balkan wars, with the American scholar and journalist Jacob Schurman (1914: 47) projecting war aims into the past: 'For ages the fatal vice of the Balkan nations has been the immoderate and intolerant assertion by each of its own claim [for territory] coupled with contemptuous disregard of the right of others.' A very similar attitude followed the just-as-devastating Greco-Turkish War (1919–22) that ultimately helped entrench the perception of the region as being characterised by incessant violence and xenophobic nationalist aspirations.[3]

Nevertheless, rather than being an omnipresent feature of Balkan history, this sudden eruption of organised violence was a completely novel product of intensive nineteenth-century state building, largely based on the Western European models. Unlike other parts of Europe, before the mid nineteenth century, the Balkan region did not have

---

[3] It is no accident that the term 'balkanisation' was coined in the aftermath of the 1912–13 Balkan wars. The stereotype of the Balkans as an inherently violent region were also reproduced in Western literature of that period as exemplified by Agatha Christie's 1925 mystery novel *The Secret of Chimneys* where the 'Balkan characters' are depicted as bloodthirsty killers ('I will slit his nose, and cut off his ears, and put out his eyes') and the region as inhabited by 'brigands' whose hobbies include 'assassinating kings and having revolutions' (Todorova 1997: 122).

a history of large-scale protracted violent conflicts as its polities did not possess even rudimentary organisational means to initiate and wage such conflicts. The direct legacy of the late Ottoman Empire's rule was almost non-existent civil service, poor transport and communication networks, no significant urban centres, dispersed and haphazard power and military structures, undeveloped banking and commerce, no proper legal system nor any significant industry.

At the beginning of the nineteenth century, the new Balkan polities had virtually no bureaucratic apparatus: in 1813 Serbia had only two dozen civil servants, the entire Dunabian Principalities (present day Romania) less than 1,000 office-holding boyars, whereas even as late as 1878 the whole of Bosnia and Herzegovina was administered by only 120 civil servants (Glenny 2000: 268; Pavlowitch 1999: 31; Stokes 1976: 4). In addition, no south east European polity had a national bank, a factory, railroad or town with more than 30,000 inhabitants until well into the second half of the nineteenth century. The mountainous terrain and the tiny network of paved roads (by mid nineteenth century, Greece had only 168 km and Serbia just under 800 km) made transport extremely cumbersome and slow (Roudometof 2001; Stoianovich 1994).

The lack of state development made violent conflict difficult; the Greek War of Independence (1821–9) and the two Serbian uprisings (1804–13; 1815–17) were largely chaotic, highly contingent events fought by disorganised and poorly armed units consisting of local notables, foreign-trained volunteers and banditry with no proper military instruction (Glenny 2000; Meriage 1977). Such weak polities could not fight large-scale protracted and destructive wars. Hence, the sporadic and disordered violence that characterised conflicts of early nineteenth-century Balkans could not, and did not, create strong states. Even in the case of the region's most intense and lengthy war, the Greek War of Independence, the war experience did not result in substantially enhanced state capacity of the new Greek polity. Thus, the idea that warfare by itself can automatically create potent states has to be questioned. Nevertheless, although this particular outcome goes against the general premise of the bellicist approach – as developed by its forbearers such as Gumplowitz (1899) or Oppenheimer (1926) or some recent articulations (Gat 2006; Carneiro 1970) – it does not really go against Tilly's thesis as his argument emphasises that low-intensity warfare is less likely to increase the organisational capacity of the state. The fact that the Greek War of Independence was militarily and politically decided by the Great Powers, and that the conflict also had all the hallmarks of civil war, complicates this issue further.

A much better testing ground for the bellicist argument in general and Tilly's thesis in particular is the end of the nineteenth and beginning of the twentieth century when one can observe a dramatic increase in the development of the organisational and infrastructural powers of states in the Balkans. Modelling their state apparatuses on the French, Belgian and Prussian examples, political elites in south east Europe managed, in a very short time, to build potent state and war machines.[4] The size of the civil service changed beyond recognition: what started off as a handful of administrators in the early 1800s grew to hundreds of thousands by the end of that century. For example, even in 1837, the Serbian civil service consisted of fewer than 500 administrators while, by 1902, over 22 per cent of all Belgrade households were inhabited by civil servants and their families. The administrative apparatus in Greece and Bulgaria underwent even greater transformation so that in less than twenty years the Greek state administration grew by 43 per cent and, by the 1930s, civil servants and their families constituted more than 650,000 in each case, which amounted to between a quarter and a third of the country's entire urban population (Roudometof 2001: 156–6; Stoianovitch 1994). In a similar vein, transport and communication networks expanded dramatically with much better roads, railway systems, and commercial shipping (i.e. Greece): between 1885 and 1912, the total length of railway lines increased by 841 per cent in Bulgaria, 613 per cent in Greece and 285 per cent in Serbia (Lampe and Jackson 1982: 211). Hence, the organisational capacity of Balkan states improved substantively.

By the end of the nineteenth century, all governments in the region were preoccupied with the greater centralisation of state power. To achieve this objective, their constitutional arrangements were modelled on the highly centralised Prussian (1850), Belgian (1831) and French (1830) constitutions (Pippidi 2010: 125). Furthermore, most states adopted hierarchical top-down models of internal organisation, often imitating French-style district prefects, and substantially enhanced the position of the top administrators. The dominant view among the political and cultural elites was that successful state building required excessive centralisation. As the onetime Bulgarian minister of education and Czech intellectual, Konstantin Josef Jireček, put it: 'Bulgarian politicians wished to arrange an omnipotent state machine on the French model, ruled by a centre with thousands of officials paid by the state and depending on it and the political parties' (Bechev 2010: 142).

---

[4] However, as I emphasise in Chapter 8, this was rather uneven modernisation as the focus was on the development of the coercive and ideological powers of the state (military, police, courts, educational system, propaganda, etc.) at the expense of nearly everything else.

Administrative expansion was paralleled with the intensive development of the military and police. Military budgets increased substantially, together with the size of the armies and officer corps. For example, at the beginning of the twentieth century, one third of Bulgaria's annual budget was allocated for the military, and other states in the region had a very similar situation (Pelt 2010: 240). The introduction of universal conscription meant that within two or three decades, the militaries of the Balkan states expanded considerably: in 1903, the Serbian army was four times larger than it was ten years earlier whereas the Greek officer corps grew between 1872 and 1895 by a staggering 240 per cent (Roudometof 2001). The military build-up was also accompanied by increasing investments in technology and industry linked to weaponry and military logistics. Hence, Romania's petrol production rose so much that by the late 1920s, the country became one of the leading petrol producers in the world. Serbia's industrial infrastructure at the same time was enlarged threefold to what it was twenty years before (Vucinich 1968).

The ultimate result of this military, bureaucratic and state expansion was the capability to mobilise large sectors of the population and field enormous armies in the two Balkan wars and World War I. It is these violent conflicts that brought about huge human casualties and material destruction never seen before in this part of the world. Hence, rather than representing an alleged continuity of violence supposedly inherent in the region's past, the proliferation of organised violence was a completely novel phenomenon emerging as a direct consequence of intensive modernisation and state building on the Western European models. In this context, the Balkan wars of 1912–13 were not a throwback to the past but a distinctly modern phenomenon. The scale of violence and destruction witnessed here was a glance of things to come, something that the rest of Europe was to experience just a year later.

The fleeting look at the two Balkan wars would suggest that their experience is fully congruent with the bellicist argument and particularly with Tilly's point that mobilisation for war and protracted warfare are likely to enhance the capacity of states: indeed what one can observe here is the parallel development of state power, war preparations and gradual pacification of domestic resistance. There is no disputing the fact that late nineteenth-century Balkan polities were much more robust state and war machines able to control resources, people and materiel, than their early nineteenth century predecessors. However, the complexity of the Balkan case challenges the simple formula that war makes states and states make war.

Firstly, it is not so apparent that warfare itself had so much impact on the state building in the region as the period of most intensive state expansion was generally characterised by prolonged peace (Malešević 2013b). In fact, in the second half of the nineteenth century, a period when the Balkan countries made most progress in enhancing the infrastructural powers of their polities, the region was involved in only three small-scale wars of very short duration: Serbo-Ottoman War (1876), Serbo-Bulgarian War (1885) and Greco-Ottoman War (1897). It is difficult to see how these rather insignificant conflicts could have had a direct impact on the dramatic intensification of state building that it took place in this period. Moreover, the large-scale protracted conflicts, such as the 1912–13 Balkan wars, World War 1 and the 1919–22 Greco-Turkish war all came after the period of concentrated state development.

Secondly, and more importantly, the outcome of these major wars provides a direct challenge to Tilly's thesis. If the central argument is that prolonged and successful war making leads not only to the creation of strong and stable states but also developed civil societies, parliamentarism and economic prosperity, than the Balkan case shows otherwise. The aftermath of all major wars fought in south east Europe at the beginning of the twentieth century shows that whether a particular state found itself on the winning or losing side made little or no difference to its post-war development. More specifically, although Greek, Montenegrin, Romanian and Serbian states were clear winners of the 1912–13 Balkan wars as well as WWI as they acquired large new territories, population and resources, their post-WWI state development was almost identical to that of the states that found themselves on the losing side: Bulgaria and Turkey.[5] In other words, instead of further enhancing their state capacities, expanding civil societies, parliamentarism and economic growth, the 1920s and 30s were periods of economic stagnation, weakening state power, curtailing of civil liberties and stifling of parliamentary institutions which eventfully ended in rigid authoritarianism. The Balkan states became heavily indebted and reliant on foreign capital and in this resembled more the colonies of imperial powers than the stable and strong sovereign states (Biondich 2011; Mungiu-Pippidi 2010; Mann 2004).

Therefore, the conventional bellicist approach seems unable to explain these different trajectories in the relationship between war and state making in the Balkans. The key question here is: Why have intensive interstate wars not created strong and vibrant polities in south east Europe? To properly answer this question, it is paramount to explore

[5] The Greek case is more complex as the state soon became involved in another large-scale conflict (Greco-Turkish war 1919–22) where it lost all its territorial gains acquired during WWI.

the internal configuration of societies in the Balkans and especially the relationship between social stratification, ideology, micro-solidarities and warfare. As the conventional bellicist approach tends to overemphasise external, geo-political and economic factors at the expense of internal sources of conflict, there is a need to go beyond Tilly's analysis. In addition to gauging coercive-organisational capacity, one has to explore the scale of ideological penetration as well as the degree to which micro-level solidarities were integrated with the wider organisational and ideological structures. Hence, the focus needs to move towards the role ideologies, especially popular ideological doctrines such as nationalism, and internal social divisions and solidarities play in mediating the relationship between state and organised violence. Much of the bellicist tradition of analysis, and Tilly in particular, downplays the role of ideological power in modernity (Malešević 2010: 79–84; Brubaker 2010). Nevertheless, to account for the Balkan case, it is crucial to take ideology and especially nationalism much more seriously than the conventional bellicist tradition does.

Rehabilitating Grounded Modernism

Sharing the general view that human beings are essentially interest driven materialist creatures, much of conventional bellicist historical sociology devotes little attention to the ideas, values, emotions, moral principles and cognitions espoused by the agents involved in various social conflicts. Charles Tilly is no exception here, as his approach emphasises the role of material interests and political institutions at the expense of collective meanings and individual perceptions. This is particularly visible in his treatment of nationalist ideology, which is never a sui generis phenomenon but rather a weak, parasitic force dependent on the actions of states and their rulers. As Brubaker (2010: 380) rightly argues, Tilly's understanding of nationalism is overly state-centred, materialist and instrumentalist: 'the theory addresses the political form of nationalist claims-making while ignoring the cultural content of nationalist sense-making'. This is not to say that humans are governed by ideas, as idealist epistemologies would imply, but only that narrow materialism is insufficient as a model of explanation. Hence, to explain persistent state weakness in the wake of intensive interstate wars in the Balkans, one needs to go beyond the coercive-organisational focus and shift attention towards the role of ideological penetration and the envelopment of micro-solidarities. In this context, I also intend to explore the links between nationalism and social stratification.

If we understand ideologies not as closed and inflexible belief systems but as dynamic changing processes through which human beings make sense of their everyday experiences, then the analysis of ideology is a precondition for understanding large-scale social processes such as war and state building. As political facts and social events cannot speak for themselves but entail a particular interpretation, we inevitably rely on different interpretative maps to understand social reality. In this sense, all human beings are ideological creatures (Malešević, 2017, 2010, 2006). More specifically, as we live in a world where the principal unit of territorial social organisation is the nation state, with much of the everyday experience articulated in nation-centric terms, it is crucial to understand how nationalism came to be and was established as the dominant source of political legitimacy in the modern world.

The classical scholars of nationalism such as Gellner (1997, 1983, 1964), Hobsbawmn (1990), Breuilly (1993) and Anderson (1981 [1983]), among others, have emphasised the inherent contingency, relative historical novelty and revolutionary character of nationalist ideology. Rather than being a natural, normal, primeval and permanent form of collective identity, national attachments are understood to be historically specific and atypical, generated by the actions of distinct social organisations, malleable and heavily dependent on on-going structural transformations such as industrialisation, urbanisation or secularisation. For Gellner, nationalism could not emerge before modernity as pre-industrial societies were rigidly hierarchical in an economic, political and cultural sense. Instead of unifying rulers and their subjects in the pre-industrial world, the culture was utilised to reinforce social distinctions between the aristocracy and top clergy on the one hand and the peasantry and urban dwellers on the other. Hence, for much of history, the dominant socio-political units were either much smaller (i.e. city states, principalities, chiefdoms, etc.) or larger than the nation state (i.e. empires). Consequently, instead of nationhood, one's sense of identity tended to be expressed in terms of locality, religion, kinship or status.

Gellner (1997, 1988) makes a sharp distinction between the agrarian and the industrial age, whereby the former is characterised by stringent hierarchies, stagnation, sluggishness and stability where 'people starve according to rank' and the latter is defined by its vibrancy, dynamism, social mobility, innovation and the striving towards continuous economic and scientific growth. The system's ingrained changeability, the clearly articulated division of labour and the demand for the constant growth enhances the role of expert knowledge. Hence, unlike *Agraria* where the work is essentially manual and discursive knowledge is ancillary if not completely irrelevant, *Industria* is dominated by semantic labour where universal, context-free literacy becomes a norm. Moreover, as the industrial world is dependent on both social and geographical mobility, with large sectors of the population moving from the countryside to the cities, there is an organisational need for greater linguistic uniformity. Consequently, the proliferation of industrial development goes hand in hand with the expansion of large-scale educational systems which ultimately turns culturally diverse peasantry into a homogenous nation. In other words, mass education does not just provide a skilled workforce necessary for the perpetuation of its industrial base but, more significantly, it also forges strong national identities that could not exist beforehand. In Gellner's (1983: 36) own words:

The employability, dignity, security and self-respect of individuals, typically, and for the majority of men now hinges on their education; ... A man's education is by far his most precious investment, and in effect confers his identity on him. Modern man is not loyal to a monarch or a land or a faith, whatever he may say, but to a culture.

Therefore, rather than preceding modernity, nationalism is a by-product of industrialisation as it is only in the modern era that trans-class cultural homogeneity makes sociological sense. In the pre-industrial era, neither peasantry nor aristocracy could conceptualise the world in national terms: while the social universe of illiterate peasants rarely expanded beyond one's village, close kinship or religious affiliation, the aristocrats and top clergy relied on culture to reinforce the internal status divide. In contrast, modernity entails a substantial degree of egalitarianism where commonly shared 'high' national culture, inculcated through the educational system and other state institutions, replaces the sea of vernacular, oral 'low' cultures and establishes itself as a principal source of political legitimacy.

Other leading scholars share many aspects of Gellner's modernist explanation while downplaying his economistic account. Instead, they argue that nationalism was an invention of political elites in times of dramatic political and social changes (Hobsbawm 1990), or a by-product of development of the modern bureaucratic state (Breuilly 1993; Mann 1993), or a new form of collective imagination resulting from the expansion of print-capitalism (Anderson 1981[1983]). This modernist paradigm, and especially Gellner's theory, has provoked a lot of criticism. Some have singled out the rampant functionalism and historical determinism that underpin the paradigm (Malešević 2007; Mouzelis 2007, 1998; O'Leary 1998), others have condemned cultural essentialism, Eurocentric assumptions and a rather nostalgic view of the European empires (Eriksen 2007; Hann 2001, 1998). Nevertheless, the most critical are the ethno-symbolists, perennialists and 'early modernists' who insist on a substantial degree of continuity between the pre-modern ethnies and modern nations and who also emphasise the role emotions play in generating nationalist action (Hutchinson, 2017; 2007; Smith 2009, 1986; Roshwald 2006; Gorski 2000; Taylor 1998). In the eyes of these critics, south east Europe stands out as a clear historical case that refutes the key tenets of modernist paradigm and in particular Gellner's theory. Hence, Drakulić (2008), Canefe (2002); Minogue (1996), Orridge (1981), Wilson (1970) and Kedourie (1960) argue that nationalism emerged in the Balkans long before any visible signs of modernity or industrialisation. For example, Minogue (1996: 120) insists that 'nationalism long precedes the coming of industrialism, as in the case of Greek nationalism', whereas Hupchick (2002: 187, 212) writes about the 'national revolutionary activity ... among the Serbs and the Greeks during the opening decades of the nineteenth century' and a 'sense of ethnic group awareness, based on recognition of a common language and shared history, [that] grew and spread among the various Balkan populations (a process termed "national revival" ...) so too did the idea of group self-governance.' In a similar way, Wilson (1970: 28) describes the First Serbian Uprising of 1804 as 'the first of the great nationalistic movements of the nineteenth century'.

The modernist response to these criticisms was either to soften their concepts and explanatory claims, to look for the exceptional historical conditions for the Balkans or to emphasise the indirect influence of modernisation on the region. Thus, Mouzelis (2007, 1998) and Hall (2010) reformulate Gellner's concept of industrialism as 'modernity' which would then be able to encompass the advent of nationalism in regions such as the Balkans, Latin America or Ireland where industrialisation arrived much later. Gellner's own defence of his theory combined the idea of unique circumstances and indirect influence. He saw the Balkan merchants and bandits as key generators of nationalist doctrine: whereas the merchants were depicted as being affected by Western ideas through international trade, the religious difference of the mostly Orthodox banditry vis-à-vis their Muslim Ottoman rulers led towards their gradual transformation into nationalist rebels. As Gellner (1997: 42) puts it:

Bandit-rebels in Balkan mountains, knowing themselves to be culturally distinct from those they were fighting, and moreover linked, by faith or loss-of-faith, to a new uniquely powerful civilisation, thereby became ideological bandits: in other words, nationalists ... these rebels and their poets did absorb and disseminate western ideas in the form in which Romanticism both inverted and continued the Enlightenment.

As Hall (2010) and O'Leary (1998) rightly point out, Gellner's defence of his argument is not only unconvincing but it is also based on highly speculative assumptions which are extremely difficult to prove. This attempt of an ad hoc justification weakens the central premise of the theory. However, expanding Gellner's concept of 'industry' to 'modernity' and searching for alternative signs of modernisation, other than industrialism, in the Balkans has not proved to be a particularly fruitful strategy either. In this sense, Gellner's approach, just as other modernist theories of nationalism, seems unable to explain the Balkan case. In other words, just as with the conventional bellicist approaches which could not make clear why intensive interstate wars did not produce strong states in the region, so the conventional modernist theories of nationalism seem resigned to the view that the Balkans are a blind spot for their approach.

Nevertheless, similar to the 'war makes states' paradigm, both the criticisms as well as the defences of the approach have been focused on the wrong target. Rather than attempting to prove the impossible – that industrialisation or modernisation were in some form present in the early nineteenth-century Balkans – the emphasis should move towards the question of whether the Balkan uprisings of the early nineteenth century and later had anything to do with nationalist ideology.

My argument is that, even more so than organised violence, nationalism was a latecomer to the region. More specifically, in what follows, I demonstrate that nationalist goals and principles were largely insignificant as a source of social mobilisation in the Balkans. This applies not only to the majority, of mostly peasant population, but also to the many members of the political elites that were at the helm of these early uprisings. Furthermore, I argue that even when the Balkan states embarked on large-scale protracted wars at the beginning of the twentieth century, nationalism still remained an ideology that influenced a minority of citizens inhabiting the Balkan states. In other words, contrary to the common understanding that the modernist theories cannot explain the Balkan case, I show otherwise. However, as classical modernism, and Gellner's model in particular, do not devote enough attention to the complex relationship between nationalism, state formation and social stratification, it is necessary to articulate an alternative, grounded, modernist explanation.

If we define nationalism as an ideology that 'rests on the popularly shared perceptions and corresponding practices that posit the nation as a principal unit of human solidarity and political legitimacy' (Malešević 2011: 75), then early nineteenth-century uprisings in south east Europe could not be described as nationalist even in a minimalist sense. One of the important legacies of life under the Ottoman Empire was the dominance of religion, kinship and status ranks over 'ethnic' attachments (Kumar 2017). The millet system fortified religious divisions and in this process subdued any sense of articulated cultural difference. For example, the Rum millet included all Orthodox Christian populations regardless of their 'ethnic' origin and the vernacular languages spoken. Since Greek became a lingua franca of the Rum millet, mastering the language well and moving to the city usually meant becoming a 'Greek'. In other words, being a 'Greek' was a status category, a mechanism for social mobility, that had neither 'ethnic' nor political meaning as an overwhelming majority of middle-class Orthodox Christians ('Greeks') had no inclination towards forming an independent Greek nation state (Kitromilides 2010; Roudometoff 2001).

In this context, the various Balkan uprisings of the early nineteenth century – such as the First (1804–13) and Second Serbian Uprisings (1815–17), Hadži-Prodan's rebellion of 1813 and the Wallachian and Cretan insurrections of 1821 – were the result of internal turmoil within the Ottoman empire, rather than what they were seen to be in the West – 'the revolutions for national liberation'. Even the largest conflict of this period, the Greek War of Independence (1821–29), had little to do with clearly articulated nationalist aspirations and much more with Ottoman internal instabilities coupled with the wider geo-political pressures of the Great Powers. The majority of participants taking part in these uprisings and conflicts had no sense of what sovereign nation meant. Even the political leadership of these movements had no ambition to establish independent nation states. All these uprisings, including the Greek War of Independence, were chaotic, highly contingent events comprising elements of social discontent, fear, opportunism and necessity, where nationalist principles were virtually nonexistent (Malešević 2013b; Roudometoff 2001).

The first two significant rebellions of the early nineteenth century, the Serbian uprisings of 1804 and 1815, were profoundly contingent historical events which were neither inspired nor undertaken in the name of sovereign nationhood. The principal leaders of the rebellions, Đorđe Petrović-Karađorđe and Miloš Obrenović, were opportune traders who quickly realised that the social frustrations of local peasantry could be channelled in a direction that would benefit their personal influence and ultimately help their ambition to establish a monopoly on pork trade with the Habsburg Empire (Meriage 1977; Paxton 1972).[6] Both leaders were

---

[6] Both Karađorđe and Obrenović were wealthy peasant pig dealers who made fortunes by exporting pigs to the Habsburg Empire. Once Obrenović established his rule in Serbia, his monopoly on pig trade made him one of the richest men in Europe: 'Miloš ... was to accumulate, by his abdication in 1839, a capital worth 1,078,000 golden sovereigns, 53 per cent in cash and 47 per cent in perianal and real property' (Pavlowitch 1981: 148).

illiterate, their lifestyle and system of rule was modelled on the Ottoman example, and instead of demanding national independence for Serbia, they were engaged in internal Ottoman conflict vouching 'to restore the order on behalf of the Sultan' and remove the disloyal and ill-disciplined ayans and janissaries (Roudometoff 2001: 231; Djordjević and Fischer-Galati 1981; Pavlowitch 1981). As there were no discernible intellectuals on the territories of Ottoman Serbia at this time, support for the uprisings came from the cultural and religious elites based in the Habsburg Empire.[7] However, even these individuals – such as the leader of the Habsburg Serbian Orthodox population, Stevan Stratimirović of Karlovac – did not envisage formation of an independent Serbian state for the Serbian nation but instead advocated establishment of a Slavic Orthodox Empire 'ruled by a Russian grand duke' (Meriage 1977: 189). Hence, neither political, cultural nor economic elites had any inclination towards national self-determination whereas the majority of the, essentially peasant, population had no understanding of what a nation is (Stokes 1976).

While there is no doubt that in the Greek War of Independence some participants among the cultural and political elites were influenced by the French and American ideas of popular sovereignty, the driving force of the conflict was more religious and social than national. Despite the later, nationalist, re-interpretation of events leading to this war and the war itself as being motivated by the clearly defined goals of 'national liberation', this is far from the truth. For example, the top Greek Orthodox clergy, wealthy merchant families and the Ottoman Christian administrators (i.e. Phanariots) were not particularly interested in the demise of the Ottoman system under which they largely prospered as the leaders of churches, trade, banking, administration and foreign policy. Moreover, both the Phanariot and Boyar (Christian) families were often the pillars of this very system, enjoying various privileges and large-scale estates. Hence, the outbreak of conflict, later dubbed the Greek War of Independence, was essentially a power struggle between the two camps of Christian elites. The uprising started not in Greece but in the Dunabian Principalities (today's Romania) and it consisted of a chaotic and messy series of events involving prolonged internal rivalry, initially between the Boyars and Phanariots and later between different sections of very diverse 'Greek society' with the final outcome decided exclusively by

---

[7] Early nineteenth-century Serbia was characterised by rampant illiteracy including the overwhelming majority of the Orthodox priests. It was only with the establishment of political autonomy that the first fully literate professionals were present on Serbia's territory. Those included Serbian-speaking teachers and administrators imported from the Habsburg Empire (Stoianovich 1994). See Chapter 8.

the direct involvement of Britain, France and Russia (Glenny 2000; Mazower 2000). The attempt to trace a direct link between these unpredictable and chaotic events with the activities of small secret societies, such as Filiki Eteria, Philorthodox Organisation, or Big Brotherhood, based outside the Greek territories which allegedly had devised plans for the establishment of Greek nation state, are largely unfounded. Prominent members of these societies advocated different and, often mutually exclusive, visions of cultural, religious or social renewal with the focus on restoration of the Byzantine Empire rather than pursuing a goal of independent Greek polity (Roudometoff 2001; Kitromilides 1994).

The traditional historiography has also made much of the role played by social bandits (hajduks, hajduts, uskoks, khlepts and kaçaks) in the early nineteenth-century Balkan uprisings, depicting them as guerillas fighting for the national cause. Nevertheless, most of these individuals were completely ignorant of nationalist aspirations, and were often simple opportunists willing to switch sides and prey on both the Muslim and Christian peasantry (Pelt 2010: 224; Glenny 2000; Pavlowitch 1999). The idea of shared national heritage and history meant next to nothing for most khlepts, hajduks and kaçaks as their worldview was much more parochial. For example, when a visiting scholar flatteringly compared leading klepht leader Nikotsaras to the ancient Greek hero Achilles, the klepht leader was insulted by this comparison: 'What rubbish are you talking about? Who is this Achilles?' (Kakridis, 1963: 252).

Since the overwhelming majority of the population in south east Europe at that time was peasants whose sense of belonging oscillated between local (kinship, village) and religious attachments (Orthodox Christianity and Islam), there was no room for comprehending the world in national terms. In this world, the networks of micro-solidarity were still disconnected from the society-wide nationalist narrative. Thus, to enhance their support in the uprisings, leaders had to rely on clan and family name recognition, religiously inspired prophecies that linked the collapse of the Ottoman Empire to the Second Coming of Christ and 'the authority of the Orthodox [Russian] tsar.. and on loyalty towards the sultan'. However, in most instances, coercion was the decisive source for mobilisation. For example, Karađorđe 'threatened to burn villages of those who did not appear [on the battlefield] ... or to decapitate Serbs [Christians] who helped Turks [Muslims]' (Stokes 1976: 83).

Therefore, the Balkan case does not falsify modernist accounts of nationalism as there was no nationalism in the Balkans before industrialisation or modernity. Not only was the majority of the population oblivious to nationalist ideology but so were, for the most part, the leaders of the early nineteenth century uprisings in south east Europe. Furthermore, Gellner's emphasis on literacy and the role of educational institutions in forging viable national identities finds much support in the post-independence period.

Although the second half of the nineteenth century saw the new Balkan states invest heavily in building large-scale nation-state-centric state apparatuses, it took a long time to create a literate and schooled citizenry. For example, as late as 1864, the literacy rate in Serbia was only 4.2 per cent while, by 1884, the literacy rate was just 4.5 per cent among men and 1.5 per cent among women in Bulgaria. Greece was in a slightly better position but the population was still overwhelmingly illiterate: in 1840, only 12.5 per cent of men and 6.3 per cent of women had basic literacy skills (Roudometoff 2001; Ekmečić 1991). The first primary Bulgarian and Montenegrin schools were opened in 1835 and 1934 respectively, whereas the Albanian-speaking population did not have a single primary school until 1887 (Biondich 2011; Lederer 1969).

As, before independence, the Orthodox Church was a most significant institution of what Gellner (1983) would call 'exo-socialisation', it is interesting to briefly explore its relationship with the nationalist ideology. Although after independence the autocephalous Orthodox Churches had become the beacons of ethno-nationalisms, during the Ottoman rule they were generally opposed to ideas and principles of national sovereignty. The Orthodox patriarchs, bishops and other senior clergymen enjoyed a privileged position within the Ottoman millet structure and were certain that independence would open the door for the potential proselytism of the Roman Catholic and Protestant churches. Furthermore, the church establishment was particularly hostile to the Enlightenment and Romanticism-inspired secularism, liberalism and republicanism that underpinned the nascent nationalist movements, and sternly resisted any initiatives that promoted the ideas and practices associated with the pre-Byzantine (i.e. pagan) traditions. Hence, the Greek Orthodox Church opposed the standardisation of Greek vernacular on its ancient model. The Patriarch Gregory V's encyclical on education (1819) strongly condemned the practice of naming children after ancient Greek heroes and denounced even rudimentary attempts to propagate republican and nationalist ideas, describing them as 'the plots of the devil that often masquerade behind the clamoring for liberty and equality' (Kitromilides 2010: 38).

Whereas the top clergy were actively hostile to nationalism, the ordinary priests were largely ignorant of nationalist ideology. As they were hardly distinct from other peasants, most ordinary priests were illiterate, lacking even basic knowledge of the Bible, were not able to deliver sermons and were often prone to combining Christian and pagan traditions. For example, as Radić (2003: 158) emphasises, 'the Serbian clergymen were almost identical to other peasants. They were farmers and herdsmen. The only difference was their clothes and beards'. In this sense, just as with the population at large, the local priests could not conceptualise the world in national terms. The ordinary priests were also indistinguishable from their fellow peasants in their understanding of the word through the prism of micro-level solidarities which remained disconnected from wider nationalist narratives. It is important to emphasise that, despite Orthodox Christianity being an important source of collective identification and probably the only pre-modern mechanism for exo-socialisation, the Church's institutional influence was very weak. Throughout the Balkans, church attendance was rather low and sporadic, confessions and communions were rare and the religious focus was on 'sin and preservation of one's honor and moral purity' and worshiping individual saints rather than on following the Christian teachings and observing Church practices (Folić 2001). Hence, before independence and the development of state apparatuses, no social institution, including the Church, was able to significantly penetrate the microcosm of the local, kinship and the village-based traditions. Simply put, there was no institutional and organisational space for nationalism in the pre-independence and early post-independence Balkans.

It is the intensive state building that took off in the second half of the nineteenth and early twentieth centuries that had direct impact on the presence of nationalist discourses. In other words, rather than being a cause of state formation, nationalism was an outcome of state building as all Balkan governments started investing a lot of energy and resources in what Mosse (1991) calls 'the nationalization of the masses'. Hence, the expansion of education, coupled with the ever-increasing literacy rates, became a crucial vehicle for the state-sponsored inculcation of nationalist ideologies. Thus, for example, the newly formed state intellectuals in Serbia were commissioned to write textbooks and other literature which depicted Serbs as the 'first and oldest people in Europe' who have 'founded Belgrade several thousand years before Christ' (Milojević 1871: 74). They also insisted that the Serbian people were very numerous in the past, have 'inhabited three continents, Asia, Africa and Europe long before Christ' and that all the peoples in the entire pre-Ottoman Balkans 'spoke old Serbian language' (Petković 1926: 57; Gopčević 1889: 12). Similarly, Greek and Bulgarian authorities financed publications of books, plays, paintings and musical creations that either traced the origins of their nations far into the past or simply glorified the 'national genius' of Greeks and Bulgarians respectively. So Constantine Paparrigopoulos's 'the History of the Greek Nation' (1865–74), which insists on the uninterrupted continuity between the ancient and present-day Greeks, was financed by the Greek government and was quickly instituted as the official account of national origin and is still used in the schools and colleges all over Greece (Roudometoff 2001: 107–10). In addition to the military, bureaucracy and police, nationalist education became a budgetary priority. Thus, Bulgaria's budget for education expanded from 1.5 per cent in 1879 to 11.2 in 1911, and it grew by a staggering 650 per cent in thirty-two years (Biondich 2011: 54; Pippidi 2010: 128). Lavish state-sponsored institutions of 'high' culture – such as national academies and learned societies, universities, theaters, opera houses, museums and concert halls – were set up in all capitals and some provincial cities throughout south east Europe. The Balkan governments provided financial support for newspapers and other mass media so that, by the early twentieth century, a large number of nationalist newspapers were in circulation. For example, by the late 1920s and early 1930s, Yugoslavia had fifty main daily papers (Case 2010: 294). The Balkan states also supported irredentist movements in neighbouring countries and attempted to project their geo-political ambitions, such as the visions of Greater Greece (*Megali Idea*), Greater Serbia (*Načertanije*) and Greater Bulgaria (*Velika i obedinena Bulgarija*), into the educational and artistic institutions (see Chapter 5). In all these cases, state elites made enormous efforts to tap into the world of micro-level groups and make ordinary individuals into loyal patriots.

Nevertheless, despite the unprecedented nationalist propaganda penetrating all state apparatuses – and especially education, mass media and civil society – nationalism remained an ideology of the elite minority, largely not shared by the rural population and urban labourers until well into the twentieth century. The intensive state building of the second half of the nineteenth century clearly privileged civil servants, the police and military establishment, state intellectuals and large businessmen. Hence, it is mostly this social strata that became fully loyal to the new nation states and it is the members of these professions that were overrepresented in the nationalist, irredentist and expansionist associations and projects. In direct contrast, the rest of the society, including the majority peasantry, manual labourers and a tiny sector of the lower middle class, for the most part did not experience any benefits from state development and as such were less enthusiastic or even hostile towards nationalist ideas. It is true that upon independence in both Serbia and Bulgaria, most peasants became de jure small landholders, while in Greece they found themselves de facto in such a position.[8] Nevertheless, these initial

---

[8] Although from 1832, land in Greece was in state ownership, farmers have taken over most of this land without any interference from state authorities (Mouzelis 1978).

gains, and further promises made by various governments, soon proved to be inadequate or unfulfilled and most peasants remained poor. With the governments' focus on state building, the true winners of this uneven modernisation were the civil servants, military, police and other state employees. In contrast, the majority of the rural population and the small but rising urban proletariat had to carry the burden of the heavy costs associated with the intensified state development and the maintenance of the enlarged state apparatus. The new states demanded cash taxation and this forced farmers to enter the market and seek credit, usually at quite unfavourable rates. Such a policy provoked deep animosity towards the city and its most recognisable representatives – the civil servants. Peasant demonstrations and occasional jacqueries expressed this in slogans such as: 'All kaputaši [wearers of city coats; townsfolk] should be killed' (Biondich 2011: 60). In other words, the swift, state-imposed modernisation and industrialisation created a sharp class polarisation with, on the one hand, an urban state-created strata, favouring further state expansion both externally and internally, and on the other hand, mostly rural (and some urban) producers, favouring state transformation or attenuation of state power. These different structural positions fostered development of different ideological orientations: whereas the state bureaucracy, police, military establishment and the state intellectuals supported étatisme and nationalism, both of which were seen as the principal source of state legitimacy, the peasantry and the urban poor were more sympathetic to religious conservatism, peasant populism and anti-statism (Stojanović 2017; 2003; Pippidi 2010; Milosavljević 2003; Roudometof 2001). In other words, the Balkan rulers and cultural elites were not successful in establishing strong links between organisational capacity, ideological penetration and the envelopment of micro-solidarity. Although nationalism expanded substantially over this period, it still was not fully grounded.

Therefore, despite their palpable visibility, Balkan nationalisms of the late nineteenth and early twentieth centuries were neither very deep nor extensively widespread. In other words, this nationalism was far from being fully embedded in the organisational, ideological and micro-interactional realms of the social order. Most peasants opposed irredentist adventures, wars of territorial expansion and urban uprisings (i.e. Serbo-Ottoman war of 1875, April Uprising of 1876, Serbo-Bulgarian war of 1885) and were often coerced to economically and politically support the war effort (Biondich 2011; Pippidi 2010). Furthermore, to make the rural population more receptive to nationalism, state authorities relied on anti-Semitism, xenophobia and the scapegoating of religious and ethnic minorities. In this sense, rather than being a spontaneous expression of 'age old' animosities and hatred, a great deal of violence was deliberately orchestrated from the top to engineer a sense of inter-ethnic fear and ultimately to provoke internal (national) cohesion. For example, in the run-up to the Balkan wars, the Greek, Serbian and Bulgarian officers and soldiers were dispatched to Macedonia to ferment inter-ethnic hostilities, and were dressed up as the indigenous brigands 'in order to conceal what was essentially state-sponsored violence' (Biondich 2011: 71). Similarly, state intelligentsia, government ministers and state-sponsored education and mass media were often the principal vehicles of anti-Semitism, Islamophobia and hatred against other mino-rities in Romania, Bulgaria, Greece and Serbia (Case 2010; Roudometof 2001; Mazower 2000).

Although by the beginning of the Balkan wars of 1912–13 and World War I, nationalist ideologies penetrated greater sectors of population and wars helped foster a degree of inter-group cohesion, even then the major-ity of the population in south east Europe was not fully 'nationalized' and most peasants and urban labourers remained skeptical if not completely opposed to these wars. For example, when a Greek activist persistently insisted on finding out whether the local peasantry of Salonika saw themselves as Greeks or Bulgarians, the peasants did not understand the question: ' ... whenever I asked them what they were – Romaioi [i.e. Greeks] or Voulgaroi [Bulgarians], they stared at me uncomprehendingly. ... Well, we're Christians – what do you mean, Romaioi or Voulgaroi?' (Mazower 2000: 50).

As Boindich (2011: 43) points out, 'in the period between 1878 and 1923, when the Balkans experienced some of its worst political violence, the bulk of population, the peasantry, still lacked a strong national con-sciousness'. Most peasant recruits were unwilling to fight, were inclined to desert or avoid conscription and were not particularly enthusiastic about the territorial expansion of their states. As well documented by Leon Trotsky's 1912–13 Balkan war correspondence, Serbian peasant conscripts were apathetic and inimical to war efforts and nationalist projects. He characterised them as 'depressed and extremely homesick for their villages' (Trotsky 1980: 121). In other words, despite years of nationalist indoctrination, Serbian peasants were still much more attached to their village or kin-based micro groups than to the imagined community of Serbs. The micro-level solidarities remained disconnected from the wider nationalist project.

Hence, south east Europe is not a blind spot for the modernist theories of nationalism. Not only was there no nationalism in the Balkans before modernisation and industrialisation, but nationalist ideology, even more so than organised violence and warfare, came very late to this part of the world. However, modernism requires some fine-tuning to account for the often inversely proportional relationship between social stratification and nationalism. While most modernist theories see nationalism as the decisive social cement that binds diverse citizenry into stable and cohesive societies able to generate economic growth and social development, the Balkan experience indicates an alternative trajectory. The nineteenth and early twentieth-century history of the region shows how, rather than acting as a cohesive social force, nationalisms in south east Europe were often a source of internal discord: state-supported irredentism and pursuit of territorial expansion were regularly perceived as ideological projects of the urban elite which could only, and usually did, bring misery to the countryside. Hence, instead of generating greater social unity and solidarity and thus potentially stimulating social development, state-enforced attempts at nationalist mobilisation tended to further polarise already extremely divided societies.

Conclusion

There is a widespread view of the Balkans as the region which, for most of its history, was brim-full of protracted violence and nationalist euphoria. From the early nineteenth century 'national' uprisings to the 1990s wars of Yugoslav secession, south east Europe has been seen as a 'powder keg of Europe' (Kaplan 1994). Moreover, both nationalism and violence are regularly singled out as the most important impediments for the social development of the region. Nevertheless, a careful historical sociological analysis shows that neither of these two common perceptions holds up well to empirical scrutiny. Instead of being an inherent feature of the Balkan landscape, both nationalism and organised violence are, historically speaking, fairly recent arrivals to the region. In a similar vein, it is not the abundance of nationalisms and wars than have stifled development of the region but, in fact, it was often the lack of their organised prevalence that hampered wider social advance. The fact that much of the warfare in the Balkans was small-scale, sporadic and disorganised meant that such wars could not help enhance the organisational capacities of states in the region. Likewise, the uneven, narrow, belated and rigid top-down spread of nationalist ideology often mitigated against the development of internal social cohesion, thus preventing the emergence of a degree of social consensus necessary for economic and political development. Nonetheless, this is not to say that war making by itself inevitably generates strong states and societies, or that the proliferation of nationalism automatically leads to societal well-being and economic prosperity.

The view of conventional bellicist historical sociology that protracted warfare is likely to eventually yield infrastructurally strong, centralised states capable of creating political stability, social order and economic growth, requires major amending. Although the institution of the state might have originated in warfare, its viability and expansion requires much more than sustained violence. Not all wars make states and even those that make states do not necessarily create strong polities. As Tallet (1992: 198) points out, Tilly's account suffers from the chicken-and-egg symptom. It is not clear what comes first: 'whether an efficient and developed bureaucracy was the precondition for the growth in size and complexity of the armies ... or whether growth in armies stimulated growth in the bureaucratic structures of the state'. Thus, warfare is better understood as a test of state strength rather than as an impetus for state formation. Balkan warfare clearly demonstrates the complexity of this relationship. Wars did not create independent polities in the early nineteenth-century Balkans. Instead, independence was a highly contingent event resulting from the combination of internal organisational structures of the weakened Ottoman Empire and the geo-political interests of the Great Powers.[9] Similarly, as they were small-scale events, the mid to late nineteenth-century wars did not forge strong states either. The beginning of the twentieth century saw south east Europe becoming an epicentre of mass-scale warfare but much of the intensive state building took place long before the 1912–13 Balkan wars and World War I. While the mobilisation for warfare certainly played a part in the centralisation of state power and the expansion of the state's infrastructural and bureaucratic capacities, the outcome of these high-intensity wars was not strong states and vibrant civil societies. Instead, both the victorious and the defeated Balkan states shared almost an identical developmental trajectory in the 1920s and 1930s: authoritarian rule, stifling of parliamentarism and civil society, huge indebt-ness to international creditors, state monopolies in the economy, rampant nepotism and corruption, heightened class polarisation and perpetual animosity between the urban and rural population.

To fully understand this particular outcome, which in many respects contradicts the central thesis of the conventional bellicist approach, it is crucial to focus on the role of nationalism and social stratification in the Balkan societies. In contrast to the normative views that see rampant nationalist attachments as an obstacle for social progress, the historical

---

[9] As Biondich (2011: 41) succinctly puts it: 'Serbia's autonomous status was achieved largely through Russian Diplomacy (1817, 1829), Greek independence (1830) through Anglo-French-Russian intervention, and Bulgarian autonomy through direct Russian military intervention followed by Great Power diplomatic fiat (1878)'.

and sociological reality indicates that a degree of national solidarity is often a precondition for effective political and economic development. The modernist paradigm in the study of nationalism, and Gellner's work (1997: 25; 1964: 114) especially, argue that not only are nationalism and economic growth fully compatible but, as the two are the main sources of political legitimacy in the modern/industrial era, they entail each other. Furthermore, and in contrast to the primordialist and perennialist accounts, the modernists rightly insist on the historical novelty of this synergetic relationship between nationalism and socio-economic development. The Balkan experience fully vindicates both of these claims.

Firstly, contrary to the primordial and perennial interpretations, the early nineteenth-century uprisings in south east Europe had nothing to do with nationalism but were a direct by-product of imperial geo-politics and internal weaknesses of the Ottoman social order. Rather than being a motivational source of state building, nationalist ideology was a consequence of state formation. Nevertheless, even after decades of intensive state-sponsored 'nationalisation of the masses', this ideology remained a profoundly weak force unable to motivate the majority of Balkan populations until well into the twentieth century.

Secondly, the corollary of the state's inability to swiftly turn peasants into Serbs, Greeks, Bulgarians or Albanians was lack of internal consensus on developmental goals and ambitions. As nationalism did not penetrate most layers of the Balkan societies, there was no adequate social glue to provide a shared vision of national solidarity necessary for radical economic, political and social reforms. This Gellnerian account of the relationship between nationalism and social progress requires an analytical extension to capture the internal dynamics of south east European societies where, rather than being a device of social cohesion, nationalism was often a source of deep class friction. Although the Balkan states invested heavily into the organisational capacity and ideological penetration of their societies, they were still unable to capture the micro-level solidarities of the different social strata.

Therefore, the popular image of the Balkan Peninsula as a historical hub of aggressive nationalisms and perpetual violence, both of which allegedly thwarted its progress, is really an inverted, camera obscura, image of the historical reality. It is really the absence of protracted organised violence and society-wide nationalisms that have heavily contributed to often sluggish development of the region.

8   Balkan Piedmont?

Introduction

At the beginning of the nineteenth century, Serbia was a puny principality that lacked most aspects of statehood. The autonomy gained in the First Serbian Uprising (1804) resulted in an entity that virtually had no military, bureaucracy, police, educational system, industry, urban centres or intellectual life. Yet only a century later, this polity developed into the strongest political entity in the Balkan Peninsula, which, by the end of WWI, controlled extensive territory and millions of inhabitants. Moreover, in this period, Serbia emerged as the rising regional power with a large and effective military machine focused on further territorial expansion. How did the Serbian state develop and expand so quickly? How was it possible for such a small entity, existing in the midst of the three great empires, to embark on 115 years of continuous territorial expansion? What role did nationalism play in this process?

In this chapter, I engage with these questions by challenging some conventional historiographic interpretations that centre on the Piedmont-style 'natural' aspirations of all Serbs to live in a single state (Pavlowitch 2002: 95; Mackenzie 1996: 203–30, 1994: 153–62). I argue that these national ambitions were not the primary cause of state expansion but that instead the expansionist nationalism was a side effect of intense and protracted conflict at the organisational core of the Serbian state. More specifically, and in line with the theoretical model articulated in the first part of this book, my argument brings together geo-political, organisational, ideological and micro-interactional factors in order to highlight the historically contingent character of state and nation formation in this part of the world. The chapter focuses on different forms of nationalism that have emerged in Serbia and among Serbian populations outside Serbia, particularly in Bosnia and Herzegovina. I argue that, while nationalism did ultimately play an important role in state formation in Serbia, this had little to do with the popular mobilisation of its citizenry and much more

188

with the internal political struggle between the supporters of the two competing royal households. In this context, nationalism in Serbia emerged as a by-product of fierce and protracted elite competition whereas Serbian nationalism in Bosnia acquired very different attributes and was shaped by the complex and contradictory ideological currents of late nineteenth and early twentieth-century Austro-Hungarian intellectual and social life.

The Improbable Rise of Serbia

Mainstream historiography interprets the First Serbian Uprising (1804–13) as a stepping stone towards an independent and inevitable statehood. Together with Hadži Prodan's revolt (1815) and Second Serbian Uprising (1815–17), these violent episodes are seen as constituting the Serbian Revolution that ultimately established an autonomous tributary principality of Serbia and in this way provided an organisational cornerstone for the future enlarged and independent Serbian state (MacKenzie 1994, Pavlowich 2002). By 1830, this political entity was officially recognised by the Ottoman rulers: the Hatt-i Sharif was issued to formally acknowledge the autonomous existence of the principality and to confirm Miloš Obrenović as its hereditary prince. At that time, the principality was confined to a very small stretch of territory: 38,000 square kilometres and a population of fewer than 700,000 people (Pavlowich 2002: 33). Over the next four decades, Serbia negotiated the withdrawal of Ottoman soldiers from its territory and expelled most of its Muslim population. By the time the state gained international recognition, at the Berlin Congress in 1878, it had expanded to 48,600 square kilometres and 1.7 million inhabitants. Upon independence, the ruling Obrenović dynasty transformed the principality into a kingdom with Milan Obrenović crowned king in 1882. Over the next three decades, the kingdom introduced parliamentary government (1888 constitution) and embarked on an intensive programme of social and economic development (Stojanović 2017: 22–47). Independent Serbia was embroiled in several conflicts, including a short war with Bulgaria (1885), one coup d'état (1903) and 'the pig war' (1906), that is, a trade embargo imposed by its main trading partner, Austria-Hungary. Nevertheless, the most significant events in the Serbian state's rise were the two Balkan wars (1912–13). The military victories in these two wars resulted in an extraordinary enlargement of Serbia's territory and population. In August 1913, the Serbian state doubled its size as it gained 40,000 square kilometres in territory and an additional 1.2 million people. This territorial and population expansion continued after the First World War with Serbs living in the territories of the former Habsburg Empire becoming a political target of the ever-expanding Serbian state. Serbia's military victories in the war proved decisive in fostering an agreement with the representatives of the Austro-Hungarian South Slavs to establish a new state – the Kingdom of Serbs, Croats and Slovenes – ruled by the Serbian dynasty, the Karađorđevićs, and with a Serbian prime minister. By now, the newly established kingdom had close to 12 million inhabitants, comprised 247,542 square kilometres and included a relative majority of all Serbs. In this context, Serbia was perceived as the Piedmont of the Balkans – a political force spearheading the inevitable and natural unification of Serbs and other South Slavs (Mackenzie 1994: 153–5).[1]

This conventional narrative of Serbia's rise is often premised on the idea that the Serbian population throughout Balkan Peninsula shared a strong aspiration towards living in an independent and unified state of all Serbs, with or without other South Slavic peoples. Hence, the dramatic expansion of the state has often been understood as due to widespread nationalist sentiment and an intense popular motivation to establish an enlarged Serbian state and in this way resurrect the pre-Ottoman Serbian empire. For example, military historian Richard Hall (2000: 2) argues that 'each Balkan people envisioned the restoration of the medieval empires on which they based their national ideas' and that 'Serbs sought to recover the extent of the [fourteenth century] empire of Stephan Dushan'. In a similar fashion, Christopher Clark (2012: 22) insists that the 'Greater Serbian vision ... was woven deeply into the culture and identity of the Serbs. The memory of Dušan's empire resonated within the extraordinarily vivid tradition of Serbian popular epic songs'.

This chapter challenges such conventional and dominant interpretations. I argue that while nationalism did play an important role in the later stages of Serbia's rise, it in itself was not the cause of state expansion. Moreover I attempt to show that, rather than being a widespread popular sentiment, nationalist ideology was quite weak among the ordinary Serbian population both within and even more outside Serbia proper. Instead, nationalism was a by-product of radically changing geo-politics as well as intensified competition within Serbian political and military elites. In other words, rather than impelling state expansion and nation building, nationalist ideology emerged as structural outcome of the

---

[1] The highly popular Piedmont thesis is built around the idea that Piedmont played a central role in the unification of Italy in 1871. However, recent Italian historiography has challenged the conventional view of the Piedmont's role in Italian unification (see Riall 2009). Arguably, Piedmont did much less towards forming a nation state than did Serbia; the hard military work was done by France (1859), Garibaldi (1860) and Prussia (1866, 1870–71). (I thank John Breuilly for this point).

transformed European and Balkan geo-political contexts, which in turn shaped the shifting dynamics of elite politics in Belgrade. More specifically, this chapter focuses on the different trajectories of nation and state building in Serbia and among the Serbian population in the rest of south east Europe. I aim to show that while in Serbia proper expansionist nationalism developed out of changed geo-politics and persistent elite conflict, Serbian nationalism beyond Serbia was much more ambiguous, contradictory and combined with other ideological currents (from anarchism to liberalism to socialism). Hence, in order to fully understand the dynamics of state and nation formation in Serbia and among Serbian populations outside its borders, it is paramount to analyse the organisational, ideological, geo-political and micro-interactional processes that shaped Serbia into a miniature rising power.

The Organisational Capacity and Geo-Politics

The relatively dramatic rise of Serbia for much of the nineteenth and early twentieth centuries is truly remarkable when measured against its extremely humble beginnings. Although the Balkans was a relatively developed area of the Ottoman Empire, as the empire experienced military defeats and economic decline and retreated from the region, the empire's organisational structure became feeble.[2] This was reflected in the distinctly underdeveloped transport, communications and civil service, as well as in the very low levels of urbanisation, industrialisation, banking and commerce. As a consequence, the semi-autonomous Serbian principality inherited an extremely weak organisational base. For example, as already mentioned in the Chapter 7, in 1815, the entire civil service of the new Serbian polity consisted of only 24 people (Pavlowitch 2002: 35; Stokes 1976: 4). The new principality had no factories, railroads, national bank or large urban centres. Its largest town, Belgrade, had fewer than 25,000 inhabitants, most of whom were not ethnic Serbs. The countryside was also thinly populated and characterised by low levels of land cultivation. There was no adequate transport system as the country boasted only 800 km of paved roads, thus making long-distance trade and travel slow, expensive and impractical. The principality had no proper military

---

[2] This is not to reproduce a popular stereotype of the Ottoman Empire as the 'sick man of Europe'. Much of recent scholarship questions such traditional interpretations of decline, presented as uniform and inevitable. Instead as Kumar (2017: 119) points out, recent findings provide 'a much more qualified picture of Ottoman "decline", suggesting reorganisation and reform as much as the signs of weakness and failure'. However, many of these reforms did not spread evenly throughout the empire and the border regions such as Serbia were substantially less affected by these changes.

or police force and the three main uprisings were undertaken by fairly disorganised and poorly armed groups consisting of Serbian and other volunteers from Austro-Hungary and other European countries, local notables, bandits and some peasants (Malešević 2012: 220–30; Meriage 1977: 189).

Such an organisationally feeble entity would never have been able to challenge the Ottoman Empire and ultimately achieve full independence but for broader tectonic geo-political changes. Both the Habsburg-Ottoman (1787–91) and Russo-Ottoman (1787–92) wars had a profound impact on the Balkans. Though the Ottoman Empire did recover most of its initial losses to the Habsburg Empire (including most of the Serbian lands), it experienced much greater territorial losses in its war with Russia and, taken together, these wars significantly weakened the Porte. The direct consequence of these wars was the Russian annexation of the Crimean Khanate and increased involvement in Balkan affairs. Russian encroachment on the Balkans also led the Habsburgs gradually to refocus their attention on the region. At the same time, the Ottoman Empire was experiencing internal turmoil with rebellions by the janissaries (a military order formed mostly of young Christians) and resistance from the Greek Orthodox hierarchy in opposition to Selim III's attempts to modernise the army and the administration. In this context, the relatively meteoric rise of the Serbian state was largely a by-product of Ottoman weakness and the growing pressure of the two neighbouring Empires: the Romanovs and the Habsburgs.

In this new geopolitical environment, the Balkan uprisings were supported and glorified in the West as the legitimate resistance of Christians against oppressive Muslim power. It is no accident that most Balkan rebellions and revolts involved a significant number of foreign volunteers and, in the Serbian case, Serb officers and soldiers from the Habsburg Empire (Malešević 2012: 220–30).

As Serbian statehood gained a foothold, its rulers invested substantial resources into state (and later nation) building. Thus, within a relatively short period of time, the Serbian state had acquired a large administrative apparatus: by 1837, the number of civil servants had grown twentyfold (Stokes 1976). In order to centralise its power and establish a monopoly on the legitimate use of violence, legislation and taxation, the Serbian state also adopted a new constitution modelled on the most centralised Western European constitutions, such as those of France and Belgium (Pippidi 2010: 125). The new, French-style administration with district prefects, tenured civil servant posts and civil codes was introduced to weaken the autonomy of local municipalities and make decision-making more effective. The government also organised population censuses, introduced registers of ownership and established title deeds on land. The infrastructure was developed immensely so that by 1883, the state had five times more paved roads that it had in the 1850s, a railroad system was put in place and between 1885 and 1912 the total length of railway lines increased by 285 per cent (Lampe and Jackson 1982: 211). The state also invested extensively in the development of industry so, whereas there was only one factory in 1847, by 1906 there were 500 large-scale industrial enterprises (Stoianovich 1994: 201–248; Djordjević 1970). Perhaps the most impressive organisational transformation was to be observed in the security sector. Even though the principality of Serbia had virtually no military or police, by the end of the century, the state was heavily militarised and policed. The government established a military academy, substantially increased the officer corps, introduced universal conscription, allocated a large military budget and created a sizable standing army (Roudometof 2001: 167). This military build-up was particularly pronounced on the eve of and during the Balkan Wars. Serbia mobilised over 255,000 soldiers for the first Balkan war and as many as 300,000 soldiers for the second Balkan war (Hall 2000: 16–18, 45, 108–19). These numbers were truly astonishing for a small state numbering only 3 million people.

The victories achieved in the second Balkan war transformed Serbia into the major military power in the Balkans. State territory doubled in size, from 18,650 to 33,891 square miles, and the country's population increased by more than 1.5 million (Hall 2000). However, this impressive and relatively swift organisational development was for the most part financed by external loans. Initially, the new state benefited from its strong economic ties with the Habsburg Empire to which most of its goods were exported (e.g. the pork trade) and from which it received substantial loans. Then, as the Serbian state strengthened and changed its alliances (i.e. from Austria to Russia and France), it borrowed money from other sources, mostly French banks, which ultimately owned more than three quarters of all Serbian debt (Antić 2006: 151–61). Thus, Serbia's military prowess remained heavily dependent on large external loans. In this context, territorial expansion was in part regarded by the political and military establishment as a way to obtain new resources to finance the existing debt.

State Formation and Nationalisms

The swift organisational transformation of the Serbian state was largely influenced by broader geopolitical changes. A small and weak polity had no chance of long-term survival in an environment where its imperial neighbours were constantly developing their military and economic capacities. However, there was another important trigger for state development: the internal elite conflict which riddled the new polity from the very beginning. It is my view that this deep internal polarisation contributed significantly to both state formation as well as to the rise of expansionist nationalism in later years. Serbia lacked a traditional aristocracy, many of whom were killed by the Ottomans during the battle of Maritsa in 1371 (Dinić and Ćirković 1978). A new political elite was forged through the two main uprisings of the early nineteenth century. The leaders of the two uprisings, Đorđe Petrović-Karađorđe and Miloš Obrenović, were the founders of two competing and deeply hostile royal houses. Karađorđe, who led the first uprising and was instrumental in setting the contours of future state structure, was assassinated on Obrenović's direct order and with the full knowledge and support of the Porte. This allowed the Obrenovićs to claim the throne but also polarised political, economic and military elites in Serbia for years to come. Although the Obrenović's royal family held power for much of the nineteenth century (from 1817–42 and from 1858–1903), the tensions between the two royal camps continued and even intensified at the end of nineteenth and beginning of the twentieth centuries.

This is not to say that the two leaders offered different nationalist visions of the Serbian state project or that their conflict was motivated by competing nationalisms. On the contrary, the initial motivation of both leaders was far from any nationalist goals. As both Obrenović and Karađorđević were wealthy pig traders who profited from trade with Austro-Hungary, their ambitions were at first centred on establishing personalised fiefdoms which would allow them an unhampered monopoly on pork trade with the Habsburgs. They were both wealthy but illiterate individuals who initially showed no interest in ideas of national emancipation and popular sovereignty. Utilising the social discontent of peasantry harassed and exploited by the renegade ayans (landlords) and janissaries, both leaders perceived these uprisings as internal conflicts within the Ottoman Empire rather than as a vehicle for 'national liberation'. For example, Obrenović insisted that he led an uprising not against the Ottoman Empire but 'to restore the order on behalf of the Sultan' (Roudometoff 2001: 24).[3] A similar justification appears in the memoires of the Orthodox archpriest Matija Nenadović who writes that uprising had nothing to do with the rejection of the Ottoman rule:

---

[3] See more about Obrenović and Karađorđević's self-perceptions as Ottoman subjects in Pavlowitch (1981).

[landlords] killed my father, knez Aleksa... many others throughout the whole pashalik, and in fact anyone they had been able to catch ... we want to defend ourselves until the sultan should come to hear of it and send some good vezir to help us, for we are not against the sultan...but have risen against the four dahis, our opressors. (Nenadović 1969: 68)

There was not much nationalism among early nineteenth-century Serbian elites. The two uprisings have managed to link the social discontent with the religious difference but in this period there was still no meaningful organisational and ideological connect with the local and kinship-based networks of micro-solidarity.

Nevertheless, their deep mutual animosities fostered intensified political mobilisation and support, both internally and externally. The main external support base in the early years shifted from the Porte to the Habsburgs as both royal families built and then broke alliances with the two neighbouring empires. In later years, Russia, France, Germany and Britain entered the picture with representatives of both royal houses courting their support.[4] Domestically, the focus was on building requisite institutional channels to establish a long-term support base. To dominate the new polity and to prevent competing dynastic claims, it was necessary to establish both organisational and ideological mechanisms for wider social and political mobilisation. In other words, the new rulers had to attain support not only from the nascent political and economic elites but also from the majority peasant population. As it is very difficult to achieve political mobilisation without adequate organisational and ideological structures, the competing royal houses had to build such institutional bases from scratch. Not only did the new Serbian polity lack most of the prerogatives of statehood, but the social base of the new society was just as poor. For example, an overwhelming majority of its population consisted of illiterate and impoverished landless peasants. At the time of the First Serbian Uprising, there were just two schools in the whole of the country and by 1830 this had only increased to sixteen primary schools with as few as 800 pupils and 22 teachers (Stoianovich 1994: 208–9). Even in 1864, only 4.2 per cent of the country's population was literate. The new principality had no home-grown intellectuals, teachers, qualified civil servants, doctors and other professionals, so it had to recruit them from the educated Serbs living in the Habsburg lands.[5] Such extremely low literacy rates did not allow development of a viable publishing industry

---

[4] The wider geo-political conditions played an important role in this process as France and Russia supported Serbia's independence as a buffer against the Habsburg and German influences in this part of Europe.

[5] For example, the intellectual founders of the Serbian nationalist project, Dositej Obradović and Vuk Karadžić, were both educated in the Habsburg lands.

and cultural products were largely reduced to the oral culture, including epic poetry, folk singing and dancing and other traditional village-centred activities. The principality had no theatres, museums, academies, concert halls or any other institutions of what Gellner (1983: 48–51) calls 'high culture', with literacy being a key prerequisite for popular nationalism. Hence, to be able to influence the masses, it was essential, on the one hand, to accommodate their social and economic grievances and, on the other hand, to try to mould them into loyal citizens of the new polity. In order to achieve these changes, the rulers were forced to imitate the more successful Western European models of state governance. In the process, they embarked on partial modernisation where the emphasis was largely on increasing military capacity, state centralisation and ideological control.

Consequently, in the 1830s, Serbian authorities initiated the programme of land redistribution as the new constitution prohibited large-scale land ownership and legalised the possession of small fields and forests by the village communities. One of the aims of this policy was to make the peasantry – that is, the majority of the population – loyal to the new state. In this way, Serbia was established as a country of peasant small holders. The abolition of the semi-feudal dependency of peasants, after several rebellions, was envisaged as an important catalyst of social change. However, appeasing the peasantry in social and economic terms did not mean, to use Eugene Weber's (1976) well-known term, an automatic transition 'from peasants into Serbs'. For one thing, the agrarian reform was not particularly successful in lifting ordinary peasants from poverty. Most peasants received very small plots of land that often proved insufficient for a household to be self-sustaining. The legal system also created various obstacles for mobility, ownership forcing these small farmers to work on the unprofitable fields. As Čalić (2004) demonstrated, up to two thirds of land plots in Serbia were very small, hovering around the existential minimum. This model of agrarian reform discouraged social and geographical mobility and in this way unwillingly maintained the persistence of traditional form of micro-solidarity centred on one's kinship and locality. Hence, instead of integrating the peasantry into the projects of state and nation-building these economic policies contributed towards the existing disconnect between the micro-level solidarities and the state-level nationalist narratives.

For another thing, the state authorities had to create an entire organisational and ideological apparatus that would, in the long-term, make these majority peasant populations into loyal and possibly enthusiastic citizens of the Serbian state. Hence, over much of the nineteenth century, the new state invested heavily into the creation of social and cultural infrastructure that would ultimately help transform peasants into nationally conscious Serbs. This is not to say that this was a simple and clearly articulated strategy of nation-building. Rather this was a messy process beset by internal conflicts, political contradictions and financial problems (Stoianovich,1994: 274–95, Stokes 1976: 135–78). As Dubravka Stojanović (2017) shows, many sectors of Serbian society, including some political and economic elites, were hostile towards any attempts to modernise institutions and infrastructure. For example, an opposition newspaper *Dnevni List* described some actions of the (ruling) Radical party as being influenced by the teachings of Russian populists (narod-niks/народники) such as Chernyshevsky. The Russian populists were known for being hostile to modernisation and capitalism and also for glorifying the communal life of traditional peasantry (Stojanović 2017: 104). However, there was a clear ambition on the part of both royal houses to foster partial modernisation in order to centralise power, increase revenue and secure the loyalty of their new citizens.

In this context, a proper state-supported educational system was put in place with standardised curricula at the primary level, and later also, at the secondary and tertiary levels. The number of primary schools increased from 143 (with 4,400 pupils) in 1843 to 344 (with 11,478 pupils) in 1858 to 441 (with 23,346 pupils) in 1870 (Ćunković 1971). Subsequently, literacy rates improved substantially: while in 1864, 95.8 per cent of the population was illiterate, by 1903, the literacy rate had jumped to 55 per cent in the cities and 24 per cent in the rural areas (Stojanović 2010: 1). Belgrade was well ahead all other towns and had a five-time higher literacy rate than the rest of the country (Stojanović 2017: 186).

The domestic publishing industry was established to produce the nation-centric and often explicitly expansionist school textbooks (Jelavich 1989). While in the early nineteenth century, the textbooks were quite basic and focused on factual events, from the 1850s onwards, most textbooks espoused a strong nationalist narrative (Roudometoff 2001: 127; Jelavich 1989: 47–75). The new state created the national institutions of 'high culture' – learned societies such as the Society of Serbian Scholarship (1841) which later became the Serbian Royal Academy of Sciences (1886), the Serbian National Theatre (1861), the National Library of Serbia (1832), the Belgrade Reading Rooms (1845), the National Museum of Serbia (1844), and several higher schools and the lyceum. The parliament was explicit in its demand that theatres show more domestic plays with national themes. Hence, in the second half of the nineteenth century, theatres were showing a number of plays focused on the Serbian history and recognisable individuals from the national cannon – Đurađ Branković (a medieval Serbian despot), *Seoba Srbalja* (a

Great Migrations of the Serbs), Maksim Crnojević (a figure from the epic poetry), Miloš Obilić (fourteenth century Serbian knight) and so on (Stojanović 2017: 209–15).

The number of daily and weekly newspapers and magazines dramatically increased, as did the state's budget for culture and education. For example, in 1905, there were only five dailies and by 1911 there were no less that twenty-three daily newspapers. The leading newspaper *Politika* sold around 14,000 copies per day. At this time, the Serbian government also allocated a substantial sum for education: whereas the education-conscious Austro-Hungarian government earmarked 3.17 per cent of its budget for education, the Serbian government went much further and devoted 7.25 per cent of the budget for educational purposes (Stojanović 2017: 244–7).

The newly created intelligentsia was particularly keen to articulate the nationalist narrative, claiming that before the Ottoman conquest all inhabitants of the Balkans 'spoke the old Serbian language' and that Serbs were 'the first and oldest people in Europe' (Gopčević 1889; Milojević 1871). In this context, the intellectuals have contributed towards the establishment of various cultural and entertaining clubs and associations focused on the promotion of the nation-centred secular and religious themes from Serbian history and contemporary life. For example, nationalist leaders introduced a popular 'competitions of the knights', which was regularly used to encourage youth to identify with their heroic ancestors. These events were popular in part because they were able to successfully tap into the microcosm of interpersonal relationships and link these strong micro ties of friendship and kinship with the larger nationalist narrative. For example, these competitions would open with the song dedicated to the founder of the Serbian Orthodox Church (Saint Sava) and would then proceed with the various sporting and artistic events including the declamation contests and the competitive singing of the patriotic songs, where friends would support each other while displaying the Serbian flag. After these events, the participants would attend the lecture on 'the love of the motherland' and the competition winners would receive prizes – patriotic books and sweets (Stojanović 2017: 349–51).

The nationalisation of the masses particularly intensified at the end of the nineteenth and beginning of the twentieth centuries, reaching its peak on the eve of and during the Balkan wars (1912–13) when the Serbian establishment put a great deal of effort into developing the ideological narratives that would legitimise territorial expansion throughout the Balkans. In this context, traditional and highly influential epic poetry and mythology associated with the Battle of Kosovo, most of which initially espoused strong religious millenarian rather than nation-focused overtones, were deliberately reinterpreted in intense nationalist terms (Malešević 2012: 220–30; Emmert 1991; Jelavich 1989). In addition, the government made the ekavian dialect of Serbian the official language in order to bring it closer to the vernaculars spoken by Slavs in Macedonia (Poulton 1995: 63). In a similar vein to its nationalising Balkan neighbours, Greece, Bulgaria or Romania, the Serbian state was also involved substantially in the financial and military support and training of various irredentist groups outside Serbia.

However, this forceful and protracted coercive-organisational and ideological offensive did not meet the expectations of the political and military establishment. Despite years of concentrated nationalist propaganda, the majority of the population in Serbia was still deeply suspicious of the Great Serbian project (Stojanović 2017: 195–235; Malešević 2012: 225–30; Djordjević 1985; Stokes 1976). As clearly indicated by the numerous peasant revolts and resistance to taxation and military drafts that plagued nineteenth-century Serbia, the state authorities were distrusted. The peasantry, who constituted the overwhelming majority of the population, were still mostly illiterate, had strong localised kinship-based attachments and were generally hostile towards the urban population. The main issue here was the legacy of uneven modernisation and state-induced nationalisation, both of which have generated deeply polarised society. Since the primary focus of the new state was to build a proper organisational structure, including the administrative apparatus, police and military, such policies tended to privilege the newly forged urban population over the peasantry. Hence, the number of civil servants increased from 492 in 1837, to 1,151 in 1842, while by 1902, Serbia had over 15,000 civil servants (Stokes 1976: 4–10). As Stojanović (2017: 117) shows, from 1885 to 1905, state administrators constituted between 22.9 and 27.6 per cent of all professions. The state's focus was on generating administrative apparatus and, in this context, the overwhelming majority of university graduates came from the legal disciplines: between 1863 and 1872, 72 per cent of students studied law (Stojanović 2017: 182). In a similar, vein the military and police forces expanded dramatically. In 1861, the government appointed a French officer, Hippolyte Mondain, as the minister of defence (1861–5) with a clear aim of modernising its military force. Between 1893 and 1903, the military grew fourfold (Roudometof 2001: 167).

Consequently, the two dominant social strata – the state employees and the relatively impoverished peasants – had very different attitudes towards the state and its ideological ambitions. Whereas the urban strata, and especially the military, police, the state bureaucracy and many intellectuals, were in favour of state-led nationalist expansionism, the rural population was generally less nationalist and more oriented towards religious conservatism, anti-statism and peasant populism (Stojanović 2017, 2003; Milosavljević 2003; Roudometof 2001). In other words, for much of the nineteenth and early twentieth centuries, nationalism and state expansion were still minority pursuits – an ideological orientation confined to the urban state-employed elite. The Serbian state still lacked stronger connection between the increased organisational capacities, greater ideological penetration and the wider envelopment of micro-solidarity. The nationalist ideology gained in influence but this was still far cry from having a well-established grounded nationalism.

In addition to this sharp class and spatial society-wide divide, Serbia was also deeply polarised at the top. What started off as a conflict between the two royal families gradually changed into a vicious and intensely violent conflict between two well-organised and mutually hostile elite groupings, a conflict which shaped much of nineteenth and early twentieth-century Serbian history. Obrenović's killing of Karađorđe and persecution of his allies allowed for his family's dominance throughout the nineteenth century. However, as Karađorđević's supporters were influential, both at home and abroad, neither King Milan Obrenović nor his descendants could rule Serbia undisturbed. Although initially the Karađorđevićs lived in exile, they maintained strong support among the military, religious, cultural and economic elites who were eager to challenge the Obrenović establishment. After Karađorđević's son Alexander returned to Serbia (from Russia) in 1840, and following popular and elite dissatisfaction with Obrenović's increasingly tyrannical rule, the Obrenovićs were forced to abdicate (first Miloš and then his son Mihailo) in favour of Alexander Karađorđević in 1842 and to go into exile. Nevertheless, this regime change intensified further political conflicts as Obrenović's supporters were profoundly dissatisfied and constantly looking for an opportune moment to remove Alexander from the throne. This came in 1858, following Alexander's miscalculated decision to support the losing side in the Crimean War (Russia). This miscalculation put pressure on Alexander to abdicate in favour of Mihailo Obrenović who was assassinated in 1868 by the supporters of Karađorđević. Mihailo was replaced by his fourteen-year-old nephew Milan who, in 1889, abdicated in favour of his twelve-year-old son Alexander who in turn was assassinated in 1903 by a group of Army officers highly sympathetic to the Karađorđević family.

This vicious cycle of forced abdications and royal assassinations was a symptom of deep divisions at the top of Serbian state. In some respects, these persistent internal conflicts indicate inherent instability of state rule but, in other respects, I would argue these conflicts and tensions stimulated the development of expansionist nationalism among political and military elites in Serbia. The internal elite struggle stimulated chronic fighting over political legitimacy. It raised questions not only about the individual claims of competing royal houses but also about the aims and ambitions of the new Serbian state. As neither royal house had deep aristocratic lineage but were the descendants of commoners, their legitimacy claims had to focus much more on the (promising) future than on the questionable (dynastic) past. Furthermore their new state was emerging in post-revolutionary Europe where popular sovereignty was gradually becoming a principal source of state legitimacy. In this context, nationalism appeared as the most plausible ideological narrative to use to boost one's credentials as a legitimate ruler (Malešević 2013a: 74–81, Breuilly 1993: 366–401, Gellner 1983: 38–47).

Since Serbia's projected 'natural' borders were largely undefined while the majority of Serbs lived outside the tiny principality, the new rulers tended to rely on expansionist nationalism to strengthen their position. For much of the nineteenth and early twentieth centuries, this nationalism had significant appeal among the political, military, economic, cultural and religious elites and was gradually gaining some impact among the slowly nationalising general population. With the infrastructural and organisational development of the Serbian state, which was accompanied by the gradual territorial expansion, the competing elite blocs tended to engage in what political scientists refer to as the outbidding model of political competition (Bloom 2004: 11–37). In other words, internal political instability and the ever-changing geo-political context fostered a structural pressure whereby the two dominant elite groupings had to, and were also willing to, demonstrate that they were more capable than their rival of achieving nationalist goals and bringing about unification of all Serbs into one state. Even though this was not an initial ambition of the two royal households, the intense dynastic struggle in the context of new state formation helped galvanise nationalist ideology as the principal source of state and royal legitimacy.

This internal dynamic was also shaped by the geo-political specificities of the Balkan Peninsula. With the gradual decline of the Ottoman grip on south east Europe, the rulers of the newly emerging Balkan polities – Greece, Bulgaria, Romania, Montenegro, Albania – all developed plans for territorial expansion: the Greek Megali Idea, the Serbian Načertanije, the Bulgarian velika Bulgariya, etc. (see Chapter 5). By the end of the nineteenth century, the focus was firmly on capturing territories belonging to the Ottomans with Macedonia emerging as a bone of contention between Serbian, Bulgarian and Greek nationalists. Now nationalist propaganda was devised by these states to justify conquests of Macedonia and other Balkan territories of the Porte. As Serbian elites were deeply divided, such expansionist nationalist aspirations were instrumental both in refocusing everybody's attention on external enemies and stimulating nationalist radicalism amongst the competing elites. With astonishing military victories achieved by the Serbian army during the Balkan wars of 1912–13, expansionist nationalism became an almost hegemonic *weltanschauung* of both competing camps within the Serbian elite. Since radical, war-centred politics was deemed universally to be a major success, it was almost impossible to challenge this ideological paradigm. After all, victories in the Balkan wars had doubled the size of the Serbian state. Nevertheless, while expansionist nationalism was not questioned, the two opposing camps became embroiled in a conflict about the speed, scale and direction of future territorial conquests. One of the main issues was whether the newly acquired territories (i.e. Macedonia, a part of sanjak of Novi Pazar and Kosovo) should remain under military rule or be fully integrated into the social and political life of the Serbian state. While the military was firm in its insistence on maintaining control of these lands, the government was eager to demilitarise the new territories (Biondich 2011: 65–80; Pavlowitch 2002: 93–110).

The second, even more important, issue was how to address the question of Serbs in Austro-Hungary and particularly in Bosnia and Herzegovina. The deep divisions over both of these issues indicated the ever-increasing dominance of the military in Serbian politics. Ever since its independence, the rulers had been keen to invest lavishly in military development and, until Alexander Obrenović's reign, the army was the most privileged institution in the state. One of the reasons Alexander was assassinated was his decision to cut the military budget and to allow officers' salaries to fall months into arrears (Clark 2012: 14). The return of Karađorđevićs on the throne signalled greater investment into the military and an increased role for top-ranking officers in decision-making. Since military officers organised the assassination of Alexander and were instrumental in bringing Peter I on the throne, the Karađorđević royal house was in many ways dependent on their support. In this context, one can understand the rise of influential secret societies and conspiratorial networks, including the most influential 'Unity or Death', *Ujedinjenje ili smrt* (Black Hand). This organisation was led by Colonel Dragutin Dimitrijević-Apis and other officers involved in the assassination of King Alexander Obrenović. Despite its clandestine structure and activities, this organisation consisted of serving high-ranking officers and active politicians and, as such, had a significant impact on government policies. Although the Black Hand was originally set up in 1901 with an aim to remove the Obrenovićs from power, it was re-established as 'Unity or Death' in 1911 with the new, ideologically more articulated, purpose: to unite all Serbs into one state. The ever-growing membership of this secret entity (around 2,500 in 1911 and at least 30,000 during the Balkan wars) signalled its influence. After the Balkan wars, the Black Hand's focus was firmly on Bosnia and Herzegovina, a former Ottoman province now annexed by Austro-Hungary, where Serbs constituted around 40 per cent of the population (Clark 2012; Okey 2009).[6]

With the slow and gradual democratisation of politics in Serbia under Peter I Karađorđević, a new constitution was introduced, parliamentary life re-established and regular elections instituted. In this environment, a majority peasant population gained a political voice of their own as their main representative – the People's Radical party led by Nikola Pašić – gained and held power for much of this period. Although Pašić was highly sympathetic to further expansionism, as Prime Minister he had had to balance the pressure of military and radical political elites with those of his own (peasant) electorate and the wider international context.[7] On one hand, Pašić had to accommodate Austro-Hungarian demands to desist from stirring ethno-nationalism among Serbs living in the empire, especially in Bosnia and Herzegovina. On the other hand, he had to demonstrate to military as well as political, religious and cultural elites in Belgrade that he was fully committed to implementing the unification agenda. Between this Scylla of external pressure and Charybdis of elite conflict, Pašić also had to satisfy his peasant constituents whose priorities were land distribution and improved living standards, not grand nationalist aspirations. Thus, Serbia after the Balkan wars continued to be a politically divided entity: while the elites were firmly in favour of further expansion into Bosnia and Herzegovina, although differing on how and when to pursue this policy, the peasant masses showed little inclination towards nationalist expansionism.

Serbian Nationalisms outside Serbia: The Bosnian Frontier

In much of contemporary historiography, Gavrilo Princip is depicted as a fanatical nationalist willing to kill and die for the cause of Serbian

---

[6] Obviously, one has to take such 'ethnic data' with a pinch of salt as they imply clear and fixed ethno-national identifications while most individuals in Bosnia and Herzegovina had much more ambiguous identities where religion, kinship and local attachments regularly trumped ethnicity.

[7] In this period, Pašić's Radical Party had little or no support in Belgrade and other urban areas and the majority of their supports were located in the rural areas (Stojanović 2017: 103).

unification (Butcher 2014; Clark 2012; Doak 2008). For example, Clark (2012: 49, 369) sees him as a Serbian ultra-nationalist formed in the world of the Serbian irredentist networks in Bosnia. He emphasises how Princip and his two co-conspirators 'read nationalist poetry and irredentist newspapers and pamphlets' and how they 'dwelt at length on the suffering of the Serbian nation, for which they blamed everyone but the Serbs themselves, and felt the slights and humiliations of the least of their countrymen as if they were their own' (Clark 2012: 50–1). The fact that Princip killed the Austrian archduke and in this way triggered events that ultimately resulted in the catastrophic war has reinforced this stereotypical perception. Moreover, the outcome of the war which saw the disintegration of Austria-Hungary, further expansion of Serbia, the establishment of monarchist Yugoslavia and the post-war glorification of the principle of national self-determination as advocated by both Woodrow Wilson and Lenin, has cemented this image of Princip as a representative of the popular struggle for national unification in the Balkans. Interestingly enough, this image of nations rising against decaying and decadent empires was equally shared by post-war liberal, socialist and communist social movements and governments, most of whom depicted the empires as 'prison houses of peoples'.

However, this picture is deeply grounded in a retrospective reinterpretation of what were in fact much more complex and messy processes, events and actors. As I argue later, Prinicip and his co-conspirators were products of a world marked by ideological confusion, changing worldviews, uncertainty and youth. While Serbian nationalism was undoubtedly a potent ideological discourse among the elites in Belgrade, there is no evidence that such sentiments were widespread among Serbs living outside Serbia. The Serb state was involved in irredentist activities and propagandistic actions throughout the region but this does not mean that such activities were welcomed wholeheartedly by the majority of Serbs outside Serbia.

Bosnia-Herzegovina is particularly interesting in this respect as it was the only region in the Balkans that was governed for substantial periods of time by the two very different empires – the Ottomans and the Hapsburgs. Moreover, with the Austrian occupation (1878) and later annexation (1908), the empire acquired a region that traditionally had a Sunni Muslim majority. Although there was some resistance to Austrian occupation by the local population, this was largely confined to a small segment of Muslim landlords. Peasant unrest taking place during this period had little or nothing to do with nationalism. Despite pronounced religious differences between the three main ethnic groups – Muslims, Orthodox and Catholic Christians – Austrian rule was not characterised by significant inter-ethnic conflicts. On the contrary, the principal tensions were much more vertical than horizontal: the peasant majority of all three groups was dissatisfied with the actions and inactions of the Habsburg regime.

One of the central bones of contention was that the new rulers had preserved the Ottoman model of land control. Under this semi-feudal arrangement, as late as 1879, 95 per cent of land was owned by Muslim landlords (agas and beys) who thus controlled 85,000 families of dependent serfs (kmets) and 77,000 free peasants, most of whom were Christian (Ekmečić 1973). Although more recent Ottoman rulers had attempted to rectify this enormous inequality by standardising the obligations and rights of serfs, including the right to retain and inherit their plots, the declining Ottoman state had no organisational means to implement these changes against landlord resistance. The Habsburg rulers decided to maintain the existing system in order not to further alienate the Muslim landlords. Although this socio-economic system affected most Christians and some Muslims, it had a particularly devastating effect on the Serbian Orthodox population who largely remained landless until 1918.

In addition to retaining the status quo on the land issue, the Austrian authorities also attempted to preserve key elements of the Ottoman religious organisational structure. As Okey (2009: viii) emphasises: 'In many ways, the Monarchy continued the Ottoman millet system of treating Bosnians as religious rather than national groups, to be governed through reshaped religious hierarchies'. In this environment, religion and social status tended to overlap as Muslims dominated towns, commerce and the remnants of Ottoman administration while the Christians were, by and large, illiterate peasants.

Hence, during the Ottoman times, peasant uprisings were often articulated as a combination of social and religious discontent. However, as this peasant world was deeply parochial and completely engrossed in everyday survival, there were no ambitions, let alone ideological and organisational means, with which nationalists could work. Even the Orthodox clergy, the only institutionally organised group among Bosnian Serbs who could potentially mobilise mass support, was largely detached from the ideas of national liberation and popular sovereignty. The main issue here was that the Ottoman millet system left Bosnian Serbs without an educated religious elite as the leading clergy in Bosnia generally consisted of Phanariot Greek-speaking bishops who could not even communicate with their flock in local vernaculars. While these bishops were largely distrusted and perceived as greedy and corrupt, the local priests could not provide much leadership as they usually were no different from their flock: most local priests were illiterate, landless peasants themselves. Even in 1882–3, 255 priests in 374 parishes were serfs. Two thirds of the 350 parochial clergy had no education and were only able to read small sections of the Scriptures, which they learned (or just memorised) from their fathers, priesthood being usually hereditary (Okey 2009: 9, 79). In this world, kinship networks and religious identification easily trumped nationhood as most peasants had little or no conception of what nation meant. Ivan Franjo Jukić, a Bosnian Catholic writer educated in Habsburg Empire, who travelled extensively throughout Bosnia, testifies that he never heard Serbian peasants using the term 'Serb' but instead that they addressed each other in terms of kinship, local or religious categories (Jukić 1973[1842]: 86). Bosnian rural society was dominated by micro-level solidarities which were almost completely disconnected from the (very weak) organisational and ideological powers.

Nevertheless, despite preserving much of the existing social and religious structure, the Austrian regime did initiate significant changes in infrastructure, administration, industry and, to some extent, education and culture. In the late nineteenth and early twentieth centuries, Bosnia and Herzegovina experienced substantial growth in all of these areas. The chief Austro-Hungarian administrator, Benjamin Kállay, was responsible for the ambitious programme of social and economic development: the railway networks and roads were built to facilitate coal and iron mining, the modern forestry industry was created focusing on paper manufacture, food processing and spirit-distilling factories were established. Nearly all of the above were owned and managed by immigrants who moved to Bosnia from other parts of Austro-Hungary (Okey 2009: 59).

Although this ambition to modernise was initially present in Kállay's vision of Bosnian educational and cultural institutions, the lack of financial resources prevented its full realisation. The inter-confessional National Elementary Schools were established throughout the country but their development was rather slow: from 42 (with 2,836 pupils) in 1882–3 to 135 (with 9,613 pupils) in 1889. Although this was a significant increase, it was still a drop in the ocean for a population of 1.5 million people (Hajdarpašić 2015: 90–98; Okey 2009: 65). As the Austrian priority was to forge a new cultural elite, most resources were devoted to secondary education. In 1889, three quarters of the education budget was spent on secondary schools, while between 1882 and 1890 more money was devoted to the Sarajevo Gymnasium and its new building than to 'all primary schools in the same period' (Okey 2009: 66).

Kállay's principal goal was to prevent the emergence of Serbian and Croatian nationalist movements in Bosnia, which would not only destabilise

Bosnia but also the rest of the fragile multi-ethnic empire. To this end, he attempted to accommodate the Bosnian Muslim elite which he perceived as the direct descendants of the medieval Bosnian nobility and saw as natural allies against the expanding Serbian state as well as rising nationalism in Croatia. Thus, in addition to preserving their land ownership rights, Kállay also attempted to forge a new multi-confessional Bosnian nation. The Austrian administration under Kállay's leadership invested a great deal of time and energy into this project, aimed at creating a unified nation out of three disparate religious groups. New history and literature school textbooks were commissioned, new pedagogical guides and handbooks for teachers were produced, new museums and archaeological sites focused on the shared past of all Bosnians were opened. However, as Austrian administrators lacked substantial financial resources, their plans largely remained limited to Sarajevo and other urban centres while the countryside, where there were very few schools, was for the most part untouched by this Bosnian-centred nationalising scheme.

In some respects, this project of forging a Bosnian nation clearly backfired as it was seen by political and cultural elites of Serbia and Croatia as an attempt to assimilate populations that they considered to be ethnic Serbs and Croats respectively. In this environment, Serbia's establishment was overtly and covertly supportive of most actions aimed at stimulating the Serbian national idea in Bosnia and Herzegovina. Pašić's government demanded that Austria allow a degree of cultural autonomy for Bosnian Serbs in the areas of religion and education. Since the Austrian authorities banned any imports from Serbia that were deemed to advocate irredentism and nationalism, much effort focused on smuggling Serbian newspapers and books into Bosnia. In the 1890s, only two newspapers from Serbia (*Naše Doba* and *Novo Vreme*), considered non-nationalist, were allowed into Bosnia. The Serbian government was well aware that non-governmental nationalist organisations such as the Society of Saint Sava were involved in illegal exports of Serbian novels, history and geography books to Bosnia.

As the Serbian Orthodox Church was a crucial institution, the Austrian authorities tried to control it through the regulation of parochial incomes, taxation and providing a life of relative privilege for bishops and priests loyal to the monarchy. With the gradual expansion of the Serbian state causing further deterioration in its relationships with Austria-Hungary, cultural propaganda was largely replaced by political and security-related activities of clandestine organisations such as the 'Unity or Death' and 'People's Defence' (*Narodna Odbrana*). The aims of these and similar organisations were much more radical and immediate: to integrate Bosnia and Herzegovina into an expanded state of all Serbs. With the victories in the Balkan wars the political, military, cultural and administrative elites of Belgrade were emboldened in their belief that unification was close and inevitable. These ideas were also shared by the government, even though Pašić had to navigate between these expansionist ambitions, the broader international environment and the more down-to-earth concerns of his peasant constituents.

While the Serbian establishment exhibited a substantial degree of unity on the question of state expansion, the picture among the Bosnian Serb population was much more ambiguous. For one thing, only after several decades of Habsburg rule was there a Bosnian Serb intelligentsia that could generate or articulate irredentist ambitions. It was only in 1886 that the first literary magazine, *Bosanska vila*, was founded and even this journal was established by Serb immigrant teachers from the Vojvodina. This magazine advocated a mild cultural nationalism which was associated more with moral progress and enlightenment than ethnic exclusivity or territorial conquests. Nevertheless, the low literacy levels and the general impoverishment of the population meant that such magazines had a tiny readership: *Bosanska vila* had only 387 subscribers in Bosnia, most of whom were based in Sarajevo (Djuričković 1975: 32). Most Bosnian Serb organisations established in this period were focused on artistic or religious activities: Serb choral societies; January concerts to honour the founder of Serbian Orthodox church, Saint Sava; theatrical performances and reading rooms. By 1908, these cultural activities and initiatives had increased substantially so in that year Bosnia had 604 clubs and societies involved in variety of events and actions. Among educated Bosnian Serbs *Prosvjeta* emerged as the leading cultural society able to secure financial aid for students and apprentices. However, the membership of this largest Serbian association was still only just over 5,100 in a Bosnian Serbs population close to 800,000 people (Okey 2009: 162). By 1907, there were also several daily and weekly papers with *Srpska riječ* and *Srpski Vijesnik* catering for a small but rising group of ethnonationally conscious urban Serbs.

While these cultural events were confined to the larger urban centres, the majority rural population was focused on everyday survival (Grandits 2014). In addition to the lack of land reform, the peasantry was also affected negatively by the gradual but constant disintegration of the traditional zadruga system of communal extended family households. With the seeds of modernisation emerging throughout Bosnia, village communal households were breaking into smaller family units which often found themselves in an economically even more difficult situation as they could not rely on the solidarity networks of the extended family households (Erlich-Stein 1964).

Gavrilo Princip and his future co-conspirators came from this deeply impoverished and radically changing social environment of the Bosnian countryside. Rather than being socialised in what Clark (2012: 22) refers to as 'memory of Dušan's [medieval Serbian] empire' these future conspirators were children of peasants who were for the most part ignorant of the Serbian national project (Hajdarpašić 2015: 100–5). In a country where even in 1910, 88 per cent of the population was illiterate (Okey 2009: 184), most peasants were preoccupied with everyday concerns such as getting enough food on their plate, having good harvests or being able to get their corn to market. As the Bosnian District Commissioner from Bijeljina described in 1913, the Bosnian Serb peasant 'is atavistically burdened by great suspicion, overall wants to hear nothing of newspapers, the efforts of Serbo-enthusiasts founder on passive resistance of the rural population' (Okey 2009: 213).

Most secondary school students were sons of peasants who left their villages to study in Sarajevo and other urban centres. The educational system they entered was characterised by excessive teaching loads, overcrowded classes, undisciplined and impoverished students, dissatisfied teachers, bureaucratic disorder and incoherent state policies. Moreover, as there was no focus on generating employment opportunities for future graduates, most students were deeply dissatisfied with the prospect of having no employment in the foreseeable future. As Bosnia was integrated into the Austro-Hungarian empire, the intellectual debates and discontents of Vienna, Budapest, Prague and Zagreb were reflected among the newly emerging educated youths in Bosnia. Hence, the general ideas of Enlightenment and Romanticism found their way into the aspirations and ideals of Bosnian secondary school students. In this environment, Young Bosnia emerged as an informal wider movement involving all ethnic groups of Bosnia and Herzegovina and aspiring to realise a variety of ideals and goals ranging from liberalism, anarchism, socialism, atheism, nationalism, anti-imperialism to romantic martyrdom. Princip, Čabrinović, Gaćinović, Grabež, Mehmedbašić and other future conspirators were all very young secondary school students influenced by all of these ideas. As Djaković (1985) shows, the average age of all those brought to trial after the assassination of the Archduke (104 accused) was 18. At this very young age, most of these students did not have a particularly developed or sophisticated understanding of the ideological currents of their time. Hence, their radicalism was generally composed of confused and conflicting ideological principles. Princip and his co-conspirator Čabrinović, were equally enchanted by anarchist literature, liberalism, socialism, syndicalism and anti-imperial nationalism. It seems that initially, anarchist principles held more sway in their belief systems as they both read and admired Kropotkin, Bakunin and William Morris's *News from Nowhere* (Hajdarpašić 2015: 148–53).

From his conversations with the prison psychoanalyst in 1916, it also comes across that Princip remained devoted to these anarchist principles until the end of his life (Smith 2009). This is not to say that young Serbian radicals were not nationalist but that their nationalism differed substantially from the nationalist ideology formulated and espoused among the political, military, religious and cultural elites in Belgrade. Whereas the former was largely an expression of youthful romantic radicalism grounded in utopian ideals that despised all authority and inequality, the latter was an instrumentally focused and well-calculated state policy bent on territorial expansion. While Young Bosnia advocated a hodgepodge of republican, socialist, anarchist, liberal and pan-Yugoslav ideas, the top echelons of Serbia's establishment wanted a monarchist mini-empire dominated by Serbs.

As the policies of the Habsburg administration in Bosnia become ever more incoherent and unresponsive to local demands, the small Bosnian Serb youth movement grew less patient and became involved in several small-scale violent actions against representatives of the empire. In many important respects, these Bosnian students, mostly but not exclusively Serb, were a direct product of the failed state-building project conducted by the Austro-Hungarian polity. In such a distrustful and deteriorating environment these youths increasingly looked to Serbia, hoping that unification of the two countries would bring about better and more equal living conditions for their peasant relatives and friends. With Serbia's gradual expansion throughout the late nineteenth and early twentieth centuries, this policy seemed to be the most realistic option for the realisation of such goals. With the decisive victories of the Serbian army in the two Balkan wars, Serbia's prestige was substantially enhanced in the eyes of most South Slavs living in the urban areas.

The ever-rising discontent of Bosnian Serb students proved to be an ideal background for the actions of several secret organisations based in Serbia. Since Apis's 'Unity or Death' was by the end of Balkan wars by far the largest and most influential such an organisation, it was capable of recruiting, training and equipping a number of Bosnian Serb youths to take part in violent actions on the territory of Bosnia and Herzegovina. Although there is still dispute among historians about whether 'Unity or Death' was the main organiser of the assassination of Archduke Ferdinand or just facilitators of actions planned by the Young Bosnian conspirators, there is little doubt that their gradual shift towards violent irredentism was deeply influenced by their further radicalisation in Serbia. In other words, rather than growing up with an aspiration towards the unification of all Serbs in a single state, these radical young Bosnian Serbs were quite quickly transformed into violent proponents of such an idea. Their radicalisation was also aided by the failures of the Habsburg state to address the key structural problems in Bosnia and by the ideological and geo-political aspirations of the rising power in the miniature – the Kingdom of Serbia. Although for much of the late nineteenth and early twentieth centuries, the two forms of Serbian nationalism exhibited profound differences, by the end of the Balkan wars the expansionist nationalism of the Serbian state project was clearly on the ascendency. Nevertheless, despite its prevalence among the political, military, cultural and religious elites in Serbia and among small cohorts of educated Serbs in Bosnia, nationalism was still relatively marginal ideological discourse among the majority of, essentially peasant, populations of both countries.

Conclusion

Ben Anderson's (1991: 12) famous quip that 'it is the magic of nationalism to turn chance into destiny' applies equally to many contemporary historiographic accounts of state formation. Such accounts tend to smooth over sharp facets of human past and transform historical contingencies into national destinies. Hence, contemporary nation states are often understood wrongly as natural and almost inevitable evolutionary developments of previous cultural identities. In this context, it seems obvious that co-nationals would always prefer to live together in a state of their own. Hence, the aspiration towards establishing such a unified and strong polity is regularly seen as a powerful motive for state expansion. From this perspective, the rise and rise of the Serbian state in the nineteenth and early twentieth centuries, does not require much explanation: it is the direct outcome of the strong and widespread nationalist sentiment shared equally by most Serbs inhabiting the Balkan Peninsula. As Mackenzie (1994: 153) puts it: 'Reborn as an autonomous principality in 1830 after four centuries of Turkish rule, Serbia played a role among the South Slavs like Piedmont–Sardinia among Italians and Prussia in Germany.' However, as I have attempted to show in this chapter, such readings of the past are profoundly mistaken. The concept of national unity and the expansion of state power in the name of shared nationhood develops very late in human history. Moreover, even when these ideas become guiding principles of political, military and cultural establishments, they largely remain unimportant to those who have not been fully integrated into the state's coercive-organisational, ideological and micro-interactional structures. Since the Balkan populations had not been exposed to this form of structural integration until the late nineteenth and early twentieth centuries, popular nationalism remained extremely weak and, as such, could not aid the state expansionist projects envisaged by the Balkan statesmen and nationalist intelligentsia. The very rapid expansion of the Serbian state was not caused by potent nationalist ideologies. Instead, most forms of nationalism emerged as a side effect of uneven state development. The rise of state power was a contingent product of geo-political, coercive-organisational and ideological factors combined with fierce domestic elite rivalries in Serbia. The ultimate outcome of these complex historical realities was nationalism centred on providing justification for state expansion in the region. In contrast to this state-led expansionist project, the Serbian population outside Serbia was even less committed to the national idea. Most Bosnian Serbs, who were still illiterate, impoverished and mostly landless peasants, largely remained indifferent towards the idea of national unification. Those among them who acquired some education became more receptive to nationalist ideas but their nationalism developed very different features to nationalist ideology dominating in Serbia. While the Serbian establishment was a chief proponent of the state-supporting nationalist project, the Bosnian youth movement was always more comfortable with the idea of anarchist, state-subverting, nationalism.

9   From Sacrifice to Prestige

Introduction

Many mainstream historians and social scientists view nationalism as an ideology that had its heyday in the previous centuries. The conventional, well-established accounts tend to identify the second half of the nineteenth century as the pinnacle of nationalism. Hence, the period ranging from the 1848 revolutions and uprisings up to the 1912–13 Balkan wars is often termed 'the spring time of peoples' rising up against a decaying imperial order (Rapport 2008: 1–2). This period of European history is associated with the 'national unification' of Italy (1859–70) and Germany (1866–71), as well as with the reorganisation of the Habsburg empire into a dual monarchy 'in recognition of Hungarian self-determination' (Kallis 2008: 512). Furthermore, the second half of the nineteenth century is depicted as a period when the nation state has finally replaced the empire as the dominant form of territorial organisation (Hiers and Wimmer 2013). In this context, nineteenth-century Balkan nationalist movements are usually perceived as being inspired by the same ideals rooted in the popular will of the people to demolish the Ottoman and Habsburg empires and establish their own independent nation states. The dominance of belligerent nationalist imagery and rhetoric in this period is taken as a sign of nationalism's strength and prevalence. Hence, nineteenth-century nationalisms are generally understood to have been potent generators of social change in the Balkans.

In contrast to their nineteenth-century counterparts, the contemporary European nationalisms are generally regarded as being less virulent. This historical change is usually interpreted as a typical shift from strong, state-seeking, violent nationalisms towards the everyday, habitual, and thus weak, articulations of nationhood associated with the established nation states. For some, the project of European integration, together with the proliferation of globalisation, have contributed towards the stifling of nationalist excesses (Giddens 2007; Held and

McGrew 2007: Beck 2006). For others, nationalism has evolved from being a violence-prone ideology towards attaining more banal features as displayed in sporting competitions, cuisine, consumerism and other everyday activities (Billig 1995; Hutchinson 2005; Fox and Muller-Idris 2008). In this context, the twenty-first-century Serbian and Croatian societies seem to represent the European standard as they display substantially less imagery associated with the virulent nationalisms of their nineteenth-century predecessors. The mass media, educational systems and civil society of contemporary Serbia and Croatia focus more attention towards the respective nation's international achievements in science, technology, sports and other fields.

In this chapter, I contest this interpretation by arguing that twenty-first-century European nationalisms are anything but banal and weak. By zooming in on the cases of Serbian and Croatian nationalisms, I aim to show how nationalisms have become stronger through organisational, ideological and micro-interactional ground-ness. Hence, the relative invisibility of aggressive nationalisms should not be confused with their weakness as European nationalisms have substantially increased their organisational and ideological capacities in the twenty-first century.

Nationhood and Nationalisms in the Nineteenth Century

The nineteenth century is often described as the age of nationalism. In conventional historiographic and popular accounts, this period is usually depicted as the springtime of small nations rising against oppressive, exploitative and decaying empires. In south east Europe, such narratives centre on the rise of Greek, Serbian, Bulgarian, Croatian, Slovenian and other national movements striving to establish independent nation states on the ruins of the old Ottoman and Habsburg empires (Hroch 2015; Rapport 2008; Smith 2010; Gerolymatos 2002). In such interpretations, empires are regularly represented as 'the prison houses of nations', whereas nationhood is understood to be a natural and normal form of group identification, best expressed through the creation of an independent and sovereign state. Long before Wilson and Lenin formulated their ideas of the right for national self-determination, the nationalist ideologues have advocated the breakup of empires and establishment of sovereign nation states. As Tilly (1993: 30) points out:

for almost two centuries this set of principles has had extraordinary force as a justification for political action by ostensible leaders of peoples who lack states, by rulers of states who speak in a nation's name, and by third parties – outside rulers, conspirators, international organisations, and many more – who intervene in the political struggles of particular states.

In this context, nineteenth-century Serbian and Croatian nationalisms are generally viewed as being rather typical of other European movements, all of which allegedly concerned with the break from the imperial dominance and the attainment of national sovereignty. Hence, the independence of Belgium (1830), Greece (1832) and Switzerland (1848), among others, have been perceived as indicating a long-term trend away from the imperial mode of rule and towards the gradual dominance of the nation-state form of territorial organisation. In all of these cases, the conventional historiography has emphasised the strength of nationalism and the weakness of imperial doctrines. Thus, the emergence of new states has traditionally been interpreted through the prism of a popular dissatisfaction with the imperial dominance and an equally strong desire to achieve political independence.

The early nineteenth-century Serbian uprisings (1804–13 and 1815–17) are often identified as 'the national revolutions' fought against the Ottoman rule and driven by the popular demand for the formation of a sovereign Serbian polity (Mackenzie 1996, 1994). In traditional accounts, the gradual rise of an autonomous Serbian state throughout the nineteenth century was directly linked to the ever-increasing nationalist aspirations built around the idea of resurrecting the medieval Serbian state under emperor Dušan (1331–46) (see Chapters 7 and 8). Although Croatian nationalism followed a different historical trajectory, it too was perceived to be strong and politically influential. As with the Serbian case, nationalist ambitions were framed in reference to the legacies of the Croatian medieval kingdom under King Tomislav's rule (910–28). Despite the fact that the Croatian nationalist movement operated in a different geopolitical context, that is, a more complex Austro-Hungarian imperial structure, it too was seen as having been quite successful in mobilising large popular support. Hence, the conventional historiography tends to portray south-eastern Europe during the nineteenth century as a hotbed of nationalisms (Pavlowitch 2002: Mackenzie 1994).

This general assumption is also rooted in some major historical events that took place during the nineteenth century. In the Serbian case, this involves prolonged struggles for autonomy and independence from Ottoman rule shaped around several key dates: the Second Serbian Uprising (1815–17) when partial autonomy was granted, 1867 when the Principality of Serbia became de facto independent, and 1882 when the Kingdom of Serbia was established. This period was also defined by several violent conflicts such as the Serbo-Ottoman War (1876) and the Serbo-Bulgarian war (1885) (Pavlowitch 2002). In the Croatian case, key events include the short-lived proclamation in 1848 by the Croatian parliament concerning the union of the Croatian provinces and their secession from the Kingdom of Hungary with the Habsburg Empire, the parliamentary act that replaced Latin with Croatian as the official language of Croatia (1847), and the 1868 Croatian-Hungarian Settlement whereby the Kingdom of Slavonia was incorporated into Croatia as an autonomous state within Hungary. As in the Serbian case, here too several violent conflicts have been singled out as the defining national events, such as the Rakovica Revolt (1871), when several politicians lead by Eugen Kvaternik declared the creation of an independent Croatian government in Rakovica, and the incorporation of the Croatian Military Frontier into Croatia-Slavonia (1881) (Magaš 2008).

In addition to these significant historical events and processes, the strength of Serbian and Croatian nationalisms is also inferred from the abundance of visual nationalist images that dominated the public sphere during the nineteenth century in south east Europe. Croatian and Serbian public spaces were different in two important senses: (1) for much of the second half of the nineteenth century, Serbia was largely an independent polity free to formulate its own national policies, while Croatian lands were still firmly integrated with the Hungarian part of the Austro-Hungarian Empire; (2) whereas Serbia was for the most part an impoverished country lacking basic infrastructure, industry and an education system, the Croatian provinces were more developed and better integrated into the economic, cultural and political networks of Western Europe. Nevertheless, despite these objective differences, their respective public spheres were saturated with very similar nationcentric images. In both cases, the focus was on the glorification of their respective medieval empires and the visions of the future sovereign and enlarged homelands. The abundance of nationalist narratives and corresponding visual imagery was present in the popular mass media, school textbooks, novels, poems, paintings, museum exhibitions, theatre performances, street names, monuments, popular events and commemorations accompanied by flags and other national symbols (Biondich 2011; Uzelac 2006; Jelavich 1990).

What particularly stands out from this period is the dominance of violent imagery: acts of martyrdom for one's nation, representations of past wars and major battlefields, forced migrations of co-nationals, the destruction of sacred places and religious buildings, a heroic military tradition and extremely negative depictions of historic enemies. For example, late nineteenth-century primary school textbooks used in Serbia all emphasise how Serbs fought bravely throughout history to protect their homeland and their culture. In this context, a geography textbook warns pupils that they have moral responsibility to preserve this tradition: 'Children! A Serb gave birth to you ... Should anyone seek to impose another name on you in place of it, you would rather die than acquiesce' (Hristić 1872: 66). History and literature textbooks contain numerous images of violent events from the nation's past. In particular, the focus is on heroic depictions of the battle of Kosovo that took place between the Serbian and Ottoman forces in Kosovo on St Vitus Day in 1389. This central event of the Serbian national mythology was also an object of numerous works of art including the frequently reproduced paintings of Serbian Prince Lazar (who died on the battlefield), Miloš Obilić (the aristocrat who allegedly killed the leader of the Ottoman forces, Sultan Murat), Kosovo maiden (*Kosovka devojka*) and various depictions of the Kosovo Field battle. In addition, Serbian mass media, textbooks and various cultural institutions were also suffused with numerous artistic and popular images of the two large-scale post-war migrations of Serbs from the Ottoman Empire to the Habsburg lands between 1689–92 and 1737–39, led by the Serbian Orthodox Patriarchs Arsenije III and IV respectively. In both cases, the imagery focuses on the tragic and violent historical context whereby Serbs were forced to leave their homesteads to preserve their lives. This emphasis on violence is also present in the sustained popularisation of traditional epic poetry, most of which depicts heroic cases of individual resistance to 'the Ottoman yoke'. The central figure in these poems is Prince Marko (Kraljević Marko) who was generally venerated as a national hero vigorously fighting the Ottomans. These epic decasyllable-poetry-reciting nights had a strong visual component as they were almost ritualistically performed in front of the entire village populations throughout Serbia. Poetry recitals were also regularly accompanied by the sound of the gusle (a two-string instrument) and the poems were often carefully memorised by children and others attending these events. These epic poetry recitals were almost exclusively centred on a detailed depiction of Ottoman misdeeds (including torture, mass killings, or taking Christian children away from their parents) and brave national heroes, such as Prince Marko, who fought the Ottoman brutes. From the mid to late nineteenth century, these images of public gatherings amid village life were regularly visualised in the mass media, school textbooks and art (Pavlowich 2002; Emmert 1991).

Although members of the Croatian public, including journalists, novelists, painters and textbook writers, had less freedom to express their nationalist aspirations in full, they too were engaged in sustained campaigns of nationcentric agitation. Hence, teachers, school textbook authors and journalists were eager to demonstrate that, despite their current predicament, Croats are an old and proud nation defined by a glorious history. For example, late nineteenth-century textbooks were saturated with depictions of Croatian achievements throughout history, including such claims as Croats 'were the first of the Slavic nations to become Christians', which ultimately proved important in their victorious resistance to the Ottomans (Jelavich 1990: 214). Textbooks were replete with graphic images of violent struggles against various enemies, where Croatian heroes such as Petar Berislavić or Krsto Frankopan were celebrated for their heroic resistance against an omnipotent enemy. In a similar fashion to Serbian textbooks, the emphasis is given to heroic sacrifice. Hence, many textbooks tell a story of how 2500 brave Croats under the leadership of Nikola Zrinski faced 100,000 Ottoman soldiers in Siget (1566) where they fought until the bitter end. According to these textbook accounts, Zrinski led a charge and was killed allegedly believing that 'there was no more disgraceful sin than the betrayal of one's homeland' (Jelavich 1990: 228). The focal point of many textbooks and mass mediated representations were the legacies of the medieval Croatian kingdom that is often depicted as a cradle of the Croatian nation. Throughout the nineteenth century, poets, novelists and painters produced numerous artistic representations of the Croatian medieval period. In particular, the focus was placed on various visual depictions of coronations of kings Demetrius Zvonimir (1076) and Tomislav (925), as well as the signing of *Pacta conventa* (1102) under which Croatia joined in a personal union with Hungary. All of these and many other medieval-themed events, including the popular paintings of other medieval kings and dukes such as Petar Krešimir IV, Trpimir I, Domagoj, Zdeslav, or Branimir, were disseminated extensively throughout nineteenth-century Croatia. The principal aim of these visual images was to highlight the link between a noble past and the foreseeable independent future of Croatia. Moreover, the proliferation of these images was also envisaged as an attempt to prove the 'thousand years of unbroken continuity' in 'Croatian national consciousness' (Malešević 2002: 225–63).

In addition to this fixation with a violent and glorious past, both the Serbian and Croatian public spheres were also infused with images centred on reconstituting new homelands. In the dominant narratives of that period, national liberation could only be complete once full sovereignty had been achieved within the confines of entire territories framed as being coterminous with the homeland. In this context, the mid to late nineteenth century was characterised by the proliferation of various maps depicting the 'natural', 'historical', 'ethnic' or 'demographic' boarders of future Serbia and Croatia. The principal idea underpinning these maps was the sense that existing borders were unjust as they did not correspond to the historical borders of these countries nor include a large number of co-nationals. Since Serbia was already an independent state developed around a small territorial core that gradually expanded throughout the nineteenth century, the idea of continuous state expansion was much better embedded in Serbia than it was in Croatia. Although there were numerous different plans for territorial expansion, as well as corresponding maps of a Greater Serbia, the most influential among such plans was that of Serbian minister Ilija Garašanin's *Načertanije* (1844), which envisaged the future Serbian state incorporating Bosnia and Herzegovina, Montenegro, Macedonia, parts of Croatia, Bulgaria and Hungary (see Chapter 5).

The idea of a Greater Croatia developed mostly in the context of the Austro-Hungarian occupation of Bosnia and Herzegovina (1878). For Croatian nationalists such as Ante Starčević and Eugen Kvaternik, this newly acquired territory together with parts of Serbia, Montenegro and Slovenia was envisaged as an integral part of the future independent Croatian state. The fact that these maps overlapped substantially, and that both sides claimed that their nation was genuine while other Balkan nations were invented, indicated that any future attempt to establish such imaginary national projects was likely to lead towards violent conflicts.

The prevalence of such bellicose imagery in the Serbian and Croatian public arenas is often interpreted as a reliable sign that virulent nationalism predominated in the nineteenth-century Balkans. Hence, over the past century and a half, south-east European history has often been described as the hotbed of 'aggressive nationalism', 'national egoism', 'ancient hatreds', and a violence-prone 'Balkan mentality'. Nevertheless, this visual abundance of violent nationalist imagery should not be taken at face value and simply read as evidence of entrenched and well-developed Balkan nationalisms. On the contrary, I would argue that this proliferation of virulent ethnocentric images indicates the weakness of popular nationalisms in nineteenth-century Serbia and Croatia, not their strength. As decades of comprehensive scholarship indicate, the society-wide pervasiveness of nationalism entails specific structural conditions, foremost among these being relatively high literacy rates, well-established and state-supervised educational systems, standardised vernacular languages, well-articulated patterns of 'high' culture, advanced division of labour, constitutionalism, organisationally centralised state governance, developed infrastructural state capacities, and the presence of reliable systems of transport and communication among others (Malešević 2013a; 2006; Mann 1993, 1986; Gellner 1983; Anderson 1981[1983]). During the nineteenth century, Serbia and Croatia simply lacked the organisational, ideological and micro-interactional constituents required to make nationalism a society-wide sociological reality. Organisational capacity was very low, ideological penetration very shallow and confined to the small sectors of population, and the envelopment of micro-solidarity was largely non-existent.

For example, as elaborated in the previous chapter, in 1830 the Serbian autonomous principality was in possession of only sixteen primary schools catering for as few as 800 students. No surprise then that literacy rates were abysmal, with over 90 per cent of the population being illiterate as late as 1864. Even in 1900, Serbia had only a 17 per cent literacy rate (Ekmečić 1991: 333). Moreover, state infrastructure was completely undeveloped. At the beginning of the nineteenth century, Serbia had only a handful of civil servants and almost no native teachers, intellectuals, doctors or other professionals (Stokes 1976: 4). The principality lacked proper roads (by 1858 there were only 800 km of paved roads), railway tracks (until 1854), as well as industry and significant urban centres. Low literacy rates also inhibited the development of sustainable publishing and media outlets, and the new Serbian state did not even have a national library (until 1832), a national museum (until 1844) or a national theatre (until 1861), all institutions generally perceived to be crucial for the development of nationalist projects. An overwhelming majority of the population were illiterate peasants for whom clan, kinship and religious attachments remained much more important than any sense of identification with the nation (Malešević 2012; Meriage 1977). This majority peasant population was deeply parochial and suspicious of any nationalist initiatives coming from Belgrade. The village-based pockets of micro-solidarity were largely disconnected from each other, thus making a synchronised (nation-centred) ideologisation almost impossible. The harbingers of nationalist zeal were largely foreign-educated intellectuals, top-tier civil servants, professional politicians and actors from the military establishment. These urban-based individuals were eager to transform peasants into nationally conscious Serbs, and were deeply frustrated that most of their co-nationals were either lukewarm or profoundly hostile towards these nationalist campaigns (see Chapters 7 and 8). Hence, despite the ever-increasing proliferation of nationalist rhetoric and imagery throughout the nineteenth century, a majority among the Serbian population were not terribly receptive to these calls, indicating that nationalism was a rather weak ideological force at this time.

Although nineteenth-century Croatia had more robust structural conditions and was more developed than Serbia, it too was largely a rural society defined by low literacy rates, conservatism, localism and weak social integration. Moreover, unlike Serbia, which lacked a traditional aristocracy, Croatia was also beset by pronounced social polarisation. Being a part of the Habsburg Empire, its internal social structure reflected a deeply stratified world of small, Vienna- and Budapest-oriented aristocracy and an impoverished and mostly landless peasantry. Despite maintaining some links with the native medieval institutions, Croatian aristocrats were for the most part integrated within the imperial order and had little sense of attachment to their 'co-national' peasantry. This was visible not only in the lack of 'national' solidarity between the two groups, but also in the pronounced diglossia whereby aristocracy communicated through Latin (and later German or Hungarian) while the majority of the population conversed in local vernaculars. This linguistic disunity was further marked by the presence of three very different dialects spoken throughout Croatia (štokavian, kajkavian and čakavian). With the rise of Hungarian dominance in the mid nineteenth century, the educational system was used as a means of Magyarisation, thus further preventing the development of Croatian nationalism. For example, in 1833, Hungarian became a compulsory language for all secondary and higher schools in Croatia. Although literacy rates were generally higher than in Serbia, the majority of the Croatian population remained illiterate until the beginning of the twentieth century. For example, by 1910 the illiteracy rate stood at only 46.2 per cent of the population (Biondich 2011). The civil service was substantially larger and better organised than that in Serbia but it was almost completely dominated by foreign professionals. Similarly, most other professional positions were filled by educated individuals from different regions of the Austro-Hungarian Empire. The imperial administration was not particularly fond of any organised attempts to foster a sense of Croatian national identity. In this context, the institutions of 'high culture' did not acquire their national names and attributes until the second half of the nineteenth century. Hence, Croatian replaced Latin as the official language of the Croatian government only in 1847, the Zagreb city theatre became the Croatian National Theatre in 1860, while most other cultural institutions were renamed Croatian by the end of nineteenth century (Biondich 2011; Magaš 2008).

This gradual rise of nationalist projects largely remained confined to upper and middle-class professionals – teachers, writers, journalists, artists and some civil servants (Biondich 2011). As in the Serbian case, the dramatic expansion of nationalist associations coupled with production and distribution of nationcentric imagery did not necessarily translate into society-wide nationalist movements. Instead, here too a majority among the peasant population remained wedded to local, kinship-based and religious group attachments. Just as in the Serbian case, these micro-level solidarities remained disconnected from each other and from the wider, society-wide, nationalist narrative. The presence of forceful nationalist images and proclamations hid the utter weakness of this ideological discourse in nineteenth-century Croatia.

Hence, despite the general perception that nineteenth-century Serbia and Croatia were both teeming with nationalism, this was not the case. On the contrary, the prevalence of violent nationalist imagery tends to hide the very low level of nationalist penetration within the broader society. The nineteenth-century nationalism was organisationally and ideologically weak and as such could not act as a society-wide social glue capable of bringing different social strata together. Rather then being firmly grounded throughout the society, nationalism was still a minority pursuit. In this context, the visual emphasis on historical glories and past sacrifices for the nation mostly acted as didactic devices centred on nationcentric socialisation of a primarily peasant population. Since the overwhelming majority of ordinary Serbs and Croats did not identify with their respective national projects, it was necessary to expose them continuously to visual bombardments of violent nationalist imagery in order to speed up the historical process of making the peasantry into nationally conscious Serbs and Croats.

Twenty-First-Century Nationalisms

For much of the twentieth century, Serbia and Croatia were a part of two joint multi-ethnic states: monarchist Yugoslavia (1918–41) and the socialist Yugoslav federation (1945–91).[1] Although these two polities were profoundly different in many respects, they were both nominally committed to developing unifying society-wide narratives intended to surpass the narrow ethno-nationalist discourses. Hence, the monarchist state deployed the idea that all of its three constitutional peoples (Serbs, Croats and Slovenes) are different branches of the same South Slavic tribe.[2] Although the socialist federation recognised and constitutionally enshrined the rights of its six constituent nations (Serbs, Croats, Slovenes, Bosnian Muslims, Montenegrins and Macedonians), it too promoted a supranational doctrine of 'brotherhood and unity'. Nevertheless, these official ideological frameworks were neither fully articulated nor were they envisaged as serious counterparts to existing nationalist discourses. In many respects, these newly formulated pan-state doctrines were largely grafted onto well-established ethno-nationalist narratives. This was clearly visible even in the case of socialist Yugoslavia, where ethno-nationalist historical mythology was gradually fused with the state socialist doctrine. Initially, this was done along

---

[1] The first joint state was established as the Kingdom of Serbs, Croats and Slovenes in 1918 and was renamed Yugoslavia in 1929.

[2] The monarchist Yugoslavia did not recognise Montenegrins, Bosnian Muslims/Bosniaks and Macedonians as distinct ethno-national categories.

Leninist lines where the ethno-national units retained cultural specificities according to the formula of being 'national in form and socialist in content'. However, after the Tito-Stalin split in 1948, the Yugoslav state developed a rather idiosyncratic model of state organisation that institutionalised ethno-national differences and also utilised periodic decentralisation strategies as means of avoiding substantive democratisation and liberalisation. In this context, much of the twentieth century was characterised by the continuous proliferation of nationalist imagery and rhetoric (Malešević 2006: 162–3; 2002).

This is not to say that there were no oscillations or changes in how national projects were articulated. Obviously, there were substantial differences between the monarchist and socialist representations of nationhood. Moreover, the socialist period was also defined by different periodic shifts in depictions of the national past. For example, the visual components of dominant nationcentric narratives changed substantially by the 1980s with less emphasis given to examples of violent sacrifices for the nation. With the political turmoil of the late 1980s and early 1990s, violent nationalist imagery re-emerged and was spread extensively by the propagandist mass media, educational systems and extremist civil-society groups. Nevertheless, with the end of wars and the gradual normalisation of social relationships, much of this virulent nationalist euphoria was replaced with a substantially softer version of national self-representations.

Thus, twenty-first-century Serbian and Croatian nationalism are less centred on the reproduction of violent imagery and more focused on the respective nations' international successes in sports, science and technology, arts, diplomacy, economy, education, tourism and other less pugnacious areas. In other words, unlike the nineteenth-century obsession with a glorious past, brutal wars, forced migrations and individual cases of ultimate sacrifice for the nation, the emphasis now is on the regional or global success achieved by distinguished representatives of the nation.

In this context, successes in international sporting competitions such as the Olympics, world and European championships loom large in the public eye. In the Croatian case, the emphasis is on the national teams' performance in the arenas of football, handball and water polo, as well as the number of Olympic gold medals Croatian athletes have won. The mass media provides extensive coverage to such events and the most memorable victories are usually celebrated with special TV and radio programmes or through exclusive newspaper and magazine reports featuring extensively illustrated articles and cover pages. For example, one typical newspaper article entitled 'They have conquered and astonished the world', lists the greatest sporting success of Croats and emphasises that – relative to its small population –Croatia proved to be 'the seventh world power in terms of the number of gold medals' at the London 2012 Olympics (Snidarić 2012). In a similar vein, achievements at the 2016 Rio Olympics were described as ultimate proof that, in sporting terms, Croatia is 'a world power': 'we knew this for years, but the Olympic games in Rio only confirmed this in the best possible way ... when the Croatian gold medals are calculated in terms of the size of its population we are the third in the world' (Besedić 2016: 12). Such newspaper articles are characteristically illustrated with numerous photographs of smiling athletes displaying their medals, along with Croatian flags and other national symbols.

In the Serbian case, sporting achievements also receive a great deal of public attention. The focus here is on team sports such as basketball, water polo and volleyball, but also on the success of individuals such as the tennis player Novak Djoković. Here too the mass media depict sporting achievements as unprecedented for the small size of the country. In a typical newspaper article from the Rio Olympics entitled 'Phenomenon in Rio: Why are we so good at sports?', the Serbian medal haul is described as the 'greatest success since independence', while 'the world public wonders how it is possible that a country with only seven million people manages to achieve such brilliant results'. This apparent success in team sports is explained by invoking a uniquely Serbian 'mentality', which is bolstered by 'discipline' and 'creativity' (Tašković 2016). Nevertheless, the main focus of Serbian mass-mediated attention in the sporting arena is centred on the performance of Novak Djoković, who is regularly portrayed as the epitome of a modern Serb. Thus, a rather typical newspaper article, entitled 'Nole, our modern champion: a new Serbian hero' describes how Djoković is not only the best tennis player in the world but also somebody who is kind, modest, hardworking, honest, intelligent, charming, funny and down to earth. All these qualities are then linked to his strong sense of 'patriotism and belonging to his nation', with this spark of virulent nationalism tempered by the claim that 'love of his own country does not mean humiliating other countries' (Mandrapa 2014). Here too sporting successes are illustrated with photographs of Djoković and other athletes triumphantly brandishing cups, medals and awards while visually framed by the national colours.

In addition to sports, the public sphere in twenty-first-century Croatia and Serbia is also saturated with images and rhetoric that celebrate national accomplishments in science, technology and education. Both Serbian and Croatian mass media regularly feature reports on the major achievements of their scientists, inventors, educationalists and various researchers. A common thread through most such reports is that the native scientists have made breakthroughs that equal or surpass those of the best researchers in the world. Hence, one long report on the main Serbian state TV channel describes how Serbian scientists discovered new technology that was later reported as a major breakthrough for Japanese scientists: 'The Japanese scientists discovery of the bacteria that can quickly decompose plastic bottles has gained a great deal of attention around the world last week. However our audience is not familiar that the Serbian chemists have been using similar technique to clean our land from oil and its derivatives and in this way are shoulder and shoulder with their colleagues from abroad' (TANJUG 2016). In a similar way, the main news programme of the influential Croatian TV channel RTL and several newspapers report on the global significance of a Croatian scientific breakthrough. The reports describe the discovery of medicine to heal bone fractures as 'a sensational success of Croatian scientists' and how 'Croats have discovered medicine for bone repair'. It is emphasised that this was achieved with 'enormous enthusiasm' against all odds and with a lot of 'hard work', 'mutual trust and wish to succeed' in order to create Osteogrow, 'the first medicine created in the [independent] Croatian state' (Jurešeko and Lilek 2016; Skorin 2016). A similar discourse appears in numerous mass media reports about 'Croatian discovery of the new material katsenit', which is described as 'likely to revolutionise [the] car industry'. A close reading of these reports makes it clear that this was result of a joint international team led by a Greek scientist, after whom the new element is named, yet the media presentations centre almost exclusively on the Croatian scientists and their importance (Arežina 2015; Matić 2015). The reports are extensively illustrated with smiling white-coated scientists working hard in their labs.

In addition, both Serbian and Croatian media feature many articles and reports focusing on the international success of pupils in various educational competitions (science, mathematics, geography, astronomy, debating etc.). In most of these reports, students are praised as exemplary representatives of their nation. One such report, entitled 'They are Croatian Pride: Geniuses from MIOC, a world champions in informatics, have returned to their homeland', reports how a group of Croatian secondary school students won gold medals at the world championships in computer science and informatics in the USA (Mesić and Bertek 2016). The report also carries illustrated interviews with students, some of whom emphasise that they have no intention of leaving Croatia despite their international success: 'I don't want to leave Croatia, I have everything here' (Mesić and Bertek 2016).

A similar information pattern is discernible in Serbia where student accomplishments are widely reported and celebrated. For example, one report that typifies this is entitled 'Serbian Mathematical Champions', which describes secondary school students who won six medals at the mathematics and physics world championship in Kazakhstan, which is then framed as the accomplishment of 'our geniuses' who 'showed the world how talented are people from Serbia' and who have made their school and the whole nation proud (Lazić and Milojević 2016).

National success in arts, literature and film also feature highly in both Croatian and Serbian public space. In particular, the winning of international awards is praised and extensively reported in the mass media. In the Serbian case, film directors such as Emir Kusturica and Goran Paskaljević are regularly described as world-renowned artists whose films have made Serbia much more visible in the world. Kusturica in particular has received a great deal of attention as somebody who has won many film awards (including at Cannes and Venice film festivals), but also as somebody who is perceived to be a 'true Serbian patriot'. The mainstream mass media regularly feature articles and interviews depicting Kusturica as the 'world renowned film director' and somebody who is dedicated to the 'Serbian cause' (Janković 2015).

In a similar way, the international successes of native artists feature prominently in Croatian public space. Newspapers and magazines dedicate long articles, always extensively illustrated, to painters, musicians, novelists, film directors and other thriving artists. One representative example is entitled 'Great International Success of our Artist: Young designer from Samobor is conquering the whole world with her illustrations', thus describing the work of Mateja Kovač, a fashion designer. The article emphasises how her illustrations were featured in many Canadian cities and how 'numerous Canadians were impressed by her work' (Bratić 2015). Similarly, several Croatian writers are depicted as having made an important contribution to world literature. In this context, Miro Gavran is described as 'the most popular Croatian writer in the world', who won twenty different awards and whose theatre plays 'were staged more than 9000 times all over the world' and 'were seen by audiences of 1.5 million' (Ožegović 2006).

When comparing nineteenth and twenty-first-century Serbia and Croatia, it becomes clear that there is a significant difference in how nationhood is represented and visualised: while the former is centred on violent imagery – a mythologised past and future greatness – the latter is predominantly occupied with peaceful and internationally recognised successes in the present. Whereas the public sphere in nineteenth-century Croatia and Serbia was saturated with aggressive imagery and rhetoric, their twenty-first-century counterparts tend to invoke much softer forms of national self-representation. This shift in visual and textual forms of representation could be seen as indicating a rapid weakening of nationalism in these two societies. The conventional interpretations might see these two cases as being rather typical European post-nationalist societies being fully integrated in the ever-globalising world (Beck 2006; Habermas 2001).

One could agree that Serbia and Croatia are not unique in this historical transition from the aggressive nineteenth-century displays of national attachments towards more habitual and trivial expressions of nationhood that characterise early twenty-first-century experience. Nevertheless, this shift in representation and visualisation of the nation should not be interpreted as a sign of nationalism's decline. On the contrary, I would argue that this major change in fact indicates the opposite: twenty-first-century nationalisms exert a much greater societal grip than was the case during the nineteenth century. In Serbia and Croatia, just as in the rest of Europe, nationalism has evolved and, in this process, has become much more grounded in the everyday life of ordinary individuals.

However, to fully understand how nationalist ideology operates, it is paramount to focus our attention on the broader structural transformations that have taken place in this part of the world. Hence, whereas nineteenth-century Balkan societies were characterised by extremely low literacy rates, un-standardised vernaculars, non-existence of society-wide uniform educational systems, weak state capacity and division of labour, poorly developed administrative structure, transport and communication networks and very scant growth of 'high' culture institutions, this is not the case with their twenty-first-century counterparts.

Even a brief look at key modernisation indicators shows that both contemporary Serbia and Croatia have become very different societies to their predecessors. For example, full literacy has become a norm in both countries (with Croatia at 99 per cent and Serbia at 98 per cent literacy rate, CIA 2016). Moreover, both states operate complex and standardised systems of primary and secondary education that encompass an overwhelming majority of its young population. This educational system is decisive in facilitating the nationcentric form of socialisation. By being continuously exposed to nationalist understandings of history, geography, literature and other school subjects, pupils become well aware of their nationhood long before they become adults. In both cases, the educational system is state supervised and state financed. In addition, this system of education together with other state institutions involves the use and policing of the official, standardised, version of national language thus maintaining a homogenised understanding of national 'high' culture (David 2014; Uzelac 2006; Malešević 2002).

Although Croatia is still ahead of Serbia on several important indicators of modernisation, both societies have made enormous progress in terms of infrastructural developments. Hence, state capacities have increased dramatically. For example, in 2014 Serbia had an enormous public sector with over 585,000 individuals employed in public administration (Verheijen 2014). The Croatian civil service was smaller but still in the range of over 388,000 employees (Bejaković 2011). The structural transformation is particularly visible in the development of transport and communication and the level of state centralisation. Despite nominal commitment to regionalisation and decentralisation, both states are highly centralised polities. Hence, all major decisions on economy, politics and culture are made by the central governments. Both countries also maintain extensive transport and communication networks. For example, contemporary Croatia possesses 2,722 km of railways and close to 27,000 km of roadways with over 1,300 km of highways (CIA 2016). Its modern highways, which connect all major Croatian cities and seaports, are generally regarded as being of very high quality. Although the standard of Serbia's roads and trains is generally lower than that of Croatia, it too maintains over 28,000 km of paved roads and 3,808 km of railways. Both countries also have advanced communication networks with modern digitalised telecommunications equipment and wireless services with national coverage and more mobile phones in use than the size of population might otherwise indicate (CIA 2016). In addition, there are numerous mass media outlets with dozens of nation-wide TV networks, many regional TV and radio stations and hundreds of newspapers and magazines. All of these significant structural developments have proved crucial in providing organisational channels for the society-wide nationalisation of the population. Unlike their nineteenth-century predecessors that lacked the organisational means to turn peasants into nationally conscious Serbs and Croats, twenty-first-century Serbia and Croatia are comprised of populations that are thoroughly nationalised. Serbian and Croatian nationalisms are now fully grounded and deeply entrenched in the institutions and the everyday life of their citizens.

According to various surveys, an overwhelming majority of the population in Serbia and Croatia considers their nationhood to be a very important source of identity. For example, in 2011, 79 per cent of respondents described attachment to their nation as being extremely or very important, with only 5 per cent stating that national identity means little or nothing to them and the remaining 16 per cent describing their attachment as being of 'medium' significance (Krstić 2011). Similarly, a large majority of Croatian respondents identify strongly with their nation (Kamenov et al. 2006) with 82.2 per cent of the population feeling proud to be Croat (Zabec 2011).

Beyond Violence and Banality: The Prestige of Grounded Nationhood

The significant difference in the way nationhood is visualised and represented in nineteenth and twenty-first-century Serbia and Croatia might indicate that this region exhibits very similar ideological patterns to those that have been identified elsewhere. In some respects this is true. Most European nationalisms have undergone a gradual transformation over the last two centuries. Whereas late nineteenth-century French or German nationalisms were celebrating martyrdom and sacrifices for the nation, today's nationalist discourses in France and Germany utilise much softer images and rhetoric. For example, nineteenth-century French art was saturated with the violent images invoking the centrality of one's nation such as Delacroix's famous paintings including Liberty Leading the People (1830) and Massacre at Chios (1824). In these paintings nationhood emerges through excessive bloodshed of innocents. Similarly, much of nineteenth-century German art had strong and aggressive nationalist articulation – from belligerent poetry of Arndt, Jahn and Schenkendorf to Wagner's operas. One of the most popular nineteenth-century patriotic lines from Schenkendorf was 'Only iron can rescue us, only blood can redeem us' (Heater 2004: 41). In contrast, contemporary nationalist discourses in France, and even more in Germany, deploy subtler ideas of nationhood. Moreover, traditional imagery of violent sacrifice and martyrdom has been replaced with the focus on nation's successes in science, technology, economy, sports, entertainment and other less bellicose areas. Hence, the German sense of national pride is now derived less from the glorious (or infamous) past and much more from the successful present including the robust world-power economy and high quality of life to the strong welfare state, advanced and accessible educational system and various sporting successes (www.theguardian.com/world/20 01/mar/25/kateconnolly.theobserver). Contemporary French nationalism operates in a similar fashion with the focus on scientific innovations, cultural, educational and artistic institutions, accessible health system and being a number one tourist destination in the world (www.thelocal .fr/galleries/news/ten-reasons-why-the-french-can-be-proud-of-france/ /10).

Since Billig's (1995) influential work, many scholars have historically traced the gradual transformation of nationalism from its traditional, virulent, forms towards more banal expressions of nationhood. While aggressive, hot, nationalism is usually associated with conflicts and the rise of national movements eager to establish independent states, banal, everyday nationalism is generally linked with the peaceful and relatively prosperous social conditions of 'established nation-states' (Fox 2017; Skey 2011). As Billig (1995: 41) put it, banal nationalism transpires when a 'nation-state becomes established in its sovereignty', thus creating conditions for the shift from the conscious display of national symbols towards unconscious daily 'flagging of nationhood'. In other words, this is 'a movement from symbolic mindfulness to mindlessness'. Although it is true that all nationalisms wax and wane and that changing geopolitical environments shape the character of nationalist experience, this simple dichotomy cannot fully capture the complex sociological features of nationalisms in general and Serbian and Croatian nationalisms in particular.[3]

For one thing, Billig's notion of banality stands for the relatively weak and unconscious reproduction of nationalist imagery in everyday life. However twenty-first-century Serbian and Croatian nationalisms are neither unconscious nor weak. On the contrary, the shift from nineteenth-century aggressive displays of politicians and intellectuals towards twenty-first-century glorifications of internationally successful scientists, athletes or artists are fully cognisant expressions of nationalism. Croatian and Serbian successes in the international arena are celebrated openly, shamelessly and deliberately. In a quasi-Durkhemian fashion, nation-hood seems to replace divinity, and as Gellner (1983: 56) put it, 'in a nationalist age, societies worship themselves brazenly and openly, spurning the camouflage'. The flags and other visual symbols are not hanging unnoticed, as in Billig's banal nationalism, but are displayed prominently, passionately and intentionally. However, these passionate displays of nationhood are generally not couched in nineteenth-century discourses of martyrdom, suffering and hostility. Instead they are centred on tangible successes in the global world.

Furthermore, this flagging of the nation is not a weak force rooted in the habits of daily routine but is a process shaped by deep organisational potency. Unlike their nineteenth-century counterparts, which had neither the organisational means nor the ideological know-how to penetrate the wider social order, twenty-first-century Balkan nationalisms are organisationally deeply grounded and ideologically rooted within the state structure and civil society networks. In this context, when an overwhelming majority

---

[3] For a more extensive critique of this hot vs. banal nationalism dichotomy, see Malešević 2013: 120–54.

of the population is already fully 'nationalised', there is no need to continuously invoke past glories and tragic sacrifices. Hence, instead of deploying nationalist imagery and rhetoric as a didactic tool of socialisation, in the contemporary context international victories are utilised as a status-enhancing ideological device. Whereas before, societywide identification with the nation was still only an aspiration, today nationalist ideology is deeply rooted and normalised as the dominant operative ideological discourse (Malešević 2006). While the nineteenth-century peasantry had to be taught who they were and who their glorious predecessors were, today's Croats and Serbs are completely familiar with, and fully immersed in, these traditional nationalist tropes. Thus, the ideological discursive field has moved not from virulence to banality, as argued by Billig and others, but towards grounded nationalisms rooted in prestige politics.

This gradual shift from nationalist ideology steeped in violence towards internationally competitive grounded nationalisms is very much in line with Max Weber's (1968: 395, 921) concept of prestige-driven nationalisms. For Weber, nations were status groups defined by their constant struggle over prestige. In his own terms: 'the significance of the "nation" is usually anchored in the superiority, or at least the irreplaceability, of the cultural values that are to be preserved and developed only through the cultivation of the peculiarity of the group' (p. 925). Furthermore, Weber emphasises that 'the prestige of power means in practice the glory of power over other communities' (p. 911), whereby political and other international successes reinforce the strength of nationalist ideology. Building on Weber's ideas, Collins (1990: 155) argues that in modernity prestige underpins nationalism and that members of the nation often resemble football fans in a sense that their loyalty is enhanced by team victories: 'A victorious state experiences the greatest nationalism ... [while] a long string of defeats saps national loyalty'. Although both Weber and Collins are right that nationalism is deeply rooted in prestige politics, they neglect how specific historical contexts shape the character of nationalisms. Rather than assuming, as they do, that all nationalisms are very similar in a sense that they are all driven by an insatiated hunger for prestige, it is necessary to differentiate clearly between early modern and late modern nationalist experiences. Nineteenth-century world populations could not resemble football fans as for the most part they did not, and could not, identify with 'their' nations. Although prestige politics was an important social driver of elite behaviour at that time, this was not the case with the majority of ordinary individuals (Mann 1993). In other words, for nationalisms to become the object of popular status competitions, it was paramount that they attain a substantial degree of organisational grounding and societywide ideological penetration.

Hence, not all nationalisms are automatically destined towards prestige competition. For this can only happen when certain organisational and ideological conditions are already in place: high literacy rates, standardised and state supervised educational systems, viable and expansive 'high culture', developed communication and transport networks and so on. In this way, twenty-first-century nationalisms easily trump their nineteenth-century counterparts: while in the early modern period only a small number of people considered themselves members of 'their' nations, today this applies to the vast majority. Although most of our daily encounters with nationhood might be shaped by unconscious habitual banality, as argued by Billig, the potency of nationalism in the twenty-first century resides primarily in its organisational, ideological and micro-interactional ground-ness. One can be more or less conscious of specific nationalist routines but the very presence of these routines is dependent on the existence of specific organisational and ideological scaffolds. In this context, twenty-first-century Serbia and Croatia are not unique as they reflect world-wide transformation of nationalisms[4]: the appearance of relatively muted and pacified nationalist imagery and rhetoric does not indicate the weakening of nation-centric perceptions of the world; instead they point towards greater structural entrenchment of nationalisms. Thus the shift from virulence and sacrifice, via banality, towards prestige entails the presence of strong organisational scaffolds, greater ideological receptiveness and the capacity to tap into the micro-universe of daily interactions. In such a highly nationalised and also competitive social environment, the successes and failures of the nation are regularly understood as directly reflecting the achievements and fiascos attributed to co-nationals as individuals and members of national 'teams'. It is only now that our nationhood resembles die-hard football fandom.

Conclusion

Much of the scholarship on nationalism coheres around the idea that contemporary nationalisms differ from their nineteenth-century counterparts in terms of rhetoric, imagery and intensity. The general perception is that whereas nineteenth-century nationalisms were defined by their popular strength, aggressive displays, violent idioms and images, most of twenty-first-century nationalisms are characterised by their anaemic

---

[4] This is not to say that all European nationalisms are identical. Obviously, specific historical and contemporary events impact on the intensity and character of specific nationalist discourse. The relatively recent wars of the 1990s certainly had an impact on the intensity of nationalist experience in Croatia and Serbia.

and moderate habitual practices of daily routine. This line of argument has been applied to different parts of the world, including south east Europe. However, this chapter challenges such interpretations by zooming in on the transformation of nationalisms in Serbia and Croatia. Contrary to conventional views that conflate violent posturing with strength, I show how nineteenth-century Balkan nationalisms were in fact very feeble. Rather than expressing popular views, such nationalisms operated largely as pedagogical devices for the political socialisation of the peasantry. In contrast to this, twenty-first-century Balkan nationalisms dispense with violent rhetoric and imagery and focus on achievements in the international arena. Nevertheless, this visual and discursive shift does not indicate the gradual weakening of nationalism or its turn towards everyday banality. Instead, this prestige-driven nationalism is much more powerful and popular as it is rooted in greater ideological penetration and the substantially increased organisational capacities of Serbian and Croatian societies.

10   Globalisation and Nationalist Subjectivities

Introduction

One of the key themes of contemporary sociology is individualisation. Over the last two decades, a variety of social theorists, including Ulrich Beck, Elisabeth Beck-Gernsheim, Anthony Giddens and Zygmunt Bauman, among others, have emphasised that the present-day world is unique in its pronounced focus on reflexive self-actualisation and self-definition. In the words of Beck and Beck-Gersheim (2002: xxii), 'the individual is becoming the basic unit of social reproduction for the first time in history'. These scholars argue that late modernity is characterised by the gradual weakening of collective identities, be they class, nation or religion, and the ever-increasing focus on fashioning one's one life according to one's individual choices, i.e. the rise of late modern subjectivities. Instead of the traditional 'social norms and regulations', 'individuals must, in part, supply ... [these norms and regulations] for themselves, import them into their biographies through their own actions' (Beck and Beck-Gersheim 2002: 2). Similarly, Giddens (1991: 75) argues that in the highly individualised world of late modernity 'we are not what we are, but what we make of ourselves'. Although Bauman is more focused on the stratifying nature of individualisation, he too is adamant that late modernity is characterised by rampant individualisation and that identities have undergone a dramatic transition from being given at birth to becoming 'a task' that one has to pursue and attain while also being encouraged to take full responsibility for this 'task' (Bauman, 2000: 31 f.).

This shift towards individualisation and late modern subjectivities is understood as being directly caused by globalisation, a phenomenon seen as historically unique in its scope and impact. For these authors, globalisation melts traditional social identities and fosters dynamic forms of subjectivity where class and nationhood lose their significance. More specifically, this view is premised on the idea that globalisation, individualisation and

234

nationalism are mutually exclusive processes. While nationalism is associated with the preservation of state sovereignty, globalisation and individualisation are understood to stand for subjectively articulated worldwide integration. Whereas globalisation and individualisation involve open borders and interchange of trade, knowledge, products, ideas and people, nationalist ideologies advocate the safeguarding of economic and political autonomy and protection of cultural authenticity.

However, in this chapter, I aim to challenge such interpretations by demonstrating how modern subjectivities, globalisation and nationalism have historically constituted each other. Moreover, the chapter makes a case that the transformation of modern subjectivities owes a great deal to the interdependence of nationalism and globalisation. The first part of the chapter offers a brief review and a critique of the approaches that overemphasise the historical novelty of individualisation and globalisation while also perceiving nationalism as an ideology in decline. The second part aims to show how and why modern subjectivities tend to be underpinned by nationalist discourses (and vice versa). The third part assesses the impact of neo-liberalism, cosmopolitanism, consumerism and religious fundamentalism on modern subjectivities and nationalist ideologies. The key arguments are illustrated with specific examples from around the world. The final part explores the historical and contemporary interdependence of globalisation and subjectivities, aiming to demonstrate how both nationalism and globalisation continue to shape the modern subject.

The Rise of the Modern Subject

The concept of subjectivity has been central to many different philosophical traditions. From Descartes and Kierkegaard, utilitarianism, phenomenology, analytical philosophy, existentialism and pragmatism, the notion of subject plays a crucial role in understanding the human condition. In contrast, mainstream social science always had a more ambiguous relationship with the notion of subjectivity. On the one hand, human subjective experience was often considered to be an important generator of social action. Hence, even the most functionalist and structuralist approaches, such as those of Talcott Parsons (1977) and Claude Levi-Strauss (1983), recognised that social relations involve a degree of inter-subjectivity. On the other hand, as social science is by definition oriented towards generalisations, the tendency is to focus on the objective parameters that shape social phenomena and, in this process, downplay the impact of subjectivity. This is particularly pronounced in positivist scholarship but is just as visible in many strands of interpretative social science. While positivists recognise the significance of human agency, they tend to treat it as a universal form of human collective behaviour leaving no room for individual differences. Interpretative-oriented approaches, such as symbolic interactionism or ethnomethodology, devote a great deal of attention to the subjective perceptions of social reality but they rarely attempt to historicise subjectivity and trace its long-term trajectories. Here too the overemphasis on generalisation has prevented development of the historically more nuanced notion of subjectivity. With the rise of anti-foundationalist perspectives in the 1980s, 1990s and early 2000s, many of which proclaimed the death of the subject, social scientists have become even more wary of any reference to subjectivity. Post-structuralism, post-Marxism and post-modernism have all dented the Enlightenment-inspired idea of the human subject as the principal agent of social change (Malešević 2004: 143–48).

Nevertheless, this anti-foundationalist onslaught, pioneered in philosophy and literature studies, has recently been challenged by several sociological approaches that have reintroduced individuality and subjectivity as the central categories of analysis. In the last two decades, one could witness growing interest in the notion of the subject within sociology. The dominance of anti-foundationalism has been contested by several sociological approaches, all of which emphasise individual action and subjectivity as the driving force of contemporary social life. In France, Alain Touraine (2009) and Michel Wieviorka (2009, 2003) developed sociology of action centred on the 'return of the subject'. The primary focus of this research is to study social movements and understand the subjective rationale of individual actors in the context of social conflicts arising in the post-industrial world. As Wieviorka (2015) insists, this type of research focuses on the personal interactions and actions: 'the individual, the particular subject (the private person), their passions, desires, calculations, fears, or emotions including the most intimate'. More specifically, for Wieviorka, subjectivity underpins much of social action. For example, in his view, violence 'refers to either impaired ability of a group or individual to become a subject or to function as such, to mechanism of desubjectivation, or to the expansion or expression of the anti-subject . . . violence is bound up with the way in which the subject is constructed, or is not constructed, in the inverted form of anti-subject' (Wieviorka 2009: 147). For Tourane and Wieviorka, the rise of the subject has shifted the focus from class and nation towards more personalised identities.

In the United Kingdom and Germany, a number of influential scholars have also shifted their attention towards subjectivity. Thus, Anthony Giddens, Scott Lash and Ulrich Beck (1994) articulated a theory of reflexive modernisation which aims to explain the transformation of human subjectivity by looking at what they see to be a radical shift in the character of modern life. More to the point, these theorists argue that one should differentiate between early and late (or second) modernity. In this account, early modernity was characterised by social and political struggles focused on civil, political and economic rights culminating in the emergence of the post-WWII welfare state. In contrast, the second modernity appears in the context of intensified globalisation where the nation state loses its supremacy as transnational corporations, regional associations and NGOs gain more power. In such profoundly changed and unstable environment, modern subjectivity becomes the centre of social conflicts as individuals are seen to be shifting their allegiances from class and nation towards different forms of cultural self-expression.

More recently, Zygmunt Bauman (2006, 2000, 1998), Giddens (2002), Beck and Beck-Gersheim (2002), among others, have extended this argument further by zooming in on the process they call individualisation. For Beck and Beck-Gersheim (2002) the proliferation of globalisation has radically changed contemporary social relations so that the individual, not the group, has become the central unit of social life. As globalisation allegedly melts borders of nation states and traditional norms, individuals become increasingly required to construct their own life-projects. In this view, individualisation is a structural feature of highly differentiated societies and as such does not necessarily mean the end of social cohesion but just its transformation into a new more-individualised form. For Beck and Beck-Gersheim (2002), this transformation is often articulated as 'institutionalised individualism', where old institutional forms are not suited anymore for building cohesive structures:

Central institutions of modern society – basic civil, political and social rights ... are geared to the individual and not to the group. Insofar as basic rights are internalised and everyone wants to or must be economically active to earn their livelihood, the spiral of individualization destroys the given foundations of social coexistence'. (Beck and Beck-Gernsheim, 2002: xxi–xxii)

Hence, the shift towards individualisation entails rethinking and reorganising existing political, economic, cultural and other structures.

All of these recent developments indicate that subjectivity has rightly become a crucial topic in sociology. There is a growing consensus that the complexity of social relations in late modernity cannot be properly explained without paying attention to the transformation of human subjectivity. However, what is missing in these contemporary sociological theories of subjectivity is the understanding that the emergence and transformation of the subject owes a great deal to the broader historical, geo-political, organisational, ideological and micro-interactional changes that have paved the way for the present articulations of subjectivity (Malešević 2017, 2013, 2010). In this context, the apparent rise of individualism cannot be reduced solely to the internal and short-term social changes taking place within specific, mostly European and North American, societies.[1] Instead, individualisation is a social product of much wider historical and geo-political processes. Hence, to fully understand the dynamics of subjectivity in late modernity, it is paramount to articulate a longue durée approach capable of tracing the historical trajectories of social change. More to the point, this entails exploring the long-term organisational, ideological and micro-interactional structures that have made the transformation of modern subjectivities possible. This means that inflexible taxonomies, such as individualisation vs. nationalism or globalisation vs. nation state, utilised by the theorists of reflexive modernisation (Beck, Beck-Gersheim, Giddens, Bauman) and the sociologists of action (Tourain, Wieviorka), require more rethinking and unpacking. In other words, I argue that the rise of modern subjectivity can only be explained in the context of nation-state transformation and the long-term historical dialectic between the polity and global order.

Instead of treating the modern subject as being completely detached from the workings of nation-states, it is paramount to recognise that modern subjectivity has largely developed through the organisational channels of the nation state as well as through violent and other interactions between nation states and other polities. Moreover, the modern subject does not transpire in opposition to nationalism; rather the modern subject is for the most part also a nationalist subject (Malešević 2013a, 2006; Wimmer 2002; Gellner 1983). In this sense, the process of individualisation does not arise as an antipode to nationalism. On the contrary, as I argue in the chapter, nationalist ideology often fosters individualisation and self-actualisation and vice versa.

Nevertheless, to historically contextualise the rise of modern nationalist subjectivity, it is also crucial to debunk the other false dichotomy advanced by the theorists of reflexive modernisation, that of globalisation vs. nation state. For Bauman, Giddens and Beck, globalisation is a distinctly novel phenomenon with no historical predecessors. In their influential account, as globalisation advances, it is bound to dissolve boundaries of nation states: state power weakens giving way to private corporations, social movements and a variety of non-governmental associations. In such an environment, as Beck and Beck-Gernsheim (2002)

---

[1] Some critics have rightly characterised these approaches as being deeply ethnocentric and blind to class differences. The critics argue that Giddens and Beck focus almost exclusively on the experiences of the European and North American middle classes while ignoring the rest of the world (Poortman and Liefbroer 2010; Bhambra 2007).

argue, traditional forms of solidarity dissipate and one's life project becomes an individualised creation – an act of self-fashioning and self-production. In this runaway world (Giddens 2002), there is no room for nationalism as globalisation generates highly individualised citizens who allegedly lose any sense of emotional or instrumental attachment to nation states. Nevertheless, both of these flawed dichotomies, individualisation vs. nationalism and globalisation vs. nation state, require much more rethinking.

Is Nationalism in Decline?

Many scholars and policy makers see globalisation and nationalism as irreconcilable foes. In this type of narrative, globalisation stands for technological progress, economic development, cosmopolitan sensibilities, interdependence of global citizens and continuous scientific innovation. In contrast, nationalism is regularly portrayed as a regressive, claustrophobic, protectionist and old-fashioned ideology which is slowly but surely losing its popular grip throughout the world. For example, one of the early analysts of globalisation, management guru Kenichi Ohmae (1995: 12), described the institution of the nation state as a 'nostalgic fiction'. The theorists of reflexive modernisation, such as Ulrich Beck (2000) and Anthony Giddens (2002), are just as explicit in their view that there is no room for nationalism in the era of globalisation. Thus, Beck argues that 'the nation-state project' has been replaced by 'the cosmopolitan project' while Giddens (2002) insists that globalisation has undermined the impact of nation states and nationalism. In his own words: 'national economic policy can't be as effective as it once was … nations have to rethink their identities now the older forms of geopolitics are becoming obsolete … most nations no longer have enemies' and 'old style territorial nationalism' is countered and replaced by 'ethically driven interventionism' as was the case in 1999 Kosovo war (Giddens 2002: 18). In a similar, albeit more critical, way, Zygmunt Bauman (2002: 84) argues that globalisation fosters individualism and consumerism so that most people are likely to behave as individualised consumers rather than as loyal patriots. As he emphasises: 'nation-building coupled with patriotic mobilisation has ceased to be the principal instrument of social integration and states' self-assertion' (Bauman 2002: 84). Even the recent proliferation of nativist populism throughout the world, ranging from the Trump election, Brexit, the dominance of BJP in India and the series of electoral success for far-right anti-immigrant parties, has not significantly dented this well-entrenched view that nationalism is bound to decline. These recent developments are often interpreted as some form of unexpected and temporary aberration that go against the unstoppable expansion of globalisation (Giddens 2017).

While Omahe and the theorists of reflexive modernisation might disagree over the question of whether globalisation benefits all or is likely to generate deeper social inequalities, these analysts generally share the view that globalisation diminishes the power of nationalist identifications. Nevertheless, I would argue that these views are premised on two wrong assumptions: that nationalism, globalisation and individualisation are mutually exclusive processes; and that the expansion of globalisation undermines the influence of nationalism. Both of these assumptions are rooted in the view that nationalism as such is an ideology in steep decline. Some analysts see the late nineteenth and early twentieth centuries as the heyday of nationalism (Giddens 2007, 2002). For others, this ideology reached its peak between the 1950s and the 1970s, following the worldwide proliferation of post-colonial independence movements (Breuilly 1993; Gellner 1983). Yet for many scholars, the wave of post-communist national revolutions of 1989–91 was the pinnacle for the ideas of popular sovereignty, national independence and cultural authenticity (Bauman 1998, Beck 2000). Once the East European countries achieved or regained their independence, the expectation was that nationalism would be confined to the dustbin of history. Francis Fukuyama's (2006[1992]) well-known notion of the end of history was largely associated with the collapse of socialist and communist alternatives to liberal democracy. Nevertheless, he fully shares the view of Omahe, Beck and others describing the rise of nationalism in Eastern Europe as a temporary phenomenon: 'the view of nationalism as permanent and all-conquering is both parochial and untrue' and nationalism has 'lost much of its ability to stimulate Europeans to risk their comfortable lives in great acts of imperialism' (Fukuyama 2006[1992]: 268, 272).[2] The continuous expansion of the European Union, reaching its pinnacle in the 2004 accession of ten new members, was perceived as ultimate proof of nationalism's deterioration and inevitable evaporation.

The rise of so-called 'new nationalism', exemplified by Donald Trump's America First policies and Brexit, is often perceived in a very similar way. The widely shared assumption is that this unprecedented shift towards economic protectionism, xenophobic immigration policies and nativism is unlikely to last as it defies the dominant economic, political and cultural dynamics of a deeply globalised world (Crouch, Sakalis and Bechler 2016). Furthermore, 'new nationalism' is perceived to be a novel phenomenon driven by social groups which found themselves on the losing end of globalisation. For example, many commentators describe 'new nationalism'

---

[2] In his recent work Fukuyama (2018) seems now to question these early assessments.

as 'broad nativist revolt' against the neo-liberal economy of unfettered free trade and unlimited immigration (Dougherty 2016; Matthews 2016).

However, this nationalism is neither new nor does it go against long-term historical trends. The unfounded assumptions about 'new nationalism' stem from the deeply ingrained, and wrong, belief that nationalist ideology has been in decline for years. Nevertheless, rather than creating an utterly new situation, Brexit and the Trump election have only made it more visible. In other words, 'new nationalism' did not come out of nowhere in 2016. Instead, this sudden escalation was rooted in well-established organisational, ideological and micro-interactional structures that have been in place for the last two centuries. Hence, nationalism was not in decline before these events: it was and remains the dominant operative ideology of modernity (Malešević 2013a, 2006). Nationalist discourses have wider reach at present than they had in the nineteenth or twentieth centuries while nationalist ideas and practices are much more institutionally grounded today than at any other point in history. For much of the nineteenth and early twentieth centuries, imperial principles and modes of legitimacy still easily overpowered the notion of popular sovereignty in practice if not in theory. This was the world run by the European empires, some of which, such as France, Britain or the Netherlands, combined the idea of national self-government at home with imperial expansion abroad while others such as Russia or Austro-Hungary attempted to integrate their diverse colonised populations by sticking to traditional imperial creeds (Malešević 2013a: 34–54).[3]

Although the second half of the twentieth century is not usually associated with strong nationalisms, this was a key period in the institutionalisation of nationalist ideas and practices. The fierce Cold War rhetoric of the period, couched in universalist discourses of liberal democracy vs. communism and socialist justice vs. capitalist inequality, often masked the ongoing subtle 'nationalisation of the masses' (Mosse 1975) which was decisive for the gradual integration of different social strata within the common nationalist narrative. In this sense, despite their mutually exclusive normative ideologies, the Cold War foes relied extensively on nationalism to boost their political legitimacy at home. Hence, the negative images of the enemy were less focused on the adversary's alleged economic failures or doctrinal inconsistencies but principally on the fact that they represented a direct security threat to one's country. In such an environment, emotion-centred patriotic calls for national unity were

---

[3] Although, as Stergar and Scheer (2018) show, in the later years Austro-Hungary was also 'enabler of nationalism' as it institutionalised and bureaucratised cultural difference within the empire.

much louder than any reasoned analyses of the adversary's flawed models of political or economic organisation (Malešević 2006: 157–84). As Fried (1999) shows in his penetrating *The Russians Are Coming! The Russians Are Coming!*, the Cold War period was critical in institutionalising ritualistic practices developed to boost American nationalism – the sanctification of the American flag, the coercively induced Pledge of Allegiance, introduction of 'Freedom Weeks', 'Loyalty Day', 'Know Your America' weeks, the travelling nationalist exhibitions (i.e. Freedom Train) and many other practices designed to foster a stronger sense of patriotic zeal among US citizens. In a very similar way, the Soviet propaganda was less focused on the inefficiencies and contradictions of the free market economics and was largely centred on glorifying Soviet nationalities and depicting the Americans and Britons as immoral and dangerous nations that present an existential threat to the Soviet way of life. For example, just as Americans, Soviet citizens were involved in large-scale, state-sponsored ritualistic exercises devised to celebrate their fatherland. As Tomiak (2016: 11) shows, Soviet nationalism permeated the educational system where children were thought to love their Soviet motherland. They were also involved in a variety of activities associated directly with nationalist ideas and practices: 'paramilitary training through the GTO programme (Ready for Labour and Defence), the Summer Lightning and Red Eaglet games, visits to battlefields and war cemeteries and the paying of homage to the heroes who died fighting against the Nazis'. Despite nominal commitment to proletarian internationalism, Soviet leaders always emphasised the cultural superiority of the Soviet Union. This was already visible in Stalin's response to Churchill's Iron Curtain speech where the soviet leader did not deploy the Marxist-Leninist discourse to delegitimise the 'evil capitalists'. Instead, he opted to described the Cold War foes as 'Anglo-Saxons' bent on destroying 'the Slavs'. In this context, the Cold War itself was regularly represented as a continuation of the 'Great Patriotic War' (Zubok 2009: 308).

What is even more important, is that the second half of the twentieth century was a period when nationalist principles were for the first time fully embraced by political and cultural elites around the world and were also gradually institutionalised through the state apparatuses of many polities (Mann 2013: 13–36). While before WWII, nationalism still remained a minority pursuit, something associated with the upper and middle-class populations, by the end of twentieth century, nationalist ideology become firmly grounded in institutional structures throughout the globe. In this historically unique organisational and ideological context, nationalism and individualisation often reinforced each other as modern citizens were able to articulate and realise their individuality through the organisational channels of the nation state.

As both Ernest Gellner (1983: 35–50) and Ben Anderson (1983) made apparent, nationalism entails modern subjectivities. There is no nationalism without high literacy rates, standardised national languages, well-established and state-run centralised educational systems, profuse nation-centric literature and mass media. Furthermore, shared nationhood presupposes the existence of vibrant civil societies and the perception that the citizens possess particular individual rights and responsibilities. Such shared liberties include a variety of civil, political and social rights: from the freedom of religion, speech, press and assembly to universal suffrage, free education and many welfare provisions. What is important to emphasise is that these rights developed together with the obligations that the nation states imposed on their citizens: to regularly pay taxes, respect law and order and fight for one's nation in times of war (Hall and Malešević 2013; Tilly 1992; Mann 1986). Society-wide nationalisation of the masses, often accomplished through the educational systems and military draft, was a cornerstone of modern subjectivity. For one could be a free and conscious agent, capable of and allowed to pursue one's goals and ambitions only through the organisational channels of a particular nation state. Moreover, since modernity was ideologically and organisationally inaugurated through the institutions of the nation state, modern subjects were inevitably also nationalist subjects.

Hence, unlike pre-modern empires, which were rooted in deeply hierarchical and often hereditary relationships and where there was no room for one's individuality, in the world of modern nation states, all citizens are regarded to be of equal moral worth. In other words, the very notion of human subjectivity could only emerge in the context of the idea of popular sovereignty and moral equality. It is no historical accident that nationalism and modern subjectivity develop and expand together: they are both built around similar principles such as autonomy, freedom, authenticity, recognition and self-expression. Despite his epistemological idealism, Kedourie (1960) was right that nationalist ideology draws as much on the Enlightenment philosophy of Kant as it does on the Romanticism of Fichte and Herder. While Kant provided the central principles of modern subjectivity (i.e. free will, reason, personal autonomy, etc.), the Romanticist movement collectivised these ideas in order to formulate nations as free, authentic and autonomous agents of history. It is in this context that one can trace the joint emergence of nationalism and modern subjectivity.

The second half of the twentieth century was a period when this ideological, nation-centric, penetration became more prevalent and more visible:

most parts of the world experienced dramatic literacy-rate increases and states all over the world poured substantial resources into building extensive educational systems with standardised national curricula including compulsory teaching of national subjects – mother tongue, history, literature, geography, etc. The outcome of these state-led, but often civil-society -supported, nationalisation drives generated new social realities where, to use Eugen Weber's (1976) famous phrase, 'peasants became Frenchman' but also Poles, Zimbabweans, Peruvians, Indonesians and so on. While before WWII an overwhelming majority of ordinary individuals in the world tended to identify themselves in terms of their locality, kinship, clan or religion, by the end of twentieth century, as various surveys show, most citizens of the world define themselves first and foremost as members of their respective nation states: Algerian, Australian, Chilean, Romanian, Japanese, etc. (Malešević 2013a: 155, 167).

This is a process which is not confined only to the newly formed polities in Africa or Asia but is a worldwide trend. As Wimmer (2018: 219) documents, several large world-wide surveys, including one conducted on a huge sample accounting for the 92 percent of world's population (i.e. 770,000 respondents), indicate that the large majority of the population across the world are proud or very proud of their nationality. Similarly, Eurobarometer surveys indicate that for most Europeans a nation remains the key source of one's social identification. Furthermore, longitudinal survey results show that one's attachment to a nation has continued to increase over the past forty years. While Eurobarometer surveys have regularly registered high levels of national identification for most citizens of Europe, these percentages have increased even more over the last thirty years. Hence, for some countries, such as Finland, Greece or Ireland, the percentages of those who express strong national pride range from 95 to 99 percent while for most other European citizens the scores oscillate between the high 80s and low 90s (Malešević 2013a: 164–7: Antonsich 2009: 281–99). This exceptionally high level of national identification is also reflected in current political events. The European project has been under severe strain for decades and the 2008 deep recession, coupled with the recent war in Ukraine, the Brexit and the immigrant crisis, further destabilised its foundations. Ever-growing 'small nation' aspirations towards independence are highly visible throughout the continent with Catalonia, Scotland and Flanders being the most prominent examples. The rise of far right and anti-immigrant parties with radical nationalist programmes has shaken domestic political life from France and Greece to the Netherlands, Sweden, Finland, Germany and Austria. The United Kingdom's decision to leave the EU and the fierce rhetoric deployed during the Brexit referendum has further polarised British and

European populations and has also made clear that nationalist discourses are firmly grounded in everyday life.

However, this strength of nationalism is not a European exception but is just as present on other continents. For example, a recent Gallup survey (2015) shows that 81 percent of Americans say that they are either extremely proud or very proud to be Americans with more than half of all respondents (54 percent) declaring themselves 'extremely proud'. Similar results have been recorded in other parts of the world. This continuous rise of nationalism is particularly pronounced among large states and rising powers such as China, India, Russia and Brazil (Duina 2018; Gallup 2015; Medrano 2009; Smith & Kim 2006: 127–36). None of this is to say that strong national attachments hamper the processes of individualisation. On the contrary, the proliferation and greater penetration of nationalist idioms and practices regularly goes hand in hand with greater individualisation. As I have argued before (Malešević 2013a: 144–52), the strength of nationalism is better gauged not by its aggressive posturing but by its invisibility. In other words, unlike hostile expressions of nationalism which often indicate insecurity and instability, habitual nationalism is more potent precisely because it is firmly grounded in everyday habitus where it becomes a second-nature, unreflected daily practice. When measured this way, bland nationalisms of liberal nation states (such as Denmark or Finland) are much more powerful than nominally aggressive nationalisms of authoritarian states (such as North Korea or Eritrea). In this context, one's sense of individuality is generally firmly linked with the organisational, ideological and micro-interactional structures of one's nation state. Polities with highly developed organisational capacities are much more capable of channelling nation-centric ideas and practices as they possess the means to do so. Furthermore, although authoritarian states such as Eritrea or North Korea often engage in permanent and very aggressive nationalist mobilisation, this nationalism lacks the degree of ideological penetration associated with polities characterised by vibrant civil societies. In other words, strong and well-grounded nationalism entails a degree of liberty where individuals can articulate their own visions of a nation. Hence, the rise of individualism does not emerge at the expense of nationalism. Instead, well-grounded nationalist ideology fosters individualisation. The US society is the best illustration of this phenomenon: deeply individualist yet intensely nationalist at the same time.

Nation States and Globalisation: Friends or Foes?

The view that nationalism has given way to globalisation is often rooted in an argument that posits a variety of globalising trends as overpowering nationalist identifications. Among those, individualist consumerism, cosmopolitanism and religious fundamentalism are identified as the principal enemies of nationalism. However, this view is largely based on the popular misconception that such phenomena are intrinsically hostile to nationalist ideologies. Nevertheless, as many recent empirical studies point out, consumerism often underpins nationalist projects. The production and consumption of national products, the branding of one's nation state and the use of national symbols for commercial purposes are widespread phenomena that have been in existence since the early nineteenth century (Skey and Antonsich 2018; Aronczyk 2013; Malešević 2013a, 120–35). The new modes of transport and communication have only helped intensify this link as most individuals can now afford to regularly consume symbols of nationhood – from US flags, badges, lapel pins, to Irish Guinness beer, to Swiss chocolates, French perfumes, Italian designer clothes to German or Japanese cars. The fact that non-nationals are also likely to consume 'our' national products further reinforces the sense of one's national pride and maintains a nation-centric understanding of social reality. More importantly, large-scale private corporations such as Microsoft, Toyota, Sinopec or Royal Dutch Shell are all popularly identified, and often marketed, as highly successful national ventures demonstrating the ingenuity and entrepreneurial acumen of their respective nations. It is no accident that several German car manufacturers, including Volkswagen and Audi, have recently started advertising their products internationally using the original German phrases such as 'Vorsprung Durch Technik' ('advancement through technology'). While most international audiences are unlikely to understand the meaning of this phrase, the use of the German expression is there to fortify the popular perception that these cars are German and that Germany makes excellent cars. While this particular marketing strategy is devised to sell cars, it also performs an important role in reinforcing a particular image of Germany as a nation state characterised by technological superiority, economic efficiency, order and scientific progress. Although most commercial adverts are created to sell specific products, they also contribute towards developing or reinforcing particular national images.

Even when individuals seem to be pacified by their lack of interest in politics and their excessive consumerist practices, this in itself does not necessarily mean that they have lost their nationalist spark. On the contrary, consumerist-oriented behaviour often goes hand in hand with periodic nationalist hysteria as citizen-consumers tend to judge their leaders on the basis of how well they produce, sell and represent their national brand (Aronczyk 2013). In this context, many governments invest into developing a unique national brand. For example, in 2003, the Polish Ministry of Commerce hired a British branding firm 'to create a new Polish national identity on the eve of the country's accession to the European Union' (Aronczyk 2013: 13). Thus, rather than undermining nationalism, consumerist practices in fact often contribute towards greater embodiment of nationalist ideas in everyday life. Consumerist individualism is rarely, if ever, an enemy of nationalism. Since capitalism and nationalism have historically developed together and have both contributed towards the rise of modern subjectivities, it seems highly unlikely that consumerist individualism will undermine nationalism (Hall 2013, 2000; Mann 2013, 1993).

The same applies to cosmopolitanism: it too does not seriously imperil nationalist ideologies. For one thing, recent cosmopolitan discourses in many important ways resemble their previous historical incarnations. Simply put, cosmopolitanism was and remains a worldview of a small, largely intellectual, minority. The idea that all human beings constitute a single moral community goes all the way back to ancient Greece, Rome and China. It is no accident that this doctrine was articulated by philosophers of stoicism and cynicism, and their predecessor Diogenes of Sinope, who also advocated the principle that only virtuous sages are capable of reasoned action. In this view, virtue was perceived as something that generates immunity to misfortune and since sages are virtuous they know how to bring about human happiness (Diogenes 2012).[4] In other words, cosmopolitan ideals have often been underpinned by elitism. This elitist ethos was noticeable, not only among intellectuals, but also among the rulers who utilised cosmopolitan doctrines to expand their power base and to legitimise their conquest of what they regarded to be less enlightened peoples. Hence, one of the leading Roman stoic cosmopolitan philosophers, Marcus Aurelius, was also a ruthless emperor responsible for the destruction of the Parthian Empire and mass killings of 'barbarian tribes' – Marcomanni, Quadi and Sarmatians. Hence, cosmopolitan ideals have historically often been grafted onto particularist projects whereby political elites camouflaged their callous politics under a veil of noble universalist ideals. This has not changed much throughout history as cosmopolitan rhetoric was regularly deployed to defend

---

[4] A version of cosmopolitan ethics developed in ancient China during the Qin and Han dynasties resembles, in some important respects, the stoic Roman tradition. It too identified the empire – Chinese instead of Roman for Stoics – with the whole world: 'the official Chinese history records are all written from the perspective of a Chinese cosmopolitan space in which all the world under the heaven is China or vice versa' (Chun 2009: 22). It also, just like Confucianism would do later, attributed special qualities to enlightened sages.

imperial projects, colonial civilising missions and more recently, humanitarian military interventions.

For another thing, many forms of cosmopolitan ideology offer highly unrealistic diagnoses of social reality. In this type of narrative, 'citizenship of the world' is directly opposed to nationalist particularisms. Nevertheless, such models of analysis privilege normative prescription over sociological realities where the nation state still remains the most powerful and only legitimate model of territorial rule. For example, despite all the talk about the unprecedented mobility of peoples 'only 3% of world's population lives outside their country of birth' (Wimmer 2018: 5). In such specific geo-political and organisational contexts, nationalist discourses are continuously reinforced in everyday activities and in a variety of banal practices (Fox & Miller-Idriss 2008, Billig 1995). Hence, while cosmopolitanism can be a choice for an elite minority, most ordinary individuals have little real opportunity to develop such a worldview or pursue such a lifestyle. As Craig Calhoun (2007: 24–5) aptly puts it: 'No one lives outside particularist solidarities. Some cosmopolitan theorists may believe they do, but this is an illusion made possible by the position of relative privilege.' Furthermore, some strands of cosmopolitan thinking, such as those articulated by Ulrich Beck (2006) and Martha Nussbaum (2006), wrongly assume that human beings can simply overcome deep political antagonisms generated through the polarising nationalist images of us vs. them. For example, Beck (2006: 137) argues that

The national outlook … fails because it cannot comprehend the new logic of power in global society. Anyone who believes that the global policeman NATO or the USA is merely pretending to play the role of global policeman while really pursuing American economic and geopolitical power interests in the powder keg of the Balkans or the Arab world not only misunderstands the situation but also overlooks the extent to which the politics of human rights (like the imposition of 'free markets') has become the civil religion, the faith of the United States itself … a new kind of postnational politics of military humanism is emerging.

The problem with this view is that it ignores the social realities of power while also wrongly assuming that nation states are driven by some postnationalist humanitarian agendas. In this sense, Beck, perhaps unwittingly, provides cosmopolitan justification for the military interventions of powerful states, a justification not very different to those articulated by Cicero, Epictetus and Marcus Aurelius almost 2,000 years ago. However, both Beck and Nussbaum conceptualise political life in sociologically unrealistic terms. As Mouffe (2005) convincingly demonstrates, there is no politics without conflict. Hence, any attempt to impose cosmopolitan virtues on nationalist publics is likely to foster new forms of political conflict. Since nationalism is sustained by the organisational, ideological and micro-interactional infrastructures of nation states, it remains the dominant operative ideology and the principal mode of political legitimisation of rule in modernity. As cosmopolitanism largely lacks such an organisational and ideological base, it is bound to persist as a minority, elite, project.

So if consumerism and cosmopolitanism are not real threats to nationalism, what about religious fundamentalism? It is true that most radical religious teachings espouse a degree of hostility towards secular nationalism (Ruthven 2007: 93). This is particularly evident among the Protestant fundamentalist sects in the USA who decry the idea of the nation state, the sections of Orthodox Judaism who oppose Zionism or the Salafist groupings who fiercely reject Arab nationalism. In all of these cases, nationalism is identified with secularity and the elevation of popular sovereignty and 'the will of the people' over that of divine authority. However, most religious organisations have tended to incorporate nationalist tenets into their religious teachings and practice. Hence, despite their nominal universalism, the Catholic, Orthodox and Protestant Christian churches have all made compromises with nationalist projects and have often acted as beacons of the national idea. The most prominent such cases include Polish and Irish Catholicism, Greek and Serbian Orthodox Christianity and Danish and Estonian Protestantism (Sanders 2015; Zubrzycki 2006; Roudometof 2001; Ruthven 2007). For example, the cornerstones of Polish nationalism are Catholic religious idioms such as the notion of Poland being the 'bulwark of Christianity' throughout the ages (*Polonia semper fidelis* – Poland always faithful), and the notion of Poland acting as 'the Christ of Nations', a partitioned land and then resurrected nation atoning for the sins of the world and enjoying the protection of its queen, the Black Madonna of Częstochowa (Zubrzycki 2006: 34). In a similar way, Shinto has been a religion highly supportive of Japanese nationalist projects throughout modern history (Benesch 2014). More recently, such a role has been assigned to Hindu teachings where Hindutva has served as an inspiration for the nationalist programme of India's ruling party, the BJP. Similarly, most strands of moderate Islam have found a way to reconcile religious and nationalist messages and many imams have acted as nationalist leaders. Even more radical groups, such as the Shia-centred Hezbollah and the Iranian ruling groups or the Sunni-centred Hamas and the Sudanese government, have developed ideological justifications capable of bridging Islamic and nationalist messages.[5]

---

[5] Ledstrup (2019) shows convincingly how the population of the United Arab Emirates successfully bridge the Islamic and the nationalist ideas and practices in their everyday life.

It is only the most radical Salafist and other purist Islamist movements which reject nationalism completely. Thus both ISIS and Al-Qaida ideologues see nationalism as a secular, Western, ideology devised to weaken the unity of global umma. For example, in his audio broadcast sermon marking the beginning of Ramadan in July 2014, the leader of ISIS, Abu Bakr al-Baghdadi, was explicit in his condemnation of nationalism and patriotism which he described as 'false slogans' spread by the enemies of Islam. He emphasised the power of ISIS as a force that has 'boots that will trample the idol of nationalism' (al-Baghdadi 2014). Nevertheless, nominal rejection of nationalism does not necessarily mean that such an ideology has no place in Salafist political projects. On the contrary, both social scientists and prominent Islamic scholars argue that ISIS and similar radical Islamist movements display a form of cryptonationalism. They point out that in the Middle East ISIS was generally perceived not as a universalist Islamist movement but exclusively as a Sunni Arab outfit where Iraqi leaders have dominated Syrians and international volunteers. Moreover, the researchers emphasise that many leading military and political positions in ISIS were occupied by former Ba'athist officers who successfully concealed their Iraqi/Arab Sunni nationalism with fierce Islamist rhetoric (Cockburn 2015). This is fully reflected in ISIS policies of ethnic-cum-religious homogenisation and the use of extreme forms of violence against all minorities (not only Christians, Yazidis or Shia Muslims but also many Sunni tribes deemed not to be loyal). Since the ISIS project did not last long, one could not assess whether nationalism would become more pronounced with the greater institutionalisation of the state structures. However, it is very likely that any attempt at forging a functioning state would involve reliance on some kind of nationalist or quasi nationalist narrative. As Khalid Blankinship (2015) argues, ISIS was

a nationalist phenomenon, even while it professe [d] to be antithetical to nationalism ... The litmus test for nationalism is statism. Is the goal of the movement a state or not? For the Taliban as for the ISIS, it certainly is their goal; therefore, they are nationalist statists, or nation-statists. In a way, they represent a movement toward the regularization of political Islam in a world dominated by nation states.

Hence, even in this most radical instance, nationalism could not simply be removed from the body politic. Although some strands of religious fundamentalisms continue to nominally reject nationalist ideologies as they operate in the nation-centric world, they cannot seriously undermine the organisational dominance of nationalism in modernity.

The Global Foundations of Nationalist Subjectivities

If various globalising trends including cosmopolitanism, consumerism and religious revival do not stifle nationalism, what is the actual relationship between globalisation and nationalist subjectivities? Obviously, globalisation involves more than changed cultural and social values; it is first and foremost a set of physical processes with concrete structural implications. It is a phenomenon that is reflected in the increased worldwide movement of trade, capital and investments, financialisation of economy, intensified migration of people, dissemination of knowledge and new technologies and many other economic and political processes. In this context, globalisation might appear as a relatively recent development standing in direct opposition to the traditional world order dominated by protectionist individual states. In this commonly shared perception, nationalist ideologies precede globalisation by several centuries and as globalisation spreads, nationalism is bound to lose its political and economic grip. However, historical sociologists have demonstrated convincingly that globalisation is a phenomenon with a long history and as such it substantially predates nationalism.

Anthony Hopkins (2006) identifies several waves of globalising trends in history starting from the archaic globalisation of early civilisations, the early modern globalisation of the seventeenth to nineteenth centuries in Europe, Asia and Northern Africa, modern globalisation spurred by the industrial revolution and culminating in the second half of the nineteenth and early twentieth centuries and the most recent globalisation accelerating at the end of the twentieth and beginning of this century. Despite popular views that see our times as unprecedented in terms of economic liberalisation and mobility of people and resources, the evidence shows otherwise: the proportion of global trade today is very similar to what it was at the beginning of the twentieth century; the statistics for both capital markets and movements of population closely resemble those that reached a peak in the 1890s; much of technology and science utilised for economic expansion is still largely produced at the national level; and despite their worldwide marketing and trade, an overwhelming majority of private companies trade solely on national stock markets (Campbell and Hall 2015: 33–40; Malešević 2010: 319–24; Hirst, Thompson and Bromley 2009; Hall 2000). As Campbell and Hall (2015: 33) show, much of world trade is not global but is in fact dominated by five nation states: USA, China, Japan, Germany and Canada. Furthermore, the economically advanced North absorbs more than half the foreign direct investment (FDI) and generates 'nearly 60 percent of the world's outflows of FDI'. Even the epitome of globalisation, the transnational corporations, are in most instances national companies that keep their ownership, assets and profits in their home countries. Furthermore, such companies regularly depend on domestic labour which is trained in national educational institutions. They also use existing national communication and transport infrastructure and still rely on state protectionism in many economic sectors deemed to be of national interest (Mann 2013; Hall 2000). Simply put, the current wave of globalisation is neither novel nor unprecedented.

Nevertheless, what is more important for this discussion is how globalisation affects nationalism. The theorists of globalisation tend to identify nationalism with strong and resilient nation states. In this, they are completely right: notwithstanding nationalists' own understanding whereby strong national feelings lead to the formation of independent polities, historically, nationalism was more often a consequence rather than a cause of nation-state formation. Nationalist ideologies are a direct product of the broader organisational transformations which led to a gradual collapse of the imperial world and development of an alternative organisational form – the nation state. However, where globalisation theorists are wrong is in their view that nation states are an obstacle to globalisation. Rather than assuming that globalisation entails weak states, it is crucial to recognise that globalisation is only possible on the back of very powerful nation states.

As Karl Polanyi (2001 [1944]) argued convincingly a long time ago, it is states that create markets and the two phenomena are mutually interdependent. From the eighteenth century onwards, the proliferation of industrialism and global capitalism went hand in hand with the rise of nation states. On the one hand, industrial (and later financial) capitalism requires the presence of strong states capable of enforcing legal agreements, maintaining fiscal control, providing adequate transport and communications, and supplying protection and viable banking systems. On the other hand, to achieve and maintain such organisational capacity, the nation states necessitate a substantial degree of popular support. Hence, the expansion of global economic trade remains dependent on the nation-state form, which in itself is dependent on the modern subjects who see their nation states as the only legitimate form of territorial rule. In other words, there is no successful globalisation without nationalism. From its early beginnings until the present day, nationalism and globalisation have tended to reinforce each other. This is not to say that nationalism emerges as a hostile reaction to homogenising tendencies of globalisation. On the contrary, the worldwide spread of nationalism ultimately generates standardised models of social organisation. As Gellner (1997: 74) recognised, there is a sharp discrepancy between the rhetoric and practice of nationalism: 'nationalism is a phenomenon of Gesellschaft using the idiom of Gemeinschaft: a mobile anonymous society simulating a closed cosy community'. Simply put, despite their rhetoric of authenticity and return to roots, once in power, nationalists tend to create nation states that in many important respects resemble each other: they develop formalised constitutional orders; introduce mass schooling organised around standardised curricula; devise long-term economic plans and demographic policies; regulate taxation, welfare provisions, heath care and so on (Meyer et al. 1997: 144–81). In other words, the global expansion of nationalist subjectivities is fully compatible with what world-society theorists call organisational isomorphism. Therefore, once generated, nationalism tends to proliferate around the world as its ideological appeal helps provide a wide-ranging popular justification for a variety of governmental actions. In this sense, as globalisation spreads so does the nationalist message: the latecomers tend to imitate the dominant nation-centric models of economic and political growth.

Hence, globalisation is not only about the opening up of economies for trade and consumption, it is also about making use of new technologies of organisation and ideological justification. It is globalisation that helps foster the greater infrastructural and surveillance powers that characterise contemporary nation states which allow greater capacity to police one's borders, to gather information on one's citizens, to increase tax intake or to utilise modern technologies to galvanise popular support (Mann 2013). There is no doubt that, in some instances, globalisation can also contribute to weakening of state power (i.e. Mexico, DR Congo, etc.), but for most of the world this has led towards increased state capacities and greater penetration of nationalist ideologies. It is no accident that there are more nation states in the world today than ever before and that more people identify in national terms than any of their predecessors. As globalisation enhances the organisational capacities of nation states, nationalism becomes more grounded in the everyday life of their citizens. The fact that outside the world's war zones nationalisms tend to be more muted and habitual should not be read as a sign of their weakness. Instead, ideological power is better measured by its ability to become normalised and naturalised (Malešević 2013a: 120–54; Billig 1995: 93–127). It is precisely when nationhood is taken for granted and perceived as normal and natural that nationalism's penetration is deeper and hence less discernible. Once symbols and practices of nationhood are reproduced daily, and often unconsciously, this is a reliable indicator of how pervasive nationalist ideology has become. As globalisation progresses, these everyday actions become ever-more grounded in the organisational, ideological and micro-interactional structures of contemporary nation states.

11 Grounded Nationalisms and the Privatisation of Security

Introduction

Capitalism is often perceived to be an enemy of nationalism. As Banton (1983: 208) noted a long time ago, 'when people compete as individuals, this tends to dissolve the boundaries that define the groups; when they compete as groups, this reinforces those boundaries'. However, as capitalism is much more than the competition of individuals in the market place, it historically was rather conducive to the proliferation of nationalist ideas. Historical sociologists have shown that the European system of nation states and their nationalisms developed not only through the proliferation of warfare but also through the expansion of market forces, banking systems and international trade (Ertman 1997; Downing 1992; Tilly 1992). Hence, for much of modern period, capitalism and nationalism sustained each other. This has not changed substantially in the early twenty-first century. Despite popular views that see globalisation and, in particular, neo-liberal privatisation as enemies of nationalism, it seems that these processes have in fact strengthened the nationalist habitus. This is visible even in the sector that has regularly been perceived as the epitome of self-interested, individualist, profit-seeking action – the privatisation of security.

Private military and security contractors (PMSCs) have regularly been described as the mercenaries of the twenty-first century whose only motivation is financial gain. Both critics and supporters of private military contracting identify strong parallels between PMSCs and their historical predecessors: corsairs, pirates, privateers, mercenaries, marauders and buccaneers. The focus here is on the similar aims of such organisations and their members: using one's expertise in organised violence for personal monetary benefit. However, in this chapter, I aim to challenge such simplified historical analogies by focusing on the different ideological and organisational dynamics of PMSCs and their pre-modern mercenary counterparts.

More specifically, I zoom in on the role nation states and grounded nationalisms play in the modern world and how PMSCs navigate these ideological and organisational obstacles in their search for profit. In particular, I focus on the substantial differences between the pre-modern mercenaries, privateers and corsairs who operated in the world of empires, city-states and other non-national forms of polity and the contemporary PMSCs who have to work in the world dominated by nation states and nationalist ideologies. In this context, unlike mercenaries who had no sense of loyalty to any nation, employees of PMSCs were born and raised in nationcentric environments. Such individuals have been socialised in education systems that glorify nationhood, have been exposed to nationcentric mass media and have often worked in national military institutions that pride themselves on promoting patriotic values. Such individuals are by definition organisationally, ideologically and micro-interactionally grounded in the world of nation states and are thus wedded to the modern ideas that define nationhood as a principal unit of human solidarity and political legitimacy. Furthermore, in such a nationcentric universe, PMSCs often have to legitimise their activities in fiercely patriotic terms, something which pre-modern mercenaries could not and did not do. The chapter explores the social dynamics of private military contracting in the world of nation states and nationalisms. I aim to show that contemporary PMSCs are very different from their pre-modern mercenary counterparts. Moreover, I argue that PMSCs and modern state militaries have much more in common than these two organisational types have with any other armed group in history.

Capitalism and Nationalism: PMSC and Ideological Change

Theorists of globalisation tend to see the nation state as an inadequate if not obsolete model of organisation for the twenty-first-century world. They also view nationalism as an ideology belonging to previous centuries and largely irrelevant in the world dominated by big corporations, incessant mobility, porous borders, accelerated economic growth, highly sophisticated technology and ever-increasing global trade networks. Regardless of their political affiliations, globalisation theorists are adamant that, in the early twenty-first century of global capitalism, economic power easily trumps political and ideological powers (Bauman 2006, 1998; Friedman 2003; Sassen 2003). However, as historical sociologists have demonstrated convincingly, capitalism and nation states have always had a much more complex relationship. The proliferation of international trade and the expansion of commercial network systems has historically been tied to state development and the nation state is itself a product of capitalist modernity (Ertman 1997; Mann 1993; Downing 1992; Tilly 1990). Since Polanyi's *The Great Transformation* (2001[1944]), it has become apparent that a free market cannot exist without political power as it is the states that create and sustain markets. The organisational and ideological backbone of nineteenth-century laissez faire capitalism was the nationalising and industrialising British state which benefited greatly from market liberalisation and the anti-protectionism policies that dominated this historical period. Mann (2013, 1993) shows that capitalism and state formation were interdependent processes as nation states were never isolated autarchies but have developed and expanded through interaction, competition and conflict with other states and global economic markets. In this context, the existence of a transnational economic space was and remains dependent on the political power of individual nation states and the changing geopolitical dynamics of state systems. Hence, there is nothing unique to the early twenty-first century: this period, too, is shaped as much by the economic networks of trade as it is by the geopolitical workings of states and other political organisations. In other words there is no capitalism without political power.

The same principles apply to the ideological realm. All social organisations including the states, private corporations, religious institutions, NGOs and many other organised collectivities have to justify their actions to others. While in the pre-modern world the mechanisms of justification might have been less robust and have been focused on the much narrower audience (i.e. the divine authority, the fellow aristocrats, the top clergy, the selected merchants, the kinship circles, etc.), in the modern age social organisations have to legitimise their actions to a much wider networks of individuals (Malešević 2002; Anderson 1991; Gouldner 1976). These ideas and practices are deployed to justify a particular course of action and are usually articulated as a set of relatively coherent normative principles and ideals that represent a specific social organisation. In other words, all modern organisations utilise particular ideological narratives to legitimise their conduct. Thus the rulers of nation states – even in authoritarian systems – have to provide some kind of justification of their actions to their citizens. The leaders of various social movements also invoke specific ideological idioms to validate their activities. The CEOs of private corporations also periodically address their shareholders and employees to attain a degree of support for their decisions. In this context, capitalist enterprises devote a great deal of resources and energy to present their actions in a positive light. Hence, the introduction of neo-liberal policies, accompanied by drives to privatise public services and assets, are usually justified it terms of efficiency and the financial benefits for all (for example, the notion of 'the trickle down economics'). However, in nearly all of these cases, and many others, nationalism also features prominently. In some instances, such as with the separatist social movements or the leaders of nation states, this nationalism is explicit and uninhibited while in other instances, including the private corporations, the nationalist narrative is often less visible but still implicitly embedded in its daily activities. For example, even the distinctly global corporations such as Levi's or Coca-Cola deploy the nationcentric advertising campaigns to sell their products or to legitimise their operations in the specific countries. Hence, even though the last American Levi's jeans factory was closed in 2004, its recent advertisements feature sparkles on the Fourth of July and the celebration of US Independence Day. Similarly, Coca Cola advertisements invoke the American hippy lifestyle and Fourth of July barbeques, thus tapping into the popular nationcentric sentiments of its US consumers (Thimoty 2017). In both of these cases, the corporations appeal to shared nationalist narratives by successfully enveloping networks of micro-solidarity – the barbecues and Fourth of July local celebrations jointly experienced by families, friends and neighbours. Smaller companies with limited global reach are even more prone to utilise the nationalist appeals. For example, Australian adventurer and businessman Dick Smith successfully advertised his food company to his Australian consumers by emphasising that his company is Australian owned and that it sells only Australian-made products (Schmidl 2012). In other words, global private corporations are not immune to nationalism. Instead, they often benefit from tapping into existing nationalist narratives. Nevertheless, the link between nationalism and capitalism is more complex than this. Let us see how this relationship operates in the social realm usually perceived to have little or nothing to do with the nationalist habitus – the privatisation of security.

Most analyses of private contractors focus on the economic rationale of their existence. They are nearly universally perceived to be organisations and individuals driven by profit maximisation. In this view, unlike regular soldiers who are associated with collective interest (i.e. defending one's country or preserving communal security), private contractors are identified as individuals motivated exclusively by personal gain. In this context, they are regularly described as 'guns for hire', 'dogs of war', 'soldiers of fortune' or 'corporate warriors' (Dickinson 2011; Singer 2008). However, the most commonly used term is 'mercenaries'. In both mainstream scholarship and the public understanding, PMSCs are perceived to be just a most recent incarnation of an age-old practice of hiring one's military skills for money. For example, the recent book by McFate (2017), entitled *Modern Mercenary: Private Armies and What They Mean for World Order*, is built on the premise that the contemporary private contractos are motivated by the same goals that inspired their traditional predecessors – corsairs, pirates, privateers, mercenaries or marauders. In his own words, 'private military organisations – from ancient mercenaries to modern private military companies (PMCs) such as Backwater USA – are expeditionary conflict entrepreneurs that kill or train others to kill' (2017: 1).

There is no doubt that financial gain has always played a crucial role in motivating individuals to join private military and security organisations, but there are substantial differences between traditional 'soldiers of fortune' and contemporary private contractors. For one thing, pre-modern mercenaries, privateers and corsairs operated in a very different historical, geopolitical and legal context where the distinction between regular and irregular soldiering was extremely vague or completely undefined. As Leira and de Carvalho (2010) show, seventeenth and eighteenth-century European privateers were often an integral part of state military undertakings. For example, in the War of the Spanish Succession (1701–14) and the War of the League of Augsburg (1688–97), 'the French navy regularly lent ships, sometimes with crews, to privateers' (Leira and de Carvalho 2010: 62). Even though most states utilised privateers, this was particularly the case with the weaker party in the conflict.

Furthermore, before the modern era, mercenaries were generally considered to be fully legitimate military forces often on equal, or even higher, footing with regular armies. Moreover, the mercenary forces were regularly prized for their military competence and as such were often preferred to more than the existing 'domestic' armies. From Roman and Byzantine emperors to the medieval rulers and Roman Popes, mercenary troops were favoured both as soldiers and praetorian guards. They were considered loyal precisely because they were paid and had no domestic attachments, thus establishing purely professional relationships. For example, between the tenth and fourteenth centuries, the Byzantine military included the Varangian Guard, composed of highly skilled Norsemen who fought for the empire but also acted as personal guards to Byzantine emperors (D'Amato 2010). In a similar vein, through much of the Renaissance period, condottieri and their companies were employed by the relatively wealthy 'Italian' city-states and were generally regarded as proficient and reliable military forces capable of defending these small polities. One of the early such Ventura companies was headed by Duke Werner von Urslingen from the Holy Roman Empire and was known for implementing a strict code of discipline and operating an egalitarian system of income distribution among its members (Mallet 1974). Another, better known and highly durable, case of traditional mercenaries, are the Swiss guards who have since the fourteenth century fought as line troops in various European armies and have also served on several European courts. In this context, the Pontifical Swiss Guards still operate as the main military force for protection of the Vatican. In all these cases, 'soldiers of fortune' were regarded as legitimate and even superior to regular armies. This stands in sharp contrast to the contemporary PMSCs who are generally regarded as profit-oriented individuals and organisations that lack political legitimacy and whose moral standing is regularly thought of as being inferior to that of national armies (McFate 2017; Kinsey 2009; Singer 2008).

For another, even more significant, thing, traditional private soldiering operated in an ideologically profoundly different world to the one we inhabit today. Although condottieri, privateers, buccaneers, mercenaries and other private military forces were just as much driven by financial gain as the contemporary PMSCs, there is a huge ideological divide that separates these two groups. Modern private contractors act in an environment where territorial sovereignty is clearly demarcated and well institutionalised, whereas in the pre-modern world this was not the case. For example, in fifteenth-century Europe, many members of nobility simultaneously held mutually exclusive claims over the same patches of territory. Moreover, the same lands could also legitimately belong to several, hierarchically ordered, aristocratic families whereby, for example, a count of Franche-Comté would control particular lands which were also concurrently owned by the duke of Burgundy as well as by the king of France (Vaughan 2002). This again differs profoundly from how territorial control is organised in the modern era where nation state stands at the epicentre of social order and where national sovereignty has primacy over all other claims to territorial rule (Malešević 2013a).

This unique organisational anchoring of nation-state order is also paralleled with the profound ideological change that separates the traditional world of 'soldiers of fortune' from contemporary private military contractors. Whereas the pre-modern ideational universe was dominated by a particular version of religious, kinship and local belief systems, the modern world is deeply rooted in nationcentric understandings of social relations that are reflected in almost every sphere of social life. As Gellner (1983) emphasised, the pre-modern world was not only defined by sharp economic and political hierarchies where a small number of aristocrats dominated an ocean of landless peasantry, but was also separated by intrinsic cultural divides. Hence, European nobility was transnational in the sense that they shared the same cultural mores, often spoke the same languages (i.e. Latin or later French) and engaged in aristocratic endogamy, all of which differentiated them sharply from their 'own' peasantry.

In this moral universe, as Gellner rightly argues, culture was not used to forge links between different strata in one's society, as is the case in the modern world, but instead cultural difference was deployed to reinforce the existing social divide between different segments of social order. In Gellner's (1983: 11) own words:

by externalizing, making absolute and underwriting inequalities, it [this social order] fortifies them and makes them palatable, by endowing them with the aura of inevitability, permanence and naturalness. That which is inscribed into the nature of things and is perennial, is consequently not personally, individually offensive, nor psychically intolerable.

Thus, the pre-modern world was defined by impregnable cultural hierarchies where aristocrats and their 'own' peasantry were almost considered to be members of different species.

In addition to this entrenched divide between the elite cultures and the peasant masses, the traditional world was also characterised by the lack of cultural homogeneity at the bottom of the social ladder. In other words, the peasants themselves were culturally diverse. Hence, instead of any sense of large-scale communality, most individuals populated a world of small-scale, vernacular, oral cultures. In many instances, these cultures were not mutually comprehensible, lacking standardised, written, idioms of expression. Thus, the primary sources of group solidarity were, as a rule, local and kinship based. Although shared religion did, to some extent, contribute to the wider understanding of the world, these shared beliefs did not foster a greater sense of societywide solidarity but were oriented towards the eschatological questions of human existence. In the European context, it is only with the wars of religion in the sixteenth and seventeenth centuries that religious denomination started becoming associated with one's polity (Hutchinson 2017; Mann 1993; Tilly 1992).

Mercenaries and other private soldiers were part and parcel of this world. In other words, their social role was conceptualised through the prism of the dominant weltanschauung of their time. Hence, rather than seeing their actions as treasonous or politically immoral, they were, for the most part, understood in relation to how they corresponded with the religious, local or kinship-based moralities of their own time. In this context, describing somebody as a mercenary was not an insult but just a description of his role in society. Moreover, to be a 'soldier of fortune' was often popularly regarded as a prestigious profession often associated with one's aristocratic lineage. In sharp contrast, the modern world has little tolerance for 'dogs of war' (Heinecken 2013; Dickinson 2011). Rather than being praised for their military skill, contemporary PMSCs are generally viewed with suspicion or outright hostility (Swed and

Crosbie 2017). Even when their role is accepted, their social standing regularly remains well below that attributed to members of national militaries.

The principal reason for such differing views of private armed forces is to be found in the ideological change that has taken place over the past three hundred years. The pre-modern and early modern universe of mercenaries, privateers, corsairs, buccaneers and other private military groups was characterised by lack of societywide ideological doctrines. This is not to say that such social orders did not possess coherent belief systems. Obviously, various religious, mythological and kinship-based doctrines were crucial pillars of everyday life. Nevertheless, what is distinct about the modern era is sustained ideological penetration of entire societies, which simply was not possible before modernity. The traditional orders were 'capstone' states where the ruling elite sat atop a series of different societies that it could not, nor was willing to, penetrate either in organisational or ideological terms (Hall 1986). In these social orders, the village and kinship-based local solidarities were not integrated with the wider societywide normative creeds. Hence, much of the pre-modern world lacked any cross-strata ideological accord that one could identify in modern nation states. Although the domestic politics of most modern states is generally defined by ideological cacophony and distinct social polarisation, unlike their pre-modern counterparts, modern populations are still largely united by a wider sense of loyalty to their nation. In contrast to the traditional identities, which for the most part were either local and kinship based or eschatological, modern individuals maintain strong national attachments (Gallup 2015; Medrano 2009; Smith and Kim 2006: 127–136). In other words, over the last three hundred years, nationalism has gradually become a principal source of one's subjectivity and by far the most significant foundation of political legitimacy. As I have argued elsewhere, nationalism is the dominant operative ideology of the modern world: while contemporary political systems might differ enormously in terms of their normative ideals, ranging from liberal democracy, theocracy, military dictatorship to state socialism and so forth, on the operative level, they all converge around nationalist principles that sustain their political legitimacy (Malešević 2013a; 2006).

In this context, private military contractors differ profoundly from sixteenth and seventeenth century mercenaries. Unlike traditional 'soldiers of fortune' who had no sense of loyalty to any specific nation as mass-level nationhood did not yet exist, contemporary PMSCs are inevitably nationcentric. Being born and raised in the world of nation states predisposes most individuals to see and understand the social world in national terms. Although individuals and organisations might be motivated by financial gain, the PMSCs inexorably operate in the wider world of nation states and as such are just as dominated by nationcentric perceptions of the world. Individuals who join PMSCs in a war-fighting capacity [i.e. as distinct from support roles which may be filled by unskilled workers] are, as a rule, former soldiers (Singer 2008: 76), who have all been socialised in educational institutions that glorify and even deify one's nation. Such individuals have also been influenced by the mass media and public sphere that is by and large nationcentric. Most of all, as former soldiers, these people were trained and worked in military institutions that are generally regarded as espousing exceptionally nationalist values (Faris 1995; Posen 1993; Burk 1989; Janowitz 1971).

As a result, most members of PMSCs see themselves as 'good patriots' who are loyal to their country and were at some point in their lives willing to sacrifice themselves for such ideals (Swed and Crosbie 2017; Pattison 2014). Even in cases where some individuals have become disillusioned with their national military forces, they often remain attached to nationalist ideals.[1] For example, one of the well-known and highly successful early private military corporations, Executive Outcomes (EO), was mostly composed of former members of the South African military. These individuals were all socialised in a nationcentric military milieu which sustained their sense of being proud South Africans. Furthermore, their involvement in apartheid's regime wars in Namibia, Angola and Mozambique was highly praised by the former government. In such an environment, these soldiers were often willing to die for their country. Nevertheless, with the collapse of the apartheid regime, their social position has dramatically changed:

Where their service had once been lauded, now it was a source of embarrassment to the South African State. The disavowal of their activities and failure to honour their losses stung those soldiers. Instead of seeing themselves as evil, they saw the operations in the border wars as a service to their nation. (Singer 2008: 103)

The fact that the apartheid order has now been dismantled and delegitimised, and its border wars criminalised, could not change the nationcentric upbringing and feelings of these soldiers. Consequently, as the

---

[1] In some cases PMSCs were led by individuals who either acted in unison with their nation's secret services or pursued their own nationalist and profit-making ambitions. For example, Frenchman Bob Denard, whose private forces fought in Congo, Angola, Gabon and Zimbabwe, was a fierce French nationalist who was eager to support the ideal of Françafrique – France's sphere of influence in its former African colonies – and who worked closely with the French intelligence. Other well-known 1960s private contractors, such as former British officer Mike Hoare and Belgian Jean Schramme, were also staunch nationalists (Weinberg 1995).

concept of a South African nation has changed and as their social status has diminished, many of these soldiers left the South African Defence Force and joined EO. However, this switch from the regular national military to PMSC has not and could not eliminate strong nationalist sentiments that underpin the ontological security of these soldiers. It is no accident that the overwhelming majority of EO personnel were South Africans, members of the SADF special forces. In addition to their shared military past, they also maintained a common language as Afrikaans was the principal mode of communication in the company and was also used by other non-white and non-Afrikaners company personnel (Singer 2008: 116).[2]

This concentration of a single nationality within PMSC is not unique to Executive Outcomes. In fact, most private military and security firms tend to be predominantly composed of members from the same nation-state. In part, this is a result of the dominance of US and to lesser extent UK-based PMSCs, which have by far the largest number of such companies, most of which are staffed by former US and UK soldiers respectively. However, more importantly as PMSCs mimic in part the regular US, UK and other military forces, they utilise practices and social values that are already familiar to the former soldiers. Therefore, to characterise PMSCs as 'dogs of war' solely driven by profit maximisation is to mis-understand the complexity of such organisations and their personnel. Rather than consisting of alienated individuals obsessed with monetary gain, most PMSCs in fact resemble national militaries in many areas. Although most PMSCs market themselves as stand-alone companies with exceptional military expertise, they in fact do not create or bring to market any new products or services. Instead, they only repackage the expertise, services and weaponry that has been already produced by the specific nation states. Moreover the key element of any PMSC, the fighters and the supporting staff, are also trained, educated and socialised into the nationcentric norms which fosters the smooth operation of PMSCs. In order to operate effectively, PMSCs cultivate a sense of organisational attachment and social cohesion that is often rooted in nationalist upbring-ing. Hence, when accomplishing military tasks, many private contractors do not separate sharply between their particular PMSC and their nation state as they regularly see themselves espousing values associated with their nation state. Simply put, US PMSC personnel tend to frame their actions in terms of liberating people from the autocratic regimes, bringing

---

[2] According to Singer (2008: 103), 70 per cent of Executive Outcomes were black Africans including Namibians, Angolans and South Africans who previously fought alongside SADF in the border wars.

American ideals of democracy, opportunity and rights, while those associated with UK private corporations often understand their actions through
the prism of British values such as fairness, honesty, justice and so on
(Pattison 2014: 44; Franke and von Boemcken 2011). As Franke and
von Boemcken's (2011: 734) survey of US private contractors shows,
96 per cent of their respondents understood their work as 'calling where
I can serve my country' and 83 per cent expressed a view that 'citizens
should show strong allegiance to their country and be willing to fight for
their country'.

Even the conventional distinction that is often drawn between the
private military contractors and regular soldiers whereby the former,
unlike the latter, are seen to be motivated by the financial gain, is not
sustainable. Although there are significant differences in their salaries,
most soldiers receive financial remuneration and in many cases they join
the military forces for this very reason. It is true that conscript armies tend
to have lower salaries but the possibility of promotion with access to
education, housing and other benefits has always been an important
factor in making individuals willing recruits. With the introduction of
professional militaries that rely on voluntary enlistment, soldiering has
largely become a well-paid job rather than a national duty. In this context,
the transition from the professional, salaried, military role to PMSC does
not represent a major change. In both cases, financial gain plays in
important role. In some instances, instrumental motives might play just
as great a role in national armies as in the private sector with soldiers being
attracted by greater job security, educational opportunities, health insurance, housing issues or even the opportunity to receive a full citizenship
(Barkawi 2010: 47). This is not to say that military service has become
just another professional occupation (pace Moskos 1981) but only that
both regular soldiers and military contractors are rather similar in being
both highly nationalistic and money oriented.

The contemporary distinction between regular armed forces and 'mercenaries', which is also enshrined in international law, is premised on the
idea that national armies are the norm while private military involvement
is an aberration.[3] However, rather than being a historical norm, this very
distinction is a product of unique historical conditions of the last three
hundred years. The idea of the national army was largely born in the wake
of the French revolution when mass conscription was introduced to
preserve the fledgling Republic. The famous Levée en masse was

[3] According to the Protocol Additional GC 1977 (APGC77) of Geneva convention, mercenaries do not possess the rights associated with regular soldiers such as to be a lawful
combatant, or to have prisoner of war status, meaning that if captured they are likely to be
treated as common criminals.

a product of modern democratic ideology that linked the political rights of citizens to their loyalty and obligations towards the new state (Conversi 2007). Unlike the traditional order where individuals (and soldiers) were only subjects of the monarchs, the modern French state was built on the principle that all citizens constitute a nation. In this context, the defence of 'the motherland' was conceptualised as a moral obligation of all citizens. Hence, a 'national army' emerges together with the rise and proliferation of nationalism as the dominant operative ideology of the modern age (see Lachman 2018, 2013; Malešević 2010: 179–200). Once this ideological doctrine became hegemonic, with other states adopting similar practices of military recruitment, it successfully delegitimised all other models of military organisation. In other words, while in the pre-national era being a 'soldier of fortune' was a legitimate and even prestigious position, in the nationalist age there is no justifiable role for privatisation of organised violence. Although conscript armies have gradually given way to professional military forces in the West and further afield, this has not substantially undermined their nationcentric foundations. Even though the organisational and ideological bases of contemporary armies and PMSCs are often very similar, the dominance of nationalist discourse makes only the former legitimate while the latter generally invokes suspicion, distrust or hostility.

PMSC and Nation States

The dominance of nationalism in the modern era does not stem primarily from the strength or authority of the ideas it promotes. While such ideas certainly contribute to the popularity of this ideology, as Mann (2006: 346–7) rightly argues, 'ideas can't do anything unless they are organised'. Thus, to understand PMSCs' rapport with nationalism, it is also crucial to explore their organisational dynamics and how they operate in the world dominated by nation states, the principal mode of territorial rule in modernity.

Historically speaking, the nation state is a rather unusual and atypical model of polity organisation. For much of their history, human beings have lived in polities that have very little in common with nation states: tribal confederacies, chiefdoms, composite kingdoms, empires, city-states, city-leagues, khanates and so on. In fact even if 200,000 years of human pre-history are excluded, the nation state period counts for less than 2 per cent of the human sedentary lifestyle (Malešević 2013a: 578). Unlike all these other forms of polity, the nation state is unique in the sense that its legitimacy is largely derived from the idea of popular consent. Obviously, this does not necessarily mean that nation states are ruled democratically but only that political sovereignty is deduced from the citizens rather than from the natural-born rights of rulers or divine authority. Thus, unlike empires which operated on the formal and informal hierarchical principles, nation states are rooted in the idea that their citizens are of equal moral worth. Furthermore, in contrast to empires or composite kingdoms which were culturally deeply heterogeneous, nation states foster a substantial degree of cultural homogeneity. This is not to say that nation states as such are culturally homogeneous. On the contrary, nearly all nation states are culturally diverse. The point is that most nation states are built around principals that privilege cultural homogeneity (Malešević 2013a; Breuilly 1993; Gellner 1983). In other words, the very existence of the nation state is premised on the idea that some group of people have the right and need to live in a state of their own and that such state should safeguard their cultural uniqueness. In this context, nationalism is the dominant legitimising principle of all nation states.

Another defining feature of this type of state is its legitimate right to monopolise the use of violence, taxation, education and legislation on its territory (Malešević 2013a, 2010; Elias 2000; Weber 1968). Although some pre-modern polities have occasionally managed to monopolise the use of violence or taxation, it is only in the modern era that this becomes a norm. Hence, when modern states lose these monopolies they are generally regarded to be 'failed states' or 'fragile states'.

As states have gradually acquired and monopolised these organisational (and ideological) features, they have also in this process managed to delegitimise alternative models of coercive and political organisation. Combining organisational monopoly with ideological hegemony, the nation state has been established as the only legitimate possessor of coercive power. In this context, any attempt to substantially privatise these public roles has been resisted and often perceived as illegitimate. Hence, since PMSCs potentially encroach on the state's monopoly on the use of violence, there is a tendency to delegitimise such organisations and individuals through the prism of being nothing more than 'profit seeking mercenaries'. The hegemonic position the nation state holds in the international system allows for the widely shared perception that national armies and PMSCs differ profoundly whereby the former is associated with kinship-like sense of group attachment and the latter with purely contractual relationships. In the dominant nationalist discourses, regular armed forces stand for the public interest – a sense of belonging and pride to one's nation linked with past sacrifices and the nation's military glories. In contrast, PMSCs are popularly associated with private self-interest – monetary transactional relationships between contractual clients. This nationcentric understanding of the two organisations is also codified in national and international legal systems where private military and security contracting is limited to some activities and strictly regulated. For example, most countries have stringent rules on fighting in 'foreign wars', while the international legal system does not make any provisions for 'fighting for profit' (Kinsey 2009; Singer 2008).

Nevertheless, if one moves away from these nationcentric definitions of social reality, it is possible to identify a great deal of similarity between contemporary PMSCs and national militaries. Moreover, I would argue that these two models of armed organisations exhibit much more similarity than any of their organisational predecessors.

Firstly, both contemporary national militaries and PMSCs share very similar bureaucratic organisational structure. In the classical Weberian (1968) sense they both differ from their patrimonial historical precursors who operated in the world where leaders invoked sacred and other traditions to rule through arbitrary decision-making and via nepotistic and clientelistic networks. Although no modern organisation is free from such patrimonial tendencies, the key feature of the most efficient modern military organisations, be they public or private, is their objective to utilise a bureaucratic model of governance. Hence, PMSCs and Western national armed forces are similar in a sense that they all operate according to the consistent system of abstract written rules and regulations, they employ highly trained professionals who have completed military academy-supervised and approved training, there is a fixed and transparent system of salaries and promotion based on merit, and there is an impersonal hierarchical system of command and control. Furthermore, both of these organisations maintain a complex division of labour and are driven by specific instrumental and value-rational goals. Thus, just like the British Armed Forces (BAF), Sandline International was an organisation engaged in various security operations ranging from military and security training and mentoring, to intelligence gathering, military operations support, international development, maintenance of military equipment, arms procurement and military actions. The organisational structure of these two coercive entities was very similar. Just like BAF, Sandline operated a public application system of recruitment and utilised existing databases to identify the skilled individuals who could be employed by this organisation. Both Sandline and BAF defined themselves as professional security organisations that operate according to legal norms. For example, in his statement to BBC, Michael Grunberg, an employee of Sandline, described this private military contractor as a commercial professional organisation that works in line with 'established sets of principles' and only employs 'professional people' (http://news.bbc.co.uk/2/hi/africa/3501632.stm). Both organisations were also shaped as bureaucratic entities focused on fostering an efficient system of governance composed of clearly defined division of labour, transparent hierarchies, written rules, merit-based systems of promotion and so on. Tim Spicer, a retired lieutenant colonel and the head of Sandline, described his organisation as 'structured' with 'professional and corporate hierarchies' covering 'training, logistics, support, operational support, post-conflict resolution' (Gilligan, 1998: 1276).

This Weberian bureaucratic model stands in sharp contrast to the traditional coercive organisations of yesteryear. For example, Sandline International was often described as a mercenary army that resembled the eighteenth-century East India Company's private presidency armies. Nevertheless, these comparisons are largely out of place as Sandline and other contemporary private contractors have very little in common with such, mostly patrimonial, models of rule. Although the East India Company was by far the most powerful and profitable organisation of its kind, which at one point controlled half the world's trade, its organisational structure and its model of governance differ profoundly from those of Sandline and other PMSCs. Whereas the East India Company's military was generally made up of makeshift units, often recruited by force or tricked into joining, Sandline operated as a professional security organisation. As Singer (2008: 47) emphasises: 'While mercenary units operate as collection of individuals, the personnel within PMFs [private military firms] are organised within the defined structures of a corporate entity. They are specifically grouped so as to operate with a set doctrine and greater cohesion of activity and discipline.' Hence, modern PMSCs like Sandline differ profoundly from pre-modern organisations such as the East India Company.[4]

Secondly, to understand this organisational similarity between private military contractors and regular armed forces, one has to focus on another significant feature of historical change: the ever-increasing cumulative coercive capacity of organisations. As I have argued in the first part of this book, one of the defining phenomena of social life throughout the course of human history has been the long-term structural process I call the cumulative bureaucratisation of coercion (Malešević 2017, 2013, 2010). By this, I mean the ongoing tendency for social organisations to accumulate greater coercive capacity and to expand their infrastructural reach, scope and societal penetration. In this context, states become capable of monopolising the use of force, taxation, education and jurisprudence, while other social organisations acquire capacity to successfully dominate their

---

[4] Although Singer differentiates sharply between contemporary national militaries and PMSCs, the evidence suggests that these two models of coercive organisation have a great deal in common.

members. This is an open-ended cumulative historical process that has been in existence for the past 10,000 years and which has resulted in the ever-increasing coercive strength of social organisations. This is not to say that coercive-organisational expansion is an evolutionary, teleological, phenomenon. It is quite clear that throughout history some social organisations have expanded while others have been destroyed, amalgamated with their previous competitors or simply weakened and disintegrated. The point is that whereas individual organisations rise and fall, expand or contract, coercive-organisational power as such has so far continued to grow (Malešević 2017, 2013b, 2010).

One can chart the cumulative, if not continuous, expansion of coercive organisational power from the early Mesolithic until the present day. As Weber (1968) was well aware, bureaucratic models of organisation have proven superior in maintaining social order and in systematically coordinating activities of huge numbers of individuals. The development of science, technology, communication and transport networks, together with the proliferation of literacy, expansion of public sphere and the professionalisation of social relationships, have all contributed towards greater coercive-organisational capacities of public and private institutions. In this context, most contemporary social organisations have greater coercive-organisational penetration then any of their historical predecessors. The Roman and ancient Chinese empires are generally regarded as the most powerful polities of the pre-modern era, with each possessing enormous militaries. For example, at its peak in 221 CE, the Imperial Roman army consisted of approximately 450,000 soldiers (Fields 2009) while its Chinese counterpart during the Tang dynasty period (618–907 CE) maintained an army composed of around 300,000 soldiers (Graf 2016: 30).[5] Nevertheless, this enormous size has generally not translated so well into empires' capacity to penetrate and fully dominate the social order they nominally controlled. For one thing, these 'capstone' states lacked the administrative machinery necessary to instantly impose their will throughout their territories. For example, the enormous Roman Empire, which at its peak spread over 3 million square kilometres encompassing over 70 million people, had no more than 400 civil servants (Mann 1986: 266, 274). Similarly, the ancient Chinese Empire, which reached a population peak during the Han Dynasty (206 BCE–220 CE) of close to 60 million people (Chang-Qun et al. 1998: 572–5) employed no more than a few thousand civil servants.[6] As Hall

---

[5] Although ancient Chinese sources often refer to millions of soldiers, most contemporary historians agree that these are inflated and exaggerated numbers.

[6] After this period, China experienced population decline until 1193 when, during Southern Song Dynasty, the population grew to 76.81 million (Chang-Qun et al. 1998).

(1988: 21) documents: 'The first Ming emperor in 1371 sought to have as few as 5,488 mandarins in government service and by the sixteenth century there were still only about 20,400 in the empire as a whole.' All of this contrasts sharply with the substantially increased coercive capacities of modern social organisations. Hence, both most contemporary militaries and large PMSCs have much greater coercive strength and infrastructural reach than their traditional imperial counterparts. Despite sometimes having smaller number of soldiers, these organisations have the capability to relatively quickly penetrate the social order under their control. In this process, they can rely on existing transport, communication and information networks as well as on superior civilian and military science, technology and industry. Thus, most mid-size and even some smaller nation states maintain armed forces that have greater coercive-organisational prowess than any of pre-modern imperial militaries. Furthermore, many large PMSCs also possess coercive capacity that regularly surpasses not only many pre-modern armies but also contemporary military forces of small states. For example, most effective PMSCs such as G4S, DynCorp, GK Sierra or ACADEMI have more contracted staff than the British Army (Singer 2008: 69). The world's largest global security corporation, G4S, employs over 620,000 people and in 2012, earned more than $12 billion. In a similar vein, ACADEMI, formerly Blackwater USA, a private military company, in 2000 was engaged in training no fewer than 100,000 sailors (www.securitydegree hub.com/30-most-powerful-private-security-companies-in-the-world/). Hence, both national militaries and PMSCs differ from their historical counterparts in terms of their shared and ever-increasing coercive capacity.

Thirdly, the organisational strength as well as the nationalist base of PMSCs stems in part from their compatibility and interdependence with the nation states and national militaries. In contrast to popular views that see private contracting as ideologically and organisationally incompatible with the nation state projects, the evidence indicates that this link is in fact very strong. Rather than competing with the national armies, most PMSCs act as an integral part of the military undertaking spearheaded by their national governments. For example, both US and UK PMSCs are largely dependent on the military and security contracts of their respective states. Large PMSCs, such as Brown & Root, BDM and SAIC, were all funded by the US government, with Brown & Root receiving over $2 billion for its reconstruction jobs in the former Yugoslavia, while BDM and SAIC received over $1.5 and $1 billon respectively in military contracts with the US Army (Singer 2008: 80). As Kinsey (2009: 24) argues and documents well, 'there was simply no need for US companies to look anywhere other than to their government for contracts ... and UK PSCs have also relied on their country's historical legacy for contracts'. Moreover, as PMSCs are for the most part composed of former national soldiers, their working practices, ethos and military knowledge tend to be fully compatible with those of national armies.[7] Hence, it is not surprising to see that private contractors share patriotic sentiments associated with national armies. Some PMSCs representatives, such as MPRI, are very vocal about their loyalty to US foreign policy aims, while others 'honestly feel that they are free from ... influence of profit concerns and that even in their private capacity they are acting in national interest' (Singer 2008: 119, 154). Most executives and even ordinary employees of the large scale PMSCs prefer to be contracted by the national armed forces as any connection with the nation state is likely to increase their external legitimacy.

All of this might indicate that private contracting is parasitic in its dependency on the nation states. Not only are such companies funded by national governments but they also rely on national infrastructure, existing state-supported systems of education and training, as well as national science, technology and industry that produce weapon systems and other military equipment. Nevertheless, this is not a one-way relationship. Contemporary militaries have just as much become dependent on PMSCs. As the technological, organisational and logistical complexity of modern wars and military interventions increases, Western and other armed forces have become dependent on private military and security contractors. In particular, without their complex operational and logistical support, the US and UK armed forces could not properly function either in Iraq or Afghanistan. As Kinsey (2009) demonstrates, the character of contemporary military action has changed, not in the sense that war has become privatised as such but that Western militaries have devolved some of their traditional logistical and operational roles to private contractors. For example, the 2003 Iraq war was conducted relying extensively on PMSCs who were involved in a variety of roles: from setting up military camps and army bases, operating digital command and control systems, setting and operating computer systems and even weapon systems to providing personal security for Iraqi politicians and so on (i.e. Kellogg, Brown & Root, Halliburton, Fluor, etc). At one point, the total number of PMSCs employees outnumbered US official troops (180,000 vs. 160,000, Scahill 2007).

---

[7] For example, the personnel of the large PMSCs such as MPRI consists of 95 per cent former US Army members (Singer 2008: 120).

This ever-increasing reliance on PMSCs stems in part from the complex division of labour and sophisticated technology involved but is also rooted in the organisational and ideological compatibility of these corporate systems. To use Gellner's (1994) memorable metaphor, one could say that both PMSCs and contemporary militaries display modular features that are characteristic of most modern social organisations. Just like modular furniture, these organisational components can be reconfigured and as such can gel together precisely because they are composed of very similar individuals and groups used to performing similar tasks in similar ways. In this context, the nationcentric primary and secondary socialisation of former soldiers contributes substantially towards their ability and willingness to switch from national armed forces to private contractors. Thus, in addition to organisational compatibility, characterised by shared military skills, weapons training, command and control practices, etc., there is also a strong degree of ideological compatibility expressed in shared nationcentric perceptions of social reality. The members of PMSCs generally tend to see themselves as loyal patriots who perhaps adapt different organisational means but are just as determined to support the national interests of their respective nation states. Moreover, as they are well aware that private contracting can be popularly understood as betrayal of one's nationhood, they are eager to demonstrate their commitment to national causes. Since public polls regularly find the US Army as one of the most respected institutions in American society, PMSCs' activities are often marketed as being fully in tune with US military undertakings. For example, Erik Prince, CEO of Blackwater USA until 2009, emphasises how his employees – former members of US Army, Marines, Navy SEALs and police SWAT team officers – were all 'proudly patriotic' and that 'everything Blackwater's men did in Iraq was by (US) State's direct command' (Hagedorn 2015: 107). In his autobiography, indicatively entitled *Civilian Warriors: The Inside Story of Blackwater and the Unsung Heroes of the War on Terror*, Prince insists that his 'life mission' was to 'serve God, family and the United States'. In other words, the influential members of PMSCs, such as Prince, see no contradiction between their lifelong commitment to, and willingness to sacrifice for, their nation states and their ambition to pursue monetary gain through private military corporations.

Conclusion

Capitalism is not necessary an enemy of nationalism. The proliferation of neo-liberal modes of organisation followed by ever-increasing privatisation of public services and public properties has not significantly dented the power of nationalist attachments in the contemporary world. On the contrary, twenty-first century global capitalism has fostered the proliferation of organisational and ideological structures that sustain nationcentric understandings of social reality. Rather than making us all into highly individualised and competitive consumers, neo-liberal privatisation has in fact provided structural mechanisms for the world-wide expansion of the nationalist habitus.

The privatisation of security illustrates all the complexities of this process. Most studies of the contemporary warfare focus only on the economic aspects of security privatisation without analysing properly its political and ideological underpinnings. In this context, the emergence and proliferation of PMSCs is understood to be a symptom of the neo-liberal shift towards marketisation of all public institutions, where even the military is not immune anymore (McFate 2017; Kinsey 2009; Singer 2008). Such influential analyses tend to overemphasise the role of economics and self interest in military and state relationships. Moreover, they regularly interpret these new developments as a return to previous historical epochs of mercenaries, corsairs, privateers and marauders. In this chapter, I have attempted to show why these views are incorrect. Although it is true that market forces have encroached on military organisations and war, the relationship between PMSCs and the nation state are more complex and more ambiguous that such analyses allow. For one thing, PMSCs share much more with the national armed forces than either of these two have in common with the mercenary armies of the pre-modern world. The economics-centred analyses which have an individual's self-interest as their focal point, simply cannot account for the long-term historical dynamics that have radically transformed the nature of social relations in modernity. Hence, unlike pre-modern mercenaries who had neither ideological nor organisational reasons to identify with large-scale abstract entities such as nationhood, modern individuals, be they employed in the public or private sector, are strongly attached to their respective nation states. This chapter zoomed in on the similar structural and ideational underpinnings of PMSCs and national militaries and aimed to show how their organisational and ideological compatibilities make the proliferation of PMSCs possible and legitimate. Thus, the often-drawn dichotomies that distinguish sharply between self-less nationally conscious and loyal individuals who join national armies and the selfish unpatriotic 'dogs of war' who are employed by the large private military corporations simply do not stand. For much of modern history, capitalism and nationalism developed together and reinforced each other and this has not changed substantially in the early twenty-first century.

Conclusion: The Omnipotence of Nationalisms

In one of his best-known statements, Max Weber (1948: 280) proclaimed that 'not ideas, but material and ideal interests, directly govern men's conduct. Yet very frequently, the "world images" that have been created by "ideas" have, like switchmen, determined the tracks along which action has been pushed by the dynamic of interest'. This passage has often been interpreted as Weber's attempt to navigate between instrumentalist and idealist epistemologies. Hence, the metaphor of the 'switchmen' stands for the notion that self-interested actions cannot be decoupled from the already-established 'images of the world' that we all have in our heads. The 'switchmen' metaphor has also been understood differently, with some, such as Parsons (1975: 668), insisting that focus on the 'world images' indicates that Weber ultimately privileges ideas over interests. Others, such as Hechter (1976), argue the opposite and see Weber as the epitome of a materialist scholar who still invokes the centrality of 'interests'. Nevertheless, these debates have overemphasised the agent's motivation and have largely neglected Weber's key point – the historicity of social phenomena. In other words, Weber makes a case for the centrality of long-term processes that shape human thinking and acting. He rightly acknowledges that social behaviour is deeply influenced by the historical 'switchmen' – the path-dependent logic of social change. Much of social science remains present centred and as such is unable to track the long-term historical dynamics of social action (Elias 1987). In this sense, Weber was absolutely right: past events and processes deeply shape contemporary social realities. Hence, to understand the character of nationhood and nationalist ideologies today, it is crucial to engage in a longue durée analysis.

However, when exploring the historical dynamics of nationalism, one should go further and perhaps stand Weber on his head by insisting that specific social structures have moulded the character of interests and 'world images' that we all now share – the idea of nationhood as a normal and natural unit of collective existence. While nationalist ideologies inevitably draw on pre-existing ideas, beliefs and practices, the dominance of nationalism in modernity cannot be explained solely through analysis of pre-existing 'world images'. Instead, nationalism is an unambiguously modern phenomenon that can only thrive in the social environment shaped by the structural forces of modernisation. More importantly, the contemporary hegemony of nationalism is firmly rooted in long-term structural transformations and especially in the character of the polity that dominates the contemporary world – the nation state. Strictly speaking, the ascendancy of nationcentric understandings of social reality stems in part from specific organisational changes whereby the nation-state model has gradually replaced all other territorial competitors and established itself as the only legitimate form of territorial rule. Hence, to understand and explain the strength of nationalism in modernity, it is paramount to explore its structural foundations. In this context, I argue that nationalism is a grounded social phenomenon which is rooted in specific historical, organisational, ideological and micro-interactional processes. Nationalism develops, expands and proliferates on the back of these social forces.

Saying that nationalism is historically grounded means that its developmental trajectory has in part determined its current configuration. Hence, since its establishment in the late eighteenth century, this ideological doctrine and social practice has largely been continuously on the rise. While one could witness cases of specific nationalist movements experiencing temporary or terminal decline, nationalist ideology as such has mostly continued to expand both vertically (across different social strata) and horizontally (across the globe). This gradual transformation hinged on the growth and expansion of organisational capacities and long-term ideological penetration that successfully brought together the world of micro-level interactions. Hence, these structural changes generated emergence of new 'world images'. Once notions of popular sovereignty, cultural homogeneity and moral equality of co-nationals spread to wider audiences, there was no turning back: nationalism became historically grounded and also a dominant form of popular legitimacy.

Nevertheless, nationalism's historical grounding was highly reliant on organisational grounding. Nationalist doctrine would have no popular impact without the development and proliferation of potent organisational vehicles – the state machine, social movements, political parties, revolutionary associations, secret societies, terrorist cells, and many other organisational forms. However, the mere presence of such organisational shells provided no guarantee that nationalist projects would succeed. Instead, what mattered more, was continuous rise in organisational capacity. Hence, the last three hundred years were characterised by an unprecedented increase in organisational capacity of many organised entities responsible for the expansion of nationalism and, most of all, the nation state. The proliferation of nationalism was possible because states and other social organisations were able to mobilise adequate financial resources from society, to administer their territories effectively, to pursue specific developmental strategies, to dominate their members/citizens through the threat of force, to establish a degree of cross-class consensus and so on. The continuous expansion of organisational power made nationalism organisationally well grounded.

While social organisations are crucial for the spread of specific ideas, they would have no purpose if there were no such ideas to spread. Thus, nationalism also entails ideological grounding. The wide appeal of nationalism resides in part in its emancipatory, egalitarian and fraternal messages. The nationalist doctrine invokes a sense of justice, individual and collective liberation and solidarity with the significant others. More than most other ideologies, nationalism invokes a sense of moral responsibility towards one's progeny and one's ancestors. In Smith's (1998) reformulation of Edmund Burke's idea, nationalism became a moral contract between 'those who are living, those who are dead, and those who are to be born'. Obviously, this is not to discount the dark side of nationalism: intolerance of difference, xenophobic in-groupism and violence against non-nationals. As many scholars of nationalism have emphasised, these two strands of nationalist experience represent two sides of the same coin – the Janus face of nationalism. Furthermore, once established, nationalism has a powerful mobilising and legitimising capacity. Unlike its historical ideological competitors, such as imperial creeds, religious and mythological doctrines, or the divine right of kings, nationalism invokes the notion of popular rule. While it is clear that in the contemporary world no state is ruled by the people as such, the idea of popular sovereignty has much more potent resonance among the citizens of nation states than any other form of political legitimacy. Hence, with the ever-increasing ideological penetration and the expansion of political, social and economic citizenship rights, nationalism has become more grounded in the everyday life of individuals.

Finally, to attain substantial and continuous influence, organisational and ideological grounding necessitates diffusion into the micro-world. Hence, nationalism is also interactionally grounded. Human beings are reflective, emotional, moral and cognitive creatures that thrive in small-group interaction. Much of our everyday life is immersed in face-to-face communication and interaction with people we know well and care about – our family members, friends, neighbours, peers, lovers and so on. Much of our moral commitment and emotional fulfilment resides in these micro-groups. Hence, nationalism can only succeed if it penetrates this micro-universe of daily interaction. Some social organisations manage to envelop the networks of micro-solidarity by mimicking the discourse of kinship and close friendships and by portraying nations as family members (i.e. 'Mother Russia' 'our Serbian brothers' or American 'Daughters of Liberty'). Others tend to benefit from the organisational inertia that reproduces nationcentric realities through everyday habitual action. Hence, nationalist discourses and practices are regularly enacted through routine talk, daily rituals, consumerism and a variety of banal practices. Although many individuals and groups can be active agents who sway, resist or subvert the dominant nationalist interpretations of reality, the historical ascendancy of organisational and ideological powers has largely restricted the scale of their influence. Hence, the longue durée organisational and ideological grounding have historically constrained attempts to transcend the world of nationhood and much of individual and collective action has focused on influencing social change within the already-existing parameters of the nationcentric world.

The strength of nationalism stems from its ground-ness: its long-term historical entrenchment, its ever-increasing organisational capacity, its deeper and deeper ideological penetration and its greater envelopment of the micro-interactional world. Hence, the rise and fall of nationalism is rarely dependent on the actions of determined elites or charismatic leaders but largely on the workings of these long-term structural forces. There is no doubt that the elites, party figures, social movement leaders and other individuals can occasionally deploy inflamed rhetoric to mobilise the large groups of people and to foster hatred against specific groups. However, such leaders cannot create nationalism at will, they can only work with something that is already there. Similarly, nationalism is not an automatic by-product of economic crises, recessions or depressions. While such economic and social turbulences can expedite more radical expressions of nationalism, economic crises do not generate nationalism by themselves. Instead, nationalist habitus has already to be present in order to be radicalised and deployed against others. The same applies to grassroot resistance. Ordinary individuals and organised groups can successfully challenge the status quo and can initiate their own interpretations of reality. They can even foster a distinct form of nationalist experience, something that the scholars of everyday nationhood call 'the practical accomplishment of ordinary people' (Fox and Miller-Idriss 2008: 539). However, they cannot surpass well-established and durable organisational, ideological and micro-interactional structures that maintain and reproduce nationcentric visions of the world. In other words, grassroots resistance, just as elite action, can lead towards the removal of a particular government, break-up of a specific state or enactment of a substantial social change but such actions can not bring about a nationless social order. Instead, as the historical record demonstrates, once in power, even fiercely anti-nationalist movements from the communists to the Islamists had no other option but to incorporate nationalism into their political doctrines and everyday activities. Hence, to fully understand the social and historical dynamics of nationalism, it is crucial not to treat nationalism as a historical anomaly caused by demagogic politicians, economic depressions and popular discontent. Instead, it is paramount to comprehend that nationalism is the dominant from of human subjectivity in the modern world. In the world where nationhood is considered to be the principal unit of political legitimacy and collective solidarity, and where the nation state is the only legitimate mode of territorial rule, one simply cannot avoid nationalism. Rather than being a temporary aberration, this ideology and social practice in fact underpins the social orders all modern individuals now inhabit. Nationalism is not something that deviates from the existing social norms; instead, nationalism is the norm.

Since the strength of nationalism resides in its ground-ness, the well-entrenched and firmly embedded nationalisms are generally less visible to the naked eye. They tend to be habitually reproduced, organisationally deep-rooted, ideologically well diffused, and also capable of penetrating successfully into the microcosm of daily routine. In contrast, less grounded nationalisms and those that undergo a substantial social transformation over a very short period of time tend to be louder and thus more visible. Such nationalist experiences are often characterised by rhetorical outbursts, radical proclamations, intolerant discourses, xenophobic rants, or mythomaniac claims and as such they attract much more attention than grounded nationalisms. However, one should not confuse ostentatiousness and brazenness with strength. Loud battle cries, verbal aggressiveness and hostile outbursts are often good indicators of anxiousness, insecurity, self-doubt and diffidence, not strength. It is the organisational, ideological and micro-interactional weakness that is more likely to generate this type of inimical reaction. In contrast, firmly grounded nationalisms tend to be inconspicuous and imperceptible, yet extremely powerful. Once fully grounded, nationalism becomes second nature, a set of largely unquestioned beliefs and social practices that underpins equally the institutional dynamics and everyday life of ordinary individuals in the contemporary world. Although the noisy, barking, nationalisms usually receive more attention, it is the tranquil, biting, nationalisms that really matter.

References

Akl, H. (2017). No 'Lawful Basis' for Compulsory Public Services Card, Expert Says. *Irish Times*, 29 August.

Al-Baghdadi, A. B. (2014). https://news.siteintelgroup.com/Jihadist-News/isla mic-state-leader-abu-bakr-al-baghdadi-encourages-emigration-worldwide-action.html.

Anderson, B. (1998). *The Spectre of Comparisons: Nationalism, Southeast Asia, and the World*. London: Verso.

———— (1991 [1983]). *Imagined Communities: Reflections on the Origin and Spread of Nationalism*. London: Verso.

Anderson, L. (1987). The State in the Middle East and North Africa. *Comparative Politics*, 20(1): 1–18.

Antić, Č. (2006). Crisis and Armament: Economic Relations between Great Britain and Serbia 1910–1912. *Balcanica*, 36: 151–61.

Antonsich, M. (2009). National Identities in the Age of Globalisation: The Case of Western Europe. *National Identities*, 11(3): 281–99.

Arežina, B. (2015). Hrvatski znanstevenici otkrili novi material – Katsenit. *Večernji List*, 25(3).

Armstrong, J. A. (1982). *Nations before Nationalism*. Chapel Hill: University of North Carolina Press.

Aronczyk, M. (2013). *Branding the Nation: The Global Business of National Identity*. Oxford: Oxford University Press.

Aronson, T. (1986). *Crowns in Conflict: The Triumph and The Tragedy of European Monarchy, 1910–1918*. London: J Murray.

Arrighi, G. (1994). *The Long Twentieth Century: Money, Power, and the Origins of Our Times*. London: Verso.

Augusteijn, J. (2002). *Irish Revolution, 1913–1923*. London: Palgrave.

Averill, A. (2018). Irish Nationalism and Globalised Society: A Study of the generation born in Ireland between 1976 and 1986. PhD thesis. Dublin: University College Dublin.

Ayoob, M. (1995). *The Third World Security Predicament: State Making, Regional Politics and the International System*. Boulder, CO: Lynne Rienner.

Bacevich, A. (2004). *American Empire: The Realities and Consequences of US Diplomacy*. Cambridge, MA: Harvard University Press.

Banac, I. (1986). The Redivived Croatia of Pavao Ritter Vitezović. *Harvard Ukrainian Studies*, 10(3/4): 492–507.

Banton, M. (1983). *Racial and Ethnic Competition*. Cambridge: Cambridge University Press.

Barbalet, J. (2002). Why Emotions Are Crucial. In J. Barbalet (ed.), *Emotions and Sociology*. Oxford: Blackwell.

(1996). Social Emotions: Confidence, Trust and Loyalty. *International Journal of Sociology and Social Policy*, 16(8/9): 75–96.

Barkawi, T. (2010). State and Armed Force in International Context. In A. Colas and B. Mabee (eds.), *Mercenaries, Pirates, Bandits and Empires: Private Violence in Historical Context*. New York: Columbia University Press.

Barnett, M. (1992). *Confronting the Costs of War: Military Power, State and Society in Egypt and Israel*. Princeton: Princeton University Press.

Barry, G., E. Dal Lago and R. Healy (eds.). (2016). *Small Nations and Colonial Peripheries in World War I*. Leiden: Brill.

Bauman, Z. (2006). *Liquid Times: Living in an Age of Uncertainty*. Cambridge: Polity.

(2002). *Society under Siege*. Cambridge: Polity.

(2000). *Liquid Modernity*. Cambridge: Polity.

(1998). *Globalization: The Human Consequences*. Cambridge: Polity.

Baumeister, R. (1986). *Identity: Cultural Change and the Struggle for Self*. Oxford: Oxford University Press.

Bechev, D. (2010). The State and Local Authorities in the Balkans, 1804–1939. In W. Van Meurs and A. Mungiu-Pippidi (eds.), *Ottomans into Europeans*. London: Hurst.

Beck, U. (2006). *Cosmopolitan Vision*. London: Polity.

(2000). The Cosmopolitan Perspective: Sociology of the Second Age of Modernity. *British Journal of Sociology*, 51(1): 79–105.

Beck, U. and E. Beck-Gernsheim. (2002). *Individualisation: Institutionalized Individualism and Its Social and Political Consequences*. London: Sage.

Beissinger, M. (1998). Nationalisms that Bark and Nationalisms that Bite: Ernest Gellner and the Substantiation of Nations. In J. A. Hall (ed.), *The State of the Nation: Ernest Gellner and the Theory of Nationalism*. Cambridge: Cambridge University Press.

Bejaković, P., G. Vukšić and V. Bratić. (2011). Veličina javnog sektora u Hrvatskoj. *Hrvatska i komparativna javna uprava*, 11(1): 99–125.

Bender, J. C. (2016). Ireland and Empire. In R. Bourke and I. McBride (eds.), *The Princeton History of Modern Ireland*. Princeton: Princeton University Press.

Bendle, M. F. (2002). The Crisis of 'Identity' in High Modernity. *British Journal of Sociology*, 53(1): 1–18.

Benesch, O. (2014). *Inventing the Way of the Samurai: Nationalism, Internationalism and Bushido in Modern Japan*. Cambridge: Cambridge University Press.

Berend, I. T. (2003). *History Derailed: Central and Eastern Europe in the Long Nineteenth Century*. Berkley: University of California Press.

Berkoff, K. (2012). *Motherland in Danger: Soviet Propaganda during World War II*. Cambridge: Harvard University Press.

Besedić, A. (2016). Sportska sila: S OI se vraćamo s rekordom i novim herojima. *24 Sata*, 21(8).

Bew, J. (2016). Ireland under the Union, 1801–1922. In R. Bourke and I. McBride (eds.), *The Princeton History of Modern Ireland*. Princeton: Princeton University Press.

Bhambra, G. (2007). Sociology and Postcolonialism: Another 'Missing' Revolution? *Sociology*, 41 (5):

Biagini, E. (2007). *British Democracy and Irish Nationalism, 1876–1906*. Cambridge: Cambridge University Press.

Billig, M. (1995). *Banal Nationalism*. London: Sage.

Bingham, H. (1898). *The Annexation of Hawaii: A Right and a Duty*. Concord: Rumford Press.

Biondich, M. (2011). *The Balkans: Revolution, War and Political Violence since 1878*. Oxford: Oxford University Press.

Blandford, S. (2013). *Theatre and Performance in Small Nations*. Bristol: Intellect.

Blankinship, K.Y. (2015). 'ISIS': A Case of Nationalism and War. www .lamppostproductions.com/isis-a-case-of-nationalism-and-war/.

Bloom, M. (2004). Palestinian Suicide Bombing: Public Support, Market Share, and Outbidding. *Political Science Quarterly*, 119(1): 61–88.

Bodley, J. (2013). *The Small Nation Solution: How the World's Smallest Nations Can Solve the World's Biggest Problems*. Lanham, MD: Alta Mira Press.

Bourke, J. (1999). *An Intimate History of Killing*. London: Granta.

Bourke, R. (2016). Historiography. In R. Bourke and I. McBride (eds.), *The Princeton History of Modern Ireland*. Princeton: Princeton University Press.

Boylan, C. (2016). Famine. In R. Bourke and I. McBride (eds.), *The Princeton History of Modern Ireland*. Princeton: Princeton University Press.

Boyle, J. (2009). Nigeria's 'Taliban' enigma. http://news.bbc.co.uk/2/hi/8172270 .stm.

Bratić, A. (2015). Veliki inozemni uspjeh nase umjetnice. *Jutarnji List*, 14(10).

Braudel, F. (1988). *The Identity of France: History and Environment*, vol 1. New York: Harper & Row.

Breuilly, J. (2017). Modern Empires and Nation-States. *Thesis Eleven*, 139: 11–29.

(1996). Approaches to Nationalism. In G. Balakrishnan (ed.), *Mapping the Nation*. London: Verso.

(1993). *Nationalism and the State*. Manchester: Manchester University Press.

Brewer, D. (2012). *Greece, the Hidden Centuries: Turkish Rule from the Fall of Constantinople to Greek Independence*. London: I.B. Tauris.

Brickman, J. and W. Zepper. (1992). *Russian and Soviet Education, 1731–1989*. London: Routledge.

Brubaker, R. (2015). *Grounds for Difference*. Harvard: Harvard University Press.

(2010). Charles Tilly as a Theorist of Nationalism. *The American Sociologist*, 41: 375–81.

(2004). *Ethnicity without Groups*. Cambridge, MA: Harvard University Press.

(1998). Myths and Misconceptions in the Study of Nationalism. In J. A. Hall (ed.), *The State of the Nation: Ernest Gellner and the Theory of Nationalism*. Cambridge: Cambridge University Press.

Brubaker, R. and F. Cooper. (2000). Beyond 'Identity'. *Theory and Society*, 29 (1): 1–37.

Brubaker, R., M. Feischmidt, J. Fox and L. Grancea. (2006). *Nationalist Politics and Everyday Ethnicity in a Transylvanian Town*. Princeton: Princeton University Press.

Brucan, S. (1993). *The Wasted Generation: Memoirs of the Romanian Journey from Capitalism to Socialism and Back*. Boulder, CO: Westview Press.

Brym, R. J. and B. Araj. (2006). Suicide Bombing as Strategy and Interaction: The Case of the Second Intifada. *Social Forces*, 84(4): 1969–86.

Burbank, J. and F. Cooper. 2010. *Empires in World History: Power and Politics of Difference*. Princeton: Princeton University Press.

Burk, J. (1989). National Attachments and the Decline of the Mass Armed Force. *Journal of Political and Military Sociology*, 17: 65–81.

Burke, P. (1986). City-States. In J.A. Hall (ed.), *States in History*. Oxford: Blackwell.

Butcher, T. (2014). *The Trigger: Hunting the Assassin Who Brought the World to War*. London: Vintage.

Calhoun, C. (2007). *Nations Matter*. London: Routledge.

(1994). *Nationalism and the Public Sphere*. Toronto: University of Toronto Press.

Čalić, M. (2004). *Socijalna istorija Srbije 1915–1941*. Belgrade: Clio.

Campbell, J. L. and J. A. Hall. (2017). *The Paradox of Vulnerability: States, Nationalism and the Financial Crisis*. Princeton: Princeton University Press.

(2015). *The World of States*. London: Bloomsbury.

Canefe, N. (2002). Turkish Nationalism and Ethno-Symbolic Analysis: The Rules of Exception. *Nations and Nationalism*, 8(2): 133–55.

Carey, H.M. (2011). *God's Empire: Religion and Colonialism in the British World, c. 1801–1908*. Cambridge: Cambridge University Press.

Carneiro, R. L. (1970). A Theory of the Origin of the State. *Science*, 169 (3947): 733–8.

Carter, M. (2010). *The Three Emperors: Three Cousins, Three Empires and the Road to World War One*. London: Penguin Books.

Case, H. (2010). The Media and State Power in South-East Europe to 1945. In W. Van Meurs and A. Mungiu-Pippidi (eds.), *Ottomans into Europeans*. London: Hurst.

Centeno, M. (2002). *War and Debt: War and the Nation-State in Latin America*. University Park: Penn State University Press.

Central Statistics Office. (2015). www.cso.ie/en/statistics/education/educational attainmentthematicreport/

Chaloemtiarana, T. (2007). *Thailand: The Politics of Despotic Paternalism*. Ithaca: Cornell University Press.

Chandra, B. (1989). *India's Struggle for Independence, 1857–1947*. New Delhi: Penguin.

Chang-Qun, D.G. Xue-Chun, J. Wang and P.K. Chien. (1998). Relocation of Civilization Centers in Ancient China: Environmental Factors. *Ambio*, 27 (7): 572–5.

Chatterjee, P. (2017). Empires, Nations, Peoples: The Imperial Prerogative and Colonial Exceptions. *Thesis Eleven*, 139: 84–96.

Chen, C. (2007). *The Prospect for Liberal Nationalism in Post-Leninist States*. State College: Pennsylvania State University.

Choloniewski, A. (2016 [1918]) *The Spirit of Polish History*. New York: The Polish Book.

Chun, S. (2009). On Chinese Cosmopolitanism (Tian Xia). *Culture Mandala*, 8 (2): 20–19.

CIA. (2016). Country Report: Croatia. www.cia.gov/library/publications/the-world-factbook/geos/hr.html.

(2016). Country Report: Serbia. www.cia.gov/library/publications/the-world-factbook/geos/hr.html.

Clark, C. (2012). *The Sleepwakers: How Europe went to War in 1914*. London: Penguin.

Clodfelter, M. (1992). Warfare and Armed Conflicts: A Statistical Reference, vol i. Jefferson, NC: McFarland and Company.

Coakley, J. (2013). *Nationalism, Ethnicity and the State*. London: Sage.

Coakley, J. and T. Gallagher (eds.). (2009). *Politics in the Republic of Ireland*. London: Routledge.

Cockburn, P. (2015). *The Rise of Islamic State: ISIS and the New Sunni Revolution*. London: Verso.

Cohen, A. P. (1996). Personal Nationalism: A Scottish View of some Rites, Rights and Wrongs. *American Ethnologist*, 23(4): 802–15.

Cohen, L. (1993). *Broken bonds: The Disintegration of Yugoslavia*. Boulder, CO: Westview Press.

Cohen, P. J. and D. Riesman. (1996). *Serbia's Secret War: Propaganda and the Deceit of History*. College Station: Texas A&M University Press.

Collins, R. (2012). Time-Bubbles of Nationalism: Dynamics of Solidarity Ritual in Lived Time. *Nations and Nationalism*, 18(3): 383–97.

(2008). *Violence: Micro-Sociological Theory*. Princeton: Princeton University Press.

(2004). *Interaction Ritual Chains*. Princeton: Princeton University Press.

(1999). *Macrohistory: Essays in the Sociology of the Long Run*. Stanford: Stanford University Press.

(1990). *Weberian Sociological Theory*. Cambridge: Cambridge University Press.

(1975). *Conflict Sociology: Towards an Explanatory Science*. New York: Academic Press.

Conversi, D. (2008). 'We Are All Equals!' Militarism, Homogenization and 'Egalitarianism' in Nationalist State-Building (1789–1945). *Ethnic and Racial Studies*, 31(7): 1286–1314.

(2007). Homogenisation, Nationalism and War: Should We Still Read Ernest Gellner? *Nations and Nationalism*, 13 (3): 371–394.

Cornell, S. (2014). *Small Nations and Great Powers*. London: Routledge.

Cramb, J. A. (1915). *The Origins and Destiny of Imperial Britain and 19th Century Europe*. New York: Dutton & Co.

Crampton, R. (2007). *Bulgaria*. Oxford: Oxford University Press.

Cronin, M. (1999). *Sport and Nationalism in Ireland: Gaelic Games, Soccer and Irish Identity Since 1884*. Dublin: Four Courts Press.

Cronin, M. and D. Adair. (2006). *The Wearing of the Green: A History of St Patrick's Day*. New York: Psychology Press.

Cronin, M. et al. (2009). *The Gaelic Athletic Association, 1884–2009*. Dublin: Irish Academic Press.

Crosbie, B. (2011). *Irish Imperial Networks: Migration, Social Communication and Exchange in 19th century India*. Cambridge: Cambridge University Press.

Crouch, C., A. Sakalis and R. Bechler. (2016). Educating for Democracy. *Open Democracy*. www.opendemocracy.net/wfd/colin-crouch-alex-sakalis-rosemary-bechler/educating-for-democracy.

Ćunković, S. (1971). *Prosveta, obrazovanje i vaspitanje u Srbiji*. Beograd: Zavod za udžbenike i nastavna sredstva.

Cvijić, J. (1922.) *Balkansko poluostrvo i Juznoslovenske Zemlje: Osnove antropogeografije*. Belgrade. Zavod za izdavanje udžbenika.

D'Amato, R. (2010). *The Varangian Guard 988–1453*. Oxford: Osprey Publishing.

Damasio, A. (2003). *The Feeling of What Happens: Body, Emotion and the Making of Consciousness*. New York: Vintage.

Darwin, J. (2013). Empire and Ethnicity. In J. A. Hall and S. Malešević (eds.), *Nationalism and War*. Cambridge: Cambridge University Press.

Daskalov, R. (2005). *The Making of a Nation in the Balkans: Historiography of the Bulgarian Revival*. Budapest: Central European University Press.

Daskalova, K. (2010). Nation Building, Patriotism, and Women's Citizenship: Bulgaria in Southeastern Europe. In J. Albisetti, J. Goodman and R. Rogers (eds.), *Girls' Secondary Education in the Western World: From the 18th to the 20th Century*. New York: Palgrave Macmillan.

David, L. (2014). Impression Management of a Contested Past: Serbia's Evolving National Calendar. *Memory Studies*, 7(4) 472–483.

Davies, N. (1982). *God's Playground: A History of Poland*, vol. i. New York: Columbia University Press.

Delanty, G. (2000). *Citizenship in a Global Age*. Buckingham: Open University Press.

de Silva Wijeyeratne, R. (2013). *Nation, Constitutionalism and Buddhism in Sri Lanka*. London: Routledge.

Despalatović, E. (1975). *Ljudevit Gaj and the Illyrian Movement*, New York: East European Quarterly.

Diamond, J. (2005). *Guns, Germs and Steel: The Fates of Human Societies*. New York: W.W. Norton.

Dickinson, L. A. (2011). Privatization and Accountability. In J. Hagan, K. L. Scheppele and T. R. Tyler (eds.), *Annual Review of Law and Social Science*, vol. 7. Annual Reviews.

Dimitrova, S. (2003). Traumatizing History: Textbooks in Modern Bulgarian History and Bulgarian National Identity (1917–1996). *Studies in Ethnicity and Nationalism*, I (III): 56–72.

Dimitrova, S. and N. Kaytchev. (1998). Bulgarian Nationalism, Articulated by the Textbooks in Modern Bulgarian History, 1878–1996. *Internationale Schulbuchforschung*, 1, 51–70.

Dinić, M. and S. Ćirković. (1978). *Srpske zemlje u srednjem veku. Srpska knjizevna zadruga.* Belgrade.
Djaković, L. (1985). *Političke organizacije bosanskohercegovačkih katolika Hrvata.* Zagreb: Globus.
Djordjević, D. (1985). The Serbian Peasant in the 1876 War. In B. Kiraly and G. Stokes (eds). *War and Society in East Central Europe: Insurrections, Wars and the Eastern Crisis in the 1870s.* Boulder, CO.: Social Science Monographs.
(1970). Projects for the Federation of South-East Europe in the 1860s and 1870s. *Balkanica*, 2: 119–46.
Djordjević, D. and S. Fisher-Galati. (1981). *The Balkan Revolutionary Tradition.* New York: Columbia University Press.
Djuričković, D. (1975). Bosanska Vila 1885–1914. In *Knjizevna Studija.* Sarajevo.
Doak, R.D. (2008). *Assassination at Sarajevo.* North Mankato, MN: Compass Point Books.
Dome, M. (2016). 10 of the Best Rock Bands from Ireland. www.loudersound .com/features/10-of-the-best-rock-bands-from-ireland.
Dorney, J. (2012). The Perfect Symbol – Italia 90 and Irish Identity. www .theirishstory.com/2012/06/18/the-perfect-symbol-italia-90-and-irish-identity/'.WvwHrYgvyUk.
Dougherty, M. B. (2016). A New Nationalism Is Rising. Don't Let Donald Trump Destroy It. *The Week.* http://theweek.com/articles/638440/new-nationalism-rising-dont-let-donald-trump-destroy
Downing, B. (1992). *The Military Revolution and Political Change.* Princeton: Princeton University Press.
Drakulić, S. (2008). Whence Nationalism? *Nations and Nationalism*, 14 (2): 221–39.
Duffy, J. (2017). *Irish Revenue Reports Reflect Strengthening Commercial Environment.* Dublin: Matheson.
Duina, F. (2018). *Broke and Patriotic: Why Poor Americans Love their Country?* Stanford: Stanford University Press.
Dukas, H. and B. Hoffman. (1979). *Albert Einstein: The Human Side.* Princeton: Princeton University Press.
Dunbar, R. (1998). *Grooming, Gossip, and the Evolution of Language.* Cambridge, MA: Harvard University Press.
Duncan-Jones, R. (1994). *Money and Government in the Roman Empire.* Cambridge: Cambridge University Press.
Durkheim. E. (1976). *The Elementary Forms of Religious Life.* New York: Oxford University Press.
Dvorniković, V. (1939). *Karakterologija Jugoslovena.* Belgrade: Kosmos.
Eagleton, T. (1999). *The Truth about the Irish.* Dublin: New Island Books.
Eckhardt, W. (1992). *Civilizations, Empires and Wars: A Quantitative History of War.* Jefferson NC: McFarland.
(1988). Wars and War-Related Deaths, 1700–1987. In R. Leger Sivard (ed), *World Military and Social Expenditures, 1987–1988.* Washington, DC: World Priorities.

Edensor, T. (2008). *Tourists at the Taj: Performance and Meaning at a Symbolic Site.* London: Routledge.

(2002). *National Identity, Popular Culture and Everyday Life.* Oxford: Berg.

Ekmečić, M. (1991). The Emergence of St. Vitus Day as the Principal National Holiday of the Serbs. In W. Vucinich and T. Emmert (eds.), *Kosovo: Legacy of Medieval Battle.* Minneapolis: University of Minnesota Press.

(1973). *Ustanak u Bosni 1875–1878.* Sarajevo: Veselin Masleša.

Elias, N. (2000). *The Civilising Process: Sociogenetic and Psychogenetic Investigations.* Oxford: Blackwell.

(1996). *The Germans: Power Struggles and the Development of Habitus.* Cambridge: Polity.

(1987). The Retreat of Sociologists into the Present. *Theory, Culture and Society,* 4(2): 223–47.

Emmert, T. (1991). The Battle of Kosovo: Early Reports of Victory and Defeat In W.S. Vucinich and T. Emmert (eds.), *Kosovo: Legacy of a Medieval Battle.* Minneapolis: University of Minnesota Press.

Endresen, C. (2013). *Is the Albanian's Religion Really 'Albanianism'?: Religion and Nation According to Muslim and Christian Leaders in Albania.* Wiesbaden: Harrassowitz Verlag.

English, R. (2007). *Irish Freedom.* London: Pan Macmillan.

EP – *Evening Post,* LXVI (16), 18 July 1903.

Eriksen, T. H. (2007). Ernest Gellner and the Multicultural Mess. In S. Malešević and M. Haugaard (eds.). *Ernest Gellner and Contemporary Social Thought.* Cambridge: Cambridge University Press.

(2002). *Ethnicity and Nationalism: Anthropological Perspectives.* London: Pluto.

Erlich-Stein, V. (1964.) *Porodica u transformaciji.* Zagreb: Naprijed.

Ertman, T. (1997). *Birth of the Leviathan.* Cambridge: Cambridge University Press.

Eurobarometer Surveys. (2010). http://ec.europa.eu/commfrontoffice/publicopi nion/archives/eb/eb74/eb74_publ_en.pdf.

Faris, J. (1995). The Looking-Glass Army: Patriotism in the Post-Cold War Era. *Armed Forces & Society,* 21: 411–34.

Fields, N. (2009). *The Roman Army of the Principate 27 BC – AD 117.* Oxford: Osprey Publishing.

Fine, J. V. (1994). *The Late Medieval Balkans.* Ann Arbor: University of Michigan Press.

(1991). *The Early Medieval Balkans: A Critical Survey from the Sixth to the Late Twelfth Century.* Ann Arbor: University of Michigan Press.

Folić, Z. (2001). *Vjerske zajednice u Crnoj Gori 1918–1953: Prilozi za istoriju.* Podgorica: Istorijski institut Crne Gore.

Foster, R. (1988). *Modern Ireland 1600–1972.* London: Allen Lane.

Fotopoulos, T. (2016). *The Revolution of the Victims of Globalisation and Neo-Nationalism.* World Financial Review.

Fox, J. (2017). The Edges of the Nation: A Research Agenda for Uncovering the Taken-for-Granted Foundations of Everyday Nationhood. *Nations and Nationalism,* 23: 26–47.

Fox, J. and C. Miller-Idriss. (2008). Everyday Nationhood. *Ethnicities*, 8(4): 536–63.

Franke, V. and M. von Boemcken. (2011). Guns for Hire: Motivations and Attitudes of Private Security Contractors. *Armed Forces and Society*, 37(4): 725–42.

Freeden, M. (1998). Is Nationalism a Distinct Ideology? *Political Studies*, 46, 748–50.

Fried, R. (1999). *The Russians Are Coming! The Russians Are Coming!* Oxford: Oxford University Press.

Friedman, T. (2003). *The World Is Flat: A Brief History of the Twenty-First Century*. New York: Douglas and McIntyre.

Frost, R. (2015). *The Oxford History of Poland Lithuania*. Oxford: Oxford University Press.

Fry, D.S. (2007). *Beyond War*. Oxford: Oxford University Press.

Fukuyama, F. (2006[1992]) *The End of History and the Last Man*. New York: Simon & Schuster.

Fukuyama, F. (2018). Identity: The Demand for Dignity and the Politics of Resentment. New York: Profile Books.

Fung, A. (2014). Online Games and Chinese National Identities. In H. Lee and L. Lim (eds.), *Cultural Policies in East Asia*. New York: Springer.

Gabriel, R. (1987).*No More Heroes: Madness and Psychiatry in War*. New York: Hill and Wang.

Gallup Survey. (2015). www.gallup.com/poll/183911/smaller-majority-extremely-proud-american.aspx.

Garvin, T. (2003). *Preventing the Future*. Dublin: Gill & McMillan.

Garwood, C. (2007). *Flat Earth: The History of an Infamous Idea*. London: Pan Books.

Gat, A. (2012). *Nations: The Long History and Deep Roots of Political Ethnicity and Nationalism*. Cambridge: Cambridge University Press.

   (2006). *War in Human Civilization*. Oxford: Oxford University Press.

Geary, P. J. (2002). *Myth of Nations*. Princeton: Princeton University Press.

   (1988). *Before France and Germany: The Creation and Transformation of Merovingian World*. Oxford: Oxford University Press.

Geertz, C. (1973). Person, Time, and Conduct in Bali. In *The Interpretation of Cultures: Selected Essays*. New York: Basic Books.

Gellner, E. (1997). *Nationalism*. London: Phoenix.

   (1996). Do Nations Have Navels? *Nations and Nationalism*, 2(2): 366–70.

   (1994). *Conditions of Liberty: Civil Society and Its Rivals*. London: Penguin.

   (1988). *Plough, Sword and Book: The Structure of Human History*. London: Collins Harvill.

   (1983). *Nations and Nationalism*. Oxford: Blackwell.

   (1964). *Thought and Change*. London: Weidenfeld and Nicolson.

Gerolymatos, A. (2002). *The Balkan Wars*. Staplehurst: Spellmount.

Giddens, A. (2017). We are suffering from 'cosmopolitan overload' and a huge task lies before us – to create responsible capitalism. https://economicsociol ogy.org/2017/11/15/giddens-we-are-suffering-from-cosmopolitan-overload-and-a-huge-task-lies-before-us-to-create-responsible-capitalism/.

   (2007). *Europe in the Global Age*. Cambridge: Polity.

(2002). *Runaway World: How Globalization Is Reshaping Our Lives*. London: Profile.

(1991). *Modernity and Self-identity: Self and Society in the Late Modern Age*. Cambridge: Polity.

Giddens, A., S. Lash and U. Beck. (1994). *Reflexive Modernization: Politics, Tradition and Aesthetics in the Modern Social Order*. Stanford: Stanford University Press.

Gilligan, A. (1998). Inside Lt Col Spicer's New Model Army. *The Guardian*, 1276, 22 November.

Glenny, M. (2000). *The Balkans 1804–1999: Nationalism, War and the Great Powers*. London: Granta.

Go, J. (2017). Myths of Nation and Empire: The Logic of America's Liberal Empire-State. *Thesis Eleven*, 139, 69–83.

(2011). *Patterns of Empire: The British and American Empires, 1688 to the Present*. Cambridge: Cambridge University Press.

Goldschmidt, A. (2004). *Modern Egypt: The Formation of a Nation-State*, Boulder, CO: Westview Press.

Goodhart, D. (2017). *The World to Somewhere: The Populist Revolt and the Future of Politics*. London: Hurst.

Gopčević, S. (1889). Makedonija: *Etnografski odnosi Makedonije i Stare Srbije*. Belgrade.

Gorski, P. (2000). The Mosaic Moment: An Early Modernist Critique of Modernist Theories of Nationalism. *American Journal of Sociology*, 105(5): 1428–1468.

Gouldner, A. (1976). *The Dialectic of Ideology and Technology: The Origins, Grammar, and Future of Ideology New York*. Seabury Press.

Graff, D. A. (2016). *The Eurasian Way of War Military Practice in Seventh-Century China and Byzantium*. London: Routledge.

Grandits, H. (2014). *Multikonfesionalna Hercegovina*. Sarajevo: Institut za Historiju.

Gullestad, M. (1997). A Passion for Boundaries: Reflections on Connection between the Everyday Lives of Children and Discourses on the Nation in Contemporary Norway. *Childhood*, 4(1): 19–42.

Gumplowicz, L. (1899). *The Outlines of Sociology*. Philadelphia: American Academy of Political and Social Science.

Habermas, J. (2001). *Postnational Constellations*. Cambridge: MIT Press.

Hade, E. (2015). RTE Still Holds the Upper Hand in TV News Battle. *Irish Independent*, 7 February.

Hagedorn, A. (2015). *The Invisible Soldiers: How America Outsourced Our Security*. New York: Simon & Schuster.

Hajdarpašić, E. (2015). *Whose Bosnia?: National Movements, Imperial Reforms, and the Political Re-ordering of the Late Ottoman Balkans, 1840–1875*. Cornell: Cornell University Press.

Hall, J. A. (2017). Taking Megalomanias Seriously: A Rough Note. *Thesis Eleven*, 139: 30–45.

(2013). *The Importance of Being Civil: The Struggle for Political Decency*. Princeton: Princeton University Press.

(2011). Nationalism Might Change Its Character, Again. In D. Halikiopoulou and S. Vasilopoulou (eds.), *Nationalism and Globalisation*. London: Routledge.

(2010). *Ernest Gellner: An Intellectual Biography*. London: Verso.

(1988). States and Societies: The Miracle in Comparative Perspective. In J. Baechler, J. A. Hall and M. Mann (eds.), *Europe and the Rise of Capitalism*. Oxford: Blackwell.

(1986). *Powers and Liberties: The Causes and Consequences of the Rise of the West*. Berkeley: University of California Press.

Hall, J. A. and S. Malešević. (2013). Introduction: Wars and Nationalisms. In J. A. Hall and S. Malešević (eds.), *Nationalism and War*. Cambridge: Cambridge University Press.

Hall, R. C. (2000). *The Balkan Wars 1912–1913: Prelude to the First World War*. London: Routledge.

Halperin, S. (2017). The Imperial City-State and the National State Form: Reflections on the History of the Contemporary Order. *Thesis Eleven*, 139: 97–112.

Halsall, P. (1997). https://sourcebooks.fordham.edu/mod/1918wilson.asp.

Handler, R. (1994). 'Is 'Identity' a Useful Cross-Cultural Concept?' In J. R. Gillis (ed.), *Commemorations: The Politics of National Identity*. Princeton: Princeton University Press.

Hann, C. (2001). Gellner's Structural-Functional-Culturalism. *Czech Sociological Review*, 9(2): 173–82.

(1998). Nationalism and Civil Society in Central Europe: From Ruritania to the Carpathian Euroregion. In J. A. Hall (ed.), *The State of the Nation: Ernest Gellner and the Theory of Nationalism*. Cambridge: Cambridge University Press.

Hannertz, U. and A. Gingrich (eds.). (2017). *Small Countries: Structures and Sensibilities*. Philadelphia: University of Pennsylvania Press.

Hardt, M. and A. Negri. (2000). *Empire*. Cambridge: Harvard University Press.

Haugh, D. (2016). Ireland's Economy: Still Riding the Globalisation Wave. http://oecdobserver.org/news/fullstory.php/aid/5456/Ireland_92s_economy:_Still_r iding_the_globalisation_wave.html.

Heaney, J. (2013). Emotions and Nationalism: A Process-Relational View. In N. Demertzis (ed.), *Politics: The Affect Dimension in Political Tension*. London: Palgrave Macmillan.

Heater, D. (2004). *World Citizenship: Cosmopolitan Thinking and Its Opponents*. London: Continuum.

Hechter, M. (2000). *Containing Nationalism*. Oxford: Oxford University Press.

(1977). *Internal Colonialism*. Berkeley: University of California Press.

(1976). Response to Cohen: Max Weber on Ethnicity and Ethnic Change. *American Journal of Sociology*, 84: 293–318.

Heimsath, C. H. (2015). *Indian Nationalism and the Hindu Social Reform*. Princeton: Princeton University Press.

Heinecken, L. (2013). Outsourcing Public Security: The Unforeseen Consequences for the Military Profession. *Armed Forces & Society*, 40(4): 625–46.

Held, D. and A. McGrew. (2007). *Globalisation/Anti-Globalisation: Beyond the Great Divide*. Cambridge: Polity.

Hengst, H. (1997). Negotiating 'Us' and 'Them': Children's Constructions of Collective Identity. *Childhood*, 4(1): 43–62.

Hennigan, M. (2007). Irish Economy 2006 and Future of the Celtic Tiger: Putting a brass knocker on a barn door. *Finfacts Ireland*. www.finfacts.com /irelandbusinessnews/publish/article_10006912.shtml

Herbst, J. (2000). *States and Power in Africa: Comparative Lessons in Authority and Control*. Princeton: Princeton University Press.

Heywood, A. (2003). *Political Ideologies: An Introduction*. London: Palgrave McMillan.

Hiers W. and A. Wimmer. (2013). Is Nationalism the Cause or Consequence of the End of Empire? In J. A. Hall and S. Malešević (eds.), *Nationalism and War*. Cambridge: Cambridge University Press.

Higgins, M. (2016). Speech at the National Flag Presentation Ceremony. www .president.ie/en/media-library/speeches/speech-by-president-michael-d.- higgins-at-the-national-flag-presentation-ce

Hintze, O. (1975). *The Historical Essays of Otto Hintze*. New York: Oxford University Press.

Hirst, P., G. Thompson and S. Bromley. (2009). *Globalisation in Question*. Cambridge: Polity.

Hjort, M. (2007). *Small Nation, Global Cinema: The New Danish Cinema*. Minneapolis: University of Minnesota Press.

Hobsbawmn, E. (1990). *Nations and Nationalism since 1780*. Cambridge: Cambridge University Press.

Hopkins, A. (2006) *Global History: Interactions between the Universal and the Local*. New York: Palgrave.

Horsley, S. (2016). Guns in America, by the Numbers. www.npr.org/2016/01/05/ 462017461/guns-in-america-by-the-numbers

Hranova, A. 2011). History Education and Civic Education. *The Bulgarian Case Journal of Social Science Education*, 10(1): 33–43.

Hristić, F. (1872). *Druga čitanka za osnove škole*. Belgrade: Državna štamparija.

Hroch, M. (2015). *European Nations: Explaining Their Formation*. London: Verso.
  (2009). Learning from Small Nations. *New Left Review*, 58, July–August: 41–58.
  (1985). *Social Preconditions of National Revival in Europe: A Comparative Analysis of the Social Composition of Patriotic Groups among the Smaller European Nations*. New York: Columbia University Press.

Hubbs, J. (1993). *Mother Russia:The Feminine Myth in Russian Culture*. Bloomington: Indiana University Press.

Hupchick, D. P. (2002). *The Balkans: From Constantinople to Communism*. New York: Palgrave.

Hutchinson, J. (2017). *Nationalism and War*. Oxford: Oxford University Press.
  (2007). Warfare, Remembrance and National Identity. In A. Leoussi and S. Grosby (eds.), *Nationalism and Ethnosymbolism: History, Culture and Ethnicity in the Formation of Nations*. Edinburgh: Edinburgh University Press.
  (2005). *Nations as Zones of Conflict*. London: Sage.
  (2000). Ethnicity and modern nations. *Ethnic and Racial Studies*, 23(4): 651–69.

(1994). *Modern Nationalism*. London: Fontana Press.

Ignatieff, M. (1994). *Blood and Belonging: Journeys into the New Nationalism*. New York: Vintage.

Iskenderov, P. (2015). The idea of a 'Greater Albania', then and now. Strategic Culture Foundation. www.strategic-culture.org/news/2015/06/14/the-idea-greater-albania-then-and-now-i.html.

James, J. (2014). Jaki McCarric: What Is It about the Irish? www.easonedition.com/jaki-mccarrick-what-is-it-about-the-irish/.

Janowitz, M. (1971). *The Professional Soldier*. New York: Free Press.

Janković, Z. (2015). Ne mogu biti izdajnik Bošnjaka kad nisam njihov. *Kurir*, 27 (7): 4.

Jelavich, C. (1990). *South Slav Nationalism: Textbooks and Yugoslav Union before 1914*. Columbus: Ohio State University Press.

(1989). The Issue of Serbian Textbooks in the Origins of World War I. *Slavic Review*, 48(2): 214–233.

Jenkinson, F., D. O'Callaghan, P. Reidy, F. Kane and S. Prior. (2017). *Strategic Public Infrastructure: Capacity and Demand Analysis*. Dublin: Department of Public Expenditure and Reform.

Johnston, I. and I. Buxton. (2013). *The Battleship Builders: Constructing and Arming British Capital Ships*. Annapolis, MD: Naval Institute Press.

Jones, E. (1987). *The European Miracle*. Cambridge: Cambridge University Press.

Jones, H. (2014). *The Media in Europe's Small Nations*. Newcastle-Upon-Tyne: Cambridge Scholars Publishing.

Jović, D. (2001). The Disintegration of Yugoslavia: A Critical Review of Explanatory Approaches. *European Journal of Social Theory*, 4(1), 101–120.

Jukić, I. F. (1973[1842]). *Sabrana Djela*. Sarajevo: Svjetlost.

Jureško, G. and M. Lilek. (2016). Senzacionalni uspjeh svjetskih razmjera. *Hrvati otkrili lijek za zarastranje kosti! Jutarnji List*, 10(9).

Kakridis, J. (1963). The Ancient Greeks of the War of Independence. *Journal of Balkan Studies*, 4(2).

Kaldor, M. (2001). *New and Old Wars: Organised Violence in a Global Era*. Cambridge: Polity Press.

Kallis, A. (2008). Perversions of Nationalism. In G. H. Herb and D. H. Kaplan (eds.), *Nations and Nationalism: A Global Historical Overview*. Santa Barbara: ABC Clio.

Kamenov, Ž., M. Jelić, A.,Huić, M.,Franceško, V. i Mihić. (2006). Odnos nacionalnog i europskog identiteta i stavova prema europskim integracijama građana Zagreba i Novog Sada. *Društvena istraživanja*, 15 (4–5), 867–90.

Kaplan, D. (2018). *The Nation and the Promise of Friendship: Building Solidarity through Sociability*. New York: Palgrave.

Kaplan, R. D. (1994). *Balkan Ghosts: A Journey through History*. New York: Viking.

Kaufmann, E. (2018). *Whiteshift: Populism, Immigration and the Future of White Majorities*. London: Allen Lane.

Kearney, R. (2002). *Postnationalist Ireland: Politics, Culture, Philosophy*. London: Routledge.

Kedourie, E. (1993[1960]). *Nationalism*. Oxford: Blackwell.

Keen, M. H. (1999). *Medieval Warfare: A History*. Oxford: Oxford University Press.

Kennan, G. F. (1993). *The Other Balkan Wars*. A 1913 Endowment Inquiry in Retrospect with a New Introduction and Reflections on the Present Conflict. Washington, DC: Carnegie Endowment for International Peace.

Kenny, E. (2015). Remarks by the Taoiseach at the Launch of Global Irish– Ireland's Diaspora Policy Tuesday, 3 March, 2015, Dublin: Government Press Centre.

Kenny, K. (2006). The Irish in the Empire. In K. Kenny (ed.), *Ireland and the British Empire*. Oxford: Oxford University Press.

Keogh, D. (1994). *Twentieth-Century Ireland: Nation and State*. Dublin: Gill and McMillan.

Keown, G. (2016). *First of the Small Nations: The Beginnings of Irish Foreign Policy in the Interwar Years, 1919–32*. Oxford: Oxford University Press.

King, J. (2005). *Budweisers into Czechs and Germans: A Local History of Bohemian Politics, 1848–1948*. Princeton: Princeton University Press.

Kinsey, C. (2009). *Private Contractors and the Reconstruction of Iraq: Transforming Military Logistics*. London: Routledge.

Kiser, E. and A. Linton. (2002). The Hinges of History: State-Making and Revolt in Early Modern France. *American Sociological Review*, 67(6): 889–910.

Kitromilides, P. (2010). The Orthodox Church in Modern State Formation in South-East Europe. In W. Van Meurs and A. Mungiu-Pippidi (eds.), *Ottomans into Europeans: State and Institution Building in South Eastern Europe*. London: Hurst.

(1994). *Enlightenment, Nationalism, Orthodoxy: Studies in the Culture and Political Thought of South-Eastern Europe*. Brookfield, VT: Variorum.

Kluipers, G. (2013). The Rise and Decline of National Habitus: Dutch Cycling Culture and the Shaping of National Similarity. *European Journal of Social Theory*, 16(1).

Kozupski, J. (2017). Irish authors and writers you should know from James Joyce to Oscar Wilde. www.irishcentral.com/roots/our-top-ten-irish-novelists-of-all-time-126080063–237787691.

Kreuzer, P. (2006). Violent Civic Nationalism versus Civil Ethnic Nationalism: Contrasting Indonesia and Malay(si)a. *National Identities*, 8(1): 41–59.

Krstić, Z. (2011). Odnos nacionalnog i evropskog identiteta Srba. *Bezbednost Zapadnog Balkana*, 6(20): 31–51.

Kumar, K. (2017). *Visions of Empire: How Five Imperial Regimes Shaped the World*. Princeton: Princeton University Press.

(2010). Nation-States as Empires, Empires as Nation-States: Two Principles, One Practice? *Theory and Society*, 39(2): 119–143.

(2003). *The Making of English National Identity*. Cambridge: Cambridge University Press.

Kymlicka, W. (1999). Misunderstanding Nationalism. In R. Beiner (ed.), *Theorizing Nationalism*. Albany: State University of New York Press.

Lachman, R. (2018). Why Privatize: The Reasons to Buy, Rent, or Create Private Militaries from Feudal Europe to the Era of American Decline. In T. Crosby and U. Swed (eds.), *The Sociology of the Privatization of Security*. New York: Palgrave.

(2013). Mercenery, Citizen, Victim: The Rise and Fall of Conscription in the West. In J. A. Hall and S. Malešević (eds.), *Nationalism and War*. Cambridge: Cambridge University Press.

Laffan, M. (1999). *The Resurrection of Ireland: The Sinn Féin Party, 1916–1923*. Cambridge: Cambridge University Press.

Laitin, D. (2007). *Nations, States, and Violence*. Oxford: Oxford University Press.

(2001). Trapped in Assumptions. *The Review of Politics*, 63(1): 176–9.

Lampe, J. R. and M. R. Jackson. (1982). *Balkan Economic History: From Imperial Borderlands to Developing Nations*. Bloomington: Indiana University Press.

Laruelle, M. 2008. *Russian Eurasianism: An Ideology of Empire*. Washington, DC: Woodrow Wilson Center Press and The Johns Hopkins University Press.

Lauenstein, O., J. S. Murer, M. Boos and S. Reicher. (2015). 'Oh Motherland I pledge to thee … ' A Study into Nationalism, Gender and the Representation of an Imagined Family within National Anthems. *Nations and Nationalism*, 21(2): 309–329.

Lazić, I. and J. Milojević. (2016). Srpski matematički šampioni. *Telegraf*, 21(1).

Leander, A. (2004). War and the Un-Making of States: Taking Tilly Seriously in the Contemporary World. In S. Guzzini and D. Jung (eds.), *Contemporary Security Analysis and Copenhagen Peace Research*. London: Routledge.

Lederer, I. (1969). Nationalism and the Yugoslavs. In P. Sugar and I. Lederer (eds.), *Nationalism in Eastern Europe*. Seattle: University of Washington Press.

Ledstrup, M. (2019). Nationalism and Nationhood in the United Arab Emirates. New York: Palgrave.

Lee, J. (2008). *The Modernisation of Irish Society 1848–1918*. Dublin: Gill & McMillan.

(1985). *Ireland, 1912–1985: Politics and Society*. Cambridge: Cambridge University Press.

Leerssen, J. (2008). *National Thought in Europe*. Amsterdam: Amsterdam University Press.

Leibold, J. (2013). *Ethnic Policy in China*. Honolulu: East West Centre.

(2007). *Reconfiguring Chinese Nationalism*. New York: Palgrave.

Leira, H and B. de Carvalho. (2010). Privateers of the North Sea: At World's End – French Privateers in Norwegian Waters, In A. Colas and B. Mabee (eds.), *Mercenaries, Pirates, Bandits and Empires: Private Violence in Historical Context*. New York: Columbia University Press.

Levi-Strauss, C. (1983). *The View from Afar*. New York: Peregrine Books.

Lieven, A. (2012). *America Right or Wrong: An Anatomy of American Nationalism*. Oxford: Oxford University Press.

Lustick, I.S. (1997). The Absence of Middle Eastern Great Powers: 'Backwardness' in Historical Perspective. *International Organization*, 51: 653–83.

Luxemburg, R. (1976 [1908]). The National Question. In *Selected Writings*. New York: Monthly Review Press.

Mackenzie, D. (1996). *Violent Solutions: Revolutions, Nationalism, and Secret Societies in Europe to 1918*. New York: University Press of America.

(1994). Serbia as Piedmont and the Yugoslav Idea, 1804–1914. *East European Quarterly*, 28(2): 153–182.

Magaš, B. 2008). *Croatia through History*. London: Saqi Books.

Malcolm, A. H. (1974). The Shortage of Bathroom Tissue: A Classic Study in Rumor. *The New York Times*, February 3: 29.

Malešević, S. (2017). *The Rise of Organised Brutality: A Historical Sociology of Violence*. Cambridge: Cambridge University Press.

(2016). Nationalism and Military Power in the 20th Century and Beyond. In R. Schroder (ed.), *Global Powers: Michael Mann's Anatomy of the 20th Century and Beyond*. Cambridge: Cambridge University Press.

(2015). Where Does Group Solidarity Come From?: Gellner and Ibn Khaldun Revisited. *Thesis Eleven*, 128(1): 85–99.

(2013a). *Nation-States and Nationalisms: Organisation, Ideology and Solidarity*. Cambridge: Polity Press.

(2013b). Obliterating Heterogeneity through Peace: Nationalisms, States and Wars in the Balkans. In J. A. Hall and S. Malešević (eds.), *Nationalism and War*. Cambridge: Cambridge University Press.

(2012). Did Wars Make Nation-States in the Balkans? Nationalisms, Wars and States in the 19th and early 20th Century South East Europe. *Journal of Historical Sociology*, 25(3): 299–330.

(2011). The Chimera of National Identity. *Nations and Nationalism*, 17(2): 272–90.

(2010). *The Sociology of War and Violence*. Cambridge: Cambridge University Press.

(2007). Between the Book and the New Sword: Gellner, Violence and Ideology. In S. Malešević and M. Haugaard (eds.), *Ernest Gellner and Contemporary Social Thought*. Cambridge: Cambridge University Press.

(2006). *Identity as Ideology: Understanding Ethnicity and Nationalism*. New York: Palgrave Macmillan.

(2004). *The Sociology of Ethnicity*. London: Sage.

(2002). *Ideology, Legitimacy and the New State: Yugoslavia, Serbia and Croatia*. London: Routledge.

Malešević, S and N. O'Dochartaigh. (2018). Why Combatants Fight: The Irish Republican Army and the Bosnian Serb Army Compared. *Theory and Society*, 47(3): 293-326.

Malešević, S. and K. Ryan. (2013). The Disfigured Ontology of Figurational Sociology: Norbert Elias and the Question of Violence. *Critical Sociology*, 39 (2): 165–81.

Mallett, M. (1974). *Mercenaries and Their Masters: Warfare in Renaissance Italy*. Rowman and Littlefield.

Mandrapa, N. (2014). Nole naš moderni junak: Novi srpski heroj. *Novosti*, 18.7.

Mandujano Y. (2014). Flagging the National Identity, Reinforcing Japaneseness. *Electronic Journal of Contemporary Japanese Studies*, 14(1).

Mann, M. (2016). Response to the Critics. In R. Schroder (ed.), *Global Powers: Michael Mann's Anatomy of the 20th Century and Beyond*. Cambridge: Cambridge University Press.

(2013). *Sources of Social Power IV: Globalisations 1945–2011*. Cambridge: Cambridge University Press.

(2012). The Sources of Social Power, vol. 3, *Global Empires and Revolution, 1890–1945*. Cambridge: Cambridge University Press.

(2006). *The Sources of Social Power* Revisited: A Response to Criticism. In R. Schroder and J. A. Hall (eds.), *An Anatomy of Power: The Social Theory of Michael Mann*. Cambridge: Cambridge University Press.

(2004). *Fascists*. Cambridge: Cambridge University Press.

(2003). *Incoherent Empire*. London: Verso.

(1993). *The Sources of Social Power II: The Rise of Classes and Nation-States, 1760–1914*. Cambridge: Cambridge University Press.

(1995). A Political Theory of Nationalism and Its Excesse. In S. Periwal (ed.), *Notions of Nationalism*. Budapest: Central European University Press.

(1986). *The Sources of Social Power I: A History of Power from the Beginning to A.D. 1760*. Cambridge: Cambridge University Press.

(1984). The Autonomous Power of the State: Its Origins, Mechanisms and Results. *European Journal of Sociology*, 25: 185–213.

Marvin, C. and D. Ingle. (1999). *Blood Sacrifice and the Nation: Totem Rituals and the American Flag*. Cambridge: Cambridge University Press.

Marshall, T. H. (1950). *Citizenship and Social Class and Other Essays*. Cambridge: Cambridge University Press.

Martins, L. (1983). *Power and Imagination: City-States in Renaissance Italy*. Harmondsworth: Penguin.

Marx, K. and F. Engels. (1998[1848]). *The Communist Manifesto*. London: Verso.

Matić, R. (2015). Hrvatski znanstevenici otkrili novi material – Katsenit. *HRT Magazin* 25(3).

Matthews, O. (2016). Beyond Brexit: Europe's Populist Backlash against Immigration and Globalization. *Newsweek*. http://europe.newsweek.com/br itain-brexit-wounds-european-nationalism-475101.

Mazower, M. 2009). *Dark Continent: Europe's Twentieth Century*. New York: Knopf Doubleday Publishing Group.

(2000). *The Balkans: From the End of Byzantium to the Present Day*. London: Phoenix.

McCarty, C. et al. (2000). Comparing Two Methods for Estimating Network Size. *Human Organisation*, 60(1)28–39.

McClelland. K. (1985). On the Social Significance of Interactional Synchrony. Unpublished paper, Department of Sociology, Grinnell, IO: Grinnell College.

McFate, S. (2017). *The Modern Mercenary: Private Armies and What They Mean for World Order*. Oxford: Oxford University Press.

McLane, J. R. (2005). *Indian Nationalism and the Early Congress*. Princeton: Princeton University Press.

McLaughlin, E. (2012). *Imitating the Continent: European Microfinance institutions in Ireland*. In B. Heffernan (ed.), *Life on the Fringe?* Dublin: Irish Academic Press.

Medrano, J. (2009). *Framing Europe: Attitudes to European Integration in Germany, Spain and the United Kingdom*. Princeton: Princeton University Press.

Mees, L. (2003). *Nationalism, Violence and Democracy: The Basque Clash of Identities*. New York: Palgrave.

Melville-Smith, A. (2014). Peace Campaigners Outraged after White Poppy Wreaths Torn Down from Aberystwyth War Memorial. www.walesonline .co.uk/news/wales-news/peace-campaigners-outraged-after-white-8123699.

Meriage, L. P. (1977). The First Serbian Uprising (1804–1813): National Revival or a Search for Regional Security. *Canadian Review of Studies in Nationalism*, 4(2): 187–205.

Merton, R. K. (1948). The Self-Fulfilling Prophecy. *Antioch Review*, 8(2): 193–210.

Mesić, M and D. Bertek. (2016). Oni su hrvatski ponos. *Jutarnji List*, 31(5).

Meyer, J. W. et al. (1997). World Society and the Nation-State. *American Journal of Sociology*, 103(1): 144–81.

(1992). *School Knowledge for the Masses: World Models and National Primary Curricular Categories in the Twentieth Century*. London: Falmer Press.

Milojević, M. S. (1871). Putopis dela (prave) Stare Srbije. I sveska. Belgrade.

Milosavljević, O. (2003). Elitizam u narodnom ruhu. In L. Perović (ed.), *Srbija u modernizacijskim procesima 19. i 20. Veka: Uloga elita*; Belgrade: Čigoj štampa.

Minogue, K. (1996). Ernest Gellner and the Danger of Theorising Nationalism. In J. A. Hall and I. Jarvie (ed.), *The Social Philosophy of Ernest Gellner*. Amsterdam: Rodopi.

Mirković, M. (1958). *Ekonomska historija Jugoslavije*. Zagreb: Ekonomski pregled.

Mock, S. (2014). *Symbols of Defeat in the Construction of National Identity*. Cambridge: Cambridge University Press.

Mommsen, W. (1982). *Theories of Imperialism*. Chicago: University of Chicago Press.

Moskos, C. C. (1981). *Institution Versus Occupation: Contrasting Models of Military Organization*. Washington, DC: Wilson Center, International Security Studies Program.

Mosse, G. (1991[(1975)]). *The Nationalization of the Masses: Political Symbolism and Mass Movements in Germany from the Napoleonic Wars through the Third Reich*. Ithaca: Cornell University Press.

Mouffe, C. (2005). *On the Political*. New York: Routledge.

Mouzelis, N. (2007). Nationalism: Reconstructing Gellner's Theory. In S. Malešević and M. Haugaard (eds.), *Ernest Gellner and Contemporary Social Thought*. Cambridge: Cambridge University Press.

(1998). Ernest Gellner's Theory of Nationalism: Some Definitional and Methodological Issues. In J. A. Hall (ed.), *The State of the Nation: Ernest Gellner and the Theory of Nationalism*. Cambridge: Cambridge University Press.

(1978). *Modern Greece: Facets of Underdevelopment*. London: McMillan.

Mullholland, M. (2016). Political Violence. In R. Bourke and I. McBride (eds.), *The Princeton History of Modern Ireland*. Princeton: Princeton University Press.

Mungiu-Pippidi, A. (2010). Failed Institutional Transfer? Constraints on the Political Modernization of the Balkans. In W. Van Meurs and A. Mungiu-Pippidi (eds.), *Ottomans into Europeans*. London: Hurst.

Munkler, H. (2007). *Empire*. Cambridge: Polity.

Mylonas, H. (2012). *The Politics of Nation-Building: Making Co-Nationals, Refugees, and Minorities*. Cambridge: Cambridge University Press.

Naughton, C. (2016). 1916 Rebellion: Six days that Shook the World. *Irish Independent*. 11 February.

Nenadović, M. (1969). *The Memoirs of Prota Matija Nenadović*. Oxford: Clarendon Press. Nicholson, H. (2004. *Medieval Warfare: Theory and Practice of War in Europe, 300–1500*. New York: Plagrave.

Nkrumah, K. (1965). *Neo-Colonialism: The Last Stage of Imperialism*. New York: International.

Nussbaum, M. (2006). *Frontiers of Justice: Disability, Nationality, Species Membership*. Cambridge, MA: Belknap Press.

Oberschall, A. (2000). The Manipulation of Ethnicity: From Ethnic Cooperation to Violence and War in Yugoslavia. *Ethnic and Racial Studies*, 23(6): 982–1001.

O'Brien, D. (2017). 101 Years After the Rising, Nationalism Is Dead and Gone. *Irish Independent*. 16 April.

(2009). *Ireland, Europe and the World: Writings on a New Century*. Dublin: Gill & McMillan.

Ó Giolláin, D. (2017). *Irish Ethnologies*. Notre Dame: University of Notre Dame Press.

Ohmae, K. (1995). *The End of the Nation-State*. New York: Free Press.

Okey, R. (2009). *Taming Balkan Nationalism: The Habsburg 'Civilising Mission' in Bosnia, 1878–1914*. Oxford: Oxford University Press.

O'Leary, B. (1998). Ernest Gellner's Diagnoses of Nationalism. In J. A. Hall (ed.), *The State of the Nation: Ernest Gellner and the Theory of Nationalism*. Cambridge: Cambridge University Press.

O'Leary, C. (2000). *To Die for: The Paradox of American Patriotism*. Princeton: Princeton University Press.

Oppenheimer, F. (2007 [1926]). *The State*. Montreal: Black Rose Books.

Orridge, A. (1981). Uneven Development and Nationalism II. *Political Studies*, 29 (2): 181–90.

Østergaard, U. (2006). Denmark: A Big Small State: The Peasant Roots of Danish Modernity. In J. Campbell, J. A. Hall and O. K. Pedersen (eds.), *National Identity and the Varieties of Capitalism: The Danish Experience*. Montreal: McGill-Queen's University Press.

O'Toole, F. (1997). *The Ex-Isle of Erin*. Dublin: New Island Books.

Ožegović, N. (2006). Miro Gavran – najpopularniji hrvatski pisac u svijetu. *Nacional*, 553, 19.6: 14.

Özkirimli, U. (2017). *Theories of Nationalism: A Critical Introduction*. London: Palgrave.

Pantelić, B. (2011). Memories of a Time Forgotten: The Myth of the Perennial Nation. *Nations and Nationalism*, 17(2): 443–64.

Parsons, T. (1977). *The Evolution of Societies*. New York: Prentice Hall.

(1975). Commentary on 'De-Parsonizing Weber: A Critique of Parsons'. *American Sociological Review*, 40(1): 666–9.

(1951). *The Social System*. New York: The Free Press.

Pathak, A. (2016). Beyond the Republic Day Parade: Looking For the Lost Ideals of the Nation. *The Wire*, 26th January. thewire.in/politics/beyond-republic-day-parade-looking-lost-ideals-nation.

Pattison, J. (2014). *The Morality of Private War: The Challenge of Private Military and Security Companies*. Oxford: Oxford University Press.

Pavlowitch, S. (2002). *Serbia: The History behind the Name.* London: Hurst.

(1999). *A History of the Balkans 1804–1945.* London: Longman.

(1981). Society in Serbia 1791–1830. In R. Clogg (ed.), *Balkan Society in the Age of Greek Independence.* London. Macmillan.

Paxton, R. (1972. Nationalism and Revolution: A Re-examination of the Origins of the First Serbian Insurrection, 1804–7. *East European Quarterly,* 6(3): 337–62.

Peleggi, M. 2007). *Thailand: Worldly Kingdom.* London: Reaction Books.

Peel, J. (1989). The Cultural Work of Yoruba Ethnogenesis. In E. Tonkin et al. (eds.), *History and Ethnicity.* London: Routledge.

Pelt, M. (2010). Organised Violence in the Service of Nation Building. In W. Van Meurs and A. Mungiu-Pippidi (eds.), *Ottomans into Europeans.* London: Hurst.

Petković, Z. (1926). *Prve pojave srpskog imena.* Belgrade.

Phelan, K. (2017). The 10 Most Famous Irish Actors in Hollywood. https://the culturetrip.com/europe/ireland/articles/the-10-most-famous-irish-actors-in-hollywood/.

Pippidi, A. (2010). The Development of an Administrative Class in South-East Europe. In W. Van Meurs and A. Mungiu-Pippidi (eds.), *Ottomans into Europeans.* London: Hurst.

Polanyi, K. (2001[1944]). *The Great Transformation.* Boston: Beacon Press.

Poortman, A-R. and A. C. Liefbroer. (2010). Singles' Relational Attitudes in a Time of Individualization. *Social Science Research,* 39: 938–49.

Posen, B. (1993). Nationalism, the Mass Army, and Military Power. *International Security,* 18(2): 80–124.

Poulton, H. (1995). *Who Are the Macedonians?* Bloomington: Indiana University Press.

Quinlan, K. (2005). *Strange Kin: Ireland and the American South.* Baton Rouge: Louisiana University Press.

Radić, R. (2003). Verska elita i modernizacija: Teskoce pronalazenja odgovora. In L. Perovic (ed.), *Srbija u modernizacijskim procesima 19. i 20. Veka: Uloga elita;* Belgrade: Cigoj stampa.

Rapport, M. (2008). *1848: Year of the Revolution.* London: Little, Brown Book Group.

Rath, R. (1964). The Carbonari: Their Origins, Initiation Rites, and Aims. *The American Historical Review,* 69 (2): 353–37.

Ratzenhofer, G. (1881). *Die Staatswehr.* Stuttgart: Cottasche Buchhandlung.

Reicher, S. and N. Hopkins. (2001). *Self and Nation.* London: Sage.

Reno, W. (2003). The Changing Nature of Warfare and Absence of State Building in West Africa. In D. Davis and A. Pereira (eds.), *Irregular Armed Forces and Their Role in Politics and State Formation.* Cambridge: Cambridge University Press.

Riall, L. (2009). *Risorgimento: The History of Italy from Napoleon to Nation State.* New York: Palgrave.

Roosevelt, T. (1910). *The New Nationalism.* New York: The Outlook Company.

Rosenthal, l. and V. Rodic. (2014). *The New Nationalism and the First World War.* New York: Palgrave.

Roshwald, A (2006). *The Endurance of Nationalism*. Cambridge: Cambridge University Press.

Rothenbacher, F. (2002). *The European Population 1850–1945*. Basingstoke: Palgrave.

Rothermund, D. (ed.). (2015). *Memories of Post-Imperial Nations: The Aftermath of Decolonization, 1945–2013*. Cambridge: Cambridge University Press.

Roudometof, V. (2001). *Nationalism, Globalization and Orthodoxy: The Social Origins of Ethnic Conflict in the Balkans*. Westport, Connecticut: Greenwood Press.

Ruthven, M. (2007). *Fundamentalism: A Very Short Introduction*. Oxford: Oxford University Press.

Rustow, A. (1980[(1950]). *Freedom and Domination*. Princeton: Princeton University Press.

Ryang, S. (2000). The North Korean Homeland of Koreans in Japan. In S. Ryang (ed.), *Koreans in Japan: Critical Voices from the Margin*. London: Routledge.

Sachs, J. (2013). *To Move the World: JFK's Quest for Peace*. London: The Bodley Head.

Sanders, H. (2015). *Religious Revivalism in Sweden and Denmark*. In J. A. Hall, O. Korsgaard and O. Pedersen (eds.), *Building the Nation: NFS Grundtvig and Danish National Identity*. Montreal: McGill University Press.

Sassen, S. (2003). Globalization or Denationalization. *Review of International Political Economy*, 10, 1 February: 1–22.

Sato, S. (1994). *War, Nationalism and Peasants: Java Under the Japanese Occupation, 1942–1945*. New York: M.E. Sharpe.

Scahill, J. (2007). A Very Private War. *Guardian*. www.theguardian.com/uk/2007/aug/01/military.usa

Schmidl, E. (2012). How Dick Smith's Business Empire Trades on Patriotism. www.smartcompany.com.au/finance/economy/how-dick-smith-s-business-empire-trades-on-patriotism/.

Schuldt, J. (2017). Iconic Ideology: Contemporary Irish Nationalism and St. Patrick's Day. Paper presented at the International Visual Sociology Association (IVSA). Concordia University, Montreal, Canada. June 20.

Schulze, H. (1996). *States, Nations and Nationalism: From the Middle Ages to the Present*. Oxford: Blackwell.

Schurman, J. G. (1914). *The Balkan Wars 1912–1913*. Princeton: Princeton University Press.

Scott, R. and J. Bedogni.(2017). *The Irish Experience: Fiscal Consolidation 2008–2014*. Central Expenditure Policy Division. Department of Public Expenditure and Reform.

Sherlock, J. (1999). Globalisation, Western Culture and Riverdance. In. A. Brah et al. (ed.), *Thinking Identities: Ethnicity, Racism and Culture*. London: Palgrave.

Shermer, M. (2007). The (Other) Secret. *Scientific American*, 1 June.

Shreeves, W. G. (1984). *Nation Making in Nineteenth Century Europe*. London: Nelson Thornes.

Simmel, G. (1955 [1917]). Conflict and the Web of Group Affiliations. *New York Free Press*.

Singer, P. W. (2008). *Corporate Warriors: The Rise of the Privatized Military Industry.* Ithaca: Cornell University Press.

Singer, J. D. (1972). *The Wages of War. 1816–1965.* Stockholm: Stockholm International Peace Research Institute.

Sission, E. H. (2014). *America the Great.* Washington, DC: Arnold & Porter.

Skey, M. (2011). *National Belonging and Everyday Life.* London: Palgrave.

(2009). The National in Everyday Life: A Critical Engagement with Michael Billig's Thesis of Banal Nationalism. *The Sociological Review,* 57(2): 331–46.

Skey, M. and M. Antonsich. (2018). *Everyday Nationhood: Theorising Culture, Identity and Belonging after Banal Nationalism.* London: Palgrave.

Skorin, I. (2016). Senzacionalni uspjeh Hrvatskih Znanstvenika: Otkrili lijek za zarastanje kostiju. *RTL Vijesti,* 10(9).

Smith, A. D. (2010). *Nationalism: Theory, Ideology, History.* Cambridge: Polity.

(2009). *Nationalism and Ethno-Symbolism: A Cultural Approach.* London: Routledge.

(2008). *The Cultural Foundations of Nations: Hierarchy, Covenant and the Republic.* Oxford: Blackwell.

(2004). History and National Destiny: Responses and Clarifications. *Nations and Nationalism,* 10(1/2): 195–209.

(2003a). *Chosen Peoples: Sacred Sources of National Identity.* Oxford: Oxford University Press.

(2003b). The Poverty of Anti-Nationalist Modernism. *Nations and Nationalism,* 9(3): 357–70.

(2000). The 'Sacred' Dimension of Nationalism. *Millennium,* 29(3): 791–814.

(1999). *The Myths and Memories of the Nation.* Oxford: Oxford University Press.

(1998). *Nationalism and Modernism.* London: Routledge.

(1991). *National Identity.* Harmondsworth: Penguin.

(1986). *The Ethnic Origins of Nations.* Oxford: Blackwell.

(1973). *Nationalism.* London: Mouton.

Smith, D. J. (2009). *One Morning in Sarajevo: 28 June 1914.* New York: Phoenix.

Smith, M. (2013). The World of Irish Dance: The Globalization of Traditional Irish Dance in the 20th Century. www.irishcentral.com/roots/the-world-of-irish-dance-the-globalization-of-traditional-irish-dance-in-the-20th-century -193820051-237575771.

Smith, T. and S. Kim. (2006). National Pride in Cross-National and Temporal Perspective. *International Journal of Public Opinion Research,* 18(1): 127–36.

Snidarić, M. (2012). Najveći uspjesi našeg sporta: Oni su pokorili i zadivili svijet. *24 Stata,* 22(8).

Snyder, L. (1968). *The New Nationalism.* Cornell: Cornell University Press.

Spiers, E. M. (1996). Army Organisation and Society in the 19th Century. In T. Bartlett and K. Jeffery (eds.), *A Military History of Ireland.* Cambridge: Cambridge University Press.

Stergar, R. and T. Scheer. (2018). Ethnic Boxes: The Unintended Consequences of Habsburg Bureaucratic Classification. *Nationalities Papers,* 46(4): 575–591.

Stephens, S. (1997. Children and Nationalism. *Childhood,* 4(1): 5–17.

Steuer, H. (2006). Warrior Bands, War Lords and the Birth of Tribes and States in the First Millennium AD in Middle Europe. In T. Otto, H. Thrane and

H. Vandkilde (eds.), *Warfare and Society: Archeological and Social Anthropological Perspectives*. Aarhus: Aarhus University Press.

Stoianovich, T. (1994). *Balkan Worlds: The First and Last Europe*. New York: M.E. Sharpe.

Stojanović, D. (2017). *Kaldrma i Asfalt: Urbanizacija i Evropeizacija Beograda 1890–1914*. Belgrade: UDI.

(2010). Institucije u Srbiji 1903–1914, *Peščanik*, 30(12): 15.

(2003). Percepcija ideala slobode, jednakosti i bratstva kod srpske elite početkom 20.veka. In L. Perović (ed.), *Srbija u modernizacijskim procesima 19. i 20. Veka: Uloga elita*; Belgrade: Čigoj štampa.

Stokes, G. (1976). The Absence of Nationalism in Serbian Politics before 1840. *Canadian Review of Studies in Nationalism*, 4(1): 77–90.

(1975). *Legitimacy through Liberalism: Vladimir Jovanovic and the Transformation of Serbian Politics*. Seattle: University of Washington Press.

Strupp, K. (1911). Unabhängigkeitserklärung Bulgariens. Proklamation des Fürsten Ferdinand vom 22 September/5 Oktober 1908. In *Urkunden zur Geschichte des Völkerrechts II*. Gotha: Friedrich Andreas Perthes.

Sombart. W. (1913). *Krieg und Kapitalismus*. Munich: Duncker & Humbolt.

Surak, K. (2012). Nation-Work: A Praxeology of Making and Maintaining Nations. *European Journal of Sociology*, 53(2): 171–204.

Suzman, J. (2017). *Affluence without Abundance: The Disappearing World of the Bushmen*. New York: Bloomsbury.

Swed, O. and T. Crosbie. (2017). Private Security and Military Contractors: A Troubling Oversight. *Social Compass*, 11(11): 1–11.

Tallet, F. (1992). *War and Society in Early Modern Europe, 1495–1715*. New York: Routledge.

Tang, W. and B. Barr. (2012). Chinese Nationalism and Its Political and Social Origins. *Journal of Contemporary China*, 21: 77.

TANJUG. (2016). *Srpski hemičari rame uz rame s japanskim – bakterijama protiv naftnih zagađenja! RTS* 15(3).

Tašković, M. (2016). Fenomen u Riju. Zašto smo tako uspešni u sportu? *Blic*. 21(8).

Taylor, B. D. and R. Botea. (2008). Tilly Tally: War-Making and State-Making in the Contemporary Third World. *International Studies Review*, 10: 27–56.

Taylor, C. (1998). Nationalism and Modernity. In J. A. Hall (ed.), *The State of the Nation: Ernest Gellner and the Theory of Nationalism*. Cambridge: Cambridge University Press.

Taylor, P. (2003). *Munitions of the Mind: A History of Propaganda*. Manchester: Manchester University Press.

Thies, C. G. (2007). The Political Economy of State Building in Sub-Saharan Africa. *Journal of Politics*, 69: 716–31.

Thimoty, S. (2017). Patriotism as a Branding Tactic. www.oneims.net/patriotism-as-a-branding-tactic/.

Thomas, W. I. and D. S. Thomas. (1928). *The Child in America: Behavior Problems and Programs*. New York: Knopf.

Tilly, C. (2003). *Contention & Democracy in Europe, 1650–2000*. Cambridge: Cambridge University Press.

(1996). The State of Nationalism. *Critical Review*, 10: 299–306.

(1994). *Durable Inequality*. Berkeley: University of California Press.

(1993) National Self-Determination as a Problem for All of Us. *Daedalus*, 122 (3): 29–36.

(1992). *Coercion, Capital and European States*. Oxford: Blackwell.

(1985). War Making and State Making as Organized Crime. In P. Evans. D. Rueschemeyer and T. Skocpol (eds.), *Bringing the State Back In*. Cambridge: Cambridge University Press.

(1975). Reflections on the History of European State-Making. In C. Tilly (ed.), *The Formation of National States in Western Europe*. Princeton: Princeton University Press.

Tin-Bor Hui, V. (2005). *War and State Formation in Ancient China and Early Modern Europe*. Cambridge: Cambridge University Press.

Tiryakian, E. and R. Rogowski (eds.). (1986). *New Nationalisms of the Developed West: Toward an Explanation*. Boston: Allen and Unwin.

Todorova M. (1997). *Imagining the Balkans*. Oxford: Oxford University Press.

Tomiak, J. J. (2016). *Western Perspectives on Soviet Education in the 1980s*. New York: Palgrave.

Tovy, H. and P. Share. (2003). *A Sociology of Ireland*. Dublin: Gill & McMillan.

Touraine, Alain. (2009). *Thinking Differently*. Cambridge: Polity.

Trotsky, L. (1980 [1913]), *The War Correspondence of Leon Trotsky in the Balkan wars 1912–13*. New York: Pathfinder Press.

Turner, J. (2007). *Human Emotions: A Sociological Theory*. London: Routledge.

Uzelac, G. (2006). *The Development of the Croatian Nation*. Lewiston: Edwin Mellen Press.

van den Berghe, P. (1981). *The Ethnic Phenomenon*. New York: Elsevier.

Vaughan R. (2002). *Philip the Good*. Woodbridge: Boydel Press.

Verheijen, T. (2014). Serbia: State Employees Galore, But Where Is the Private Sector? World Bank: IBRD, IDA.

Viroli, M. (1997). *For Love of Country: An Essay on Patriotism and Nationalism*. Oxford: Calderon Press.

Vucinich, W. (1968). *Serbia between East and West: The Events of 1903–1908*. New York: AMS Press.

Wallerstein, I. (1987). The Construction of Peoplehood: Racism, Nationalism, Ethnicity. *Sociological Forum*, 2(2): 373–88.

(1980). *The Modern World-System*, vol. II: *Mercantilism and the Consolidation of the European World-Economy, 1600–1750*. New York: Academic Press.

(1974). *The Modern World-System*, vol. I: *Capitalist Agriculture and the Origins of the European World-Economy in the Sixteenth Century*. New York: Academic Press.

Ward, L. F. (1913). *Dynamic Sociology*. New York: Appleton.

Watson, I. (2003. *Broadcasting in Irish: Minority Language, Radio, Television and Identity*. Dublin: Four Courts Press.

Watterson, J. (2016). Olympics: Michelle Smith Saga still Divides 20 Years On. *Irish Times*, 30 July.

Weber, E. (1976). *Peasants into Frenchmen: The Modernisation of Rural France, 1870–1914*. Stanford: Stanford University Press.

Weber, M. (1968). *Economy and Society*. New York: Bedminster Press.

Weinberg, S. (1995). *Last of the Pirates: In Search of Bob Denard*. London: Pantheon.

Weininger, E.B., A. Lareau, & O. Lizardo Ritual, Emotion, Violence: Studies on the Micro-Sociology of Randall Collins. London: Routledge.

Weiss, J. (2014). *Powerful Patriots: Nationalist Protest in China's Foreign Relations*. New York: Oxford University Pres.

Wieviorka, M. (2015). Towards a Global Sociology of Social Movements Today. http://futureswewant.net/michel-wieviorka-global-sociology-english/.

(2009). *Violence: A New Approach*. London: Sage.

(2003). Violence and the Subject. *Thesis Eleven*, 73: 42–50.

Wilson, D. (1970). *The Life and Times of Vuk Stefanović Karadžić, 1787–1864: Literacy, Literature and National Independence in Serbia*. Oxford: Clarendon Press.

Wimmer, A. (2018). *Nation-Building: Why Some Countries Come Together while Others Fall Apart*. Princeton: Princeton University Press.

(2012). *Waves of War: Nationalism, State Formation, and Ethnic Exclusion in the Modern World*. Cambridge: Cambridge University Press.

(2002). *Nationalist Exclusion and Ethnic Conflict: Shadows of Modernity*. Cambridge: Cambridge University Press.

Wittek, P. (1938). *The Rise of the Ottoman Empire*. London: Royal Asiatic Society.

World Value Survey. www.worldvaluessurvey.org/WVSNewsShow.jsp?ID=154.

Woodhouse, C. M. (1969). *The Philhellens*. London: Hodder and Stoughton.

Wolf, N. M. (2014). *An Irish-Speaking Island: State, Religion, Community, and the Linguistic Landscape in Ireland, 1770–1870*. University of Wisconsin Press.

Wulff, H. (2008). *Dancing at the Crossroads: Memory and Mobility in Ireland*. New York: Berghahn Books.

Yack, B. (1999). The Myth of the Civic Nation. In R. Beiner (ed.), *Theorizing Nationalism*. Albany: State University of New York Press.

Zabec, K. (2011). Časnici priznali: Dobre veze u stranci znače i više činove. *Jutarnji List*, 3: 1.

Zarinebaf, F., J. Bennet and J. Davies. (2005). *A Historical and Economic Geography of Ottoman Greece*. Princeton: American School of Classical Studies.

Zerubavel, Y. (1994). The Death of Memory and the Memory of Death: Masada and the Holocaust as Historical Metaphors. *Representations*, 45(1): 72–100.

Zhao, D. (2014). *The Confucian-Legalist State: A New Theory of Chinese History*. Oxford: Oxford University Press.

Ziegler, C. (2009). *The History of Russia*. Westport: ABC Clio.

Zielonka, J. (2006). *Europe as Empire: The Nature of the Enlarged European Union*. Oxford: Oxford University Press.

Zubok, V. M. (2009). *A Failed Empire: The Soviet Union in the Cold War from Stalin to Gorbachev*. Chapel Hill: University of North Carolina Press.

Zubrzycki, G. (2006). *The Crosses of Auschwitz: Nationalism and Religion in Post-Communist Poland*. Chicago: University of Chicago Press.

Index

Acton, Lord, 1
Afghan nationalism, 38
Africa, 82, 87, 94, 117, 126, 127, 130, 164, 181, 244, 251, 280, 290, 299, 302
Albanian Fascist Party, 123
Albanian nationalism, 124
Albanians, 123, 132, 187
Alexander of Battenberg, 103
Alexander the Great, 62, 66
Al-Qaida, 250
American Revolution, 2, 11, 30, 80, 138
ancien régime, 9, 72, 103
Anderson, Benedict, viii, 1, 2, 9, 23, 26, 27, 30, 32, 36, 54, 59, 79, 84, 98, 138, 148, 173, 174, 211, 219, 243, 257, 280
Angola, 263
Annales school, 47, 51
April Uprising of 1876, 183
Arab Spring, 2
Armenia, 117
Armstrong, John, 40, 41, 42, 68, 280
Arrigi, Giovanni, 48
Asia, 24, 32, 82, 117, 119, 127, 164, 181, 244, 251, 280, 288
Aurelius, Marcus, 247, 248
Australia, iv, 60, 71, 87, 94, 126, 127, 130
Austria, 81, 107, 126, 189, 193, 204, 207, 244
Austrian Freedom Party, 3
Austrians, 104
Austro-Hungary, 192, 203

Bahrain, 26
Balkan nationalisms, 111, 112, 118, 131, 183, 219, 230, 233
Balkan wars (1912–3), 108, 161, 198
Balkans, ix, 15, 18, 58, 91, 98, 99, 101, 103, 112, 113, 114, 115, 118, 121, 124, 125, 126, 129, 131, 132, 133, 140, 160, 161, 164, 165, 166, 167, 168, 169, 171, 172, 175, 176, 179, 181, 184, 185, 186, 190, 191, 192, 193,
198, 204, 213, 219, 248, 281, 282, 285, 287, 289, 290, 291, 295, 296, 297, 299, 300, 303
Bannon, Stephen, 3
Banton, Michael, 255, 281
Basque country, 2
Basques, 111, 137
Bauer, Otto, 1
Bauman, Zygmunt, 157, 234, 237, 238, 239, 240, 256, 281
BDM, 271
Beck Gernsheim, Elisabeth, 234
Beck, Ulrich, 86, 157, 214, 227, 234, 236, 237, 238, 239, 240, 248, 281, 289
Belarus, 28
Belfast, viii, 127, 140
Belgium, 17, 113, 115, 117, 126, 192, 215
Belgrade, 37, 129, 161, 169, 181, 191, 197, 203, 204, 208, 210, 220, 283, 285, 289, 291, 297, 299, 302
Berislavić, Petar, 218
Berlin Congress (1878), 189
Bharatiya Janata Party, 3, 239, 249
Big Ditch thesis, 46
Billig, Michael, 13, 35, 142, 214, 229, 230, 231, 232, 248, 253, 282, 301
Bismarck, Otto von, 73
Blackwater USA, 271, 273
blocking presentism, 40, 41, 51
Boko Haram, 23
Bolivia, 113
Boru, Brian, 138
Bose, Chandra, 12
Bosnia and Herzegovina, 120, 203–211, 222
Bosnian Muslims, 120, 222
Boulanger crisis (1889), 82
Braudel, Fernand, 47, 48, 53, 282
Brazil, 71, 245
Breuilly, John, viii, 9, 23, 30, 36, 44, 54, 76, 86, 90, 92, 138, 173, 174, 190, 201, 240, 267, 282
Brexit, 2, 7, 135, 239, 240, 241, 244, 296